Fashion
Drawing

OUTWEAR COLLECTION '08

Fashion Drawing

Illustration techniques
for fashion designers

Michele Wesen Bryant

Laurence King Publishing

Published in 2011 by
Laurence King Publishing
361–373 City Road, London
EC1V 1LR, United Kingdom
T +44 20 7841 6900
F +44 20 7841 6910
enquiries@laurenceking.com
www.laurenceking.com

A catalogue record for this book is available
from the British Library.

ISBN: 978 1 85669 719 4

Development Editor: Anne Townley
Senior Editor: Zoe Antoniou
Designer: Paul Tilby
Picture Researcher: Emma Brown
Copy Editor: Angela Koo
Proofreader: Liz Jones
Indexer: Sue Farr

Printed in China

Prelims illustrations by: p. 1 Laurie Marman; pp. 2–3
Sylvia Kwan; p. 4 Richard Rosenfeld; p. 5 bottom Steven
Broadway; p. 5 top Eri Wakiyama; p. 6 bottom left Alfredo
Cabrera; p. 6 bottom right Anna Kiper; p. 6 top Michele
Wesen Bryant.

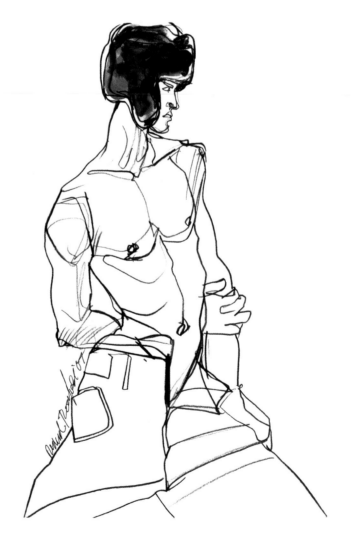

Contents

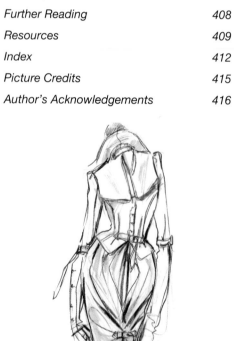

Related study material is available on the Laurence King website at
www.laurenceking.com

Introduction

A fashion drawing is a bit like a fairytale—an imaginative invention that incorporates just enough reality to tell a convincing story. While tradition calls for elongating the limbs and the rigorous editing of visual information, the key message of this book is that there is no right or wrong way to draw fashion.

In Part I, the exploration of figure proportion avoids establishing set rules. Firsthand observations from live fashion model drawing are used to discover the foreshortening and balancing of figures.

Part II focuses on drawing as a function of the garment design process with instruction for drawing construction details and silhouettes—how they are combined is up to you.

In Part III, demonstrations for rendering different types of fabric use a wide variety of media and techniques; examples are presented with varying degrees of completion relative to different job descriptions.

Throughout this book instruction is supported with a broad array of illustration styles by many different artists. The goal is to develop a unique visual language of your own.

Who This Book Is For

This is a textbook for aspiring designers that will also be of interest to illustrators, stylists, merchandisers, and anyone else in need of an immediate and effective means of visualizing concepts.

Many other books available on this subject either present a drawing course with a single point of view or an anthology of exquisite examples. This book combines step-by-step instruction with exemplary artwork from all over the world. A more inclusive aesthetic discourages the judgments and preconceived notions that can inhibit truly creative expression.

Although the easy-to-follow instructions, assignments, and examples provided here will quickly bring your skills up to speed, fashion drawing is a discipline that requires constant observation and you should expect your results to be gradual and cumulative. However, once these skills are developed they can be used for problem solving, communicating ideas…and pleasurable pursuits!

How To Use This Book

The content of this book is set out across 12 chapters that, depending on previous experience and focus, can be read in any order.

There are proportion templates for drawing women, men, and children that can be adapted according to your intuition, market category, and for various customers such as curvier girls, petites, and even for the "bump." Supplemental assignments provide for further exploration and development of skills. An illustrated glossary of details and silhouettes will help to build a broad vocabulary for garment design. Although there is no real substitute for working with

▲ In this illustration by Laura Laine, the combination of abundant hair offset by tiny feet creates an extreme overhead point of view. Exquisite attention to detail is used to supernatural effect; garments are presented as being both beautiful and edgy.

actual swatches, the photographic gallery of fabrics at the end of each chapter in Part III can be used in lieu of hard-to-find swatches for rendering practice. Finally, a discussion of different specializations (also in Part III) can be used to guide decisions about a more focused course of study or the development of a portfolio for a specific career path.

It is my hope that working with this book will help you to develop a drawing style that is as unique as your signature. Only through practice and ongoing experimentation will you be prepared to work with the spontaneity and imagination required for fashion.

Part I of this book provides examples and instruction for drawing stylized versions of women, men, and children. The development of customized templates will help you to determine and maintain a consistent proportion for these figures. The basic rules for balancing and foreshortening the figure are then introduced to guide the creation of poses. Both the figure proportion and the poses can be adjusted to convey different ideals and concepts. Decisions about emphasizing certain shapes, colors, and patterns are important because they affect the way that a fashion design is perceived—both before the garments are created (in the designer sketch) and after (in fashion journalism).

Looking Back

A quick look back in time reveals that figures, layout, and media change in response to the same considerations that affect garment design. For instance, the popularity of new activities (such as eighties' rollerblading) not only requires new apparel, but also new figures and poses for the illustration of design concepts. The gestures of the figures reflect the social conventions of a particular era (for example, the sixties' sexual revolution caused fashion drawing to become more risqué). Demographics that shape evolving standards of beauty also determine the ethnicity and age of figures used in fashion sketches. The same aesthetic applied to the cut of the clothes affects the way that the garments and figures are drawn. Technology is also in the mix, evident in alternately precise or expressive line quality and providing new means for graphic reproduction.

Given the number of choices available in fashion today, it may surprise you to discover that a single trend once held sway for an extended period of time, further influencing the way that fashion was represented on the page. A brief review of the twentieth century will explain how and why fashion drawing evolves so that you can develop a personal style that is evocative of your own times…and the future.

La Belle Epoque (1890–1914)

At the turn of the century, daily and weekly editions of illustrated journals were the sole source of news. As a result, fashion icons of the period were brought to life by illustrators such as Charles Dana Gibson, J.C. Leyendecker,

◄ *(Previous spread) An artistic interpretation of garments can be used to position fashion in a specific and unique context. Illustration by Alfredo Cabrera.*

▲ *Contemporary designers often revisit both the fashion and the visual culture of another era as inspiration. (For examples of images from the first luxury fashion magazines see p. 12.) Here, Anna Sui*

explains her designs: "For Spring…I was looking at reproductions of the French fashion magazine, La Gazette du Bon Ton (1912–25). I was excited by the vivid, saturated hand-painted colors."

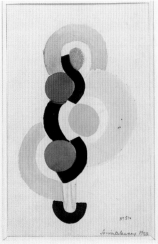

◀ Coles Phillips's exquisite attention to garment detail made fashion central to compositions for his "Fadeaway Girls" (so-called because they "faded" into their painted background). Illustrations were used to tell complex stories in a way that anticipated twenty-first-century graphic novels.

◀ Heavily boned foundations for women cinched the waistline and forced a full upper body forward while sending shoulders and hips to the rear. Drapery and lace were used to emphasize the fullness of the lowered "monobosom."

▼ Russian émigrés living in Paris brought with them an exotic fusion of costume, music, and dance that influenced fashion. This colorful costume design by Sonia Delaunay is entitled Robe simultanée et rythme sans fin, costumes, 1923.

and Coles Phillips. Illustrations not only documented but also dictated fashion. The all-American "Gibson Girl" inspired fashion trends for suffragettes—long gored skirts and high-collared embroidered blouses with necktie, cravat, or jabot completing the look.

Paris was established as the international fashion capital and French fashion dictated a mature hourglass shape in the West. Both Edwardian women and men aspired to the wasp waist. As intercontinental travel by new superliners afforded increased exposure to the East, styles began to change. **Orientalism** was becoming a parallel force in fashion, prompting Paul Poiret's introduction of a less constricting cylindrical form—his **Directoire** line.

Fashion illustration from the Belle Epoque featured a great deal of shading to emphasize the dimensions of the hourglass form. The "pouter pigeon" look, achieved with heavy corsetry in real life, was easily and more fully realized in drawings. Inert figure poses and stiff drawing technique mirrored the mannered and rigid social structure of the Edwardian era.

When Orientalism hit fashion, it also had a major impact on illustration. Figures took on the new cylindrical form. Poses became less static and a more sensual drawing style was used to prioritize the decorative pattern, color, and drape of exotic textiles. Granted new prestige, fashion was repositioned and reviewed as art in the very first luxury fashion magazines. *La Gazette du Bon Ton* and the *Journal des Dames et des Modes* included the illustrations of artists such as Georges Barbier, Eduardo Garcia Benito, Bernard Boutet De Monvel, Georges Lepape, and Gerda Wegener (see p. 12). Compositions featured the bright colors and decorative motifs inspired by Orientalism.

World War I (1914–18)

Attitudes and lifestyles changed dramatically after the onset of World War I. Privilege associated with the Belle Epoque became a thing of the past. Women and children dressed in work clothes and uniforms as they assumed men's jobs on the home front. The austerity of wartime was soon expressed in the elimination of social dress codes and the appearance of trench coats and other military and utilitarian fashions. As a consequence, wartime fashion drawing was limited in scope. What little there was reflected influences from the East and the new silent screen, with emerging fashion icons such as Rudolph Valentino (also known as "the Sheik") and the erotic Theda Bara ("the Vamp").

▼ *Public service and fashion comingle in a recruitment poster circa 1916.*

▲ *The precise and descriptive line used by Gerda Wegener conveys a theatrical gesture that is borrowed from the exaggerated display of emotion on the silent screen.*

The Roaring Twenties

Twenties' fashion evolved in tandem with **Art Deco**, jazz, and the emancipated flapper. The modern era had been ushered in by the Bauhaus mandate for form to follow function and fashion designers responded in kind. Madeleine Vionnet's innovation of the **bias cut** (1922) allowed new freedom of movement and would become wildly popular in the thirties (for more about the bias cut see pp. 260–67). Coco Chanel's "little black dress" was both a symbol and an extension of the new modernity. Tight-fitting "jazz suits" for men passed quickly in and out of fashion, replaced by roomier clothing required for dancing the Charleston and the Lindy Hop.

After years of women's suffrage and a shift in gender roles during the war, the twenties' ideal woman was an androgynous *garçon*. New elastic foundation garments minimized the same parts of her body that corsets had previously emphasized. Waistlines dropped and then disappeared altogether, making a sudden reappearance at the end of the decade. Abbreviated hemlines for day and evening revealed turned-down hose and powdered knees. Emancipation also prompted greater participation for women in outdoor activities—golf, archery, tennis, and sunbathing—and a new vogue for sportswear was part of the fitness trend.

While the genesis of women's fashion came from Paris, men looked to London for sartorial cues. Students at Cambridge and Oxford rejected Edwardian morning and evening dress codes, choosing instead to remain in flannel trousers and soft collars throughout the day. Plus fours (knickerbockers lengthened by four inches), popular on the golf course and forbidden in the classroom, were often concealed under full-cut trousers called "Oxford bags." American Ivy League students were now traveling abroad and were quite taken with British fashion.

Hailing from stage and screen, fashion icons such as Louise Brooks, Josephine Baker, and Anna May Wong reflected the relaxed social structure and exotic tastes of the twenties. In a decade dominated by women, male icons were scarce, although writer F. Scott Fitzgerald with his wife Zelda came to symbolize the excesses of the Jazz Age.

▲ *Following the discovery of King Tut's tomb in 1922, Egyptian influences started to appear in decorative patterns for textiles, embellishments, and jewelry. While Orientalism was impacting the West, a reciprocal fashion influence was underway in the East.*

Twenties' fashion drawing reflected an increasingly mechanized lifestyle that now included mass-produced clothing. The frenetic *joie de vivre* of the first youth cult, living in the modern city, was conveyed with youthful active figures. Orientalism prevailed and the proportion of fashion figures changed to a more cylindrical form. The size of the head was reduced as per the bobbed hair and cloche hats then in fashion. Compositions featured the bright colors and flat geometric forms associated with Art Deco.

▼ *Casual daywear for men and boys in the twenties featured soft-shouldered sports jackets, pullover sweaters, and soft caps, as illustrated by J.C. Leyendecker.*

▼ *Dresses for girls featured the same lowered waists and raised hemlines as for adult flappers. Tight-fitting cloche hats created the appearance of smaller heads sitting atop cylindrical bodies.*

▲ *The exploration of the subconscious mind had an enormous influence on both fashion and illustration. René Magritte worked as a fashion illustrator in Brussels before coming to Paris in 1927 to join the Surrealists.*

The Thirties

After the stock market crash of 1929, Hollywood movies (now enhanced with sound) provided diversion from tough economic realities. Gilbert Adrian's costumes for Jean Harlow, Greta Garbo, and Joan Crawford set the new standard for thirties' women's fashion. Fred Astaire's ability to dance served as the great social equalizer. Swing dance required freedom of movement, and long, baggy pants, with zippers replacing button flies, were popular for men—and daring women. Newsreel appearances had similar fashion clout. The pattern mix favored by Edward VIII, when Prince of Wales, was all the rage. Amelia Earhart's aviator cap and flight jacket would be an ongoing source of inspiration for decades to come.

On screen and off, fashion began to reject the default styles of the twenties. Garments for women became extremely feminine and glamorous. The natural waist returned and darts were replaced with soft gathers.

Peplums and flounces were added to suits, dresses, and gowns. Chanel replaced her little black dress with a long white gown for swing dancing. The revealing bias drape sculpted a more naturalistic figure with large shoulders, lowered bust, and narrow hips—an ideal difficult, if not impossible, to attain naturally.

Examination of thirties' fashion drawing reveals an elongated figure proportion and painterly rendering appropriate for feminized fashion. Greater consideration was given to light and shadow, with a gradual shift to a less precise and more impressionistic drawing style.

By 1934, the military style of World War II (1939–45) was anticipated in a more severe and masculine silhouette. An inverted "V" shape became the ideal, achieved with extreme shoulder emphasis, braided trim, tight skirts, shoulder bags, and sturdy flat shoes. Men's suits were modified with shoulder pads, high armholes, tapered sleeves, and peaked lapels to create the appearance of a large torso.

▶ In this illustration by Gerd Hartung from 1932, it is apparent that Hollywood glamor had a strong influence on thirties' body-skimming fashion.

▼ Clothing for girls reflected a more masculine silhouette with exaggerated shoulder emphasis.

◀ The popularity of double-breasted suits in Hollywood gangster films sparked a new trend in men's fashion. Looser-fitting zoot suits were adopted by the jazz subculture.

World War II (1939–45)

During and after World War II, fashion design was affected by the rationing of raw materials and natural fibers reserved for the war effort. Civilians were asked to "make do and mend." Rationing prompted women to wear short tight skirts and men to favor shorter jackets, narrow pants, or trousers, and the total elimination of vests, or waistcoats, vents, pleats, and cuffs. Style for women and men was largely demonstrated through imaginative accessories.

Wartime fashion, though limited in scope, continued to be monitored by illustration. Iconic images of Rosie the Riveter were used to recruit women for factory work as part of the war effort. Beginning with the publication of *Esquire* in 1933, centerfold pinups of the airbrushed "Petty Girl" (named after her creator, artist George Petty) raised soldiers' morale and were often reinterpreted as nose art decoration of airplanes.

The inverted "V" silhouette, intended to emphasize physical prowess, continued to be reflected in the stylized figure proportion used for drawing men, women, and children.

◀ There was a marked rebound from thirties' naturalism with padding, corsets, and girdles used to achieve broad shoulders, conical breasts, small waists, and suppressed hiplines.

▶ American utilitarian looks featured solid or striped T-shirts, originally military issue, and overalls (dungarees) worn by women and children working on wartime assembly lines.

Carefree play clothes by Blue Bell

Smart, thrifty and carefree—jeans for you, play overalls and dungarees for your youngsters. BLUE BELL play clothes are more than a match for the most boisterous wear. And their low cost saves you money; their rugged construction cuts mending chores to a minimum. Overall suspenders are adjustable, easy to fasten. Points of strain reinforced with no-scratch rivets or strong cross sewing. Snap-fastener closures. Kiddies' dungarees and elastic back overalls, sizes 1 to 5, about **$1.25 to $1.69**; girls' and women's Jeanies, about **$1.98 to $2.98**, depending on fabric. At better stores everywhere. Sanforized. Guaranteed the best made, best fitting you can buy—or your money back! Blue Bell, Inc., 93 Worth Street, New York 13.

Wranglers — Western jeans in heavy 11-oz. Sanforized denim. Kiddies', boys', men's sizes, from about **$1.79 to $3.29.** Styled by Rodeo Ben, tailor to top rodeo stars!

Boxer shorts, 2 to 12, and bib shorts, 2 to 6. Let your youngsters romp through summer days in these cool, comfortable play shorts. Made to take rambunctious wear!

There's a BLUE BELL for every job, indoors or out. Roomy and comfortable; sturdily sewn for long, carefree wear. In sizes for all the family.

BLUE BELL

WORK AND PLAY CLOTHES

WORLD'S LARGEST PRODUCER OF WORK CLOTHES

Bib overalls, dungarees, women's blue jeans, Wrangler Western jeans, work shirts, work pants, matched pants and shirts, unlined and blanket-lined coats, Cossack and Western jackets, coveralls, children's play clothes.

The Postwar Era (1945–59)

Postwar fashion from France brought a rediscovery of female curves with an artificial sculpting of the body. Dior's **"New Look"** was emphasized by a slouch posture as characteristic of the new restrictive styles as the clothing itself. Stiletto heels, invented by Salvatore Ferragamo in 1955, finished off the look. The conformity of wearing a uniform during the war carried over to civilian life where men now dressed for success in single-breasted gray flannel suits. The postwar population grew exponentially and "baby boomers" were the first generation to experience the luxury of an extended childhood—with ample time for rock and roll, teenage rebellion, and a new preoccupation with fashion. The casual American teenage style quickly spread worldwide.

◂ *Al Pimsler's drawing captures the conformity of the fifties' corporate "boys' club." While women's fashion increased in volume, men's suiting became quite streamlined with single-breasted jackets (sans shoulder pads) layered over shorter slimmer pants.*

▾ *Economic prosperity was celebrated as per Dior's "New Look" with extravagantly full skirts that fell just below the knee. Illustration by Gerd Hartung.*

Biomorphic shapes dominated all "Atomic Age" product design, including curvaceous evening and cocktail dresses designed by Charles James. Softer versions by Claire McCardell provided women with a more comfortable choice for active lifestyles. By the mid-fifties, the introduction of the **sack dress** (Cristóbal Balenciaga, 1955) and **trapeze dress** (Yves Saint Laurent for Dior, 1957) spurred yet another rebound to naturalism. In menswear, slim high-fashion suits were coming into favor with young British "Mods" and the Las Vegas "Rat Pack."

Fashion icons continued to hail from the mass media. Forties' pinup girls morphed into openly sexual movie bombshells such as Marilyn Monroe, Sophia Loren, Brigitte Bardot, and Bettie Page. Audrey Hepburn's elegant gamine was muse to Givenchy and the shape of things to come. James Dean and Marlon Brando immortalized the combination of motorcycle jacket, white T-shirt, and jeans as the male uniform of rebellion.

Fashion drawing in the aftermath of World War II reflects the influence of Abstract Expressionism; crisp accuracy gave way to the vague description of surface and garment details. Poses and backgrounds presented fashion in the context of unprecedented leisure time and social mobility.

At the beginning of the decade, a more voluptuous fashion figure corresponded to aspirations for postwar prosperity and a return to traditional gender roles. By the end of the decade, fashion figures began to slim down in anticipation of the sixties' youth cult.

In 1957, the dress worn by Marilyn Monroe in *The Seven-Year Itch* came directly off the rack. The American ready-to-wear industry, which expanded out of necessity during the war years, was about to explode.

▼ *One of Cristóbal Balenciaga's many fashion innovations included a square coat with sleeves and yoke cut from a single piece of fabric. In this illustration by Gerd Hartung you can see how many other designers looked to Balenciaga for inspiration in the late fifties. His protégés, Hubert Givenchy, Emanuel Ungaro, André Courrèges, and Oscar de la Renta, went on to establish their own couture houses.*

◀ *When the Beatles' appearance on* The Ed Sullivan Show *launched the British Invasion, television and rock music began to trump the salon for fashion influence. Both the men and the women in this illustration by Joanne Landis have the same unisex haircut inspired by Beatlemania.*

The Sixties

The revolutionary sixties were a combustible mix of accelerating technology and youthful rebellion. The baby boomers, now an international youth cult, began to challenge the establishment and, in doing so, initiated an upheaval in the social structure, politics, and the arts. Sixties' fashion reflected this broadening of horizons and rejection of tradition. The Space Race sparked the imaginations of futuristic fashion designers André Courrèges, Pierre Cardin, and Mary Quant. The sexual revolution found expression in androgynous clothing. A subversion of dress codes provided new choices for women

that now included miniskirts, paired with newly invented pantyhose (tights), and pants for all occasions.

Left-leaning politics challenged elitism and by extension, the **haute couture**. Working out of London boutiques, young designers such as Ossie Clark and Mary Quant offered unfitted shapes, knitted suits, and the freedom of the **chemise** as an alternative to staid looks from the salon. Yves Saint Laurent revolutionized couture with references to Pop Art and the uniform of student protest: military surplus, sweaters, and jeans. His source of inspiration would soon expand to world cultures with gypsy, Cossack, tuxedo, and safari looks. In menswear, minimalist Mod looks—with and without **Nehru collars**—shortly gave

way to the bright colors and Edwardian suits of the
Peacock Revolution. Hippy Flower Power followed
thereafter with psychedelic, paisley, and floral patterns.

Sixties' fashion icons included Twiggy, the
quintessential gamine and first supermodel. Owing to the
growing civil rights movement, African-American models
Naomi Sims and Pat Cleveland appeared on the covers of
top fashion magazines. First lady Jackie Kennedy came
to symbolize the Americanization of fashion. Cads ruled
men's fashion, with Mick Jagger, the androgynous bad boy,
and Sean Connery as James Bond, the dapper sexual
adventurer and Cold War spy.

In fashion illustration, the mature elegance of the fifties
gave way to the appearance of perpetual adolescence.
Androgynous female figures had small bosoms, natural
waists, and elongated limbs, not unlike the twenties'
garçon. Wide-eyed faces bore more than a passing
resemblance to the waifs portrayed in Margaret Keane's
kitsch paintings. Elongated menswear figures, now sporting
long hair and purses, were an indication of the blurring of
gender roles. Pop Art's use of commercial reproduction
processes was evident in the decorative use of line screens
and benday dots.

◀ *The mainstreaming of erotic content
in the sixties caused fashion illustration
to become more sexually suggestive.
Later in the decade the elimination of
foundation garments marked the return
of naturalism.*

▲ *Antonio Lopez's use of psychedelic
imagery is borrowed from rock music
posters and album art. Impressionistic
drawing styles from the fifties were
replaced with flat expanses of color
defined by carefully plotted line work
made possible by new technical pens and
transparent color film.*

The Seventies

Whereas the sixties' youth cult had embraced technology and rejected tradition, in the seventies there began a new preference for historic preservation, natural materials, and evidence of the hand. Fashion became retrospective, influenced by Victoriana, Art Deco, and the golden age of Hollywood. Thrift store finds were blended with do-it-yourself handicrafts and multicultural exotica for the new Bohemian **vintage chic**. The hippies' sampling of folkloric references was mirrored in naive drawing styles for fashion.

The sixties' space-age cylindrical form now morphed into a more feminine and elongated trumpet silhouette reminiscent of thirties' fashion. The subversion of dress codes culminated in the widespread acceptance of pants for women (now low-rise, with flared bottom hems) and jumpsuits, workwear, and knitted leisure suits for men. Streamlined sharkskin suits gave way to new softer Italian tailoring with suppressed waists, wider lapels, and a lower button stance.

The constant presence of television, radio, and print media caused rebounding fashion cycles to accelerate. By the late seventies, Studio 54, a club in New York City, spawned a new disco culture with an entirely different fashion sensibility. Body-conscious clothing made of synthetic fibers featured Art Deco-inspired prints made possible by new heat-transfer technology. Giorgio Armani's new suits for men and women featured sizable shoulder pads. The trumpet shape popular at the beginning of the decade was turned upside down to form a "V" in anticipation of eighties' power dressing.

A preference for the exotic carried over from the sixties and Grace Jones, Paloma Picasso, and Tina Chow were the first of "Antonio's Girls." Music and fashion formed ever tighter bonds. The Sex Pistols, outfitted in costumes from Vivienne Westwood and Malcolm McClaren's Seditionaries store, launched the punk movement. Art-rockers such as David Bowie and Patti Smith were established as androgynous fashion icons.

The lithe figures used for the illustration of feminized clothing for men and women eventually became less suitable as the baby boomers matured. Drawing styles shifted from naiveté to glamorous sophistication. Then in the mid-seventies, the harsh reality of unflattering portrait painting by Lucian Freud, Francis Bacon, and R.B. Kitaj provided fashion artists with a new subversive genre to reference for the representation of "anti-fashion"—deconstructed, fetish, and Goth clothing.

In anticipation of the coming digital age, fashion drawing ultimately became more premeditated and controlled. Simulated airbrush art, created with aerosol cans of compressed air and new spray markers, was both high-tech and a throwback to forties' pinup art. Postmodernism was on its way.

▶ *The relationship between fine art and fashion intensified in the seventies. Here, in this fashion forecast for the* New York Times *circa 1976, Barbara Pearlman's inclusion of giant birds is both a reference to surrealism and the altered perceptions associated with psychadelic drug experiences.*

▶ *George Stavrinos's illustration recalls the airbrushed pinup art of the thirties and forties. At the end of the seventies the more realistic figure proportion that began to emerge for "power dressing" had a defined waist, accentuated by higher-rise seams.*

▼ *In the mid-seventies, the discovery that some of the best design was industrial led to an ad hoc modernist mix for home décor. In fashion, authentic workwear garments, such as cooks' jackets and auto mechanics' overalls, were incorporated into blue-collar looks for men and women.*

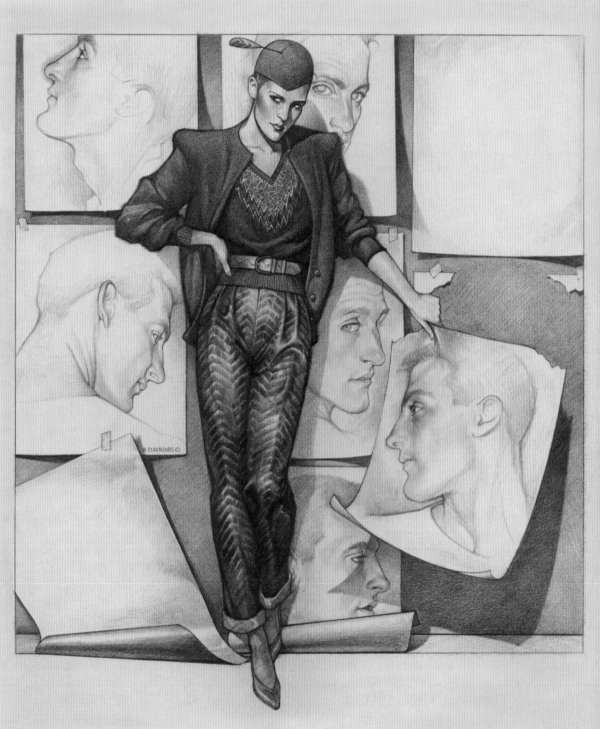

▲ During the eighties Milan became a creative hub for interdisciplinary design, where proponents of the "Memphis" movement used color and materials for emotional impact. Memphis found expression in MTV graphics and soon after in fashion drawing. Illustration by Albert Elia.

The Eighties

The arrival of the eighties brought extravagant materialism, a new cyberaesthetic, and street culture into fashion. "Ghetto fabulous" looks decorated with counterfeit status logos were wry commentary on the proliferation of designer label chic. Everyone affected the appearance of luxe, wearing designer clothing from new secondary **bridge collections** (diffusion lines). Television and rock music continued to be the genesis of mainstream and anti-fashion trends with over-the-top, retro, and new wave looks seen on MTV and nighttime soaps such as *Dallas* and *Dynasty*.

The use of personal computers in everyday lives put an end to linear thinking and this triggered an overlapping and

▶ *In this illustration, Antonio Lopez exaggerates the garment's increased shoulder presence both as a postmodern reference to forties' fashion and to emphasize the notion of power dressing. Graphic color-blocking was also frequently incorporated into eighties' fashion design.*

▼ *South Beach fashion as worn by Don Johnson on* Miami Vice *was extremely popular for menswear. A more realistic figure proportion, characteristic of the eighties, is evident in this illustration by Sharon Watts.*

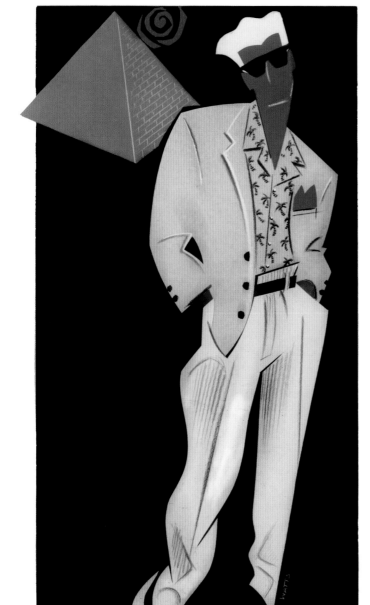

contradiction of trends. Performance artist Leigh Bowery's fetishist designs straddled the line between fine art and fashion. Deconstructed looks by new Japanese and Belgian designers featured voluminous garments literally turned inside out, upside down, and torn apart. The postfeminist agenda was responsible for the return of corsets and crinolines. Ruffled pirate looks for "New Romantics" were a reflection of the illegal "sampling" of music off the radio. Christian Lacroix entered haute couture with a wild postmodern mix of patterns and signature pouf skirts. The ad hoc use of materials in high-tech interior design was reflected in high-fashion garments made of ripstop parachute cloth and sweatshirt fleece. The one connection between the disparate trends was volume.

In menswear, tailoring was softened by new microfiber polyester and then deconstructed for pastel color "Miami Vice" jackets. Hip hop culture called for velvet tracksuits, the "sagging" of oversized pants and luxury car hood ornaments worn as jewelry.

Eighties' fashion illustration gave visible form to changes in technology, society, and politics. Branding strategies for corporate fashion were now aimed at a larger and more diverse consumer base, and as a result the facial detail in fashion sketches was abstracted so as to appeal to the broadest possible audience. There was also a new mandate to sell lifestyle (such as street culture) with social setting implied or drawn in detail.

The cold anonymity of slick digital graphics eventually prompted a new appreciation for Outsider and graffiti art, reflected as naive tendencies in fashion illustration.

The Nineties

Owing to the collapse of the stock market on Black Monday in 1987, the economic austerity of the early nineties called for politically-correct minimalism in fashion. Miuccia Prada and Helmut Lang conjured up utilitarian chic with fashionable high-tech lab coats. The Gap was hugely successful in marketing American basics such as overalls (dungarees), jeans, khakis, and cargo pants.

The shift to a new digital "information society" brought about significant changes for fashion. Telecommuting for all or part of the workweek redefined career wear.

▼ *Minimalist fashion called for an economy of line and brushstrokes. Because fashion traditionally becomes retrospective at the turn of a century, illustration continued to call upon its own vernacular in the nineties for the representation of postmodern fashion.*

◀ *Digital processes revolutionized the creation and reproduction of commercial art and textiles.*

Pre-millennium fears about computer failure in Y2K prompted a new trend for "cocooning" that expanded the market for "at home" apparel. "Bricks and mortar" retail was supplemented by 24/7 virtual shopping on the home shopping network and the Internet. The wide dissemination of fashion information, previously available only to the trade, resulted in a nearly simultaneous offering of fast-fashion knockoffs. Couture houses, now part of monolithic fashion corporations, sought reinvention in the recruitment of young fashion designers such as John Galliano, Alexander McQueen, and Tom Ford.

As fashion cycles continued to accelerate and overlap, it became difficult to launch a single vision into the global mass market. The impact of subcultures, now referred to as "tribes," increasingly carried more weight, and **cool hunting** drove mass-market fashion. Grunge hailed from the Pacific Northwest with oversized plaid (tartan) shirts, concert tees, and cargo pants for boys and inverted flowerpot skirts layered over pants for girls. A wacky combination of traditional Japanese clothing, Western style, and cyberpunk was favored by gothic Lolitas in Tokyo's Harajuku district. The anticipated success of the dotcom startups prompted a trend for geek and nerd chic—complete with black glasses and three-button suits.

The fusion of fashion and music intensified, with the waiflike Kate Moss paired with rapper Marky Mark in Calvin Klein's controversial advertising campaigns. Computer gaming and graphic novels produced more voluptuous and militant fashion icons such as Tank Girl and Tomb Raider's **avatar**, Lara Croft.

Eclecticism in fashion was mirrored in a broad variety of digital and manual drawing styles. Computers were not only used to render photographic fiction, but also to simulate naturalistic art media.

Relative to minimalist fashion, illustration lightened up both in terms of proportion and media used to convey the fluid drape of new textiles. **Manga** and **anime** inspired obsessive fans (known as **otaku**) and were extremely influential for drawing styles used to describe anti-fashion in underground subcultures.

◀ *Comfort and familiarity were key to nineties' fashion. A mix of classic silhouettes and industrial workwear was reinterpreted with new fabric finishes and garment washes to suggest wear, fatigue, and distress.*

▼ *Amy Davis tracked the subculture for the "Style Fiends" section of* Paper Magazine. *There was a general trend in fashion illustration toward larger heads, shifting focus to the individual and the appearance of youth.*

Twenty-first Century and Beyond

In the twenty-first century, print magazines struggle to compete with online fashion coverage where bloggers— self-declared experts—express personal points of view in real time. Fashion drawing has also become more immediate, used for live runway reports, observations from the street, and interactive animations.

As work and recreation increasingly take place in virtual environments, fashion figures reflect the influence of customized avatars. Photoshop allows for the seamless fusion of photography and illustration. The magic of digital photo-editing has extended careers in front of the camera and, owing to the aging baby boomer demographic, many of the nineties' supermodels are making a reappearance. Glossy magazines, accused of promoting anorexia, campaign for all-inclusive fashion with special "Size" issues. Along with Internet sensation Lady Gaga, both Beth Ditto and Crystal Renn deserve mention as fashion icons for the "noughties" decade. **Masstige** is also part of the democratization of fashion with design teams such as Proenza Schouler and Rodarte creating capsule collections for Target and other superstores.

It has become common practice to cross boundaries between disciplines, and conceptual fashion is barely distinguishable from fine art. Moreover, fine artists such as Andrea Zittel and Alex Katz (see p. 188) are involved with fashion projects. The cult following for "Project Runway" has helped to elevate do-it-yourself fashion to the status of Outsider art. Fashion illustrators such as François Berthoud and Grayson Perry straddle commercial and fine art, with representation at international art galleries, and even Art Basel in Miami.

In facing the realities of twenty-first-century globalization, a call for the preservation of cultural diversity has yielded a blend of traditional techniques with technology. Garment details, color, and sizing are being adapted for specific markets. As you will see in examples throughout this text, fashion artists have also responded in kind with imaginative drawing styles that reflect personal experiences and different world cultures.

◀ *"Designerman" Richard Haines illustrates observations of street fashion for his blog "What I Saw Today." The absence of tactile experiences has created a preoccupation with surface and a desire for evidence of the hand.*

▲ Designer versions of modest Islamic dress by Christian Dior, Nina Ricci, Alberta Ferretti, and Blumarine were recently presented on the Paris catwalk with sponsorship from Saks.

◄ Mark Grady creates fashionable avatars for virtual environments. Real world fashion designers such as Jean Paul Gaultier and Calvin Klein have crossed over into "Second Life" to advertise real and virtual products.

CHAPTER 1
DRAWING WOMEN

▼ *Most people really measure about seven and a half heads. The head and torso together comprise one half of the total height.*

The ancient Greeks considered beauty to be a matter of correct proportions. As such, classical figure drawing uses the head, seen in relation to the body as a whole, as a unit of measurement to determine landmarks and widths for different parts of the body. The ideal classical figure is thought to be eight heads tall.

In comparison to fine art, fashion drawing requires fewer reality checks. The fashion figure, or **croquis**, is infinitely malleable, ideal for visualizing beauty standards that are often unattainable. The stylized proportion can be anything you want it to be so long as it works well with the design concept, remains consistent within a multi-figure composition, and reflects **customer profile**.

Planning

The proportion of the figure is one of several premises on which your fashion fiction is built. And since the figure is ultimately a tool for visualizing design concepts, the way that you stylize it should serve your purpose. For instance, miniaturizing the torso to a point where it might become difficult to fit in construction details would not make sense. It is also crucial that the stylized proportion of your fashion figure has some relationship to reality so that the concept sketches approximate the realization of the garments. It is important to try to invent multiple views of this fashion fiction to fully convey all aspects of garment construction.

As you begin to develop a variety of poses, it will be challenging to keep the proportion of your figure consistent. Drawing the figure from head to toe is an acquired skill. Cropped figures are much easier to manage—you do not have to worry about the relationship between all of the parts. But because fashion is concerned with the coordination of different garments and accessories, drawing the figure in its entirety is a required skill for designers and illustrators. At first, do not be concerned with drawing facial features. Focus instead on the proportion and movement of the body as a whole.

◄ *Eri Wakiyama's concept sketches of her garments show multiple views. These designs are for the Swarovski crystal design competition at Parson's School of Fashion, New York.*

Eight, Nine, or Ten Heads?

This is an extremely personal decision. Even when students attempt to use the identical proportion, everyone's figure still turns out differently. Today fashion illustration incorporates a diversity of figure proportion as never seen before.

The key is to experiment and then pick a proportion that works for you. As best you can, remain as loose as possible. You can facilitate fluid drawing and consistent figure proportions by using a template, a guide that will be especially useful for the development of the **high hip** and turned figures. As your skills improve you will be able take even greater creative license, but following some of the traditional conventions is a great place to start. The template can be created from scratch or by analyzing one of your existing drawings.

▶ ▶▶ *Although Niloufar Mozafari (right) and Anna Molinari (opposite) both use eleven heads for their stylized fashion figure proportion, the distribution and widths of the body parts are dramatically different. Each designer establishes a distinguished and unique figure proportion to convey their vision of fashion.*

ABITO IN DUCHESSE
COL. RUBINO

FALL-WINTER 2007-2008

Blumarine®

▲ ▶ *Fashion illustrators Andrea Marshall (above) and Laura Laine (right) both have extremely personal and stylized fashion figure proportions.*

Traditional Fashion Figure Proportion

To start from scratch, one of many good formulas for a modern fashion figure is a nine-head template (see p. 39). Note the vertical landmarks and widths for the different parts of the body. You can recreate the guide in the size that works best for you by measuring or folding nine equal spaces (see p. 182). Everyone has a different drawing size that is comfortable for them. It is a good idea to get accustomed to working on a standard paper size, such as 11 x 14in. or its closest European equivalent, A3 (11.64 x 16.54in./297 x 420mm). You will want to think ahead to the size and orientation of your portfolio and plan your figure accordingly, making sure to use the full height of the paper size you choose. If you are considering an e-portfolio, the aspect ratio of computer monitors will also factor into the planning of compositions. Whereas portrait used to be the orientation of choice for portfolio presentations, landscape is now thought to be best for the wide variety of manual and digital portfolio formats. All of this may seem premature, but the emotional impact of original art in your portfolio should not be underestimated. If you get used to drawing in a uniform size from the start, you will not have to reproduce drawings at another scale when the time comes to consolidate your work in a portfolio.

You will gain a better understanding of the general construction of the woman's figure by breaking it down into simplified geometric forms. The torso can be divided in half, with the ribcage and pelvis represented by two trapezoids.

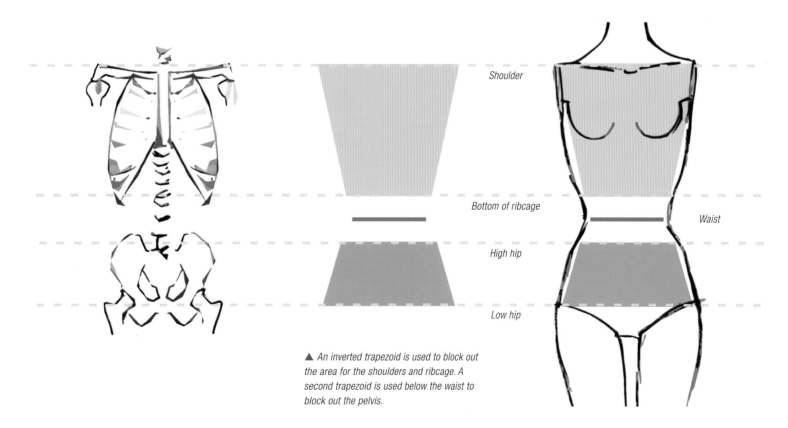

Shoulder

Bottom of ribcage

High hip

Low hip

Waist

▲ An inverted trapezoid is used to block out the area for the shoulders and ribcage. A second trapezoid is used below the waist to block out the pelvis.

Blocking in the Geometric Forms for the Rounded Figure

Refer to the simplified geometric forms (right) much as you would an articulated poseable artist's mannequin. Using a proportion template as a guide, draw the forms of the fashion figure, noting their order and location in space (for example, above or below eye level).

1 Working with all-purpose paper, divide the sheet vertically into nine equal spaces. Drop a red vertical line through the center of the measured spaces to establish a "plumb" or **Balance Line** (BL). Then mark off the vertical landmarks and widths for the different body parts as indicated on the example of the figure proportion template (second from left).

2 Place a sheet of tracing paper over the template. Secure the overlay so that it does not shift while you draw. Drop a red Balance Line. Working with a #2 or HB pencil, draw an oval for the head. Begin to sketch in the other geometric forms. The elbows and wrists have a constant relationship with the body, located slightly below the waist and hips respectively. Indicate this relationship with a dashed arc at both landmarks. Once you are satisfied with the blocking of these forms, you can use the drawing as the basis for a rounded figure.

3 Working with a second sheet of tracing paper, begin to draw your figure. It is helpful to look at various photo references as you begin to draw the body. Take care not to make your drawing overly realistic or too muscular.

NOTE Drawing the forms is vital to honing your skills. Resist the temptation to trace!

GEOMETRIC FORMS

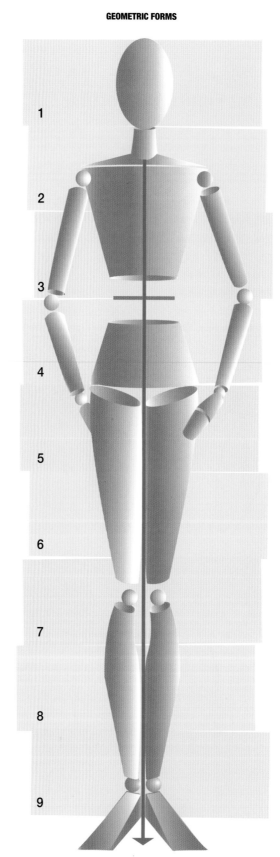

1

2

3

4

5

6

7

8

9

*Shoulders 1½ heads wide
@ 1½ heads*

*Bottom of ribcage
Waist ¾ heads wide
@ 3 heads
High hip*

*Low hip 1¼ heads wide
@ 4 heads*

Knees @ 6½ heads

Heels @ 9 heads

BALANCE LINE

PROPORTION TEMPLATE: NINE HEADS

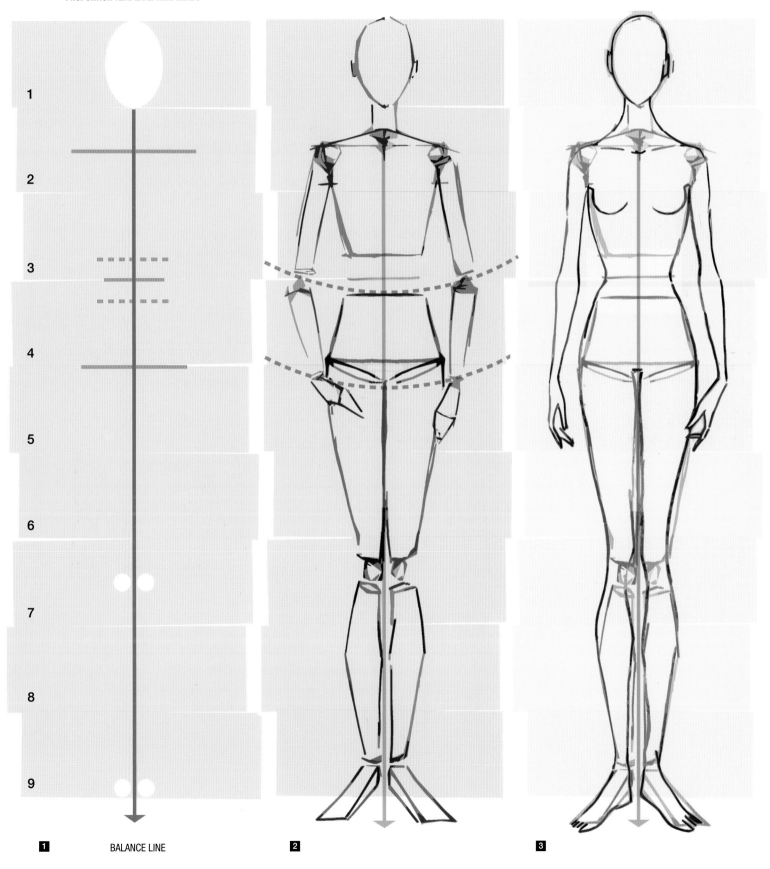

1

2

3

4

5

6

7

8

9

1 BALANCE LINE

2

3

Fashion models typically have a slim appearance to allow for better garment drape. In a traditional front view fashion figure, the expression of the bust does not extend beyond the edge of the ribcage. In drawing the front view, light and shadow are used to define form and volume. As a rule, the shape of the bust only becomes apparent in the silhouette as the body begins to turn. Based on your personal aesthetic and customer profile, you can choose a more voluptuous proportion for your figure.

As you gradually refine your sketch you will want to include more detailed information about garment fit lines. You can indicate the **apex**—the high point on the bust—and the **Center Front** (CF) line in blue. The Center Front line is fixed upon the body (almost like a tattoo), a landmark for garment details such as buttons and zippers and not to be confused with the Balance Line (indicated in red). The Balance Line is architectural in nature, always straight and perpendicular to the ground plane. For the moment, the Center Front and Balance Lines coincide, but they will part ways when the distribution of body weight begins to shift.

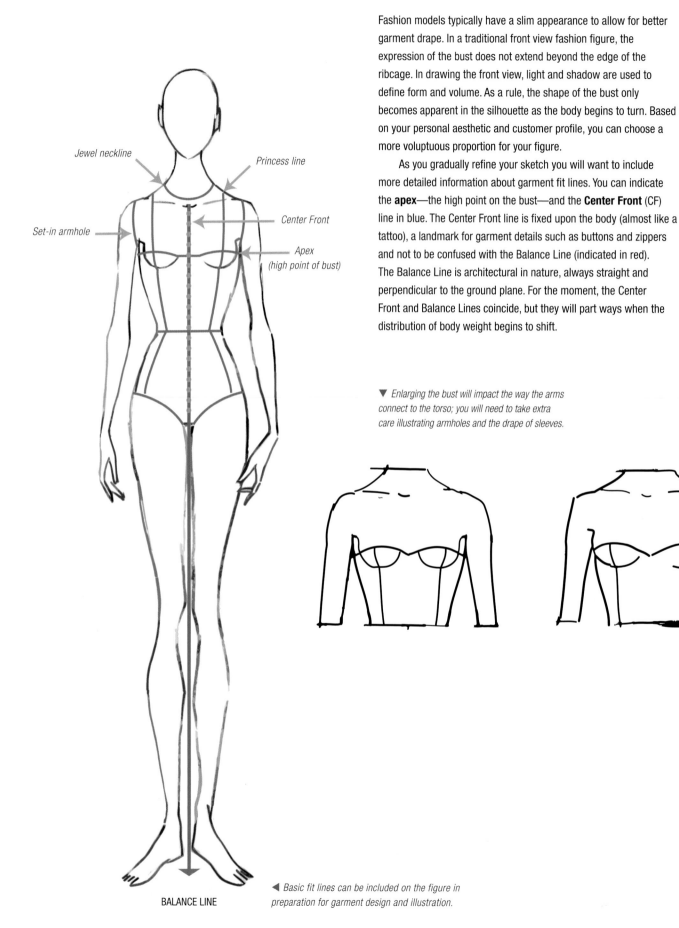

▼ *Enlarging the bust will impact the way the arms connect to the torso; you will need to take extra care illustrating armholes and the drape of sleeves.*

Jewel neckline

Princess line

Set-in armhole

Center Front

Apex (high point of bust)

BALANCE LINE

◄ *Basic fit lines can be included on the figure in preparation for garment design and illustration.*

The Flats Figure

The best way to describe a **flat** (technical drawing) is to think about what your clothing looks like when you are not in it—flat and a bit wider owing to the fabric allowance for the front-to-back dimension of your body. Flats are used for presentation and production, where a greater degree of technical information is required. Designers and illustrators typically use a flats figure to help keep the proportion of their sketches uniform. This figure can mirror the more realistic proportions of a **fit model** who approximates the measurements of your target customer (a runwalk model is more extreme). Develop your own figure for this purpose by tweaking the proportion of your rounded figure almost as if you were flattening her with a rolling pin. Take care to keep her fashionable. Presentation flats often support and amend illustrations on the stylized fashion figure. If you have an extremely esoteric drawing style for your figures and your flats are extremely realistic, there may be a disparity between the two. Take care to establish some visual connection between them.

▼ *Like many designers, Hae Won (Anna) Lee uses a flats figure to maintain a consistent and relative proportion for her flats. Although the drawings are quite technical, her personality is expressed via the line quality and designs.*

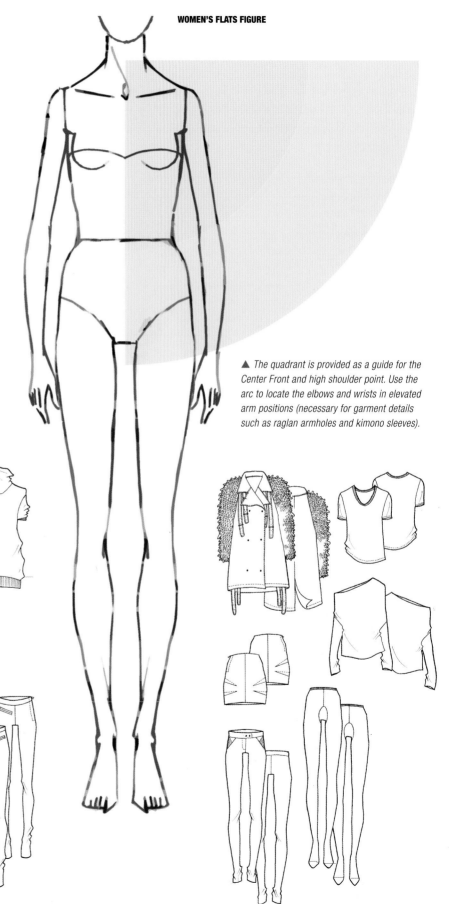

WOMEN'S FLATS FIGURE

▲ *The quadrant is provided as a guide for the Center Front and high shoulder point. Use the arc to locate the elbows and wrists in elevated arm positions (necessary for garment details such as raglan armholes and kimono sleeves).*

Intuitive Sense of Figure Proportion

You may be surprised to find that you already have an innate sense of proportion. On the first day of class students are often asked to do a quick fashion sketch to assess their intuitive fashion drawing skills. The "pretest" usually elicits groans, but these drawings are a great guide for the evaluation of what is truly unique in each artist. If the pretest is deemed a success, students have the option of using these drawings as the basis for building their figure proportion templates.

Analyze the proportion of your fashion figure

1 Working with a tracing overlay, measure the size of the head on your drawing. Then block off the number of heads in your figure.

2 Drop a Balance Line. Determine appropriate landmarks and widths for the shoulders, waist, and hips. In this example Jessica's figure is distinguished by an exaggerated fullness through the thighs. An additional guideline for the width of the thighs is used to facilitate proportion consistent with her pretest drawing. Establish the vertical landmarks for knees, heels, elbows, and wrists.

3 Then, interpret the geometric forms using your own figure proportion.

4 Use the geometric forms as the basis for your customized rounded figure.

NOTE   Take the time necessary to experiment. Periodically, your perception of proportion will shift. No matter how extreme, any figure proportion that you choose is valid. By using a customized template you will be able to develop a variety of poses while maintaining a personal and constant figure proportion. For those new to fashion drawing, try a quick fashion sketch to discover your intuitive sense of proportion. If this seems intimidating, you can draw on a small scale, almost like a doodle, experimenting with different proportions. If you hit upon something workable you can always enlarge the image on a photocopier or scanner.

▼ *Jessica Strimbu demonstrated an unconventional (and totally charming!) sense of proportion in her pretest. When stylizing the figure, it is important to consider the relationship between the parts. Shortening the torso creates the appearance of lanky arms.*

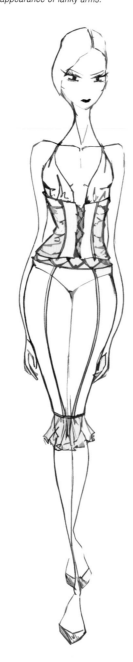

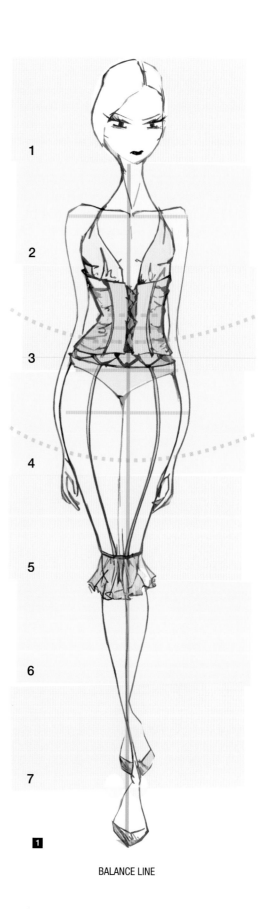

BALANCE LINE

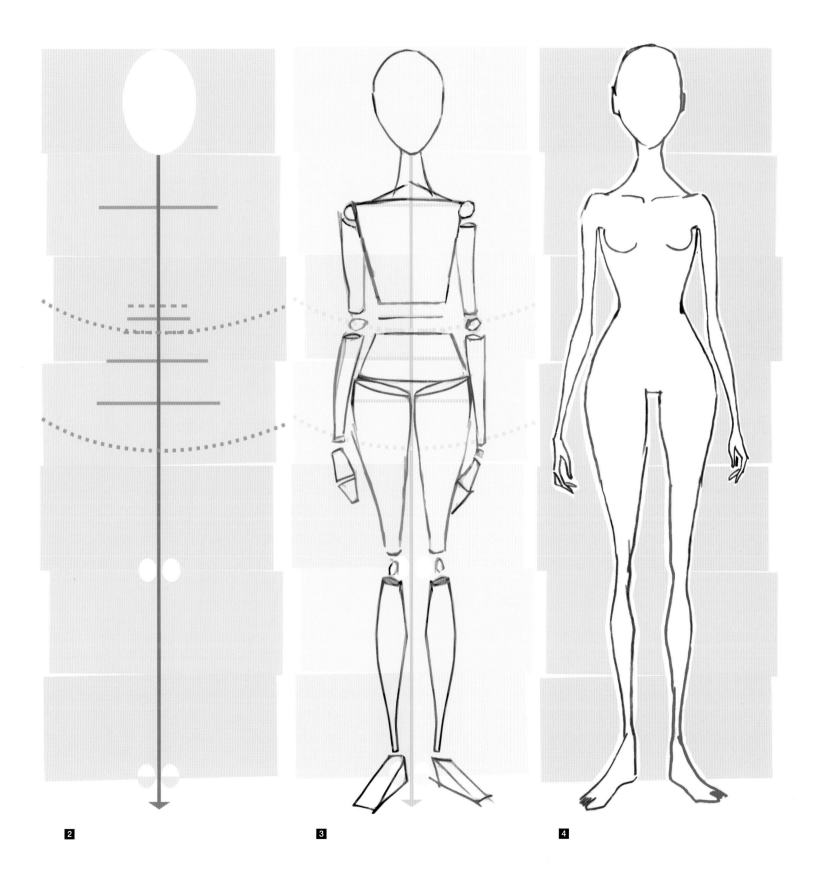

2

3

4

Balancing

Once the proportion has been determined, it is time to get some movement into your figure. The front view with even weight distribution was helpful to determine overall proportion. But this figure seems rather static when compared to the action you see on the catwalk. Once again, you will defer to classical drawing, which dictates that in order to give the body motion, one must first show the figure at rest. In the "high hip" pose, known more formally as **contrapposto**, the body weight rests on one leg.

In preparation for balancing the figure, it is helpful to stand in front of a full-length mirror and watch what happens to your own body when you shift your weight from side to side. Notice how the angles of your shoulders and hips work in opposition; how your entire body moves in the direction of the weight-bearing leg. After you shift your weight over to one leg, look straight down and observe how the foot of the weight-bearing leg is positioned directly beneath your chin on an imaginary Balance Line.

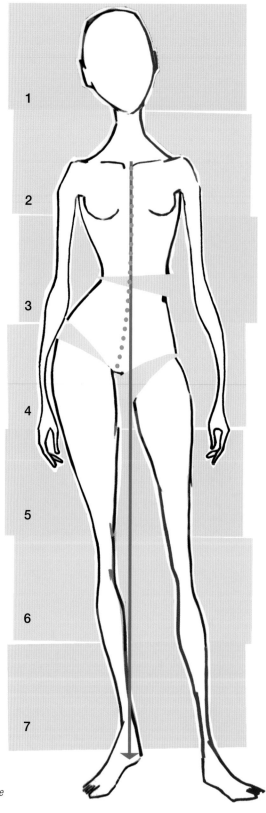

▶ *You can manipulate the parts of your intuitive figure to create a preliminary high hip pose.*

BALANCE LINE

Blocking in the Forms for the High Hip Figure

Returning to the block geometric forms will help you to better understand body movement and to develop a wide variety of poses. Working with your template, draw the geometric forms (right), adapting them as necessary for your customized proportion. As you draw, make sure that the arrangement of the forms is consistent with the rules of contrapposto.

Checklist for the High Hip Figure

✓ The CF line swings in the direction of the weight-bearing leg.

✓ The head is directly over the foot of the weight-bearing leg.

✓ The opposition of the upper and lower forms of the torso counterbalances the body.

✓ The weight-bearing leg is straight (in fact it is awkward to bear weight on a bent leg).

✓ The angle of the knees is parallel to that of the hips.

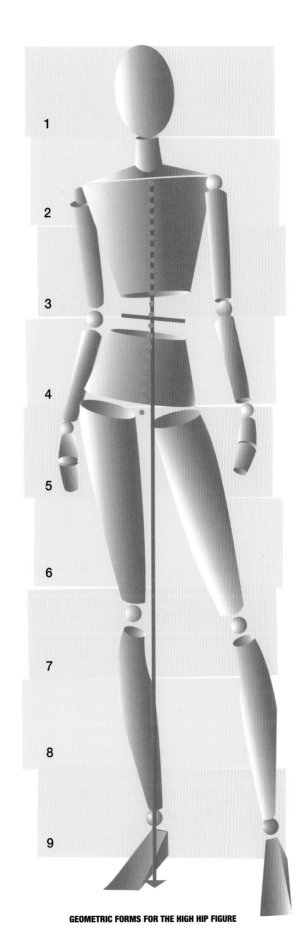

1

2

3

4

5

6

7

8

9

GEOMETRIC FORMS FOR THE HIGH HIP FIGURE

▲ *Before you begin drawing the high hip figure, analyze the pose using a small stick figure.*

Drawing the High Hip Figure

Your drawing of the forms can then be used as the basis for a first high hip figure. Slip the sketch under several sheets of tracing paper. The underdrawing should be only a vague reference since, once again, you are not tracing but drawing.

1 Using a color pencil or felt tip marker, analyze the pose as follows:
a. Drop a Balance Line from the pit of the neck perpendicular to the ground (note how this line intersects the foot of the weight-bearing leg.)
b. Plot the Center Front line by connecting the pit of the neck with the belly button and then the crotch.
c. Diagram the angle of the waist and hips, then the shoulders and bust line.
d. Finish up your analysis by plotting the location of the knees and feet, noting their relationship to the angle of the hips and proximity to the Balance Line.

2 Begin to rough out your high hip figure, guided by the various landmarks. Take care to distribute established widths for shoulders, waist, and high and low hip evenly on the Center Front line. Do not confuse Center Front with the Balance Line.

3 Indicate the collarbone, apex, and top of the legs.

4 Add the neck, bust, and arms; refine the legs.

5 Refine your drawing, using a second sheet of tracing paper as necessary, and add fit lines (see p. 40).

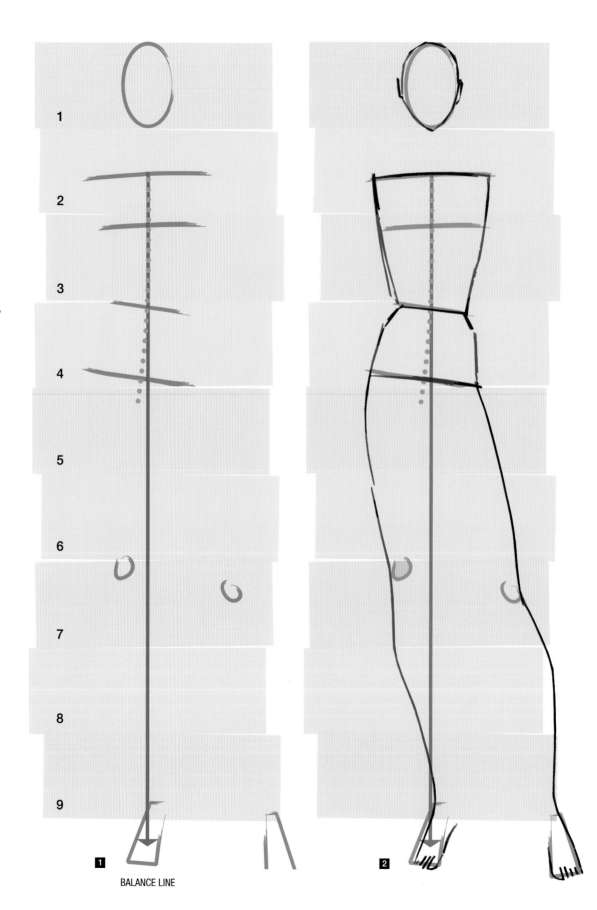

BALANCE LINE

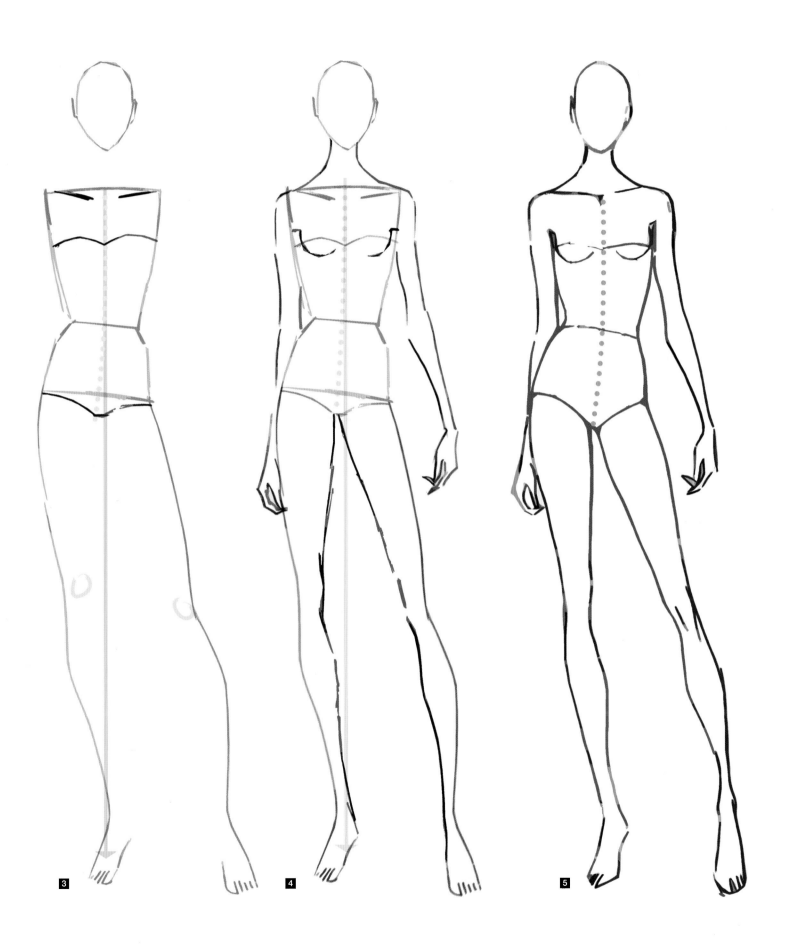

3

4

5

Variations

Once you are satisfied with your drawing you can begin to develop other poses by flopping the image and experimenting with various arm and leg positions. Try not to be overly ambitious and keep in mind that, moving forward, garment design will ultimately dictate the pose you choose for your figure.

As you can see (opposite right), contrapposto is in fact a universal pose. When the body weight rests entirely on one leg, the action of the non-supporting leg is completely arbitrary. The opposing forms of the upper and lower torso combine with the straight supporting leg to form the basis of both the relaxed and action poses (opposite left and center).

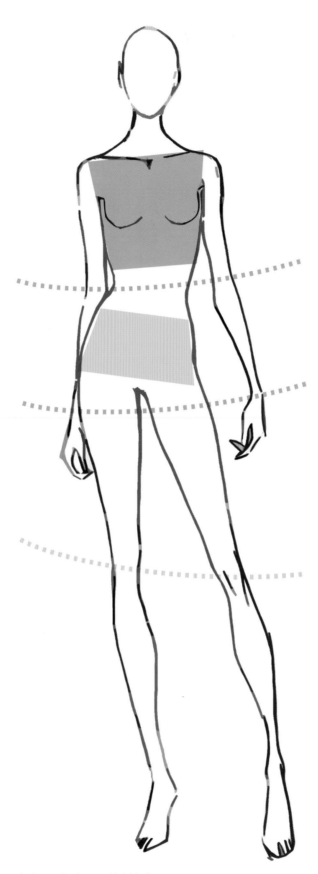

▲ As you develop your high hip figure, note how the angle of the elbows and wrists corresponds to that of the shoulders; how the angle of the knees parallels the action of the hips.

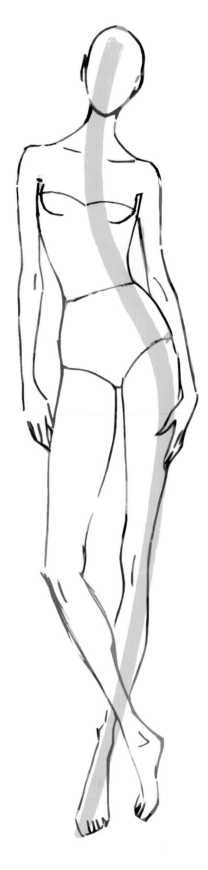

▲ The insinuation of the S-curve, which accommodates shifts in the body's weight, will lend rhythm to the final version of your drawing.

▲ The relaxed pose.

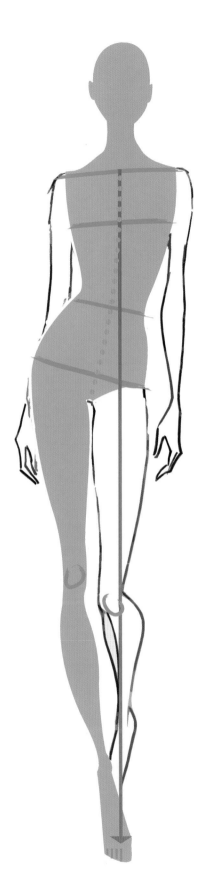

▲ The action pose.

▲ The high hip figure is extremely versatile
and can be adapted for a variety of relaxed
and walking poses.

Drawing the Back View Figure

Following the same steps as for the front view high hip figure, establish a back view. Working with your template and a tracing paper overlay:

1 Drop a red Balance Line. Then draw the back of the head in pencil. The back of the head is more circular than the front, which is an oval shape. Plot the **Center Back** (CB) line, shoulders, bust, waist, hips, knees, and the feet.

2 Begin to rough out your back view high hip figure, guided by the various landmarks.

3 Refine your drawing, using a second sheet of tracing paper as necessary; be sure to maintain the movement of the S-curve.

NOTE In some instances, although the weight of the body has shifted in one direction, it still is shared by both legs, although disproportionately; therefore the Balance Line will fall closest to the foot bearing the greatest burden. In this drawing, the foreshortening of the non-supporting leg gives it the appearance of receding into the background.

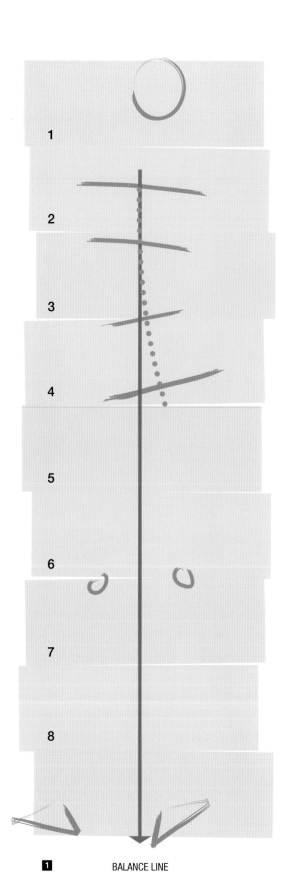

1 BALANCE LINE

2

3

Inventing the Skeletal Structure

Because the idealized fashion figure is quite slender, you would expect to see some expression of the bone structure. Which is not to say that you need to articulate each and every bone, as this would make the figure look quite old or emaciated. Nor should you arbitrarily add lumps and bumps to your drawing. In order to make your drawing more convincing, there should be some indication of bone structure derived from classic anatomy and adapted for your own fashion proportion.

For this next exercise, you will use your high hip figure as the basis for a study of the bones. Discovery of the individual bones and their relationship to one another will give you a better understanding how the body moves and is balanced. There is no reason to take the rules of contrapposto on faith; by studying the bones you will see why the shoulders and hips work in opposition, how the angle of the knees is governed by the angle of the hips, and so on. When you analyze a pose, you are in fact plotting the various joints and bones. For instance the plotting of the Center Front line is really for the spine, the plotting of the hips for the top of the butterfly-shaped pelvis, and so on. You should do some preliminary research in a basic anatomy book to gain an overall impression of how the skeleton works. There are also some good anatomical charts on the Web. Your approach to this drawing should be casual, with gesture prioritized over accurate representation of individual bones. Referring to a model or photo reference, observe how the bones affect the shape of the figure and where they find expression just under the skin.

1 Place your high hip figure under a tracing overlay. As you refer to an anatomical chart begin to roughly construct a skeletal structure that corresponds to the proportion of your high hip figure.

2 Refine your drawing; the bones should be accurately drawn and the action of the spine should correspond to the S-curve. The Center Back line reflects the action of the spine.

3 Use your front view skeleton as a guide for the back view. The back view of the spine should also convey the S-curve.

1

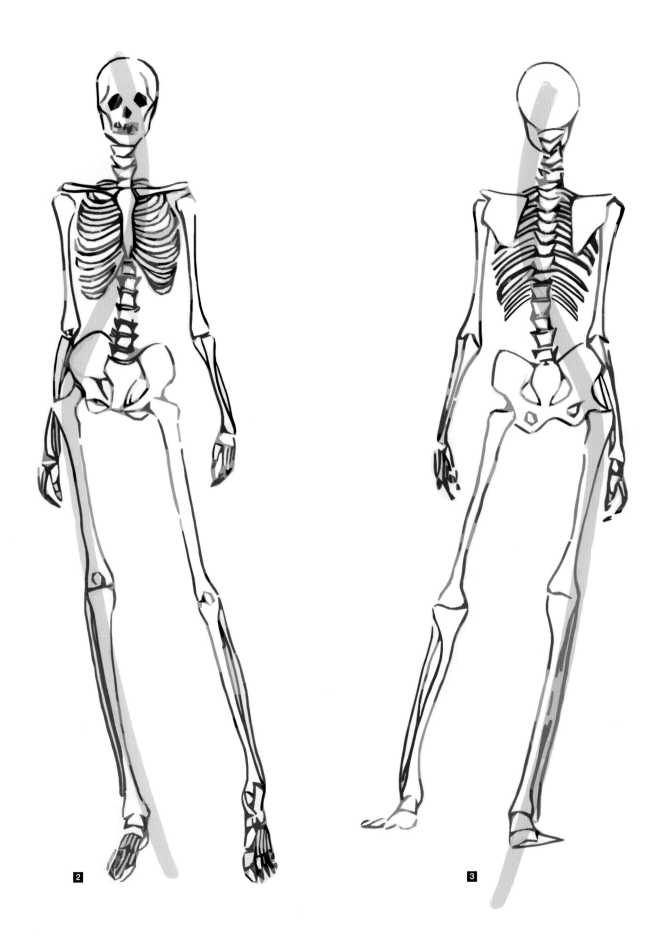

Turning

Having established your figure's relationship to gravity (balancing) you can now move on to the next premise for your drawing— perspective. In order to convincingly rotate the high hip figure, you will need to create the illusion of depth. But some basic spatial relationships need to be established first.

While fashion illustration does not necessarily require mechanically accurate perspective, a good drawing will have some indication of depth. Decide for yourself to what degree reality will come into play. You can take a flattened decorative approach as was popular in the twenties (see p. 13) or use light and shadow in conjunction with the rules of perspective as was popular in the thirties (see p. 14). Either way, a general understanding of the principles of perspective will help you to achieve roundness and a layering of the forms as they advance and recede in space.

For the purposes of fashion illustration, the rules of perspective can be distilled into very general terms. Simply stated, your eyes perceive the size and shape of an object in a way that gives you information about its location. For instance, as an object moves away from you it will appear smaller; conversely as it moves toward you it will appear larger. Your perception of that object will also change depending on whether it is viewed from above, below, or head on.

The appearance of the different parts of the fashion figure (and eventually garment details) will also vary depending on their location relative to the level of the viewer's eye. So in order to represent your figure convincingly in space, you must make decisions about the location of eye level in the **picture plane**.

When you are first beginning to draw the figure, it is best to avoid more extreme points of view. A simple approach is to plot eye level at the hips. Everything above the hips/eye level will be represented with a convex line and everything below the hips/eye level will be represented with a concave line.

The partially turned figure allows for a more comprehensive view of garment details featured on the side of the body (such as, racing or tuxedo stripes, peekaboo openings, and **engineered prints**) without sacrificing information about the front view. As the body begins to rotate, the side moving away from view appears to decrease in size. This visual distortion, known as **foreshortening**, will be simulated in your drawing so as to suggest the illusion of depth. Although the vertical landmarks remain the same, the widths of the shoulders, waist, etc. are foreshortened by the body's rotation in space.

Note how the side of the body turning away from view appears to shrink (opposite right). The distribution of the widths of the forms on the Center Front is no longer symmetrical—instead they are foreshortened on the side receding into space. The rules of contrapposto still hold true: the Balance Line runs from the pit of the neck through to the foot of the weight-supporting leg; the opposing angles of the shoulders and hips act to counterbalance the body. As the body turns, the vertical landmarks remain constant but the receding forms are now seen in a new layered order (the neck is in front of the bust is in front of the shoulder, and so on).

Advancing

Receding

Below Eye Level

Above Eye Level

←TURNING LEFT

TURNING RIGHT→

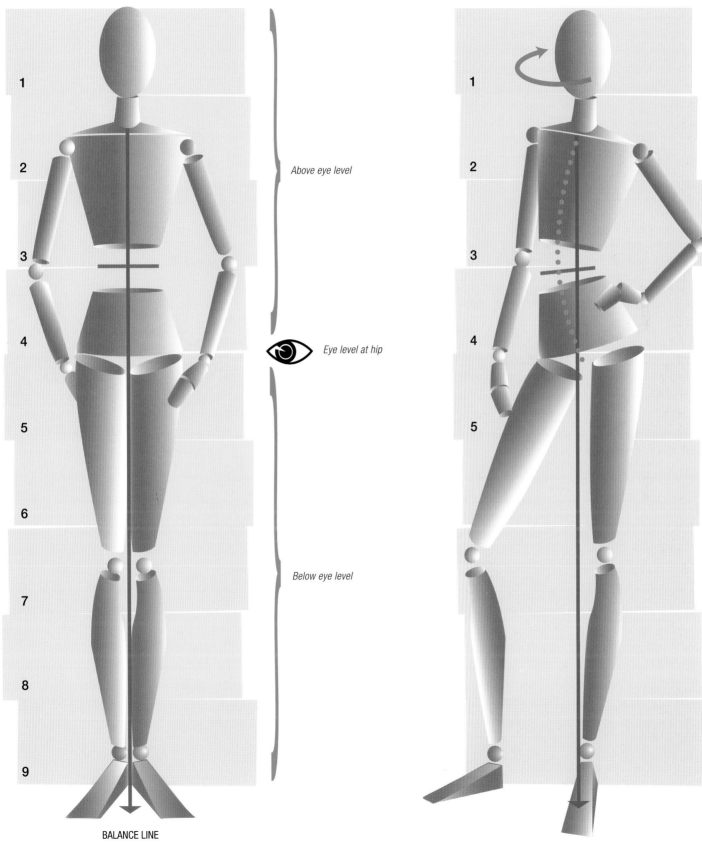

1

2   *Above eye level*

3

4   *Eye level at hip*

5

Below eye level

7

8

9

BALANCE LINE

ESTABLISHING EYE LEVEL

GEOMETRIC FORMS FOR THE TURNED FIGURE

Drawing the Turned Figure from a Photo Reference

In an effort to create a more convincing fashion fiction, it is best to work from a model so that you can see the physical mechanics of contrapposto. A photograph is also extremely helpful. Try to find an image or magazine **tear sheet** that features a head-to-toe, three-quarter view of the figure. Work with your proportion template slipped under a sheet of tracing paper.

1 Using a colored pencil or felt tip marker, analyze the photo as follows:
a. Drop a Balance Line from the pit of the neck (this line intersects the foot of the weight-bearing leg).
b. Plot the Center Front line by connecting the pit of the neck with the belly button and then the crotch.
c. Diagram the angle of the waist, hips, shoulders, and bust line. Order is important here since the volume of the hair often obscures the angle of the shoulders. By analyzing the waist first, you know by default that the angle of the shoulders will be in opposition.
d. Plot the location of the knees and feet, noting their proximity to the Balance Line.

2 Working with your template and a tracing overlay, use the established landmarks to reinterpret the analysis of the pose. Foreshorten the widths of the shoulders, waist, and hips on the side turning from view.

3 Sketch the head and torso, then add legs and feet. Referring to the photo, sketch the hand in position on the hip using the landmarks.

4 Refine your drawing to include the basic garment fit lines.

NOTE Drawing the hands in position before the arms eliminates guess-work. Using the photo as a guide, block in the negative space between the arm and the body with a colored marker; then draw the inside of the arm from the wrist up.

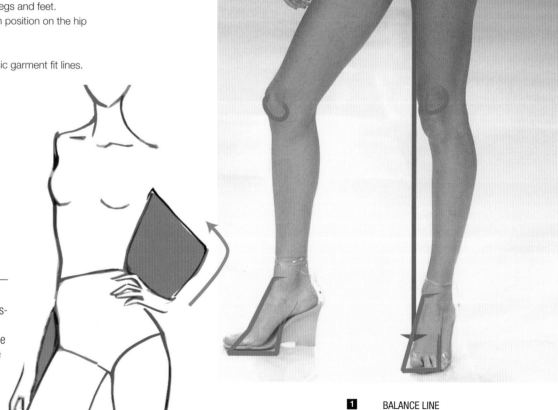

1 BALANCE LINE

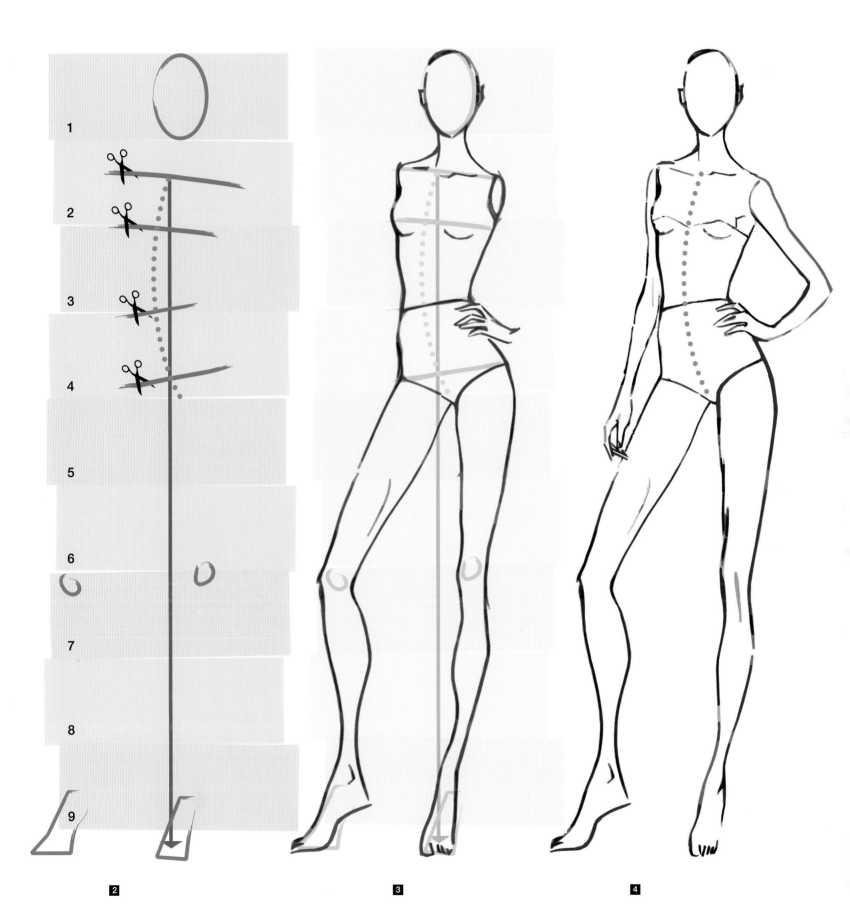

1

2

3

4

5

6

7

8

9

2

3

4

ASSIGNMENT 1

The two hemispheres of the brain that process words and images operate in very different ways. When you struggle with your drawing, in all likelihood it is because the hemisphere of your brain that deals with words has assigned a name, and the various attributes associated with that name, to the troublesome part of the drawing. These preconceived notions interfere with your ability to objectively observe shape and form. A quick fix for this problem is to turn both your drawing and your photo reference upside down, abstracting the image. When you cannot "name" them, you will find it much easier to redraw the difficult parts (such as face, hands, and feet). The upside-down method is not good for establishing the whole, though, since you need to be more subjective when stylizing the proportion. Working with the photographs here (right and opposite), analyze and reinterpret the poses using your proportion template. Then double-check and refine your work by turning both the photo reference and drawing upside down.

▶ ▶▶ *Photographs of runway presentations for swimwear are a good resource for figure references. Here are photos for a back view walking pose (right) and the high hip figure at rest (opposite).*

To begin developing a facility with markers, and to reinforce an understanding of balancing and foreshortening the figure, sketch the high hip (left), turned, and profile figures wearing one-piece swimsuits. Design the swimsuits using only the fit lines indicated on p. 40. Bisect the garments on the Center Front line with color blocking. You may want to do a preliminary rough sketch on tracing paper. Then finish your sketch on marker paper using an HB or colored pencil or fine felt tip marker for the outline. Applying color directly over pencil or ink is a tricky affair; you can pretty much rely on a smudged mess. To avoid this problem, render colored marker on the reverse side of the paper (Bienfang Graphics 360 Marker Paper is especially good for this technique.) See Part III for more tips on rendering.

The integration of your manual drawing and digital skills will optimize both. After you have finished your pencil sketch of the swimsuits from Assignments 1 and 2, scan and export the drawings to either Photoshop or Illustrator. You can then experiment with the various pen and brush tools, fills, filters, effects, and layer blending modes to render your drawing. The Cutout filter in Photoshop, with its varying degrees of abstraction, is a personal favorite. The Live Trace option in Illustrator is a great way to preserve the spontaneity of a pencil sketch when converted to the appearance of an inked drawing. There is also the added bonus of being able to edit the vector image.

Drawing the Women's Profile Figure

Using the method established for the other views, you can now complete the rotation of your figure with the profile figure. Once again, refer to the block geometric forms (right).

1 Using your proportion template, plot the half-widths on one side of the Center Front line.

2 Sketch the figure using the established landmarks and widths.

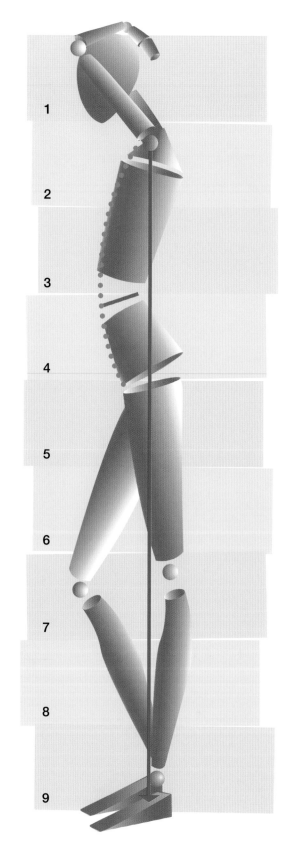

PROFILE GEOMETRIC FORMS

NOTE Note the location of the Center Front line; the profile figure is literally one half of the front view.

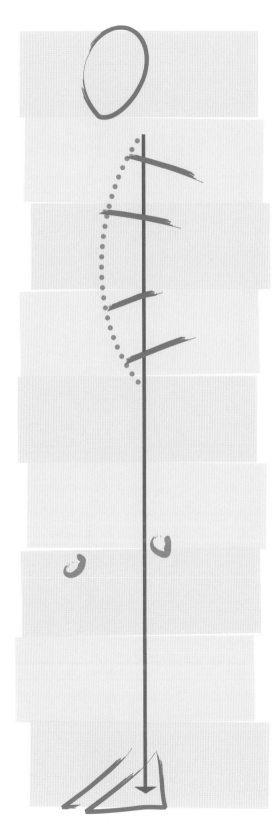

1

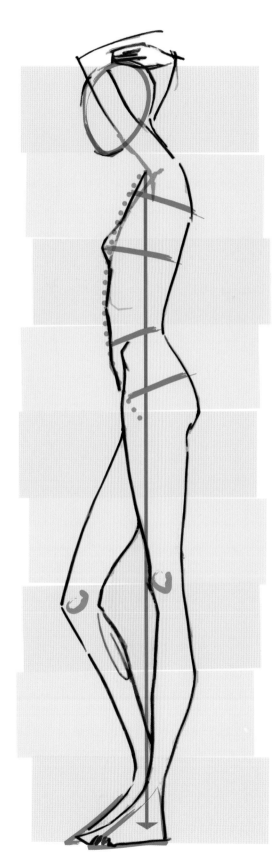

2

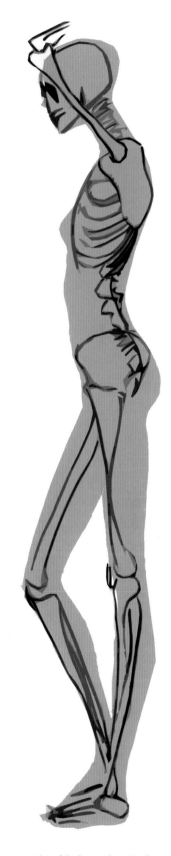

▲ *The expression of the bones closest to the surface is most apparent in the profile view.*

▼ *The front-to-back and side-to-side movement of the spinal column is the genesis of the S-curve.*

▼ *The position of the foot is critical to the profile view. Standing on tiptoes with the weight borne by the ball of the foot shifts the upper body forward.*

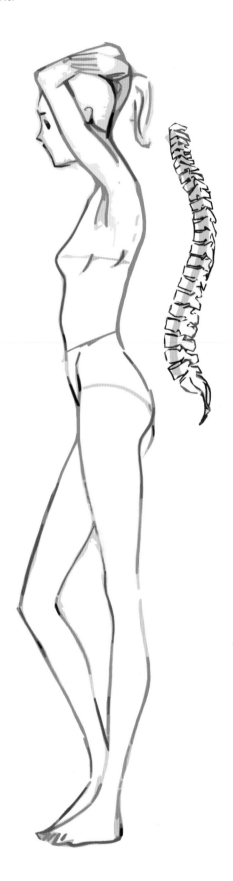

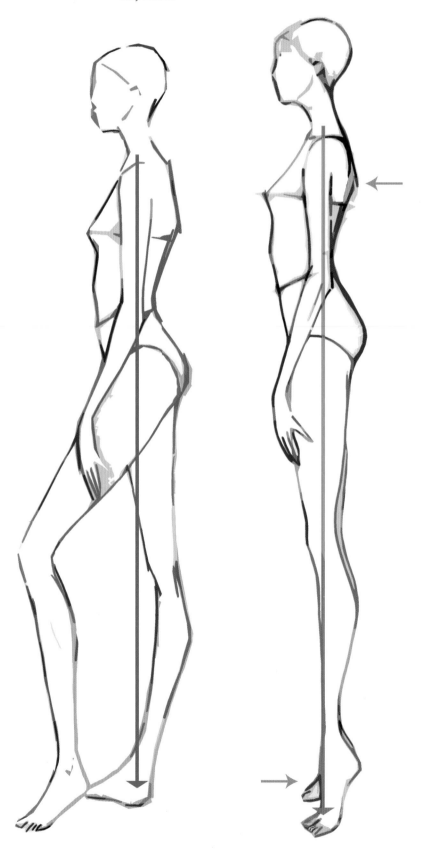

Posing

As you become more adept at drawing the figure you will want to experiment with more ambitious poses. For extreme foreshortening it is best to refer to a photograph or live model (for more about foreshortening and model drawing see Chapter 5). Although you can get away with making up poses from your imagination, it really is better to have a photo reference in order to evoke the experience of real bodies. An accumulation of magazine tear sheets in a **swipe file** is invaluable for working in the absence of a model. There are also lots of images available online—retailers of high-end intimate apparel and swimwear are especially good for figure references. Subscription Web sites specifically geared to the needs of artists provide 360-degree virtual poses (although these are not fashion models). Stock photo Web sites are also exellent resources. Keep in mind that if you do not require high-resolution images most will be royalty free.

When selecting a photo, look for a head-to-toe pose where the figure is not obscured by layers of clothing. You may need more than

▶ *Illustrator Andrea Marshall uses an artful composition, props, accessories, and a dynamic pose to showcase a simple garment silhouette.*

one photograph; one for face and hair, another for shoes. Because the camera is likely to have been positioned differently in each photo, your reference materials may have multiple points of view. Here is where the eye level "premise" of your drawing will come into play and unify point of view. When evaluating a photograph, ask yourself: does the figure truly appear to be standing up? A pose that contradicts the rules of contrapposto (even if it occurred in a moment frozen by the camera) may not be believable in a drawing. On the other hand, a figure that is slightly off balance can be used to dramatic effect—you do not know until you try. Not every pose need be overly complicated. Figures that are extremely contorted can actually obscure and distract attention from the garment. The use of a static figure with small gestures can be very effective in offsetting more dynamic poses in multi-figure compositions.

When working from a photo, resist the temptation to trace or exactly duplicate what you see. Rather, the photo is your jumping-off point, to be reinterpreted via the drawing premises established in this chapter. Your goal is to search out the facts of your photo and then use them to create a believable and fashionable fiction.

◀ *If the figure is leaning on a table or against a doorway, you must be sure to include it or a substitute prop in your drawing or she will appear to be falling over.*

▲ *Kelly DeNooyer's garment designs and illustrations are inspired by Scott Radke's marionettes. The poses—also in keeping with her inspiration—could not be freestanding without the support of the marionette strings.*

ASSIGNMENT 4

Working with your proportion template and a variety of photo references, develop six new figure poses. Experiment with more dramatic foreshortening, props (below), and accessories, as well as the pairing of figures with shared gesture and balance.

▲ The addition of appropriate accessories and props will also add visual interest to your compositions.

▶ You can experiment with a pair of figures that have a shared gesture and interdependent balance (see Chapter 5 for how to try this out in the model-drawing studio). Design and illustration by Eri Wakiyama.

Adjusting

After working in fashion for a period of time you will begin to notice how different figure proportions go in and out of vogue. For instance, eighties' power dressing called for fashion figures that were about eight heads tall. By the mid-nineties there was a new figure proportion of ten heads. The dawn of the twenty-first century called for one more reconsideration, with nine heads thought to be the ideal proportion. You must be prepared to periodically renew your girl by reassessing her figure proportion.

Breaking the Habit

The "habituated" eye is not just a problem for fashion drawing veterans. If you are brand new to fashion drawing but have extensive training in fine art you will have a strong tendency toward more classic (robust) proportions. No matter what the reason, if you have become stuck on a certain proportion and want to change in order to accommodate trend, customer profile, or perhaps a personal statement, digital manipulation is a great aid to breaking visual habits.

There are many other reasons for adjusting the proportion of your figure. You may happen upon a new figure proportion purely by accident, out of the blue, drawing a quirky figure unlike anything you have ever done before. A life model might inspire such a change in proportion. The method described for intuitive fashion proportion (see p. 42) will also help you to adapt and perpetuate the lucky accident.

Relative Proportion

Then there is the case of relative proportion. The descriptive terms "plus" and "petite" imply larger or smaller than what is deemed to be average. Of late, fashion has developed a greater awareness of the many body types and varied perceptions of beauty. It is possible that you will either want or need to reflect these differences in your fashion presentations. Customer profile is very much at issue—there are plus women and plus juniors; petite is not junior, but rather an adult woman's frame with shorter stature. The approach to garment design will vary for these distinct customer profiles and it is very important to have the right figure on which to visualize concepts. The plus and petite figures are variations on a theme—take care to use the same economy of line, stylization, and elegance as in your other fashion drawings.

▼ *One of the premiere life models on the New York drawing scene, Aviva Stone's robust figure has appeared in drawings and paintings by hundreds of artists as well as French* Vogue.

NOTE   There are many names for the different size ranges in the marketplace. The average woman's (5'4"–5'7"/162–170cm) sizes are 0/2–14, XS–L (UK 4–16). The fuller figure sizes are 14–20, XL–4X (UK 16–22). The petite figure (4'11"–5'3"/150–160cm) sizes are 0–20, XXS–XL.

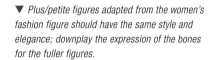

ASSIGNMENT 5

The challenge in drawing the relative proportions of the plus and petite figures (below right) is that as you adjust one part of the body, the size of the other parts will appear to be thrown off. There is quite a bit of trial and error involved in these drawings. Begin experimenting with adjusting proportions using Photoshop to adapt your "average" women's fashion figure. Scan your high hip figure and open the document in Photoshop. Then, select and transform the waist, hips, thighs, etc. for the plus and petite sizes. For the petite figure, adjust the vertical landmarks. Conversely, for the plus size figure the vertical landmarks remain constant with an adjustment made to the widths of the various parts of the body. Avoid a blanket transformation of the entire figure. Instead, adjust the individual parts of the body for an idealized plus and petite form. When you are satisfied with your figure, you can use it as the basis for a new proportion template.

▶ *The petite customer should not be exempt from edgy fashion—concepts can be visualized in a relative drawing style. Illustration by Elisabeth Dempsey.*

▼ *Plus/petite figures adapted from the women's fashion figure should have the same style and elegance; downplay the expression of the bones for the fuller figures.*

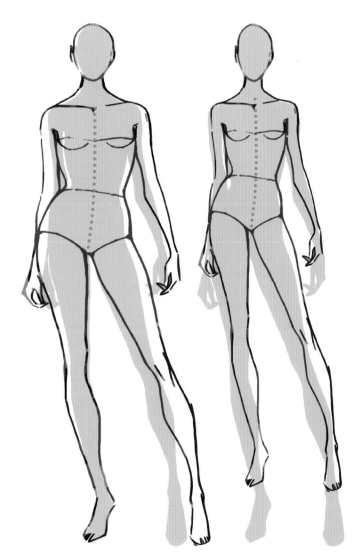

Drawing the Turned Plus Size Figure

Fine art gives us many examples of the glorification of the fuller figure, such as the paintings of Peter Paul Rubens and Niki de Saint Phalle. You must seek out the beauty in the more robust form. For this next exercise, follow the steps for drawing a turned figure, taking care to foreshorten the side of the body receding into space.

1 Create a proportion template for the plus size figure based on your digital manipulation of the "average" figure in Assignment 5.

2 Working with your plus size template and a tracing overlay, drop a red Balance Line and then, using pencil, draw a fuller oval for the head and plot the shoulders, bust, waist, hips, knees, and feet. Remember to foreshorten the body widths on the side turning away from view.

3 Begin to roughly sketch the plus size turned figure, guided by the various landmarks.

4 Refine your drawing, using a second sheet of tracing paper as necessary; be sure to maintain the movement of the S-curve. Experiment with different hairstyles and arm positions. Remember that the non-supporting leg is also a variable.

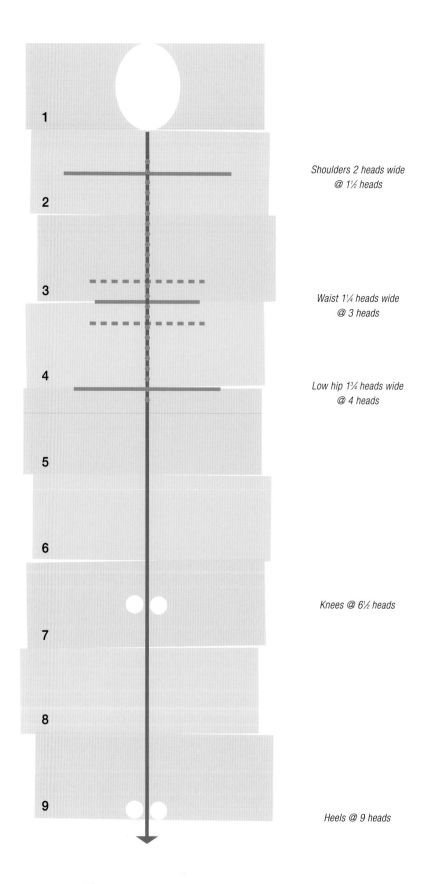

Shoulders 2 heads wide @ 1½ heads

Waist 1¼ heads wide @ 3 heads

Low hip 1¾ heads wide @ 4 heads

Knees @ 6½ heads

Heels @ 9 heads

1 BALANCE LINE

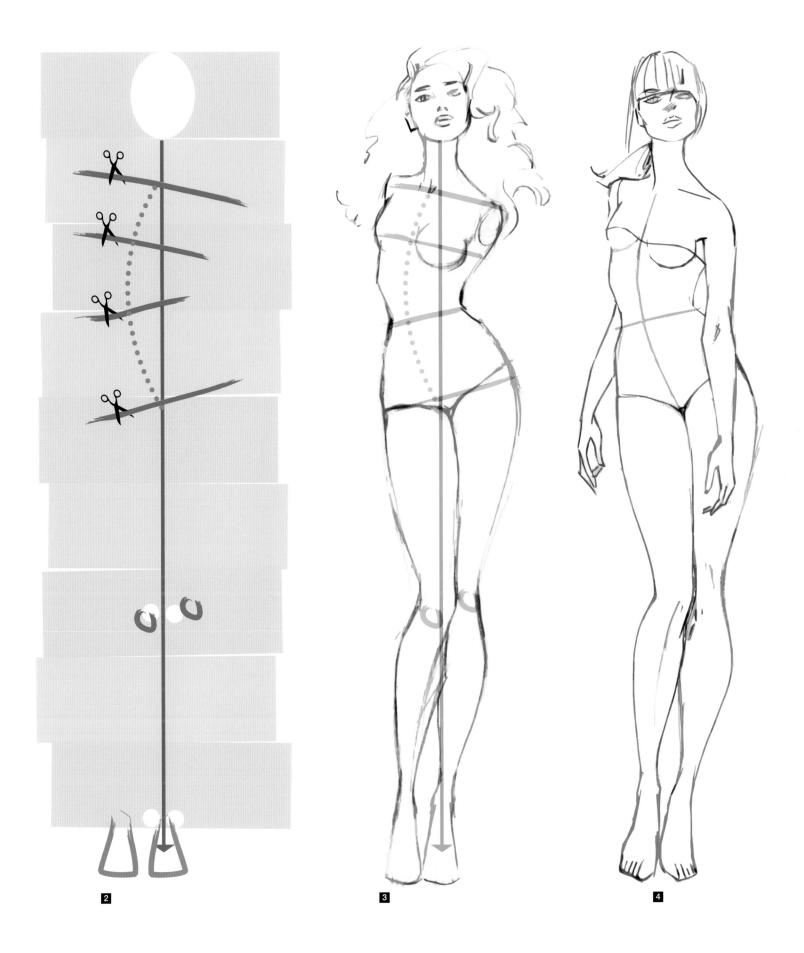

2

3

4

Drawing the High Hip Petite Figure

Create a proportion template for the petite figure relative to the nine-head "average" fashion figure. A more compact torso can be achieved by slightly raising the landmarks for waist and hips; the limbs will be abbreviated in comparison to the average women's figure.

1 Working with your petite size template and a tracing overlay, drop a red Balance Line and then, using pencil, plot the landmarks and widths for the various parts of the body.

2 Diagram the angles of the shoulders, bust line, waist, and hips, then plot the location of the knees and feet.

3 Roughly sketch the figure, guided by the various landmarks. The preliminary pencil sketch of the petite figure should begin to capture subtle gestures such as a slightly turned foot.

4 Refine your drawing, using a second sheet of tracing paper as necessary.

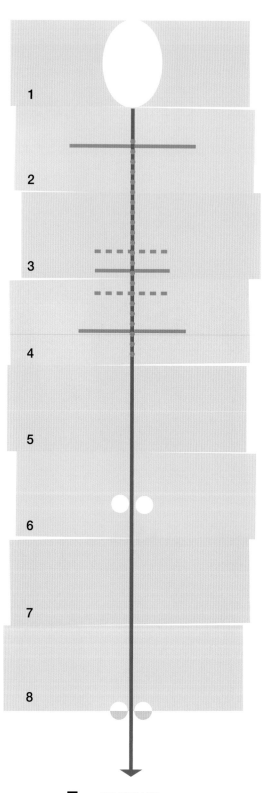

1 BALANCE LINE

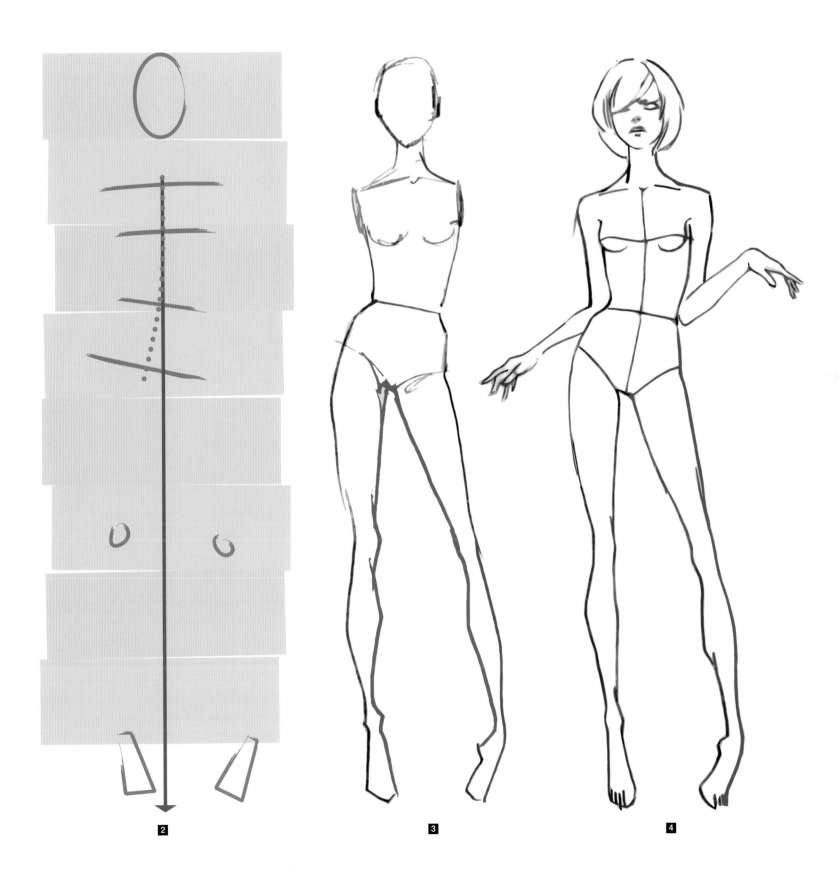

2

3

4

The Bump

In recent years, the pregnancies of high-profile celebrities have pushed maternity apparel into the fashion forefront. Part of this new sense of prenatal chic is an entirely different sensibility about expectant mothers' bodies. As compared to the past, when pregnant women cloaked their bodies in voluminous drapery, women today often dress in body-hugging silhouettes that accentuate their growing form. Designer Liz Lange pioneered trend-driven maternity, and these days a pregnant woman can easily flaunt her bump in clothing that mirrors the latest runway looks. Even Agent Provocateur, makers of scandalous intimate apparel, now offer pre- and postnatal collections.

The glamorization of maternity begins with concepts visualized on an appropriate figure. The maternity figure must be just as stylized and fashionable as your regular fashion figure—just with a bump! Subtlety is not a good idea here since you do not want this figure to be confused with the plus size. The turned and profile views are ideal for emphasizing the fashionable bump.

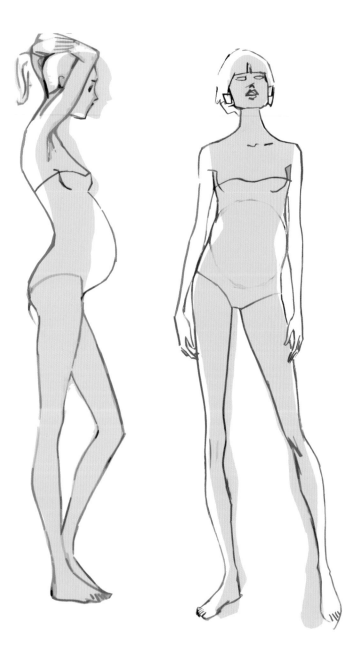

◄◄ *The upper body shifts backward to counterbalance the additional weight of the "bump." The high hip maternity figure will have less opposition between the upper and lower torso and a slightly wider stance.*

◄ *Model Jourdan Dunn on the catwalk wearing a signature look by Jean Paul Gaultier adapted for her bump.*

▲ *Illustrator Muntsa Vicente portrays maternity à la mode—in the context of a modern urban lifestyle.*

CHAPTER 2
DRAWING MEN

As in the case of the women's figure, design philosophy, prevailing fashion trends, and customer profile will all be determining factors in the representation of your men's figure. For instance, if the garment designs tend to be more experimental, presentations are also likely to be unconventional, both in terms of figure proportion and media. On the other hand, a classic design philosophy would dictate a more traditional approach. Garment specialization will also influence visual presentation. For instance, performance apparel geared to a specific sport would be best illustrated on more athletic figures in active poses.

◀ *Designers Nina Donis apply the same aesthetic to clothing for men and women.*

▶ *Dylan Taverner uses an edgy drawing style and a figure proportion suited to young designer fashion for men.*

▶ *A more muscular physique is preferred for modeling athletic clothing and swimwear. In reality, the figure measures about seven and a half heads tall. Note how the head and torso together comprise one half of the total figure height.*

▲ *Howard Tangye uses an expressive line quality to illustrate men's fashion. Menswear designers such as Hedi Slimane, Kris Van Assche, and Thom Browne prefer a slim, androgynous body.*

▶ *Richard Haines uses a gestural drawing style to convey impressions of fast fashion for men.*

▲ *Paula Sanz Caballero uses innovative media choices to illustrate fashion-forward suiting.*

Planning

Any stylized proportion that you choose is acceptable—in fact, there is typically a broader allowance for the male ideal. Designers such as Nina Donis often establish a relative proportion between their men's and women's figures. It would make sense that if you prefer to draw a large head for the women's figure, you will be inclined to follow through with a similar proportion for the men's. The overall height of the men's figure is often scaled to be somewhat larger than that of the women's. If your women's figure has a proportion of nine heads, so too would your men's—but the heads used as a unit of measurement will be slightly larger.

WOMEN   **MEN**

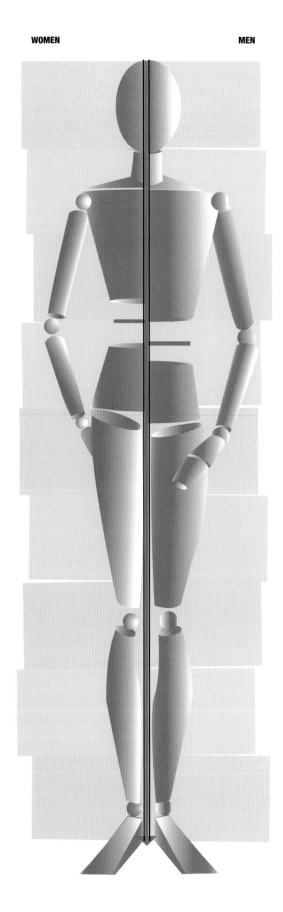

THE GEOMETRIC FORMS COMPARED

▲ *Fernanda Guedes uses a relative figure proportion for her illustrations of men and women. Less closely cut contemporary urban streetwear requires a more robust form and the suggestion of contemporary lifestyles for context.*

Obviously, there are many other gender-based differences and these become immediately apparent with the geometric forms (left). Relative to women's figures, men have more developed and consequently prominent skeletal and muscular structures. Facial features are chiseled and the jaw square. (For more about drawing men's faces see Chapter 4.) The men's figure will also be wider through the shoulders and chest. Men have longer torsos with lowered waists and narrowed hips. However, the appearance of masculinity for fashion does not necessarily translate as bulk.

The purpose of your sketch will also be an influencing factor. Fashion designers, for instance, face the unique challenge of visualizing garments that do not yet exist beyond their imaginations. An extremely stylized figure proportion used for sketching initial concepts may later cause a disparity between roughs, finished figures, flats, and, ultimately, the realization of the garment. Illustrations created for advertising, magazines, and blogs have an entirely different set of parameters. Fashion illustrators such as Richard Haines (see p. 76), may have greater creative license in the representation of existing garments. Artwork can be less specific and more experimental in terms of proportion and media choices. But the fashion illustrator must also satisfy the demands of the commissioning client. A certain number of revisions may be part of the contractual agreement. And since perceptions of artwork can be quite subjective, satisfying both the client and yourself requires a skillful balance.

◀ ▲ *Seksarit Thanaprasittikul's initial concept sketch features a restrained stylization to better predict realization of the garments.*

Traditional Fashion Figure Proportion for Men

If you prefer to use the nine-heads template for your women's fashion figure it would make sense to use a similar formula for the men's. You can use the nine-heads template for the men's fashion figure provided. Recreate this guide in another size that works better for you by measuring off or folding your drawing paper into nine equal spaces. If you prefer to use a customized proportion for the women's figure, you will want to adapt it for men by scaling up the head size and modifying the width of the shoulders, extending the length of the torso, and emphasizing expression of the muscles and bones.

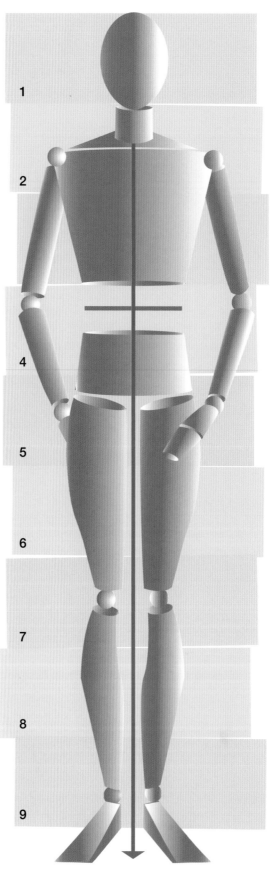

GEOMETRIC FORMS

BALANCE LINE

MEN'S PROPORTION TEMPLATE: NINE HEADS

Blocking in the Geometric Forms for the Men's Rounded Figure

Refer to the diagram of the geometric forms for men much as you would an articulated poseable artist's mannequin. Using the men's template as a guide, draw the forms for the male fashion figure noting their order and location in space (for example, above or below eye level). (For more about spatial relationships and foreshortening see pp. 54–55.)

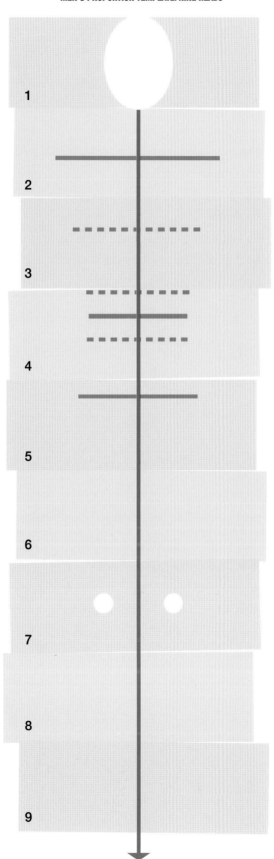

Shoulders 2 heads wide @ 1½ heads

Bottom of pectoral muscles @ 2⅓ heads

Bottom of ribcage @ 3 heads

Waist 1¼ heads wide @ 3¼ heads

High hip @ 4½ heads

Low hip 1⅓ heads wide @ 4¼ heads

Knees @ 6½ heads

Heels @ 9 heads

1 Place a sheet of tracing paper over your template and drop a red vertical line through the center of the measured spaces to establish a "plumb" or Balance Line. Working with a #2 or HB pencil, draw an oval for the head and then work your way down the body indicating the geometric forms for the men's fashion figure.

2 Once you have established the forms, roughly block in the shoulders, chest, and abdomen on a second tracing overlay. Remember that a masculine fashion physique is not necessarily bulky.

3 Loosely sketch the rest of the figure.

4 Refine your drawing to include details for the face, hands, and feet.

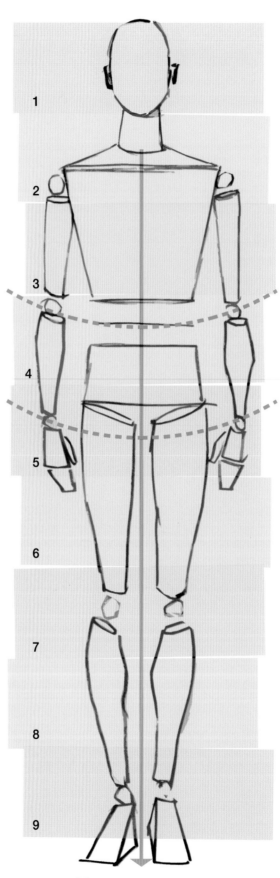

1 BALANCE LINE

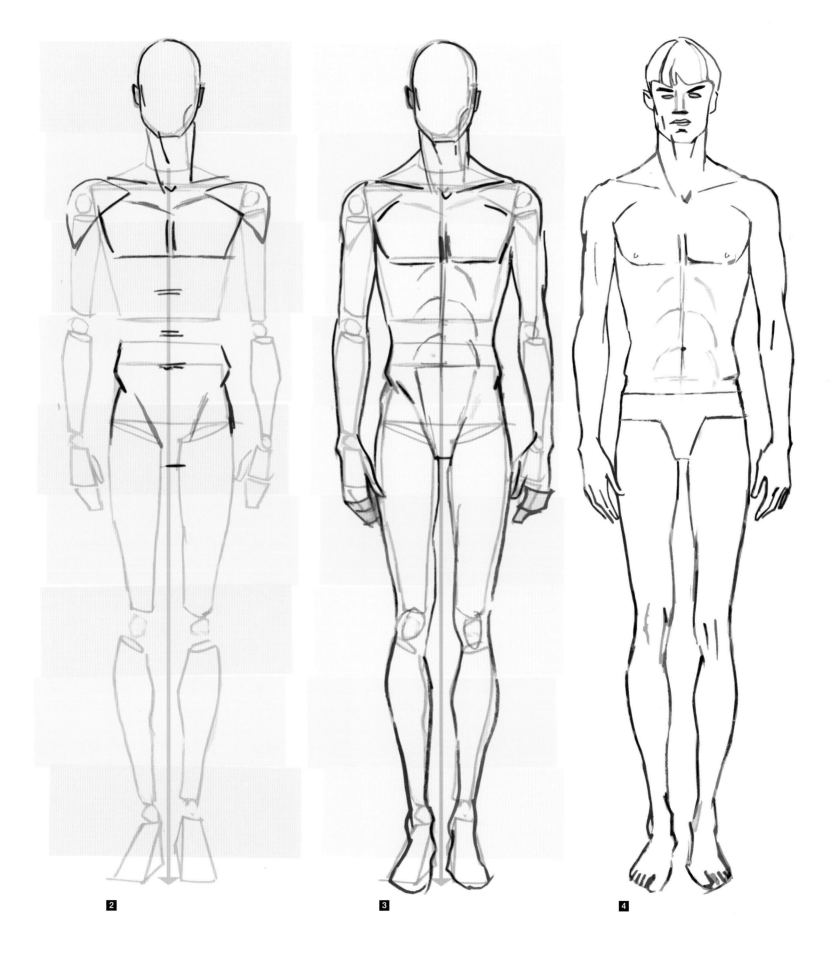

2   3   4

The Flats Figure for Men

Flat sketches, which visualize how a garment looks off of the body, are integral to the design and production of menswear. While the stylized fashion figure is used to idealize and predict how a garment will drape, flats are more effective for communicating technical information about construction. Flats used for garment specification in **tech packs** must be quite literal since they serve as a blueprint for the creation of first samples. A greater degree of imagination comes into play when flats are used for initial concept development—in fact many menswear designers often design on the flat. Presentation flats, used for merchandising and sales, can also be more inventive. An illustrator may be hired to reinterpret the fashion designer's concept for a promotional presentation. Details are sometimes intentionally obscured in such presentations to protect designs from being copied.

A flats figure can help to maintain a uniform proportion between the different garments in a collection. By adapting the stylized front view men's figure for this purpose, you can establish a relationship between the fashion and flats figures. Because clothing is fitted to accommodate a three-dimensional form, garments will appear wider when laid out flat, off the body. As such, the flats figure will also be a bit wider. The position of the legs should be hip-width apart and the arms parallel to the Center Front. That way if you have occasion to fill your flats with pattern, the body and sleeves of the garment will have the same pattern direction.

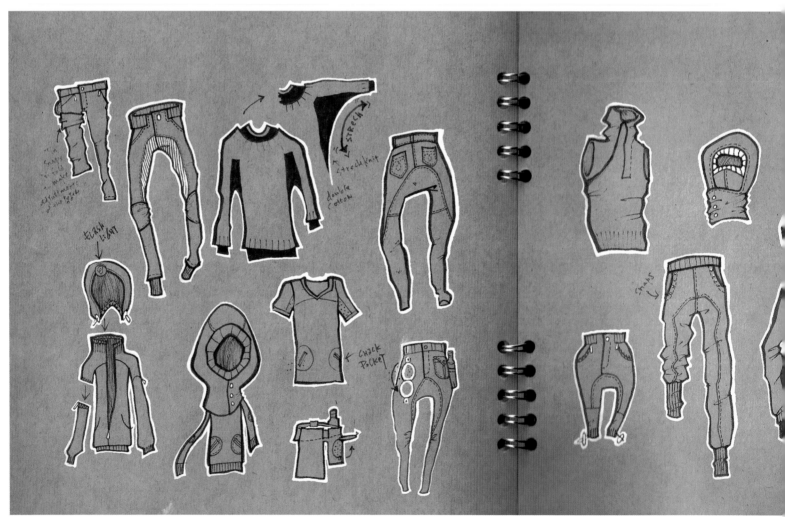

THE MEN'S FLATS FIGURE

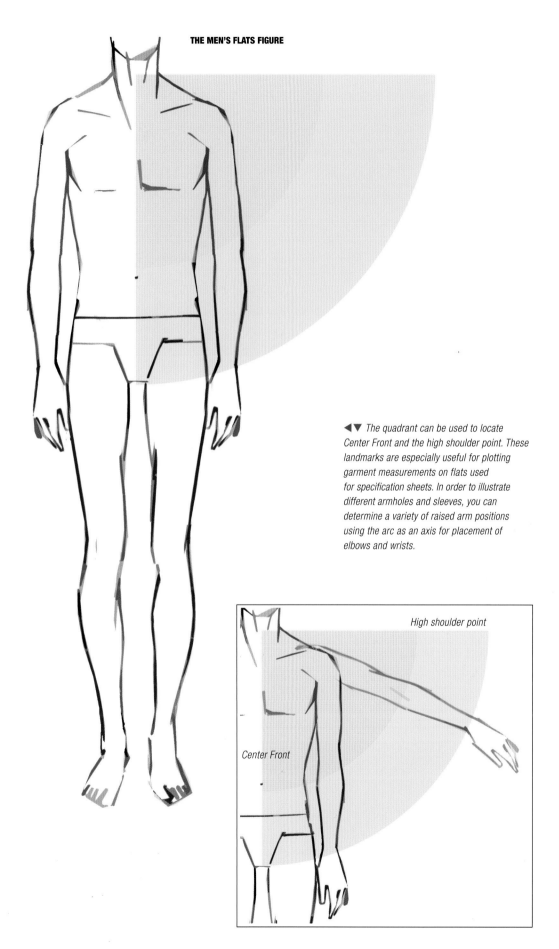

◀ *Peter Clark re-imagines the motorcycle jacket as fine art. A collage done on the flat can inspire garment design.*

▼ *Diana Lin uses animated flats for her active sportswear collection.*

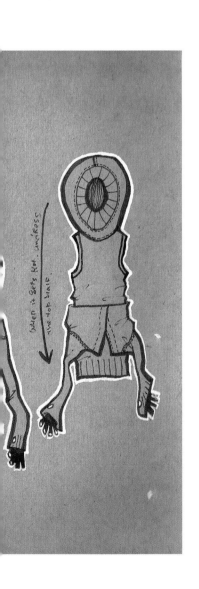

◀▼ *The quadrant can be used to locate Center Front and the high shoulder point. These landmarks are especially useful for plotting garment measurements on flats used for specification sheets. In order to illustrate different armholes and sleeves, you can determine a variety of raised arm positions using the arc as an axis for placement of elbows and wrists.*

High shoulder point

Center Front

Proportion Derived From Model Drawing

New students often have preconceived notions about fashion drawing based on exposure to artwork that, in all probability, inspired them to become fashion artists in the first place. As a consequence, the novice will often attempt to draw the way he or she thinks they should. Working within the conventions of the discipline is well and good for the development of drawing skills. The methodology of teachers also leaves a lasting impression. But it is also possible to create a perfectly wonderful fashion drawing that does not look like anything you have ever seen before. If you are to achieve any level of creative autonomy, it is imperative to remain open and not dismiss such "quirky" drawings out of hand.

Observations from life, which are invaluable for the development of your figure drawing skills, are most likely to produce unpredictable (and desirable) results. Because of the finite amount of time allotted to capture the likeness and gesture of the live model, you draw more quickly and without hesitation. As a result, the outcome is less premeditated—it is through model drawing that you are most likely to discover your intuitive sense of proportion. You may also react in a unique way to different models that embody distinct and varied customer profiles. While there is virtuosity to extensively working and reworking a drawing over many hours, the immediacy and spontaneity of a timed model sketch best captures the essence of fashion.

Because of the differences between drawing from life versus a photo or even the imagination, many people experience a major disconnect when working under disparate circumstances. More often than not, the figure proportion established for drawings created without the benefit of a model does not quite match up to that of figures drawn from life. You might be very accomplished at life drawing and yet struggle when you have to work without a model (or vice versa). Discoveries from model drawing can (and should) be carried over to the other modes of illustration. You can facilitate a seamless transition between the different drawing modes by analyzing the proportion of one of your life drawings and applying it to a new proportion template. Then, when you draw from a photo reference or your imagination, you can use the template derived from life drawing to achieve a new proportion, one perhaps better suited to a particular customer profile or garment specialization. (For more about model drawing see Chapter 5.)

▶ *Richard Rosenfeld expertly captures the likeness of the model in an extremely foreshortened pose.*

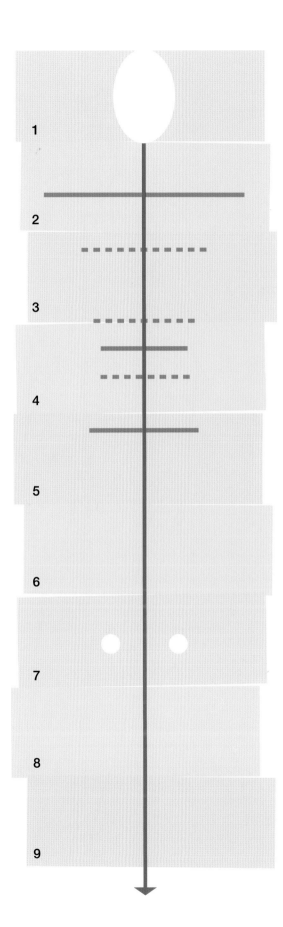

▲ *A more extreme proportion emerges in a timed model drawing.*

PROPORTION TEMPLATE DERIVED FROM MODEL DRAWING

Shoulders 2¼ heads wide @ 1⅔ heads

Bottom of pectoral muscle @ 2¼ heads

Bottom of ribcage @ 3 heads

Waist 1 head wide @ 3⅓ heads

High hip @ 3⅔ heads

Low hip 1¼ heads wide @ 4¼ heads

Knees @ 6½ heads

Heels @ 9 heads

Balancing

Before you begin manipulating the men's figure into a high hip pose, make sure you have read the in-depth explanation of balancing the figure in Chapter 1. Since gravity has the same effect on men and women, the rules of contrapposto will apply to both. Just as for women in the relaxed pose, the angle of the men's shoulders will be in opposition to that of the hips. As the lower torso shifts in the direction of the high hip, the head will be positioned directly over the foot of the weight-bearing leg. There is also an insinuation of the S-curve—although to a lesser extent than for women.

There are, of course, many gender differences. Compared to women, men have more developed musculature and skeletal systems. As a consequence, they have comparatively less flexibility and, when their weight shifts, the opposition between the upper and lower torso will not be so extreme. Stances and hand and foot gestures are also gender specific—for example, figure poses with even weight distribution are perceived to be more masculine.

Drawing the Men's High Hip Figure

Using your proportion template and the checklist for the high hip figure (see p. 45), draw the men's high hip figure at ease, both front and back. The beauty of working on tracing paper is that once you are satisfied with these drawings, you can flop them to create additional mirror-image figures.

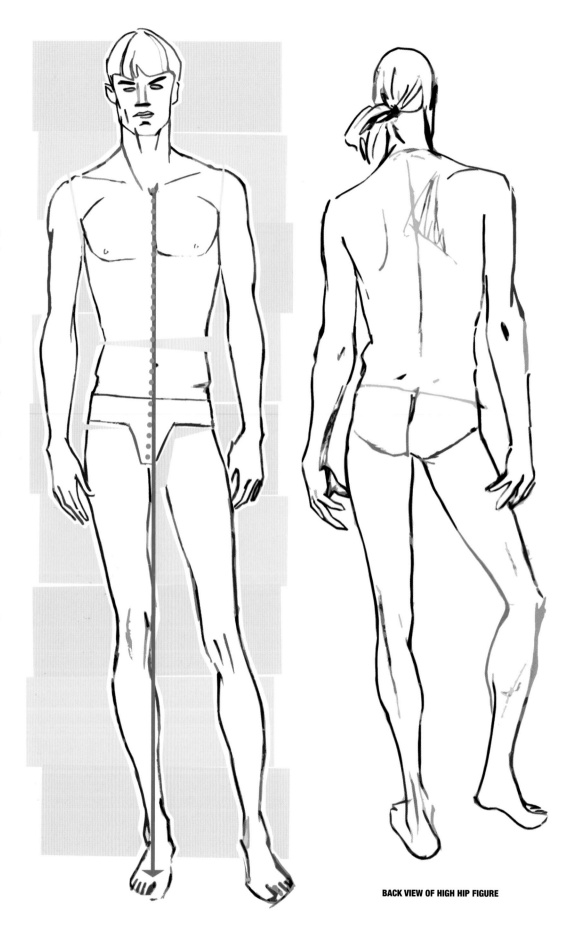

▶ *You can manipulate parts of the front view static figure according to the rules of contrapposto to create a high hip pose.*

BACK VIEW OF HIGH HIP FIGURE

Inventing Muscles and Bones for the Men's Figure

Once you have determined overall proportion, you can then invent the muscles and bones for your men's fashion figure. Place your figure under a tracing overlay. Referring to an anatomical chart (there are many good diagrams available on the Web), reinterpret the skeletal structure according to your stylized figure proportion. Then draw the muscles on a second tracing overlay. Studying the muscles and bones—which find greater expression in the male figure— will be invaluable to the development of the men's figure. Your placement of shadows and highlights on the skin (or body-hugging clothing) will be informed by your knowledge of key muscle groups.

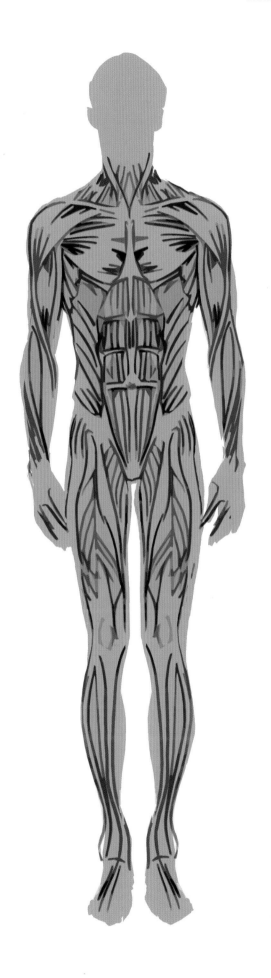

▶ *Reinterpreting the musculature for a stylized figure proportion.*

Adapt the proportion you have established for your men's figure to accommodate a variety of customer profiles and garment specializations (for example, a young, streamlined athletic form for activewear, this page and opposite), or a more mature figure that would be appropriate for conservative tailored clothing).

▶ Working from life, illustrator Richard Rosenfeld's observations of diverse figure proportions relate to a wide variety of customer profiles.

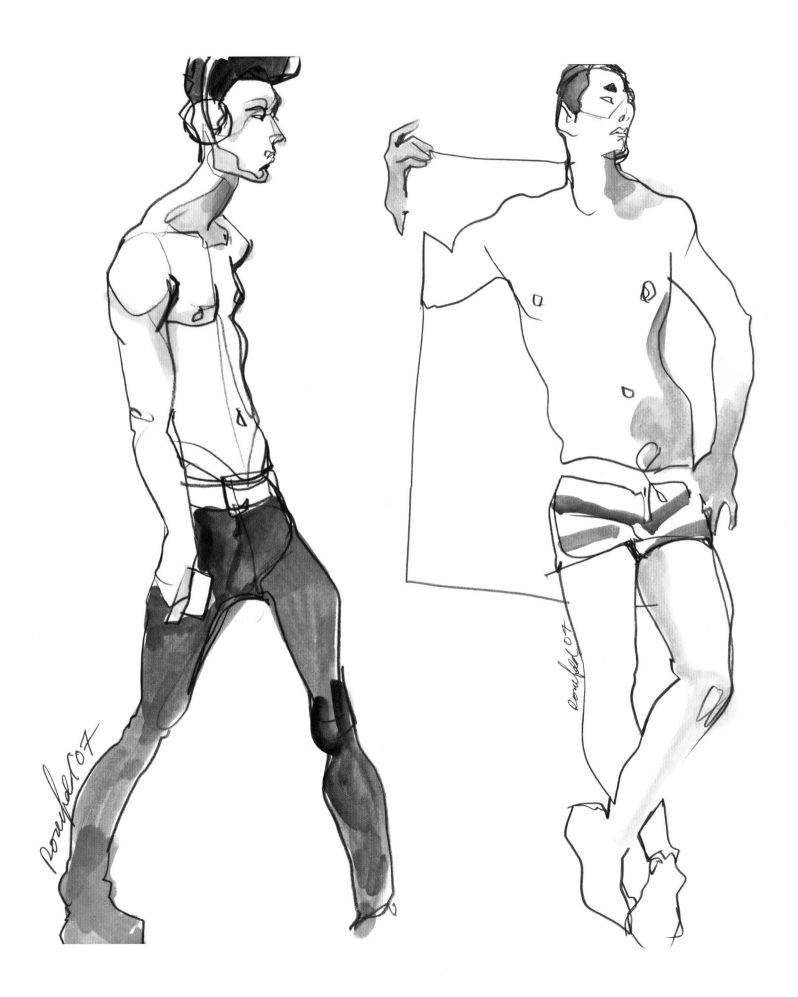

Posing

As discussed in Chapter 1, the high hip figure is really a universal pose that can be infinitely adapted so long as you respect the rules of contrapposto. The weight-bearing leg must be straight, with the foot positioned directly under the head; the action of the non-supporting leg, however, is completely arbitrary. You might want to capture the action of the runway with a walking pose (see below). In the end, garment design will ultimately determine the pose. For instance, the sleeves of a tailored blazer, set in high at the armhole and close to the body, would restrict the full range of motion for the arms. There are also certain behaviors and demeanors associated with different garment specializations. Again, using the tailored blazer as an example, you would probably choose a more dignified and reserved pose.

The Walking Pose

Fashion runway photos, available in print and on the Web, are excellent references for walking poses. Swimwear collections are particularly good to use, with the proviso that these models tend to have more muscular physiques. Take care to develop a figure that is fashionable and not a bodybuilder! As in previous chapters, you are cautioned not to copy or trace the photo. Your objective is to reinterpret the pose via the stylized fashion proportion you have established for men. (For more about working with photo references see p. 56.)

Working with a photo reference and your men's proportion template slipped under a sheet of tracing paper:

1 Analyze a photo reference of a walking pose; determine the Balance Line, Center Front line, and the angle of the shoulders and hips. Then plot the location of the knees and feet.

2 Reinterpret this analysis by indicating the same landmarks on your proportion template. Then establish the forms for the upper and lower torso, knees, and feet.

3 Roughly sketch the body as a whole.

4 Refine your sketch to include details for the face, hands, and feet. Take care to establish spatial relationships, foreshortening the parts of the body that advance or recede into the picture plane. Articulate the muscles using an economy of line to create an appropriate physique for fashion. Evaluate the figure as it relates to your design philosophy, customer profile, garment specialization, and relevant fashion trends.

1

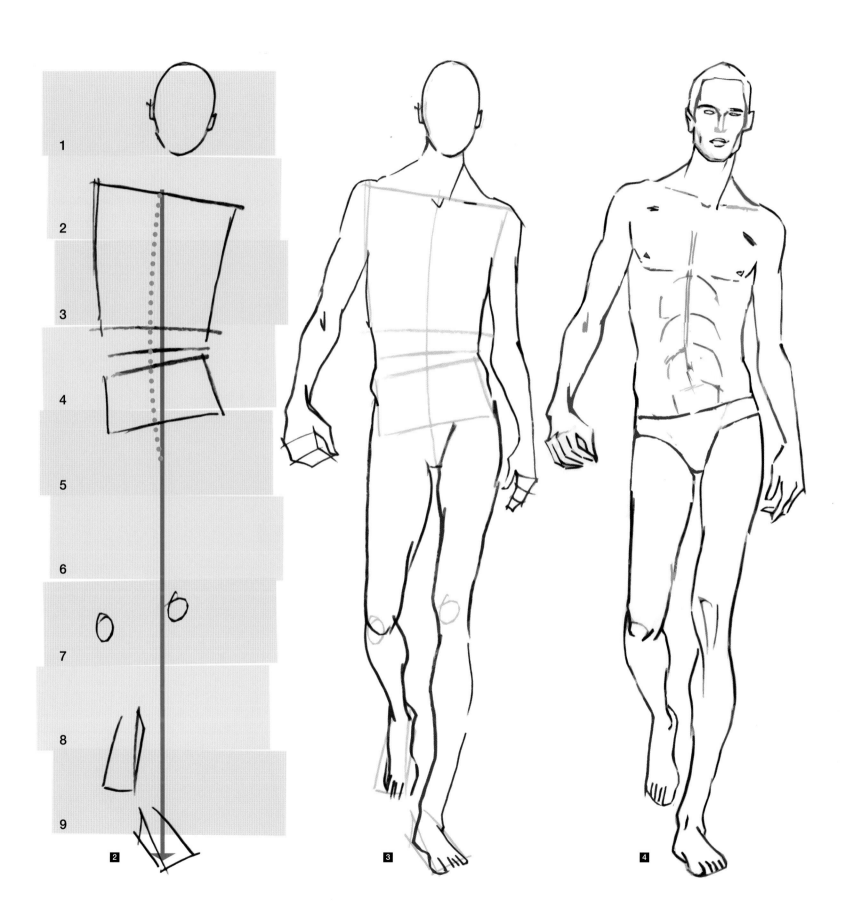

1

2

3

4

5

6

7

8

9

2

3

4

Turning

Before attempting to turn the men's figure, be sure to read about spatial relationships and foreshortening in Chapter 1 (see pp. 54–55). Turned figures are used to emphasize construction details featured on the side of a garment. For instance, a concept sketch might feature a turned pose to draw attention to the eccentric placement of a contrast racing stripe on a pant outseam.

A good place to begin turning the men's figure is with a three-quarter pose.

1 Working with your proportion template slipped under a sheet of tracing paper, plot the analysis of the pose, taking care to foreshorten the parts of the body that are turning away from view. Then refine your drawing, using a second and third tracing overlay as necessary.

2 Experiment with different degrees of rotation so that you will have just the right figure to emphasize a wide assortment of garment details. A profile view is handy for providing information such as racing stripes and satin piping on outseams.

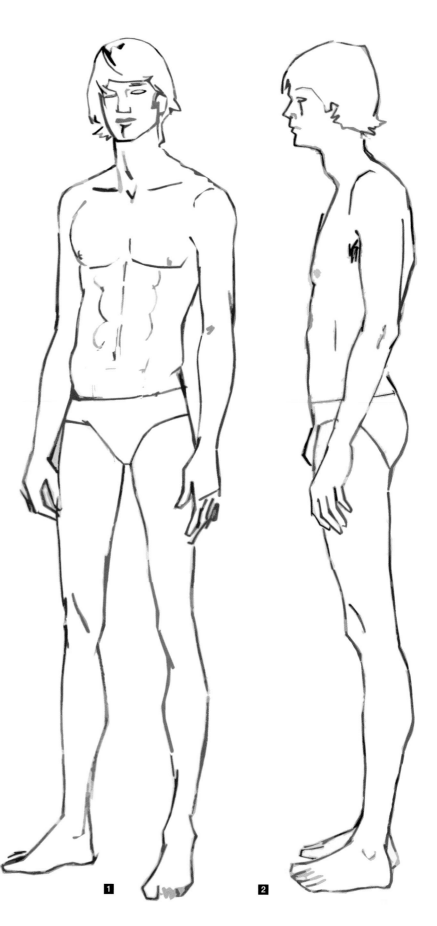

1   **2**

Design and illustrate a small collection of men's performance apparel using at least three different poses (right). (See Chapter 6 for more information about drawing basic garment details.) Sports such as cycling and running, which require body-hugging silhouettes and athletic poses, will really test your ability to draw the men's figure. Thermal base layers for skiing and snowboarding are also a challenge. The garment designs should be quite simple with minimal seaming, perhaps utilizing seamless knit technologies and color blocking.

▼ *Dylan Taverner uses a more androgynous men's figure proprtion for illustrating his young designer sportswear.*

▲ *Howard Tangye uses a landscape page orientation and a seated pose to achieve an artful composition.*

ASSIGNMENT 3

Working with a model (above) or a variety of photo references, develop six new men's figures. Experiment with more dramatic foreshortening (opposite top) and the use of props to imply a narrative.

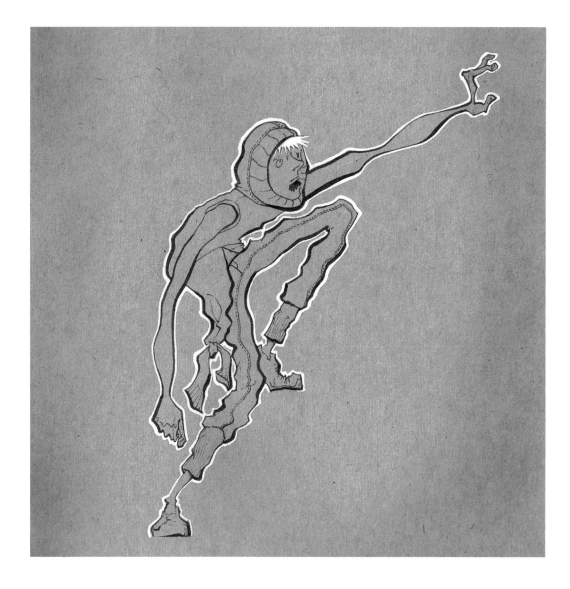

◀ *Diana Lin uses a dynamic and foreshortened figure to illustrate clothing for extreme sports.*

ASSIGNMENT 4

Repeated redrawing tends to inhibit immediacy and expression: the very qualities that characterize good fashion drawing. If you have a basic understanding of Illustrator, you can use the computer to preserve the freshness of your original drawing as you move into finished art. Working with any of the figures developed in previous assignments, scan a pencil sketch (before color is applied) and open the document in Illustrator. Then, select the drawing and go to Object>Live Trace>Make. Once you have completed the Live Trace, you can expand the object and render color and pattern with Live Paint tools. If you are not familiar with the Live Trace and Live Paint, use the Help menu to guide you. As an alternative, you can also print out the Live Trace line art on marker paper and render by hand with markers. Never hesitate to integrate manual and digital techniques. Take care to test your markers beforehand as various brands react differently to inkjet and laser inks. (Copic and Prismacolor are the brands recommended for this purpose.)

◀ ▶ ▼ *Childrenswear illustrations need not be saccharin-sweet. Here, Sarah Beetson creates a relative figure proportion for different age groups: a tween (opposite), big girl (right), and toddler (below).*

CHAPTER 3
DRAWING CHILDREN AND YOUNG ADULTS

For the design and illustration of childrenswear, you can (and should!) work with greater creative license. If your approach is too realistic, the children can end up looking overly mature and serious—more like miniature adults. You will be better served by a lighter, more imaginative approach, inspired perhaps by antique or collectible dolls, puppets, licensed characters (**licensing**), or comics (including manga). Naive art and children's picture books are other sources of inspiration. A narrative or "back story," achieved by featuring children of different ages as they interact with one another in a specific activity and setting, can enhance your childrenswear presentations.

Media choices should also be expanded to facilitate more imaginative compositions (you could add dimension to your work with collage or overstitching, for example). You may also want your illustrations to effect the appearance of a child's drawing. Interactive presentations, such as pop-up books, are also particularly engaging. For a futuristic approach, check out avatars in virtual environments and computer games geared especially toward kids. As with the adult figures, it will be important to support illustrations with flats. (For more about flat sketching see Chapter 2, pp. 84–85.)

In determining the proportion of your children's figures, it is important to take into consideration that physical growth occurs at a variable rate. Kids who are small for their age at one point can experience dramatic growth spurts in the years that follow. The same is true for developmental milestones. Babies, for instance, may take their first steps anywhere from nine to fourteen months of age. Both physical and developmental growth have enormous impact on figure proportion, poses, and garment design. Because of the variable growth rate, it is impossible to establish the figure proportion of a child at a specific age. But what you can do is develop a figure that approximates a range of ages. These ranges will also correspond to clothing sizes offered by the various markets for childrenswear.

Since design briefs for childrenswear often require the representation of more than one age/size group, it is especially important that the figures for the different age/size ranges have proportion relative to one another. The size of the head, seen in relation to the body as whole, will be critical to the establishment of proportions for the different ranges. At twelve months, an infant's head measures roughly two-thirds the size of an adult's. Since the baby's head is so large, over time growth will occur mostly in the torso and—to an even greater extent—the limbs. Therefore, if you draw the head very large in relation to the body, your figure will have a more youthful, even babyish appearance. Your stylized figure proportion can be easily modified for the older age/size ranges by increasing the number of heads for the total height. Take care that an extremely exaggerated figure proportion does not interfere with its function as a tool for visualizing children's garment designs. There should be a strong visual relationship between the concept sketch and realization of the garment.

As with the development of adult fashion figures (see Chapters 1 and 2) the proportion of the younger figures is left entirely up to you. Work with the templates provided in this chapter to achieve more lifelike children's proportions. Alternatively, allow your imagination to run free—your first children's figure may actually begin as a doodle. As you experiment, allow yourself to stylize the figure to the extreme. When you are satisfied that your "fashion fiction" is both imaginative and believable, adjust the proportion for the various age/size ranges. Be sure to establish believable spatial relationships by determining eye level—typically positioned at the hips. Take care, too, to foreshorten the side of the body turning away from view. (For more about foreshortening see Chapter 1, pp. 54–55.)

Since kids rarely stand still for any extended period of time, photo references will be invaluable. It is important to refer to your own life experience in order to develop a unique and personal design philosophy. Take the time to research family photos and even your own baby pictures! Photographic studies that document phases in the development of growing boys and girls are especially useful. Pictures of the same child taken under precisely the same conditions over a period of years provide a direct comparison for the proportions of children and young adults. The Muybridge series (see Further Reading, p. 408) is one such study and will be particularly helpful in this regard.

NOTE All of the figures in this chapter have a relative proportion to one another. They do not, however, have a consistent relationship to the adult figures (Chapters 1 and 2) which have been scaled to fit the page size of this text. For more information about drawing children's faces and limbs see Chapter 4.

◄ *Sungeun Kim modifies her naive drawing style to convey the figure proportions of little girls and toddlers.*

Babies

The range for babies is divided into infants and toddlers. Both the age and clothing sizes for infants are calculated in three-monthly increments from newborn to eighteen months with U.S. sizes from 3M to 24M. (In Europe, measurements may also be given in centimeters.) Toddlers' ages are given in years from one and a half to three years with U.S. sizes 2T to 4T.

▼ *Placement and allover prints are prominently featured in designs for toddlers. For more about prints, see Chapter 11. Illustration by Sarah Beetson.*

▲ ▶ *Yuki Hatori's illustrations feature character imagery that might also be incorporated as appliqué, placement, or allover prints into layette.*

Infants

An infant's head is quite large in comparison to the body and constitutes slightly more than one quarter of the total height. A tiny neck supports this relatively big head. Infants have a plump U-shaped torso and short limbs. The forms appear to be quite chubby because the skeleton is protected by so much baby fat. There are few gender differences at this age—rely on the cut and color of the child's clothing for visual cues as to its sex. Both boys and girls have short "baby-fine" hair that falls forward; the amount of hair increases with age. To draw the infant figure, start by establishing measurements for proportion:

1 Decide how tall you want your figure to be and draw a vertical line for that height. Then divide the height into four equal spaces. Indicate the head as an oval in the top space. The width of the figure at the shoulder line is equal to the height of the head. Position this measurement vertically at 1¼ heads. Using the landmarks and widths indicated, plot the location of the waist, hips, and knees to complete your infant proportion template.

2 In preparation for the construction of your figure, search out the geometric forms using your proportion template and a tracing overlay. This diagram will serve as the basis for your infant's figure.

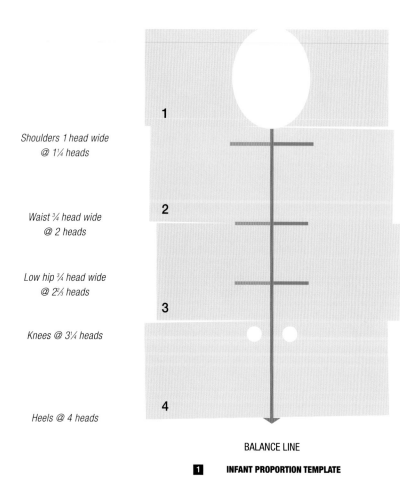

Shoulders 1 head wide
@ 1¼ heads

Waist ¾ head wide
@ 2 heads

Low hip ¾ head wide
@ 2⅔ heads

Knees @ 3¼ heads

Heels @ 4 heads

BALANCE LINE

1   **INFANT PROPORTION TEMPLATE**

GIRL   BOY

2   **GEOMETRIC FORMS FOR THE INFANT'S FIGURE**

3 Place a second sheet of tracing paper over your template and, referring to the geometric forms, roughly sketch the standing figure.

4 Refine your drawing to include details for the face, hands, and feet. Keep the drawing simple with very few shadows. (For more information about drawing babies' faces and limbs see Chapter 4.)

When you are satisfied with the front view, experiment with turning the figure (for example, three-quarter and profile views). Take care to use appropriate foreshortening. (For more about spatial relationships see Chapter 1, pp. 54–55.)

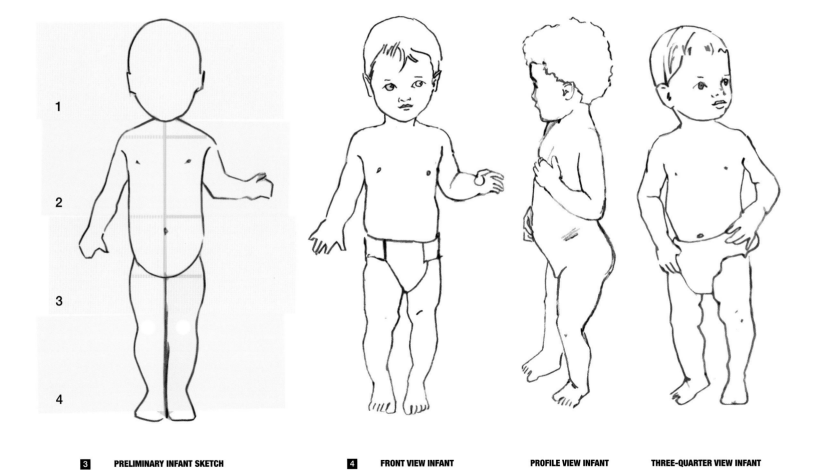

3 PRELIMINARY INFANT SKETCH

4 FRONT VIEW INFANT   PROFILE VIEW INFANT   THREE-QUARTER VIEW INFANT

Drawing the Seated Infant

When posing the infant figure it is important to take into consideration that the baby's muscles have only just begun to develop. In fact, most infants do not have the leg strength to stand unsupported until around eleven months. Therefore, **layette** (a collection of essential apparel and linens for newborns) is often illustrated with the baby crawling, lying down, or in a seated position.

1 Working with a tracing overlay and your proportion template, block in the head and torso using the same landmarks and widths as for the standing pose.

2 Most seated poses require foreshortening of the legs as they recede into space. This will vary for different poses. Roughly block in the limbs noting the position and order of the forms in space. The total height of the seated figure is approximately three heads.

3 Refine and finish your seated pose.

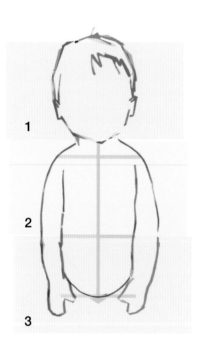

1   **SEATED POSE: THREE HEADS**

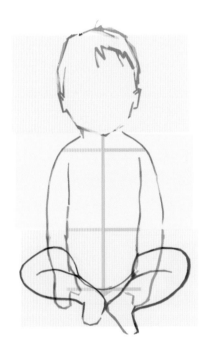

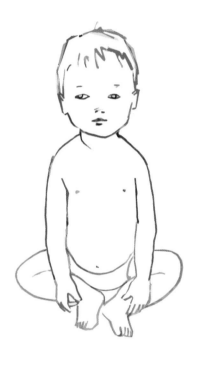

2 **FORESHORTENED LEGS**

3 **SEATED INFANT**

SEATED PROFILE

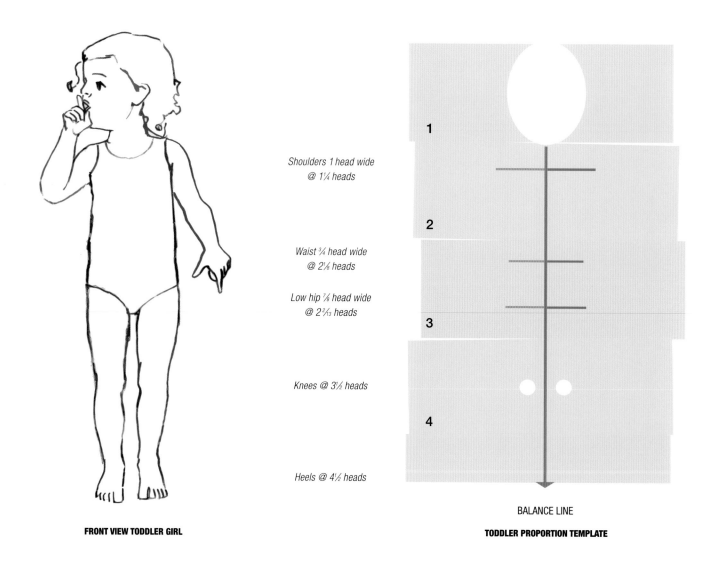

Shoulders 1 head wide
@ 1¼ heads

Waist ¾ head wide
@ 2⅛ heads

Low hip ⅞ head wide
@ 2⅔ heads

Knees @ 3½ heads

Heels @ 4½ heads

BALANCE LINE

FRONT VIEW TODDLER GIRL

TODDLER PROPORTION TEMPLATE

Toddlers

Toddlers are aptly named because they are new to walking and their balance is not the best. The head is similar in size to that of the infant. The toddler's limbs and torso begin to elongate and there is a total height of four and a half heads. The overall impression is still quite plump and you can adapt the geometric forms used for the infant by elongating them ever so slightly. To draw the toddler, follow the same procedure as for infants (see pp. 102–3). First determine the measurements for your toddler proportion template (use the information provided above right). Then block in the geometric forms, which will be the basis for your preliminary sketch. Once you refine the sketch you can move on to other views and variations of the figure. When posing the toddler, make sure that the feet are firmly planted—reserving dramatic weight shifts for bigger kids.

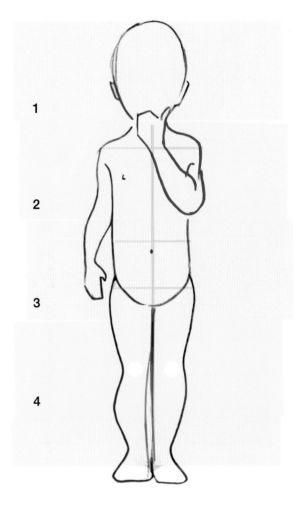

1

2

3

4

PRELIMINARY TODDLER SKETCH

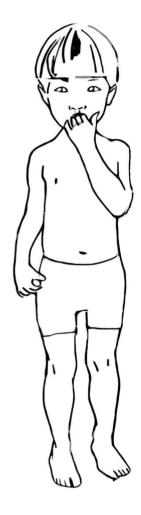

FRONT VIEW TODDLER BOY

BACK VIEW TODDLER BOY

Children

The range for children includes little girls and boys and their older counterparts big girls and boys. In the U.S., "little" girls and boys aged four to six years old wear sizes 2 to 6X and sizes 2 to 7 respectively. "Big" girls and boys aged six through eleven years old wear sizes 7 through 16 and 8 through 16 respectively. As baby fat begins to slowly melt away, subtle gender differences start to emerge, with a slight expression of the hips for girls and more developed muscles for boys.

▲ *Tina Berning uses observations from life to capture an individual likeness for each of these girls.*

◀◣ *Because they are often featured together in children's presentations, big and little kids should have a relative proportion. Illustration by Antonio Lopez (top right) and Kathryn Elyse Rodgers (opposite).*

▶ *Childrenswear often reflects trends in adult fashion. Here, Joey Casey's high-fashion sportswear for boys.*

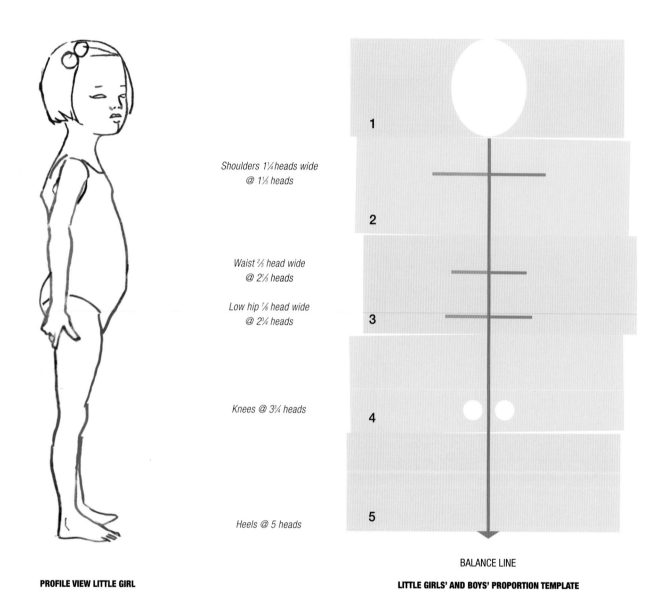

Shoulders 1¼ heads wide
@ 1⅓ heads

Waist ⅔ head wide
@ 2⅓ heads

Low hip ⅞ head wide
@ 2¾ heads

Knees @ 3¾ heads

Heels @ 5 heads

1
2
3
4
5

BALANCE LINE

PROFILE VIEW LITTLE GIRL   **LITTLE GIRLS' AND BOYS' PROPORTION TEMPLATE**

Drawing Little Girls

As growth in the limbs accelerates, the head now constitutes one-fifth of the total height. To draw little girls, follow the same procedure as for infants (see pp. 102–3). First determine the measurements for your little girl's proportion template (use the information provided above right). Then modify the infant's geometric forms for an elongated figure. This will lay the groundwork for your preliminary sketch of the little girl. Once you refine the drawing you can move on to other views and variations of the figure. Little girls have developed surer footing, so poses can become more ambitious, reflecting greater activity.

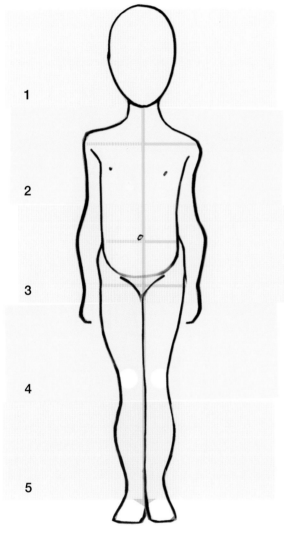

1

2

3

4

5

PRELIMINARY LITTLE GIRL

FRONT VIEW LITTLE GIRL

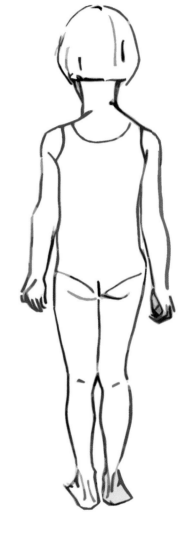

BACK VIEW LITTLE GIRL

Drawing Little Boys

Although there are small gender differences (the boy will have a slightly longer torso) you can use the same general figure proportion for both little girls and boys. To draw a little boy, follow the same steps as for the infant (see pp. 102–3). You can use the same measurements as for your little girl's proportion template (see p. 110). Then block in the geometric forms as groundwork for your preliminary sketch. Once you have refined the sketch you can move on to other views and variations of the figure. Although the little boy's figure has begun to mature and elongate, the belly is still quite round—especially when seen in profile.

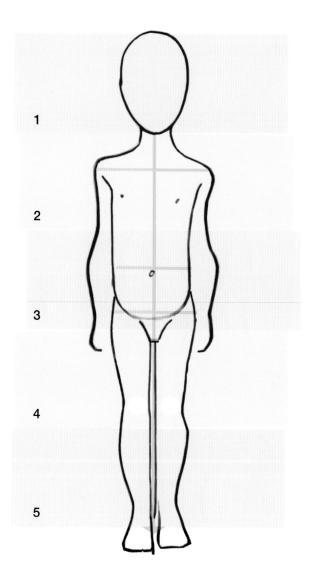

PRELIMINARY LITTLE BOY

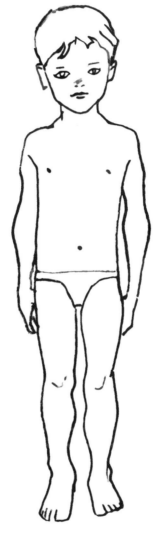

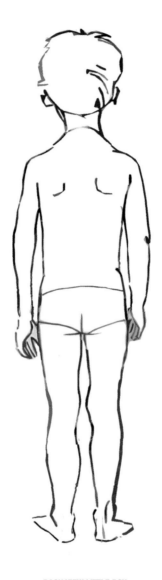

FRONT VIEW LITTLE BOY

BACK VIEW LITTLE BOY

PROFILE VIEW LITTLE BOY

Drawing Big Girls

Big girls have somewhat cylindrical bodies and a total height of six and a half heads. There begins to be a very slight definition for the waist, and the lower torso flares a bit at the hip. To draw big girls, first determine the measurements for your proportion template using the information provided below. In searching out the body shape, you can begin to utilize the more angular geometric forms associated with development of the adult figures. These will serve as the basis for your preliminary sketch of the big girl. Once you refine the drawing you can move on to other views and variations of the figure (see p. 116).

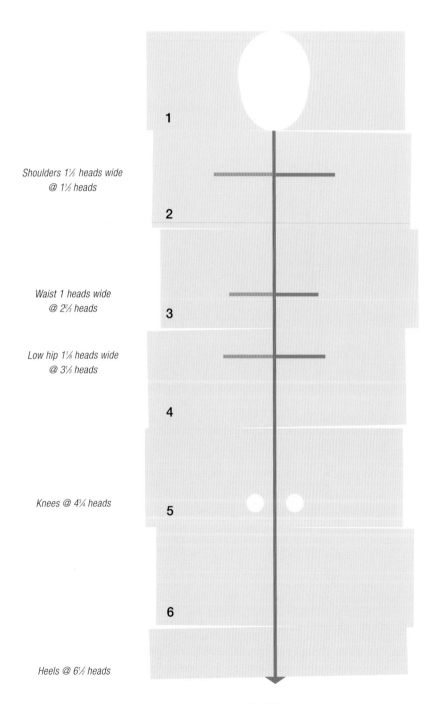

Shoulders 1⅓ heads wide
@ 1½ heads

Waist 1 heads wide
@ 2⅔ heads

Low hip 1⅛ heads wide
@ 3⅓ heads

Knees @ 4¾ heads

Heels @ 6½ heads

BALANCE LINE

BIG GIRLS' AND BOYS' PROPORTION TEMPLATE

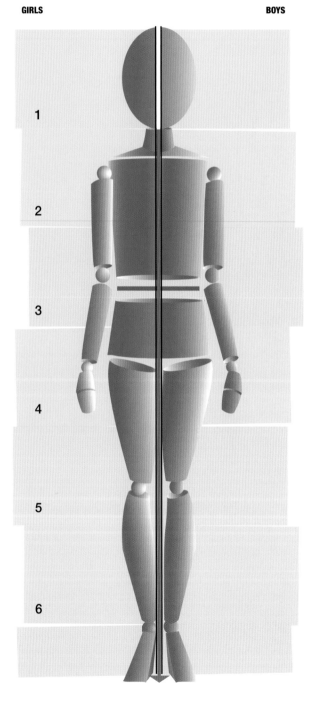

GIRLS   BOYS

THE GEOMETRIC FORMS FOR BIG GIRLS AND BOYS COMPARED

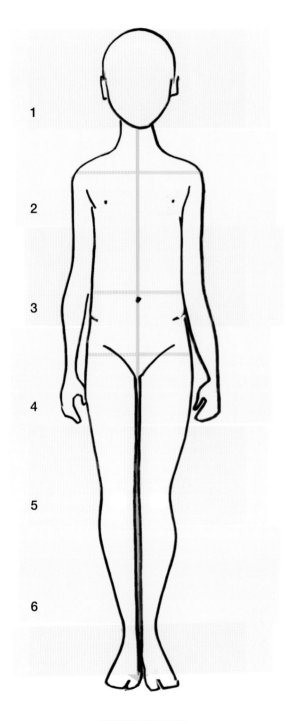

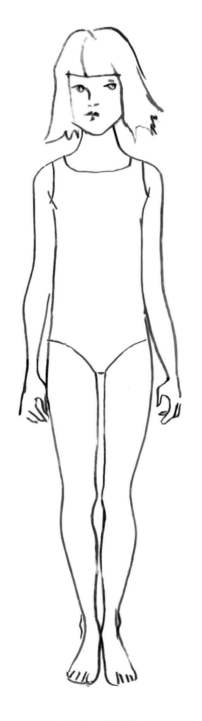

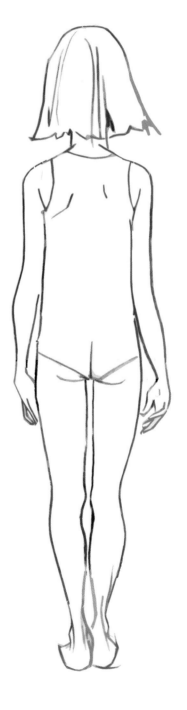

1

2

3

4

5

6

PRELIMINARY BIG GIRL

FRONT VIEW BIG GIRL

BACK VIEW BIG GIRL

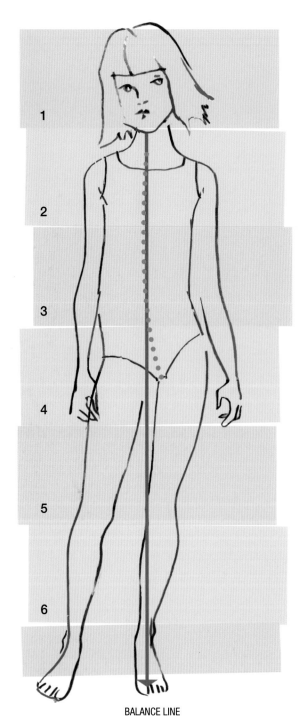

1

2

3

4

5

6

BALANCE LINE

PRELIMINARY HIGH HIP FIGURE

THREE-QUARTER VIEW BIG GIRL

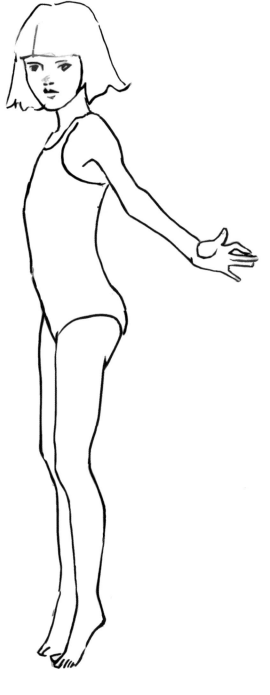

▲ *Big girls are bursting with energy. Hand and foot gestures convey attitude and femininity.*

Drawing Big Boys

Big boys have cylindrical bodies with little or no indentation for the waist. The torso is a bit longer than the girl's and slimmer through the hip. The shoulderline, which is still quite narrow, begins to flare as muscles and skeletal structure find greater expression. Despite these few small differences, the overall proportion for big girls and boys is pretty similar and you can use the same template and geometric forms for both (see p. 114). Behavior, however, will be a strong signifier; rely on the poses you choose to convey femininity or masculinity. (For more about gender-specific poses and gestures see Chapter 2, p. 88.)

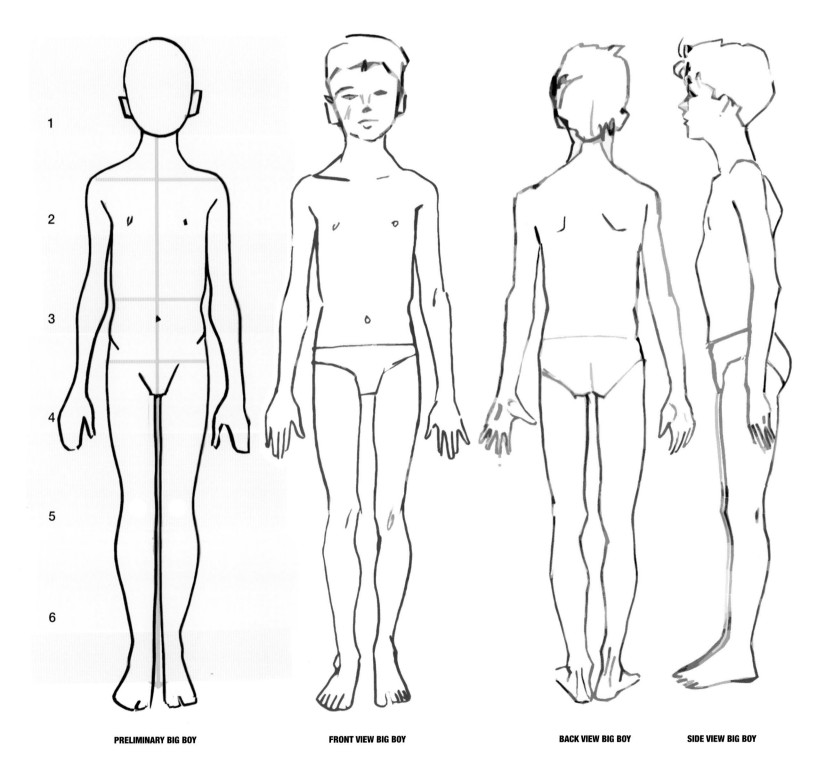

PRELIMINARY BIG BOY   FRONT VIEW BIG BOY   BACK VIEW BIG BOY   SIDE VIEW BIG BOY

▲ *Attitude and gesture are best captured from life.*

ASSIGNMENT 1

In order to capture more authentic gestures, try quickly sketching children at play. While most parents will not be comfortable having strangers photograph their children, they are less likely to object to an artist's sketch (above). The energetic activity on display in schoolyards, playgrounds, and at the beach provides a terrific opportunity for you to practice quick drawing. (For more about drawing from life, see Chapter 5.)

ASSIGNMENT 2

Using an interactive format, such as a pop-up book or graphic novel (left and below), create a presentation for a childrenswear collection. You will find that the back story and sense of place may actually inspire an entirely new direction for your garment designs. Just remember that these elements are meant to support, but not overwhelm, your garment designs.

◀ ▼ *Illustrator Antonio Lopez portrayed fashionable kids in the context of sixties' Pop Art. A serial comic strip format suggests both place and narrative.*

Tweens

In the past, tweens have gone by many different names—subteens, preteens, and so on. There is conflicting opinion as to when this age range actually begins. Some marketing experts say tweendom begins as early as eight years old, leading up to the age of fourteen. But no matter what you call them or how you determine their age, preadolescents comprise a distinct and booming segment of the childrenswear market. For the purposes of fashion drawing, eleven to fourteen years of age will work quite nicely for the tween figures with sizing from 8 to 16 for both tween girls and boys.

Tweens no longer think of themselves as children. Rebellion and cool hunting, which will intensify in the late teens, begins in earnest. Tweens have yet to achieve the sophistication of juniors and their interest in the opposite sex is usually limited to an obsession with a celebrity or pop star. They are quite fashion conscious and have a lot to say about clothing choices which, for the most part, are governed by the opinions of their friends. Tweens are big on attitude and your portrayal of them should be a bit edgier than that of younger children. Adult fashion can trickle down, but the tween market has its very own trends. Whereas the entire children's market is influenced by licensed imagery, characters such as Hello Kitty are especially appealing to tweens.

◢ *Steven Broadway uses graphic elements associated with different pop music genres (such as hip hop, electronica, and dub) to provide an edgy context for tween boys' fashion.*

◣ *Fashion-forward accessories are key to achieving the total look for tweens.*

Drawing Tween Girls and Boys

Tween bodies and limbs continue to elongate and the head is now nearly full-grown. Their total height measures seven heads. Faces are beginning to show signs of maturity—thinning out and elongating through the lower front portion of the skull. Gender differences become more pronounced; a small bust begins to develop in the girls, and boys have increased body mass and slightly longer torsos. To draw the tween figures, follow the same steps as for younger kids.

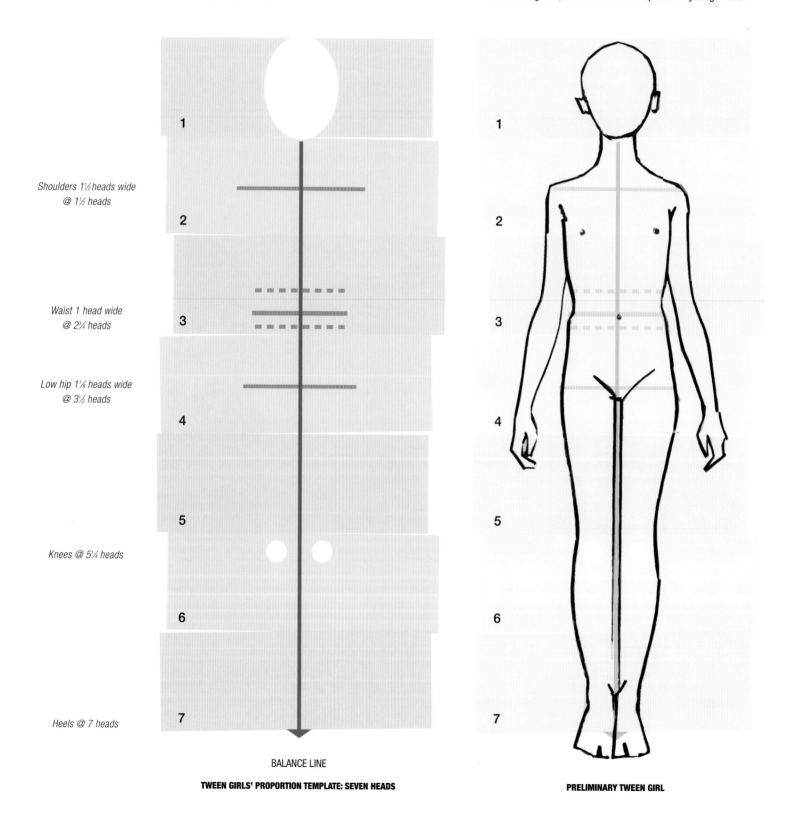

Shoulders 1½ heads wide
@ 1½ heads

Waist 1 head wide
@ 2¾ heads

Low hip 1⅛ heads wide
@ 3½ heads

Knees @ 5¼ heads

Heels @ 7 heads

BALANCE LINE

TWEEN GIRLS' PROPORTION TEMPLATE: SEVEN HEADS

PRELIMINARY TWEEN GIRL

You will first need to determine the measurements for the tweens' overall figure proportion, creating two distinct proportion templates with different landmarks and body widths for girls and boys. The geometric forms for the big girls and boys (see p. 114) can be adapted for the tweens. Once you have blocked in the forms you can then move on to preliminary sketches and from there to other views and variations of the figures (see pp. 122–23).

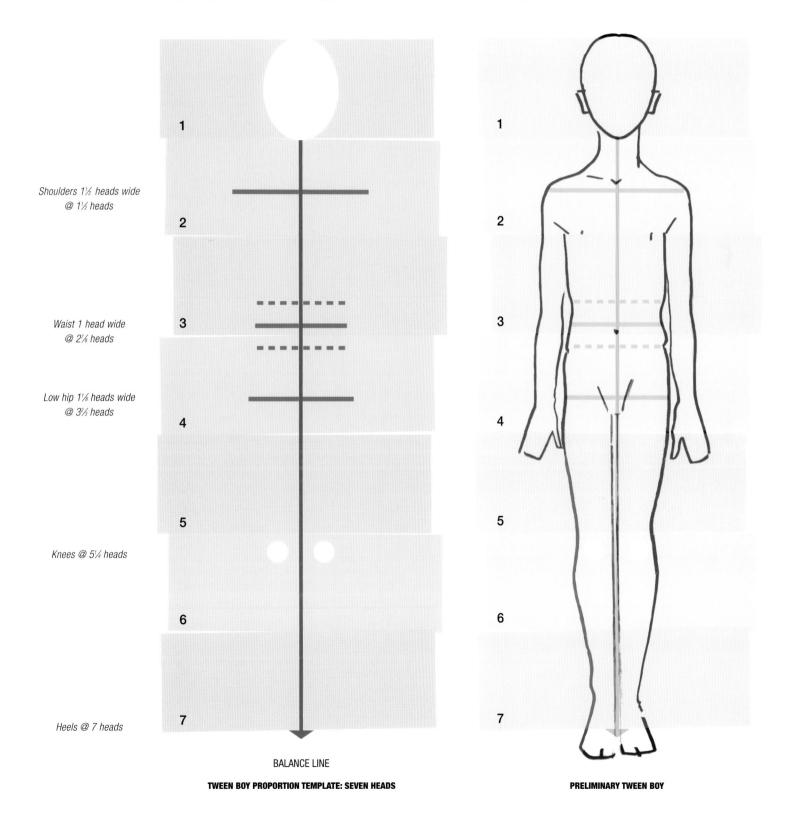

*Shoulders 1½ heads wide
@ 1½ heads*

*Waist 1 head wide
@ 2⅞ heads*

*Low hip 1⅛ heads wide
@ 3⅔ heads*

Knees @ 5¼ heads

Heels @ 7 heads

BALANCE LINE

TWEEN BOY PROPORTION TEMPLATE: SEVEN HEADS

PRELIMINARY TWEEN BOY

ASSIGNMENT 3

Can you think of a licensed or comic book character that would not only appeal to tween sensibilities but also influence the way you draw them (below)? Once you adjust your tween figure to reflect this character, develop a variety of views consistent with this proportion.

▼ *The artwork associated with DJ mixtapes can inform your knowledge of tween and junior sensibilities. Illustration by Lubo Vladov.*

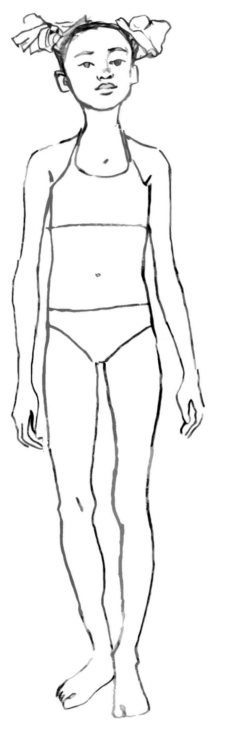

FRONT VIEW TWEEN GIRL

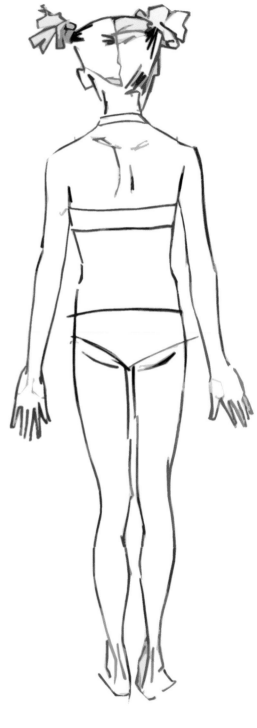

BACK VIEW TWEEN GIRL

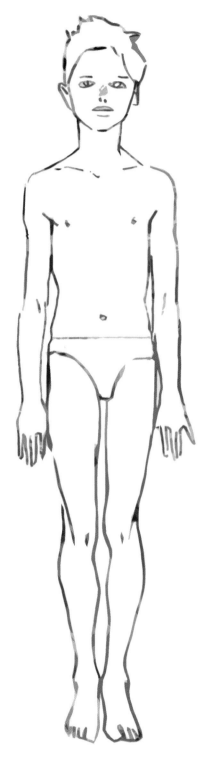

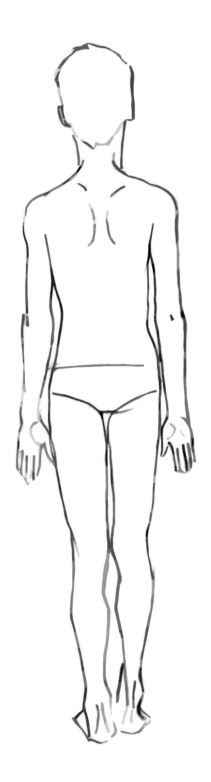

FRONT VIEW TWEEN BOY

BACK VIEW TWEEN BOY

Juniors

The junior range in the U.S. encompasses young adults from ages sixteen to eighteen. Sizing will vary for younger and older juniors and according to gender and garment type. Clothing can be designated as S, M, L, XL, or sized according to the neck, chest, or waist circumference as well as the length of the arms and legs. Whereas the sizes for adult women are given in even numbers, sizes for junior girls are given in odd numbers (sizes 1, 3, 5, etc.). Young juniors' sizings are given as a combination of odd/even numbers (for example, 1/2, 3/4, and so on).

▼ *Junior trends are closely tied to popular music and street style. Illustration by Fernanda Guedes.*

▲ *Illustrations of junior fashion should have lots of attitude, here conveyed via facial expression and gesture. Design and illustration by Eri Wakiyama.*

Juniors are likely to adhere to a rebellious dress code as prescribed by their social peers. Sketching from life will help you to capture juniors in the context of contemporary lifestyles (for more about drawing from life see Chapter 5). Teen magazines, street style journals, as well as music-related publications (see Further Reading, p. 408) also provide unlimited figure references and information about trends. Graphic novels, edgier comics, grafitti, and virtual avatars are additional sources of inspiration.

The proportion of the junior figures is quite similar to that of the adults—just one head shorter. Gender differences will require two distinct proportion templates for junior girls and boys.

▲ Rebellious male juniors may sport facial hair or an extreme hairstyle (including, but not limited to, mohawks, buzz cuts, afros, mullets, dreadlocks, you name it). Experimentation with hair color, piercings, and tattoos are also part of the juniors' rites of passage. Illustration by Lubo Vladov.

▶ Juniors often follow dress codes as determined by fashion tribes. Here, Richard Haines documents street style for his blog, "What I Saw Today."

▲ There is reciprocal influence between real world and virtual fashion environments. Here, a virtual gothic Lolita by Mark Grady.

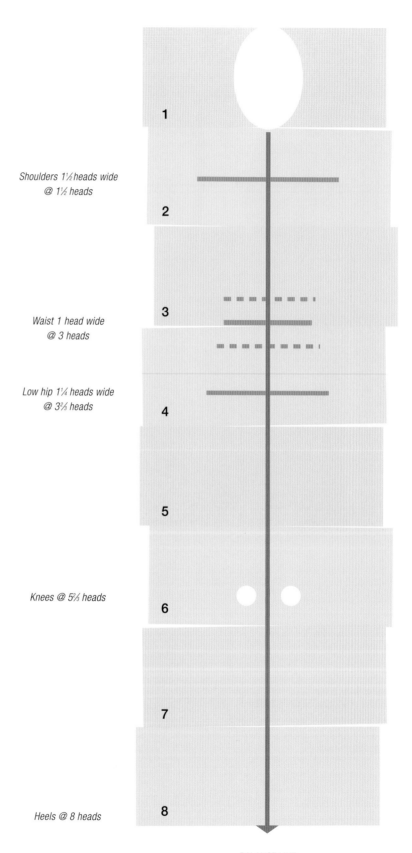

Shoulders 1½ heads wide
@ 1½ heads

Waist 1 head wide
@ 3 heads

Low hip 1¼ heads wide
@ 3⅔ heads

Knees @ 5⅔ heads

Heels @ 8 heads

BALANCE LINE

JUNIOR GIRLS' PROPORTION TEMPLATE

Drawing Junior Girls

In comparison to the women's figure, the junior girl has a higher and smaller bust, is shorter through the torso, and slimmer through the hip. Since many high-fashion models begin their career as teens, there is often no discernible difference between women and juniors in fashion photography. For fashion drawing, however, the figure used to design and illustrate apparel for juniors should be differentiated from the one used for adults.

To draw the junior girl, use the same steps as outlined in Chapter 1 (see p. 38). You will need to determine the measurements for the overall figure proportion. Since the junior girl is almost fully mature, you can refer to the geometric forms used for development of the women's figure (see pp. 38–39). You will need to adapt the forms, blocking them in according to your junior proportion template. Using these forms as the basis of your figure, you can then move on to a preliminary sketch. Once you have refined your front view junior girl you can begin to experiment with other views and poses (see opposite, middle and right). (For more about balancing and turning the figure see Chapter 1.)

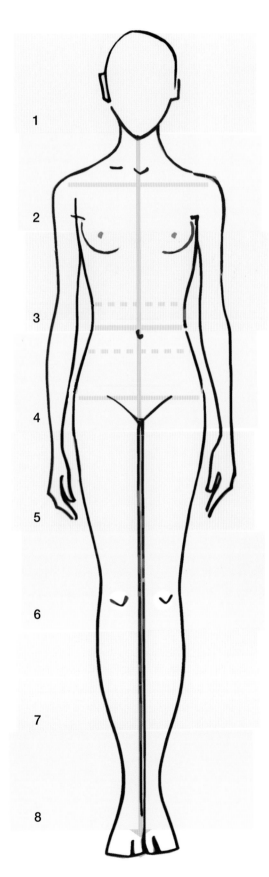

1

2

3

4

5

6

7

8

PRELIMINARY JUNIOR GIRL

FRONT VIEW JUNIOR GIRL

BACK VIEW JUNIOR GIRL

▲ Shona Reppe's "Cinderella" puppet provides a wonderful example of how the figure may be imaginatively stylized.

▶ Graffiti art (here by street-art team Herakut) can inspire an edgier approach to illustrating children's fashion.

▲ Marina Bychkova's exquisite "Enchanted Dolls" are made of porcelain with movable parts that can be manipulated for lifelike poses.

ASSIGNMENT 4

Working with a doll (above left and center), puppet (above right), or graffiti art (opposite) as inspiration, develop a more stylized version of a junior figure. Then, modify this figure according to age and gender for the other childrenswear size ranges. Take care not to simply splice a highly stylized head onto a conventional body; the overall figure proportion must also reflect your inspiration.

Drawing Junior Boys

The junior boy is not a fully developed adult (there is quite a bit of filling out to come). However, a significant increase in body mass distinguishes juniors from younger boys. Faces become more angular, with a lengthening and squaring of the jaw. The junior boy is eight heads tall and has broad shoulders, a long slim torso, and narrow hips. Although both junior boys and girls have a figure proportion of eight heads, the boy's head size is slightly bigger and so the overall height will also be greater.

To draw the junior boy, follow the steps outlined for the men's figure in Chapter 2. You will need to determine the measurements for the overall figure proportion. The geometric forms for the men's figure (see p. 80) can be adapted according to the proportion for junior boys. Once you have blocked in the forms, you can then move on to a preliminary sketch and from there to other views and and poses (see pp. 132–33). (For more about balancing and posing the figure see Chapter 1.)

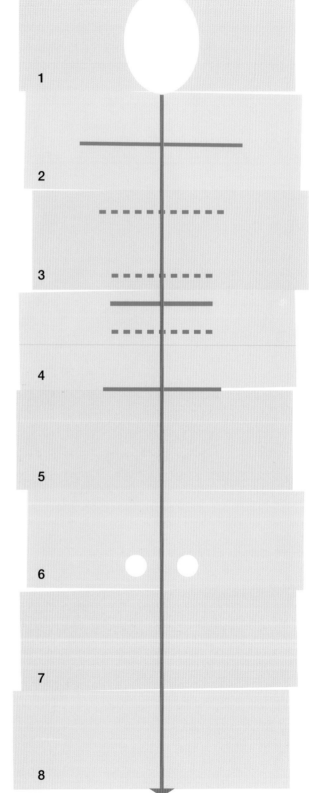

Shoulders 1¾ heads wide
@ 1½ heads

Waist 1 head wide
@ 3⅛ heads

Low hip 1¼ heads wide
@ 4 heads

Knees @ 5¼ heads

Heels @ 8 heads

BALANCE LINE

JUNIOR BOYS' PROPORTION TEMPLATE

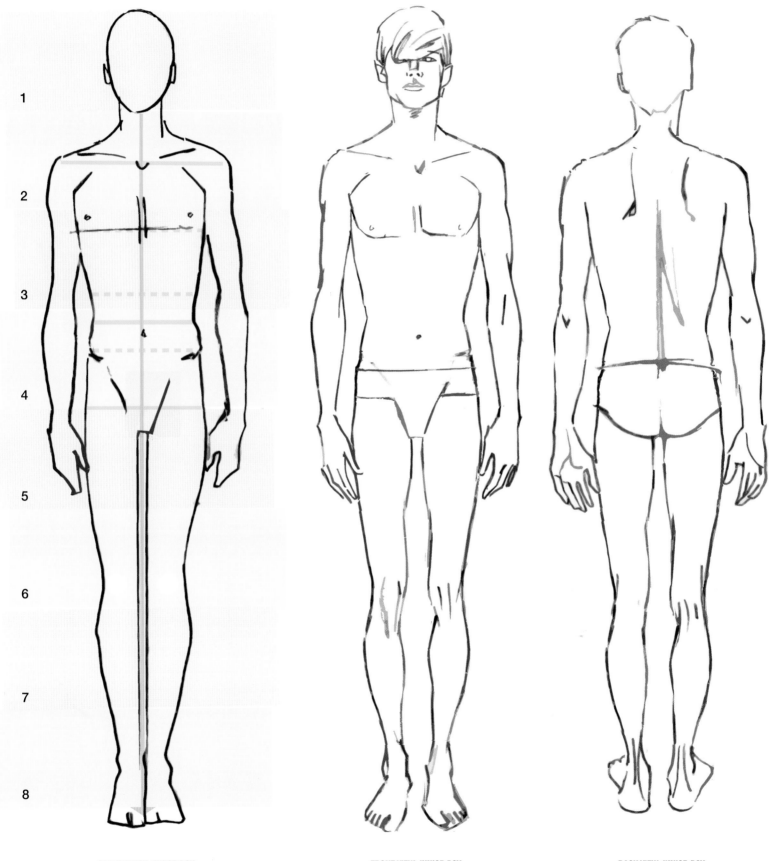

1

2

3

4

5

6

7

8

PRELIMINARY JUNIOR BOY   **FRONT VIEW JUNIOR BOY**   **BACK VIEW JUNIOR BOY**

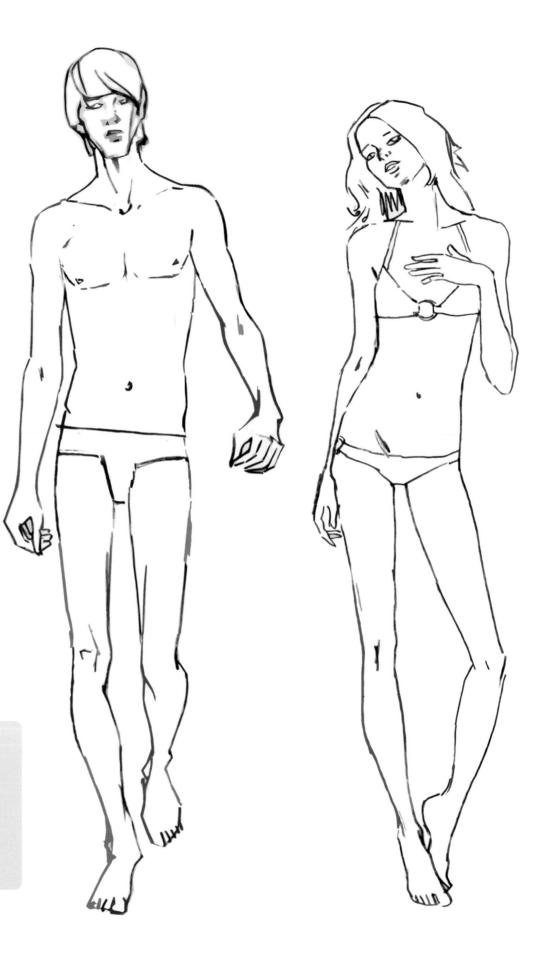

▶ *Here are some variations on junior girls and boys to help develop different poses.*

ASSIGNMENT 5

Working with several photo references, create a variety of figures suitable for the junior market (for more about drawing from a photo reference, see pp. 56-57). Develop several junior variations (right).

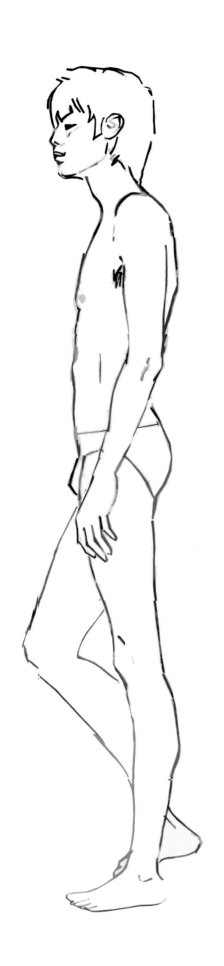

CHAPTER 4
ZOOMING IN

While the initial chapters of this book have dealt with establishing overall figure proportion, the focus of this chapter is on drawing individual parts—the face, hands, and feet. Decisions about hair, makeup, and shoes are used to design the figure from head to toe and so drawing faces, hands, and feet is quite important. The techniques and measuring cues that follow in this chapter are intended to help with drawing these parts. If one area proves to be difficult, focus extra attention on the trouble spot so that it does not block the flow of your drawing. Your focus should be sharpest at the beginning—do not save the hard parts for last! With practice and perseverance you are sure to achieve a harmonious and proportionate arrangement of beautifully drawn parts.

Just as for drawing the fashion figure as a whole, there is no right or wrong way to draw the parts. Your goal is to create a believable fiction that conveys your personal perception of beauty and a sense of the person you imagine might wear your designs (or those of your commissioning client). Capturing the essence of your "girl" is not limited to the drawing the head. Along with facial expressions, gestures of the hands and feet not only provide information about the person, but also suggest a narrative.

◀ *When drawing the head, your approach should be the same as for any other part of a fashion figure—you must distill a great deal of visual information in stylizing your ideal. Illustration by Tanya Ling.*

▶ *Vivienne Westwood's runway presentations typically include imaginative accessories.*

Drawing Heads

Perhaps because identity is so closely tied to the face, a great deal of importance is assigned to drawing heads. Preconceived notions can interfere with observation and the imaginative portrayal of the face. Models on the catwalk look very different at various runway presentations. Similarly, the way you draw faces should also vary according to design development. The skillful illustration of hair, makeup, and shoes can really help sell the presentation of your design concept. Moreover, the face should reflect a specific customer profile.

While some artists are quite good at working strictly from their imagination, in the beginning it is advisable to work from a broad range of photo references and life. Your goal, however, is not a photographic likeness but rather an ideal expressed with an economy of line. A fair amount of invention and editing will be required. The visual information you choose to eliminate is key. For instance, the vertical creases that form on either side of a smiling mouth can make even a child appear old, similar to a marionette. Also keep in mind that unless you are doing a larger portrait, the size of the head in a full figure drawing will not allow for a lot of facial detail.

The drawing style must correspond to customer profile and garment design (a more conceptual design would require an extremely imaginative presentation, for example). No matter how you choose to stylize the head, consistency within multi-figure compositions will be equally important. The governing principles that follow will help you to establish the size and location of the individual features. When rotating the head in space, take care to create the illusion of foreshortening (see p. 54). Also, be cautioned that an errant line or shadow can belie your ideal or create an unintentional expression of emotion (such as, a downward tilt of the innermost edges of the eyebrows, which can indicate distress or anger).

But above all, take care to approach this task in your own unique way. There is no denying that draftsmanship is important, but authenticity will be the true key to your success. Draw with ease and authority in a way that feels natural to you. Take the time to experiment with different customer profiles and explore a variety of media choices.

▼ *In this illustration by Julie Johnson an immediacy and economy of line convey a wealth of information about the target customer (such as attitude and look).*

▲ The scope of a designer's vision does not end with the garments. Here, Fabiola Arias actually incorporates the same materials used for her garment designs into a three-dimensional fashion portrait.

▶ ▶▶ Drawing styles can run the gamut from an extremely detailed rendering to a slight indication of the features with varying degrees of abstraction and broad choices for media. Shown here (left) is an expressive ink and wash drawing and (right) a more realist charcoal sketch on vellum.

▲ Graffiti artists Hera and Akut (Herakut) combine their artistic skills to create exquisite street art and gallery installations. Their work blurs the line between graffiti and fashion art.

▶ Angelique Houtkamp's unique illustration style is derived from her experience as a tattoo artist, along with micro-references to mythology, dreams, nautical iconography, and Hollywood nostalgia.

Drawing Women's Heads

Over time your personal style will begin to emerge and the way you draw women's faces will become unique and natural to you. As with all fashion drawing, a certain measure of reality will be required. Begin by formulating a template so that the location and size of the features will be consistent in all of your fashion drawings. Keep in mind that observations and visual information that might otherwise be included in a classic life drawing will be omitted or stylized for the portrayal of a fashionable ideal.

The Front View

The front view is uncomplicated by foreshortening and is therefore a good place to start. The skillful placement of shadows and highlights will be used to define facial features seen head-on. Although faces can vary widely and the movement of the features is in constant flux, there are some basics that can help you establish and maintain a consistent proportion. Approximate vertical landmarks and widths for adult features are as follows:

Relative proportion and landmarks for facial features

1 Divide the height of the head in two; the eyes are located at the halfway mark.
a. From the hairline down, divide the height of the head into three equal parts; the eyebrows are located at the bottom of the first third.
b. The nose is located at the bottom of the second third.
c. Divide the area between the bottom of the nose and chin into thirds; the upper and lower lips will meet at the bottom of the first of these thirds.
d. The tops of the ears roughly line up with the eyes, the bottom with the nose.
e. Although in reality the eyes are one-fifth the width of the head, they are usually enlarged for fashion drawing. No matter the size, be sure to space them one eye-width apart.

2 The width of the mouth can be determined by dropping a line down from the inside of each iris.

3 The width of the nose can be determined by dropping a line down from the tear ducts.

4 The width of a long, graceful neck approximates the distance between the outer edges of the eyes.

These measuring cues will yield a somewhat lifelike drawing. You may want to take even greater creative license with your fashion head (such as drawing an unnaturally large iris in reference to Manga and anime, see p. 143).

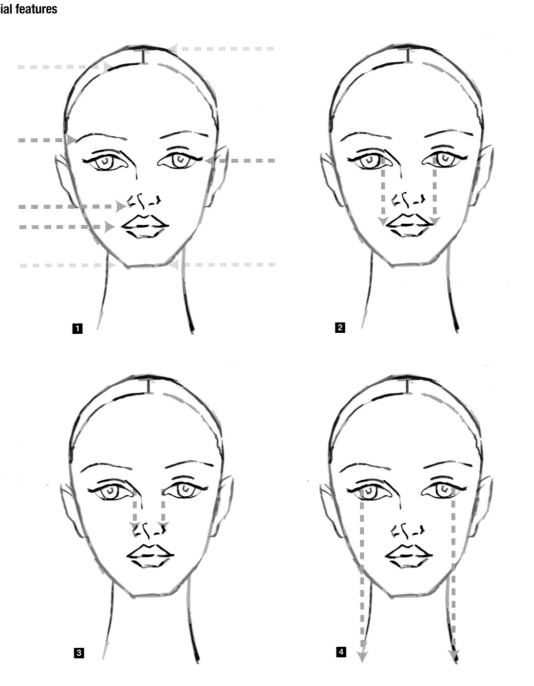

Creating a Front View Template for a Woman's Head

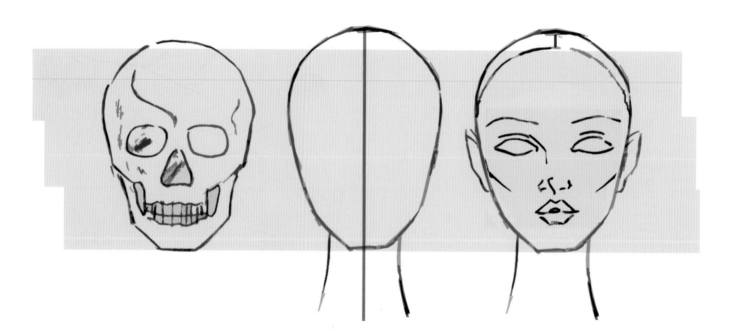

1 Begin with a rectangle that has a 2:3 aspect ratio. Then pencil in an egg shape, with the wider end at the top and the tapered end at the bottom.

2 As with the figure, it is important to have a working knowledge of the skeleton. The skull finds subtle expression on a woman's face. Note how the hinged jaw is the only moving part.

3 Refine the egg shape, articulating the cheekbones and jawline with soft undulating curves. Establish a Center Front line to facilitate the symmetrical placement of the features.

4 Sketch in the hairline. Divide the face into three equal parts from the hairline down. Roughly sketch in the features as per the measuring cues given on p. 139. Note their relative proportion and location—for example, the tops of the ears line up with the eyes.

Drawing the Individual Features in the Front View

You can use this generic template to create a more specific study of the face by refining features and then adding hair and makeup. A step-by-step guide for drawing the individual features in the front view follows.

The eye

The eyes are spheres set deep into two recesses of the skull. Fashion tends to emphasize and enlarge the eyes, although the size will vary according to personal drawing style.

1 Draw concentric circles for the iris and the pupil.

2 Next, draw an almond shape, adding a tear duct at the innermost corner of the eye. Pencil in the upper lid. Note, the iris is partially obscured by the upper eyelid; leaving white space above the iris will suggest an expression of fear or surprise.

3 Lengthen the line at the outermost edge to suggest eyelashes.

The nose

Defining the nose in the front view will require the use of shadows and highlights.

1 Draw only one side of the bridge of the nose. Carefully place a soft shadow just above the base to suggest a slight upturn.

2 Indicate the nostrils. Note, the width of the nose is roughly equal to the distance between the eyes.

The mouth

For fashion drawing, it is best to draw the mouth closed.

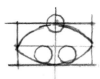

1 Begin with a rectangle. Divide the shape in half vertically and horizontally. Draw an almond shape within the rectangle.

2 Indicate a small circle centered above the upper half so that it creates a semicircular depression in the upper lip. Add two small circles to the lower half.

3 Follow the contour of the small circles to refine the shape of the top and bottom lips. The corners of the mouth should have a slight upturn for a neutral facial expression.

NOTE Should you have need to draw a broad smile, take care to flatten the stretched lips and simplify the teeth.

The Neck

Before moving on to other views, it is important to understand how the head is mounted on the neck. As observed in the initial development of the figure using geometric forms, the neck can be represented as a cylinder. This cylinder connects the head and torso in such a way that it is shorter in the back and taller in the front. Take care not to draw the neck and shoulders at a right angle—capturing the graceful slope between neck and shoulders is key to successfully drawing the front, turned, and especially, back views.

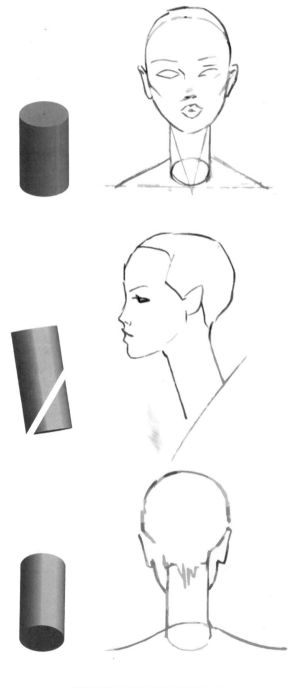

CYLINDRICAL PERSPECTIVE FOR THE NECK

Hair and Makeup

Once your template is established and you are comfortable with drawing the individual features, you can begin to experiment with different hairstyles and makeup. Try working from your imagination, photographs, or from life. Remember that you are not after an exact likeness and that your stylized ideal should work with garment designs targeted to a specific customer.

When drawing hair, take care to first establish an overall shape. Then indicate the mass and texture (curly versus straight) with highlights and shadows. And while drawing individual hairs is ill-advised, you will need to give some indication of their direction. The hair should appear to be growing outward from an organic, irregular hairline, with shadows cast near to the face and neck. There are of course exceptions for hairdos that obscure the hairline, such as bangs (a fringe). Keep in mind that textures achieved with irons (tongs) and chemical processes can take hair from unnaturally straight to curly and vice versa. No one hairstyle will be appropriate for all design concepts and you must not allow yourself to fall into a rut. Initial attention to detail on the head sets up the presentation of your total design concept.

Think about designing the head in relation to the body. For instance, the appearance of a small head was key to the twenties' *garçon* look, achieved with a closely cropped bob hairdo and a tightly fitted cloche hat (for more about drawing hats, see pp. 161–65). The relative proportion between the head and the body will appear completely different depending on the hairstyle—for instance, a heightened crown can be achieved by backcombing the hair.

History shows that hair and makeup evolve in tandem with garment design. In the fifties, hairstyles, makeup, and clothing were as carefully prescribed as the social mores for nuclear

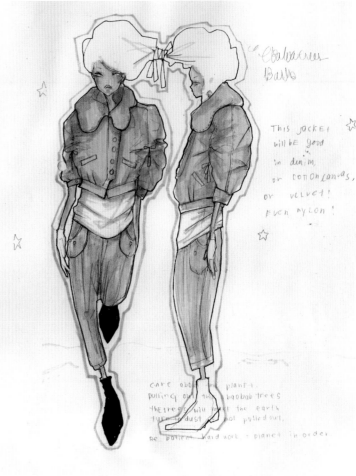

▲ The inspiration for a design collection can (and should) find expression in the stylization of the head. Design and illustration by Eri Wakiyama.

families. In the late seventies, punk culture prompted a taste for the unnatural colors of urban decay in hair and makeup, with postmodern blonde bombshells sporting ironic black roots. Just as different parts of the body are emphasized by garment design during historical periods, so too are different facial features. For example, the sixties' gamine look was all about emphasizing the eyes with false lashes and a pale mouth.

Think about your personal vision of contemporary beauty as it relates to a specific garment design: which features should be emphasized and how? Is the look natural or artificial? Is it a modern variation of a historic style? Does your image convey and speak to your target customer? What media choices best communicate your message?

Take care not to overwork your drawing with pencil as this will interfere with the application of color. Residual pencil marks tend to make the finished illustration look dirty and can have an aging effect on drawings of the face. Reserve shadows, highlights, and makeup for color rendering. Sometimes it is hard to know where drawing ends and rendering begins. For example, you might want to reserve indication of the iris for rendering in color.

◀ Here, Frank Nathan uses a line-art portrait to offset and prioritize jewelry and accessories.

▶ The otaku culture of manga and anime has had a significant impact on both fashion and illustration. Sweet and gothic Lolitas wear artificially colored wigs and contact lenses to effect the appearance of cartoon characters.

◄ In this illustration by Laurie Marman, the customer profile is distinguished by more extreme hair and makeup choices.

▼ A study of the high-fashion head, drawn from life. Elisabeth Dempsey's choice of media and drawing style help to convey customer profile.

ASSIGNMENT 1

A fashion drawing of the head should convey a distinct customer profile. A classic customer may reflect a timeless standard of beauty, a high-fashion customer (right) can be more of the moment, while a more stylized customer could favor a look that is ephemeral or extreme (above). Working with a variety of photo references, draw a series of front view faces representing distinct customer profiles. Use hair, makeup, and accessories to communicate the profile.

ASSIGNMENT 2

The spontaneity of doodles and quick sketches (this page) can sometimes point you in the direction of a freer, more imaginative drawing style. With that in mind, do quick small studies of faces wherever and whenever you can. The drawings can be based on observations from life or from your imagination. Try to search out what is natural for you.

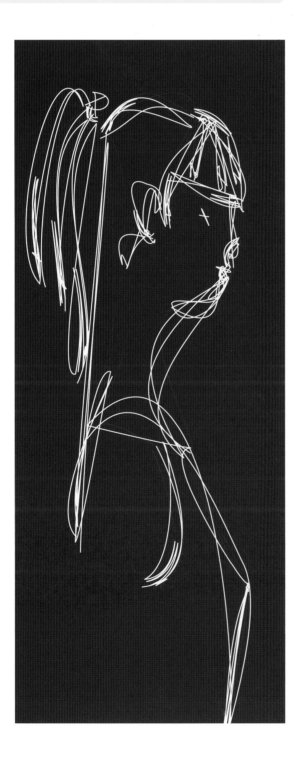

▲ Observations from life will inform your fashion drawings; these two sketches were created on the fly by Richard Haines using his iPhone and the "brushes" app for drawing and painting.

◀ A quick computer sketch created with Adobe Illustrator can have the same immediacy as a manual life drawing.

Turning the Woman's Head

Based on your experience of rotating the figure, can you predict what will happen to the appearance of the head as it turns in space? The vertical landmarks you have established for the features will remain constant with the lateral rotation of the head. The widths of the features, however, will become foreshortened as they turn from view. You will also notice that the forms will be seen in a new layered order: the head will be seen first, then the neck, and finally the shoulder.

The partially turned head is perhaps the most challenging view because of the varying degrees of rotation (as compared to the front and profile views, which are absolute). In order to be able to draw the many variations, it is important to understand how the appearance of the features and shape of the face will be altered by foreshortening. The face, which actually looks quite slim in the front view, will appear to grow wider as the back of the skull comes into view.

◀ *An imaginative rendering of the face need not be restricted to standard flesh tones. Illustration by David Bray.*

▶ *As the head turns, the back of the skull gradually comes into view. The rectangle, which is the basis of the drawing of the face, will become progressively wider as the degree of rotation increases. Divide the rectangles in half horizontally to locate the eyes and the tops of the ears. Then divide the lower half again, to locate the tip of the nose. Subdivide the lower quarter into thirds to establish a landmark for where the upper and lower lips meet.*

▲ *Necklines and dramatic collars, which frame the face, can be used to achieve innovative page layouts for fashion portraits. Illustration by Laurie Marmon.*

▶ *Illustrator Tina Berning is able to capture the essence of a specific individual with precious few brushstrokes.*

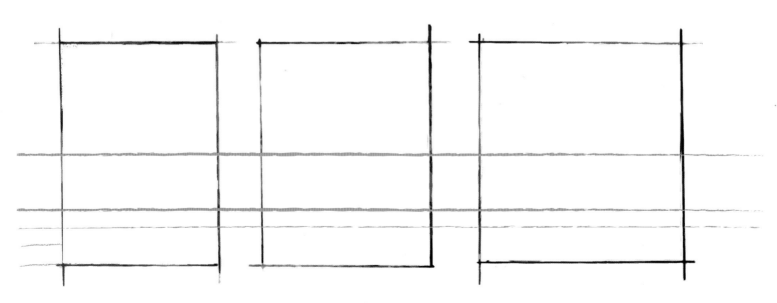

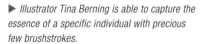

GUIDES FOR FRONT, THREE-QUARTER, AND PROFILE

Creating a Three-quarter View Template

Because the head appears to grow wider with greater degrees of rotation, you will need to begin the three-quarter view with a rectangle that is slightly wider than the one used for the front view. The Center Front line, which appeared to be straight in the front view, becomes curved and moves with the rotation of the head. The two halves of the face no longer appear equal—one side will become foreshortened as it turns from view.

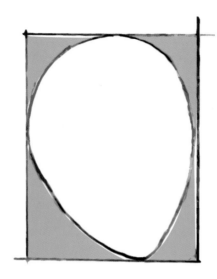

1 Having established your rectangle, draw an egg shape. This time the egg will be tilted so that the placement of the chin is closer to the lower right-hand corner of the rectangle.

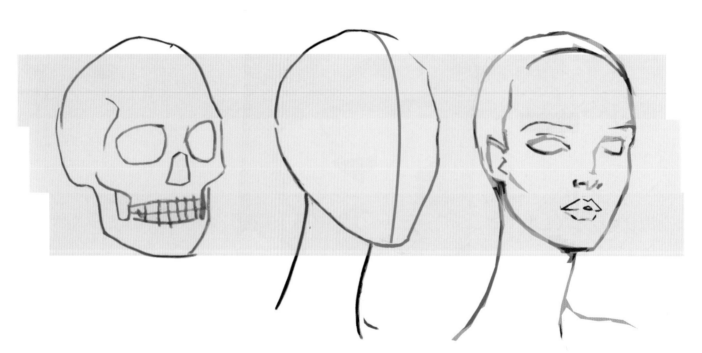

2 It is important to understand how the skull becomes foreshortened and finds expression in the three-quarter view. The edge of the face on the side turning from view is defined by the hollow of the eye socket and the cheekbone.

3 Draw a curved Center Front line positioned closer to the right. Mark off vertical landmarks (the same as those established for the front view) for the eyes, nose, and mouth.

4 Refine the shape of the face and add features, taking care to foreshorten the side of the face turning from view. Indicate a small indentation near to where the eye socket and cheekbone meet. Note how the features are now seen in a new layered order (the nose will partially obscure the eye on the turned side). You will also see that the ear now falls within the overall outline of the head.

5 You can then modify this generic face to be more specific, refining facial features and adding hair and makeup.

Drawing Individual Features in the Three-quarter View

The three-quarter eye

Draw as for the front view, but so that it is slightly rounder.

The three-quarter nose

The shape of the nose is more defined and only partially in view. The bridge hides part of the eye on the turned side of the head.

The three-quarter mouth

The near side of the mouth is drawn the same as for the front view. The far side of the mouth will be foreshortened, indicated with a half ball shape.

Creating a Profile View Template

For this view you will require a square as your starting point.

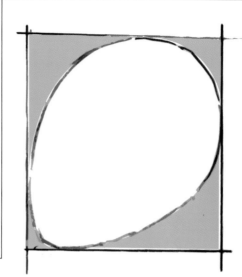

1 Draw an egg shape positioned within the square so that the chin will be in the lower left corner.

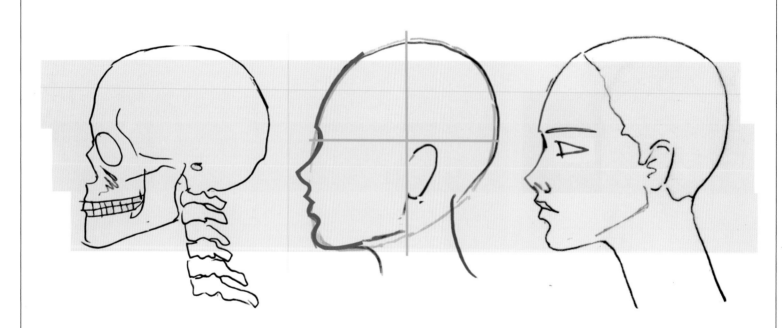

2 It is important to understand how the spine connects to the skull, as this determines the graceful angle of the neck.

3 Bisect the egg shape horizontally to locate the eyes and the tops of the ears. Bisect the egg vertically to position the end of the jaw. The intersection of these two lines will determine the location of the ears. The vertical placement of the features will be consistent with the front view. Draw the edge of the nose, lips, and chin to form the shape of the profile, which coincides with the Center Front line. Only the nose will extend beyond the confines of the egg shape.

4 Draw the foreshortened features, placing them on the same vertical landmarks as for the front and three-quarter views. Roughly indicate the hairline.

▼ *Variations on the profile.*

Drawing Individual Features in the Profile View

The profile eye

For the profile view, you will draw exactly half of the eye. The iris becomes foreshortened as an ellipse and the lower lid follows the line of the cheekbone. The eyebrow is set in front of eye.

The profile nose

The shape of the nose has the greatest definition and is actually part of the Center Front line in the profile view.

The profile mouth

In this view the mouth is equal to half of the front view. It looks something like a heart rotated sideways.

▲ *Creating a reality for your fictionalized fashion face requires interpretation of a specific set of features at varying degrees of rotation. Illustration by Howard Tangye.*

ASSIGNMENT 3

Practice drawing the head in various degrees of rotation (above). Experiment with different customer profiles and, for a more ambitious challenge, try to capture the same likeness viewed at different degrees of rotation.

Drawing Men's Heads

Drawing men's heads can be quite freeing; the ideal is far less prescribed and there is less editing required than for women. Character lines and shadows will help to define the expression of the men's more highly developed skeletal structure. The overall shape will be much more angular with the squaring of the jaw, and straighter lines will be used to define the features and suggest bone structure. Otherwise, many of the basics for drawing the women's head will apply to the men's.

▼ *In this illustration by Ferdinand, the men's profile is reduced to the simplest of forms, described with a minimum of line work. (For more about alternating line and mass see Chapter 5, pp. 188–89.)*

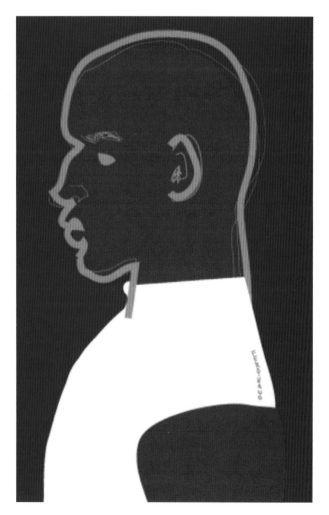

▲ *Just as for women, style and imagination will be required for idealizing men's faces. Illustration by Wyatt Hough.*

Creating a Front View Template

Just as for the women's head, the front view is a good place to start. Approximate the same vertical landmarks and widths for adult features as indicated on p. 139. Use shadows and highlights to accentuate a more chiseled bone structure and prominent features.

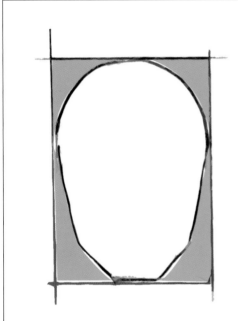 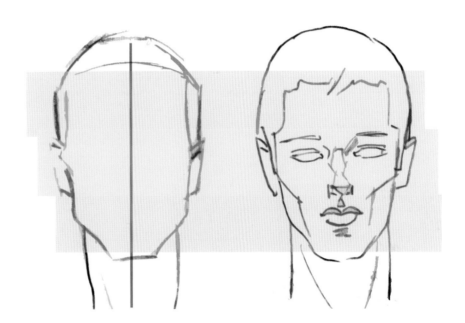

1 Begin with a rectangle that has a 2:3 aspect ratio. Then draw an egg shape that is slightly wider at the top, and tapered and flatter at the bottom.

2 Draw a Center Front guideline to facilitate the symmetrical placement of the features. Refine the shape of the face, indicating a more angular jaw line than for the women's head.

3 Sketch in the hairline. Roughly sketch the features using the established vertical landmarks. In comparison to the women's features, the men's lips are somewhat flatter and the eyes, unadorned by makeup, will appear to be smaller. A careful indication of the spatial planes can be used to define the structure of a more prominent nose.

Creating a Three-quarter View Template

As noted in turning the women's head, vertical placement of the features will remain constant for lateral rotation. The Center Front line will turn with the head; the two halves of the face will no longer be equal in appearance as the side of the face turning from view becomes foreshortened. The Center Front line, which appeared straight in the front view, becomes curved for the three-quarter view.

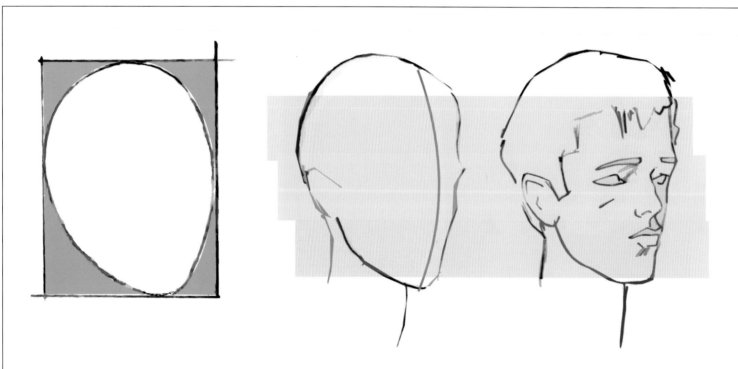

1 Begin by drawing a slightly wider rectangle than for the front view. Draw an egg shape tilted so that the placement of the chin is closer to the lower right corner of the rectangle.

2 Draw a curved Center Front line positioned closer to the right. Mark off the constant vertical landmarks for the eyes, nose, and mouth. Indicate the ear, which is now placed within the overall outline of the head.

3 Refine the shape of the face and add features, taking care to foreshorten those appearing on the side of the face turning from view. Indicate a small indentation near to where the eye socket and cheekbone meet. Keep in mind that the features are seen in a new layered order with the nose partially obscuring the eye on the side of the head turning from view.

For this assignment, you will take a cue from the working methods of artist Peter Clark (right). Using magazine tear sheets and novelty papers, create a composition for a man's head. For an added challenge, reinterpret your collage in a different medium, such as gouache, marker, or colored pencil.

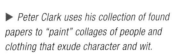

▶ *Peter Clark uses his collection of found papers to "paint" collages of people and clothing that exude character and wit.*

Creating a Profile View Template

Just as for the women's profile, you will require a square as your starting point.

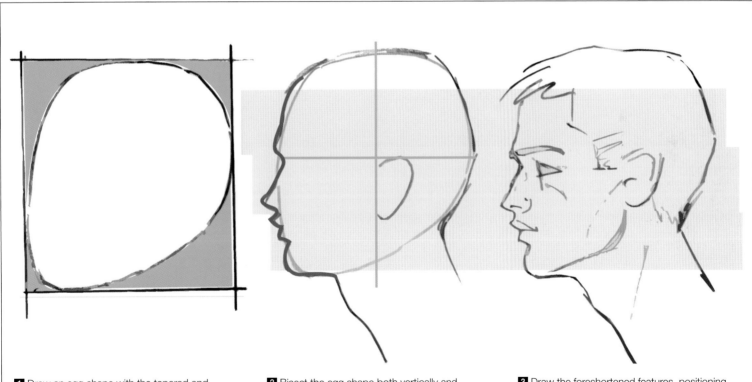

1 Draw an egg shape with the tapered end positioned in the lower left corner of the square.

2 Bisect the egg shape both vertically and horizontally to determine the location of the ear. The vertical placement of the features will be consistent with the front view. Draw the edge of the nose, lips, and chin to form the contour of the profile (this line also corresponds to the Center Front).

3 Draw the foreshortened features, positioning them on the established vertical landmarks. Roughly indicate the hairline. Note how the head is thrust forward in relation to the neck. Facial features will be foreshortened as for the women's profile view.

Drawing Children's Heads

The design and illustration of kids' clothing tends to be more imaginative and whimsical and so when it comes to drawing children's faces you will want to take similar creative license. Overly realistic drawing tends to age the appearance of children's faces. As well as being stylized, your illustrations should also convey attitude.

A consistent drawing style must be adapted for the different age groups. As noted in Chapter 3, during infancy the head is extremely large in relation to the body. The ratio of head to body size changes as the baby matures. For example, an infant's head is one-quarter of its total body height; by age five or six, the head equals one-sixth of the height. You are under no obligation to precisely duplicate this ratio. But no matter what head-to-body ratio you choose, there should be a relative proportion between the age groups.

The face must reflect other developmental changes, too. Children's faces not only grow larger but also longer over time. The bridge of the nose, which is barely visible in infancy, becomes more defined. Faces become increasingly distinguished by gender. Boys' heads take on a more rectangular appearance as the jaw becomes

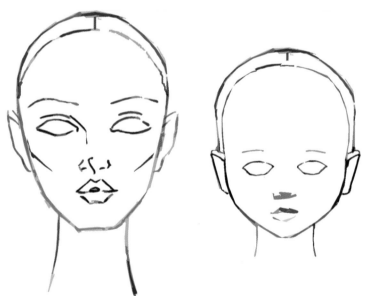

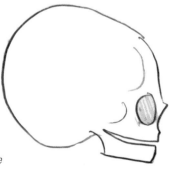

▲ *Stylization must be brought consistently across all age groups.*

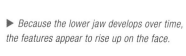

▲ *Relative proportion of adults' and little kids' heads.*

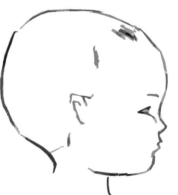

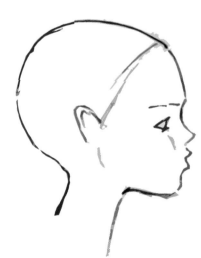

▶ *Because the lower jaw develops over time, the features appear to rise up on the face.*

▲ Dana De Kuyper's "Damned Dollies" subvert conventional notions about girls.

▶ A drawing style inspired by Herakut's graffiti art would be well suited to the tween and junior categories.

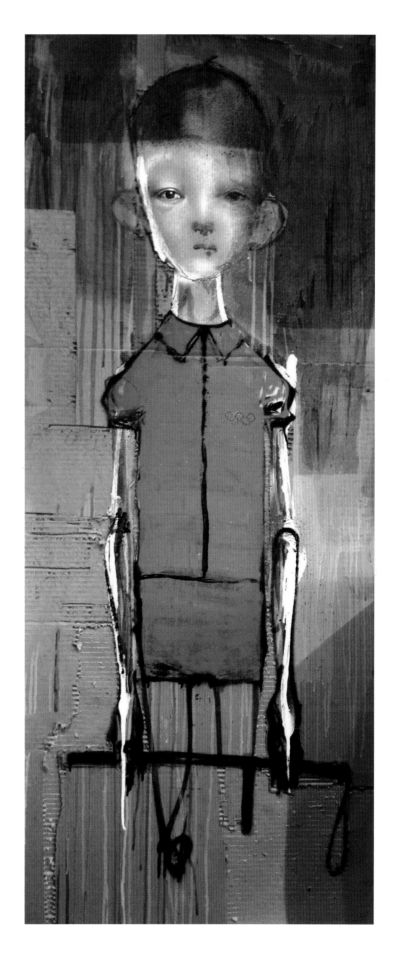

square. Girls' faces take on a soft oval shape. The junior fashion head is similar to that of an adult, distinguished by attitude, hairstyle, and accessories.

The size, shape, and location of the features will also change as the child matures. In comparison with an adult head, an infant's features appear to sit lower on the face because of an undeveloped lower jaw. All of the features are smaller than for the adult, with rounder eyes and a barely defined nose. The overall shape of the head is wide through to the cheekbone and abruptly tapers to a very tiny chin. As the baby grows into a child, the jaw develops and the features appear higher on the face. The infant's large head sits on a delicate, almost non-existent, neck. There is not too much hair in the beginning, with only a slight indication of the hairline and eyebrows. On the whole, everything should seem rounded and small.

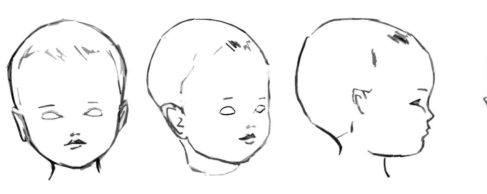

INFANTS' HEADS

▲ *With scant hair, infants often wear hats to keep their heads warm.*

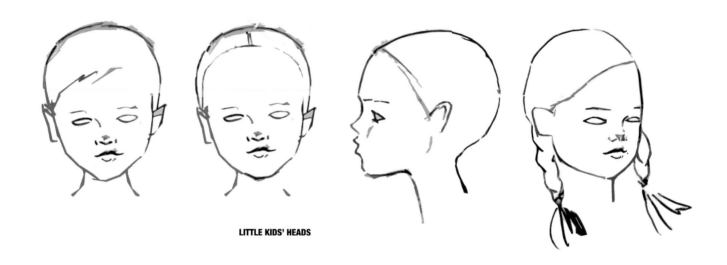

LITTLE KIDS' HEADS

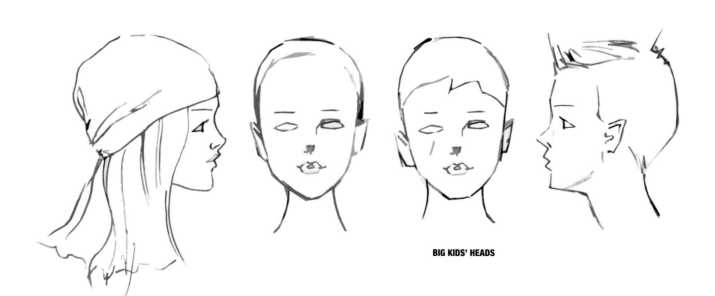

BIG KIDS' HEADS

Front to Back Rotation

Tilting the head downward or upward results in a foreshortening of the shape and location of the features. A downward tilt causes a greater portion of the top of the head to be visible. The forehead appears to elongate and the features look flatter and sit lower on the face. The neck is concealed by the downturn of the chin and the ears appear higher in relation to the eyes. Conversely, when the head tilts upward, a smaller portion of the forehead is visible. The features appear to be higher on the face and the ears seem lower in relation to the eyes. The under surfaces of the jaw, nose, lips, and brow come into view.

▼ *Experiment with different hairstyles and variations for the little kids' three-quarter view.*

▲ *Big kids' facial expressions can be used to suggest a specific customer profile and the circumstances under which (s)he might wear the clothing (such as playtime versus school).*

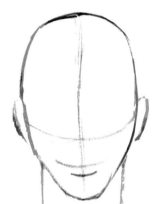
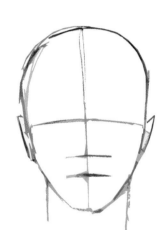

DOWNWARD, NEUTRAL, AND UPWARD TILT

FORESHORTENING THE FEATURES

As mentioned in Chapter 3, your drawing of children and young adults should not be overly sweet. Licensed characters and dolls such as Blythe and Emily Strange are good examples of the successful edgier depiction of children. Working with a doll (left), graffiti (below), or Japanese anime as your inspiration, develop a more extreme and imaginative drawing style for the faces of children and young adults.

▲ *Handmade dolls can be a wonderful source of inspiration. Marina Bychkova's handcrafted porcelein "Enchanted Dolls" feature a lifelike articulation and exquisite detail that has inspired equally beautiful illustrations by her ardent fan base.*

▶ *Look to graffiti art to help you develop an alternative approach to the portrayal of children. Graffiti art by Herakut.*

Drawing Hats

Once you have some command over drawing the head, you can move on to hats. There are many varieties: hard/soft, knit/woven, and so on. No matter what the style, placement of the hat on the head is key to the design. Placement is determined by the size of the circumference of the hat. The amount of space between the top of the head and the crown of the hat will also vary according to design. Hats come with and without brims, the shape and scale of which will also be determined by specific design. Depending on size and location, brims and visors may obscure the eyes and cast big shadows on the face. Observation will be key to your success in drawing hats. Take care to collect a deep swipe file of different styles and fabrications for ongoing reference. Remember to exaggerate your drawing of a hat, just as you would any other part of a fashion drawing.

◀▼ *Hats with a large circumference sit lower and cover a larger portion of the head. Conversely, hats with a small circumference sit very high and only cover a small portion of the head. Illustrations by Antonio Lopez (left) and Ferdinand (below).*

Drawing a Soft Hat

For this exercise you will draw a Tam o' Shanter (soft round hat) on a three-quarter view head.

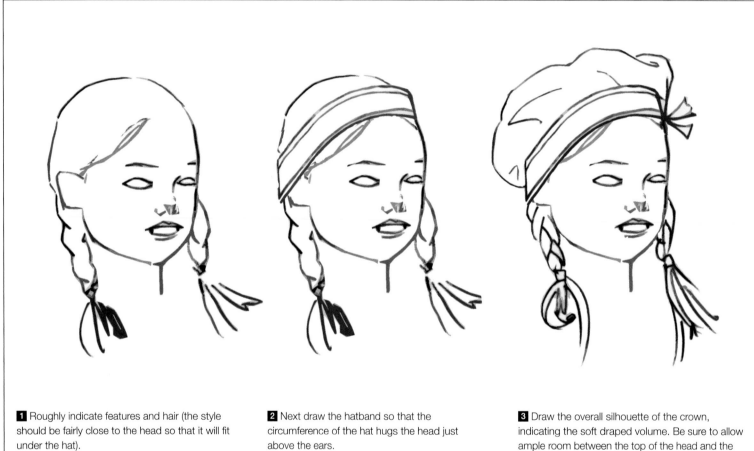

1 Roughly indicate features and hair (the style should be fairly close to the head so that it will fit under the hat).

2 Next draw the hatband so that the circumference of the hat hugs the head just above the ears.

3 Draw the overall silhouette of the crown, indicating the soft draped volume. Be sure to allow ample room between the top of the head and the crown of the hat. The pompom traditionally featured at the top of a Tam o' Shanter would not be visible above eye level.

Drawing a Hat with a Visor

For this exercise you will draw a newsboy cap (a fuller, paneled version of the flat cap) with a full soft draped crown and visor.

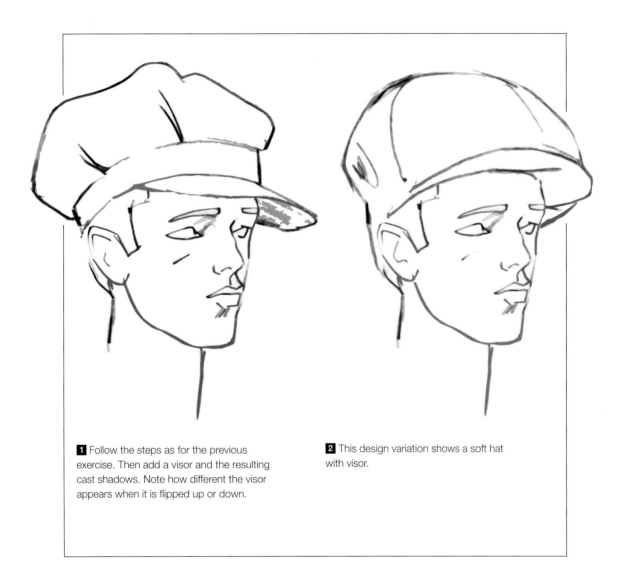

1 Follow the steps as for the previous exercise. Then add a visor and the resulting cast shadows. Note how different the visor appears when it is flipped up or down.

2 This design variation shows a soft hat with visor.

Drawing a Hat with a Brim

For this exercise, you will draw a fedora, a brimmed felt hat with a crease in the crown.

1 Working with a front view head, roughly indicate the facial features and hair. Place the bottom line for the circumference of the hat to fit the head snugly just above the temples. Draw a second parallel line for the top edge of the hatband.

2 Next draw the crown of the hat, allowing ample room for the top of the head.

3 Complete the drawing by adding the brim. Be sure to add shadows cast on the face by the brim. In some instances, larger brims may obscure the eyes.

▶ Design variations for a structured hat: an upturned brim with low crown (left), and a small brim with high crown (right).

Drawing Eyeglasses

Fashion branding extends to eyeglasses, with sunglasses in particular as key items for the luxury market. Some glasses are designed to make a strong visual statement, while others are so understated as to be nearly invisible. The size of the lenses will vary according to design— for example, seventies' granny glasses featured small lenses with wire frames whereas fifties' iconic Ray-Ban Wayfarers featured larger lenses with thick black frames. For this exercise, you will draw a pair of classic aviator glasses.

1 Working with a three-quarter view, roughly indicate the features and hair. Leave your drawing of the eyes quite vague as they will be obscured by lenses and their reflection of the light.

2 Draw the overall shape of the glasses to project beyond the edge of the head on the side turning away from view.

3 Add the remaining details to the frames. To complete the drawing, add diagonal hard shadows and highlights to indicate a reflective surface.

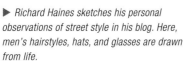

ASSIGNMENT 6

Working from a variety of photo references and life, draw three views of the head with different hats and hairstyles (right), and makeup for women.

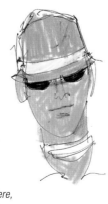

▶ *Richard Haines sketches his personal observations of street style in his blog. Here, men's hairstyles, hats, and glasses are drawn from life.*

Drawing Hands

Drawing a hand for the fashion figure will be significantly different than for classic life studies. The complex network of bones and knuckles must be stylized for fashion with consideration given to movement and position. What would this fashionable hand look like if placed on the hip? How would the hand look holding a cell phone or waving goodbye? Stored visual observations will be helpful, but these must be filtered through an exaggerated drawing style. A facility for drawing different hand gestures is essential for communicating emotion, attitude, and even gender. For example, a "thumbs up" hand gesture suggests approval, while graceful finger movements are typically reserved for women. The position of the hands can also be used to draw attention to a specific detail.

You should have some understanding of the bones and knuckles of the hand in order to portray natural movement. The bones of the hand radiate from the wrist, with the fingers fanning out from the knuckles. The hand and wrist move as one part, with the muscles of the wrist controlling all movement except for twisting, which is controlled by the forearm. When seen from the knuckle side of the hand, the thumbs point to the body. When seen from the palm side, the pinky fingers are closest to the body. When viewed from the underside, fingers appear shorter because of a seamless blending with the pads of the palm. Because of the hand's wide range of motion, you will seldom see all five fingers at once and the fingers you do see will often be foreshortened. As in all fashion drawing, it will be necessary to eliminate some anatomical detail in order to create an idealized form. But take care not to eliminate too much structural detail as this will create the appearance of a rubber glove!

Observation will serve you well so long as you stylize in a consistent manner. Mannequin parts are terrific to work from in that they are already re-proportioned for fashion. Practice drawing different hand positions, avoiding unnatural, self-conscious, or distracting gestures. The small bones and knuckles of the hand present a visual complexity that can be a bit overwhelming at first. Working with the techniques that follow (and lots of practice) you will be able draw hands with ease and authority in no time.

▼ Beginners reliably draw the hands (and feet) too small in relation to the rest of the body. The hand is actually equal to the height of the face excluding the hairline.

▲ Just as for other parts of the body, there is a relative proportion between the head and the size of the hand. Illustration by Glen Tunstull.

Drawing Women's Hands

In order to understand the three-dimensional volume, first analyze
the hand in terms of simple geometric forms.

1 Begin by drawing two inverted wedges to represent the hand and fingers. Then add the thumb. Indicate the wrist as a ball socket attached to the forearm.

2 The knuckles of the hand and fingertips follow an arc. Each finger has three joints with the length of each segment conforming to the arcs. Roughly block in the overall shape of the hand, fusing the two middle fingers. Then add the thumb, the top of which should be aligned with the first joint of the fingers.

3 Refine the drawing by articulating each finger. Be sure to indicate a delicate bone structure and graceful gesture.

▼ When drawing gloves show the seams as well as the soft folds created by the movement of the wrist, hand, and fingers.

▲◥ In order to deal with the visual complexity of the small bones and knuckles of the hand, first seek out the overall shape and then subdivide it to indicate individual fingers.

ASSIGNMENT 7

Working from life or a photo reference, draw women's hands in a variety of positions (above). Experiment with different gestures and points of view. For a more ambitious challenge, illustrate the hands wearing gloves (far left) or gripping an object.

Drawing Men's Hands

Men's hands are more square in appearance, with knuckles and bony structures having greater prominence. Following the same steps as for women, draw various views of men's hands.

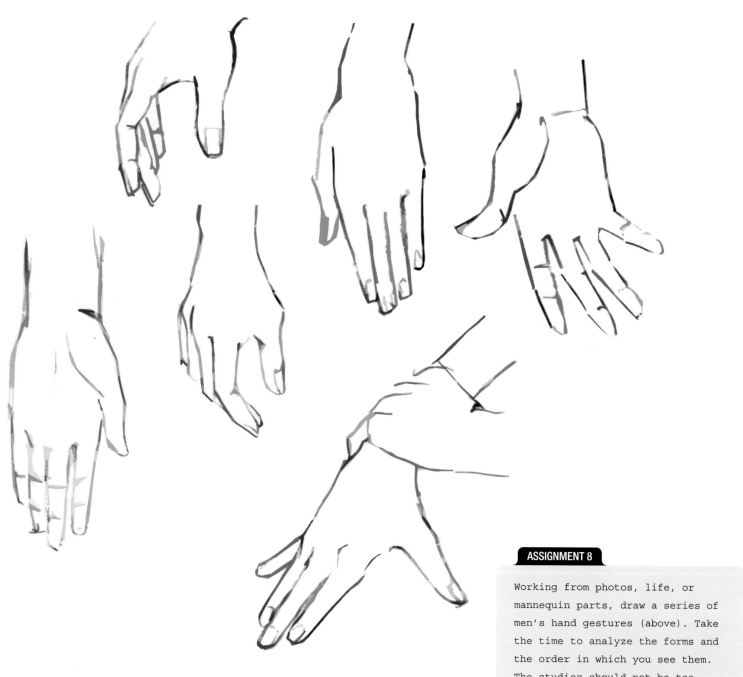

Working from photos, life, or mannequin parts, draw a series of men's hand gestures (above). Take the time to analyze the forms and the order in which you see them. The studies should not be too large, approximating the size the hands would be in a head-to-toe figure drawing.

Drawing Children's Hands

Infants' and children's hands must also be highly stylized for fashion drawing. As children mature, the size, proportion, and structure of their hands changes. Babies and younger kids have short, round fingers and chubby knuckles which slim and elongate with maturity. By the time a child reaches seven, the shape of the hand is quite similar to that of an adult, only smaller. The younger the child, the shorter and rounder the fingers. A child's hand gestures reflect a specific level of dexterity depending on their age. (For more information about drawing hands from life, see Chapter 5, p. 186.)

(For more information about drawing hands from life, see Chapter 5, p. 186.)

ASSIGNMENT 9

Working from a photo reference or from life, draw a variety of infants' and children's hands (below), searching out suitable gestures for each age group (for an infant, draw chubby hands crawling). If the child's hand is holding something, draw the object first and then observe how the hand conforms to the object.

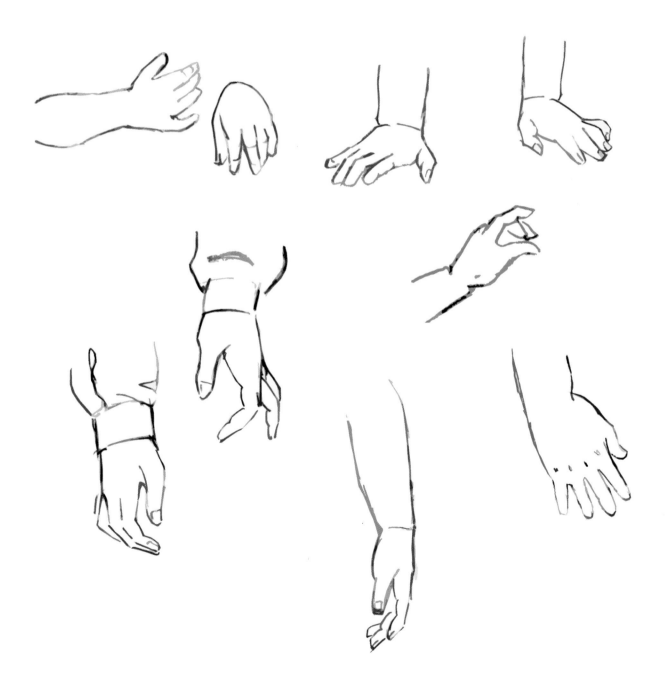

Drawing Feet

As with other parts of the body, it will be helpful to imagine a geometric shape—a wedge—as the starting point for drawing the foot. The relative proportion of this wedge compared to the total body height will be key. When first beginning, there is a tendency to draw very small feet.

As with other parts of the body, you must have a working knowledge of the movement of the foot and leg. For example, when the heel is flat on the ground, the foot and leg come together at a right angle. As the heel elevates, this angle is expanded and, when viewed from the front, more of the instep becomes visible

and the ankle is raised. Conversely, when the foot is flat, there is a foreshortening of the instep in the front view and a lowering of the ankle.

The right and left foot are seldom seen in the same position or from the same point of view. For example, the right foot may be seen head-on (front view), while the left is partially or fully turned. The leg and foot positions in your fashion drawing should seem natural, corresponding to the rotation of the rest of the body. The way in which you stylize the foot should also have a relationship with the rest of your drawing.

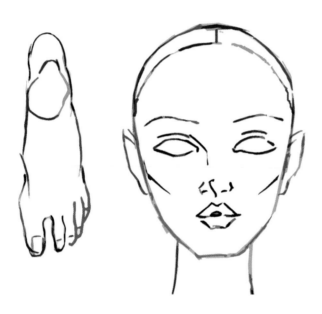

▲ The length of the foot is actually equal to the height of the head.

◥ While the leg bones are usually thought of as being straight and rigid, they actually form a subtle inward curve from the knee down. The foot is an extension of this S-curve. Note the difference between flat (left) and elevated (right) heel positions.

▲ The ankle bones fit neatly into the curve of the instep; the protrusion of the ankles is higher on the inside of the leg.

▶ Elevation of the heel changes the appearance of the foot (a greater portion of the instep comes into view).

Drawing the Side View Foot

The inside and outside edges of the foot are anatomically different, so you must first decide which foot (right or left) you are drawing and from what point of view. While the outside edge of the foot makes full contact with the floor, the inside edge has a slight elevation in the center where the arch forms a bridge between the ball and heel. Turning the foot affects the order in which you see the toes. For the interior side view, the big toe is seen first and largely obscures the other four toes. For the exterior side view, the pinky toe comes first in the visual ordering of the forms.

▲ *Think of the foot as a triangle or wedge, and imagine how it would look from different points of view.*

EXTERIOR AND INTERIOR VIEWS OF THE LEFT FOOT

▲ *The Achilles tendon and heel are seen first, head on, in the reordering and foreshortening of the forms for the back view.*

Drawing Men's and Children's Feet

Advice for drawing men's and children's hands will carry over to the feet. The men's foot will be less delicate and more square. For infants and children, the relationship between the feet and the body as a whole will change as the child matures. Babies and little kids have relatively large and chubby feet. Since very young infants are unable to walk, they are usually drawn in sitting or crawling positions, and the bottoms of their feet are often in view. For bigger kids, the foot begins to thin and is smaller in relation to the body as a whole. Shoe styles (see p. 173) also become more sophisticated as the child moves toward adulthood.

MEN'S FEET

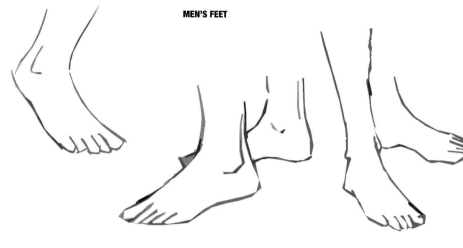

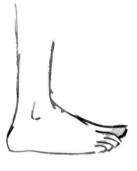

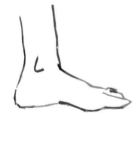

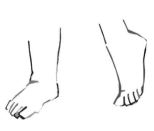

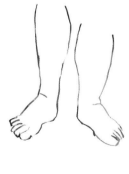

INFANTS' AND KIDS' FEET

Shoe styles (see p. 173)

ASSIGNMENT 10

Depending on your area of specialization, draw a variety of foot gestures for women, men (above), or children (left).

Drawing Shoes

As you probably know from personal experience, although the foot must fit inside a shoe, some designs bear little or no resemblance to the natural shape of the foot. The choice of shoes will determine overall posture and is therefore a determining factor for balancing the entire figure (see p. 62). Shoes come in all shapes and sizes. There are "flats," such as delicate ballet slippers and heavy-soled construction boots. "Heels," such as 4in. (10cm) stilettos, raise the heel to give a woman additional height. Thick-soled "platforms" also provide additional height. The toe of the shoe may be round, pointy, square, or even split with divisions for groups of toes. Shoes can make a design concept more or less sophisticated, casual, and so on. The shoe is a significant consideration in determining overall silhouette and is an important extension of the design concept. For example, the Maison Martin Margiela design collective is as famous for their iconic split-toe *tabi* boots as for their garment designs.

Just as hats can be used to change the apparent size of the head, shoes can also make the foot appear small or large in comparison to the body. The way the foot is positioned in the shoe will radically affect its overall appearance. For instance, the elevation of the heel brings a greater portion of the instep (both shoe and foot) into view. Try to imagine the shoe in a box to approximate believable perspective.

In the past, the laws of physics governed placement of the heel in both the design and drawing of shoes. State-of-the-art technology now allows for shoe designs that are limited only by your imagination. Just as with the most experimental architecture, some shoe designs actually appear to defy gravity. So when you design or draw a shoe, your only requirements are to make sure that there is a (comfortable) way for the foot to fit into the shoe and that your drawing conforms to a stylized proportion and foreshortening.

▲ *Technology affords nearly unlimited options for shoe design as demonstrated by these imaginative platforms by Alexander McQueen.*

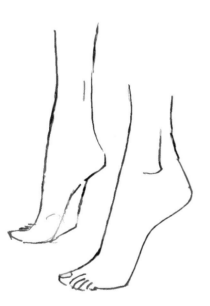

▲ *When drawing a shoe from your imagination, first draw the foot in the position it would assume in the shoe, and then draw the shoe around it.*

▲ *Whether drawing from a photo reference or a model, try to see the foot and shoe as a composite of abstract shapes.*

ASSIGNMENT 11

Practice drawing different foot gestures and shoes from photos (this page and opposite). Take care to stylize just as for any other aspect of a fashion drawing.

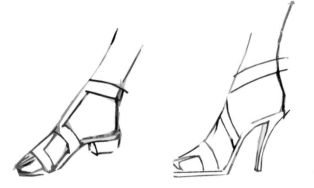

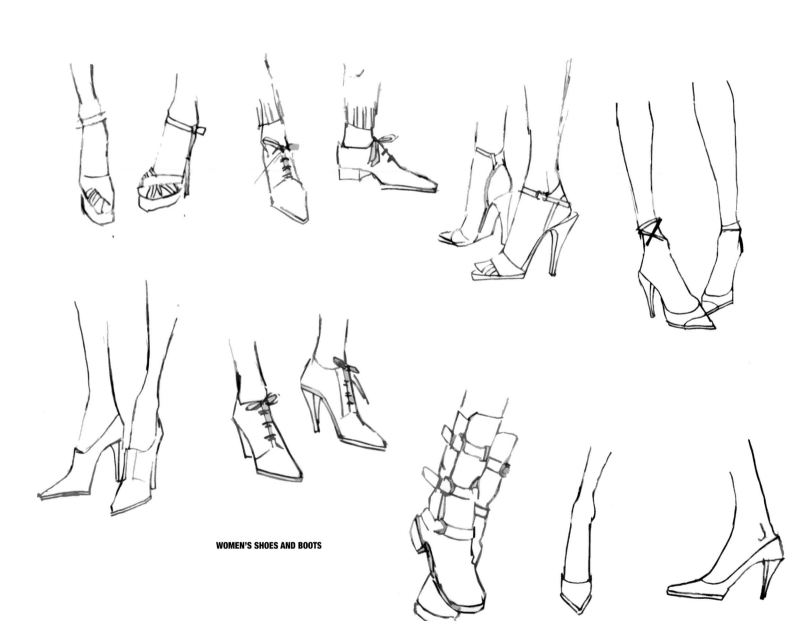

WOMEN'S SHOES AND BOOTS

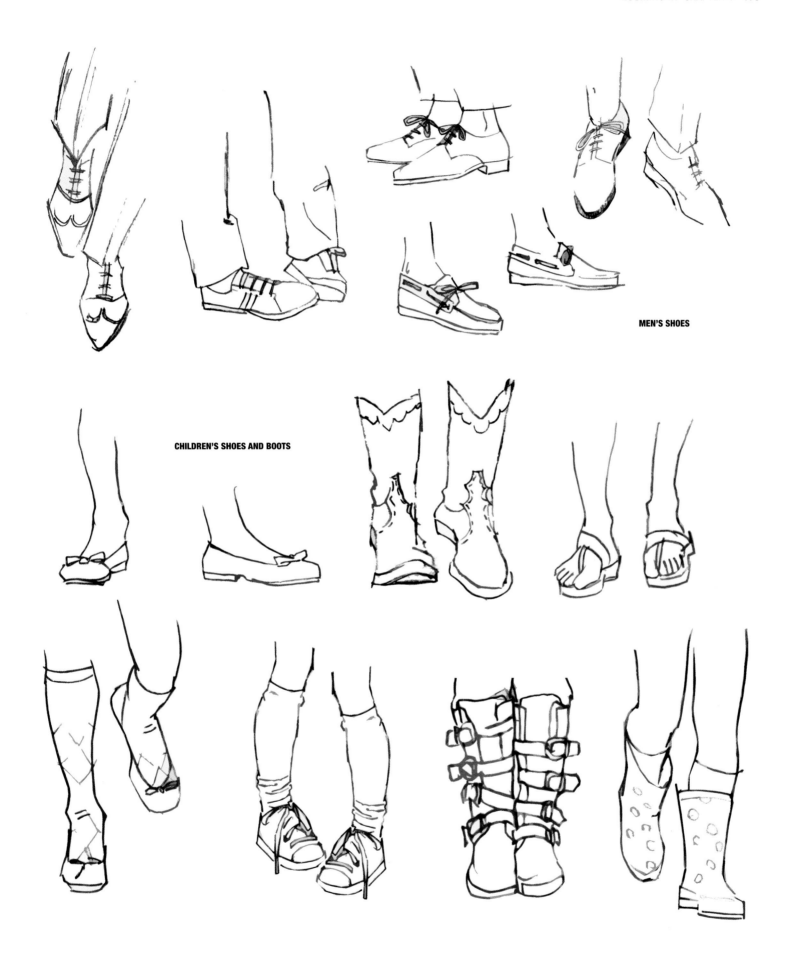

MEN'S SHOES

CHILDREN'S SHOES AND BOOTS

CHAPTER 5
WORKING FROM LIFE

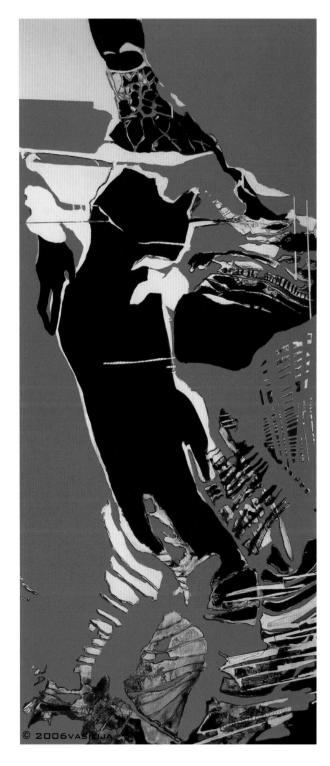

▼ *The spontaneity, movement, and line that distinguish good fashion drawing originate from the direct observation of life. Painting by Vasilija Zivanic.*

This chapter deals with drawing from a live fashion model. Observations from life will ultimately inform all of your fashion drawings, including those created without the benefit of a model. The preliminary exercises provide firsthand experience of the basic principles for figure proportion and balance introduced in Chapter 1. The second series of exercises address right/left brain function and are designed to eliminate frustration and allow you to draw what you see. The concluding exercises bring everything together; drawings are refined and incorporated into innovative compositions.

Getting Started

The whole point of fashion model drawing is learning how to see. Everyone has different perceptions and a designer must come to their own conclusions about what they see and want to create. While drawing from a photo reference is extremely useful in the development of your figures, such studies are based on secondhand perceptions. The image of a "frozen moment" has already been manipulated by the photographer and computer technician. You can never really treat a photo as fact. With all this in mind it is a good idea to work from a model as often as you can. The curriculum for most fashion design programs requires drawing from live models, and many schools have open drawing sessions. You can also form your own group and pool resources to hire a model, or even draw one another. As with all of your work, model drawing should be a personal expression, not an imitation of another artist's style. Over time, practice, patience, and discipline will yield cumulative progress and increased spontaneity.

◀ *Illustration by Janae De Laurentis.*

▶ *While the model is resting, take the opportunity to draw other artists in your group.*

Setting Up a Studio

When drawing from the model, you are best served by setting up an area within your studio or classroom dedicated to this purpose. An optimum studio situation should have good light and airflow, with access to a sink. There should be a space where the model has privacy to change costume. You will also need spotlights, a platform to elevate the model above eye level, some kind of sound system, a chart of the human muscular system, and, if possible, a model of a skeleton. Classical schools of drawing recommend drawing from casts and sculptures. For fashion, there is similar benefit to sketching from mannequin parts while your model is on break. This will help you to ease into stylized proportions. Listening to music enhances concentration, with the proviso that you must be considerate of others. Stick to instrumentals as words/lyrics can be distracting.

Choosing Materials

Since you will be doing lots and lots of drawing, chose an inexpensive pad of newsprint or Manila paper in a size that allows you to work comfortably in the landscape orientation. Each figure will fill the page from top to bottom and you should be able to fit five figures across for quick warmup gestures. (For more about paper and art supplies, see Introduction to Part III.)

As for media, avoid art supplies that do not allow for an expressive line (such as mechanical pencils and ballpoint pens). Begin with charcoal pencils; by holding them at different angles you can achieve the various line qualities needed to describe the surfaces and textures of apparel. Caran D'Ache Neocolor II water-soluble crayons can be sharpened with a razor blade or craft knife for color line work. Adding water to the shavings turns the crayons into paint; Dr. Ph. Martin's and Luma dyes afford especially vibrant color. Pastels can be very freeing.

▲ The rendering techniques and art supplies that you choose are directly related to the garment and market category being illustrated. For example, Noriko Kikuchi renders her more conceptual designs using unconventional materials such as collage.

Selecting/Working With a Model

In selecting your fashion drawing models, keep in mind that the perfection of a photography model is not required. You can reinvent this person as you draw and very often the "flaws" that may prevent the model from working in front of a camera can be far more interesting to an artist. Because (s)he will be the embodiment of your fantasy customer, (s)he should have character, style, and graceful body movement. You can never be quite sure who will be your muse; some models will surprise you with an indescribable quality that is not apparent until you begin drawing them. The whole experience of model drawing pivots on the rapport between model, artist(s), and, if present, an instructor. It is a good idea to assemble a diverse stable of models. Be spontaneous and collaborative. Create scenarios by juxtaposing garments that suggest a narrative (for example, layer a trench coat over lingerie). You will find that more extreme, over-the-top fashion is easier to draw than more subtle variations.

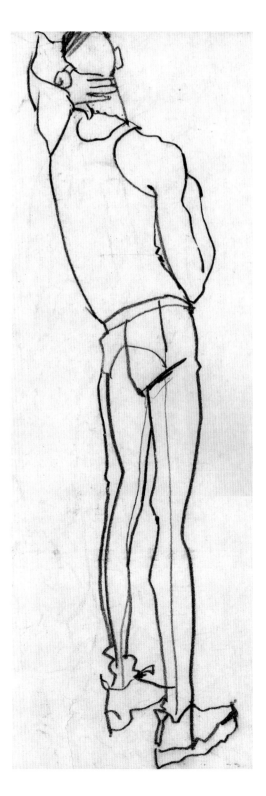

◀▼ *Be sure to draw petite and plus size models from time to time, as interpreting different figure proportions in your personal drawing style is a special challenge. The same goes for drawing men and children.*

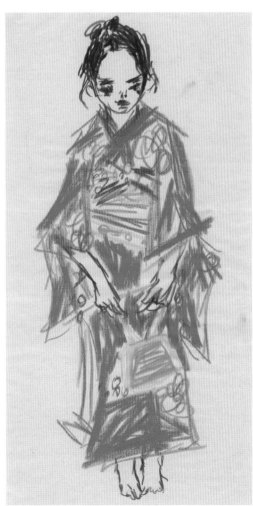

▶ *The immediacy of Erika Kobayashi's sketch captures a fleeting moment of stillness for this little girl.*

Professional artists' models usually pose for twenty minutes at a time with five minute breaks in between poses. It is important to bring a timer to your sessions so that you can monitor the length of the poses. Depending on your rapport, you can leave it to the model to time themselves. Position her/him on a platform above eye level in the center of the room to allow for a 360-degree view. Alternatively, move the platform in front of a mirror to create both a front and back view for a single pose. While the model is posing, move around the room to experience different points of view. The model should assume a pose that is natural for her and if she needs help, you can make some suggestions. You can get ideas for poses from current and vintage fashion magazines. Warm up with a combination of one-, two-, and five-minute gesture poses. Then move onto ten- and twenty-minute poses.

The increasingly frenetic pace of daily life—fast cuts in action movies, Web animations, videos—has made concentrating for longer periods of time difficult. The ability to maintain your concentration for longer poses will develop with practice over time. Eventually the forty minutes required for a more extensive rendering will fly by, but in the beginning it can seem like an eternity.

▼ ▶ *The shapes, colors, and textures featured in Sofia Enlund's imaginative and expressive model drawings inspire her garment designs.*

Take care that poses are not overly ambitious for their duration. Both model and artist should try to anticipate the effect of gravity on the figure. Draw the part most likely to be affected by gravity first (an extended or elevated arm or leg perhaps). For longer poses, mark the platform with taped landmarks so that your model can assume the same pose after the break. As you become more accomplished, begin to experiment with props, drapery, and lighting.

The exercises that follow are not meant to be one-off. The exploration of garment details and fabric rendering techniques in Parts II and III of this book can be incorporated into the various premises given for each of the exercises. You can then observe what the details and fabrics really look like when draped on the model.

Basic Principles

Model drawing must be seen as a process of improving your ability to observe detail. Fashion sketches drawn from life will tend to be less calculated and more emotional than those done without the benefit of seeing the model. The quick decisions made during a timed pose will sharpen critical thinking and thus enhance problem-solving skills. While only a small percentage of model drawings are usable as preliminary sketches for portfolio presentations, the stored memories of direct observations are an invaluable resource. The use of experimental materials in model drawing can be the jumping-off point for an extremely imaginative composition and future garment design. You may also discover an entirely new figure proportion.

▶ *Sara Harper's loose and expressive line work is ideal for capturing the model's gesture in quick timed poses.*

▼ *Model drawings can be used as studies for poses, a likeness, or facial expression, worked up at a later date for finished presentations of garment designs.*

Unleashing Your Imagination

In fashion model drawing, you extrapolate what you see and filter it through the lens of an idealized figure proportion. In subsequent exercises you will make a conscious effort to establish and maintain a consistent fashion proportion for your model drawing. But before you begin training your eye, it is important to determine your innate sense of figure proportion. For this exercise, sketch freely from the model without any specific guide or prejudgment. Observe what you see without regard for technique. If you have had prior training in fine art, your understanding of anatomy and how the body moves will be an asset.

As previously discussed in Chapter 1, the proportion of the fashion figure has very little to do with reality. Through model drawing, you may discover an entirely new proportion for your fashion figure. For your initial sessions have the model wear a leotard with a contrasting color belt to emphasize the movement of the waist. If she has long hair, have her pin it up so that it does not obscure her shoulders. Working in charcoal pencil on newsprint:

1 Warm up with quick sketches, known as gestures. Have the model do a series of ten two-minute poses. Allow for honest first impressions. Draw quickly and confidently—as if you were running a race—to help eliminate the second-guessing that interferes with visual perception. The rhythm of the music you choose can help you to pick up the pace.

2 Do a contour drawing—using a single continuous line to describe the model. Keep your eye up and concentrate on searching out the edges. For the longer poses, make corrections without erasing your mistakes. Mistakes are, after all, your best learning tools. You can edit them more effectively by manipulating the image at a later time in Photoshop.

▲ *Do not allow preconceived notions about traditional fashion drawing to inhibit your imagination.*

Maintaining a Constant Proportion

Once you have decided how you want to stylize your fashion figure, try to apply this proportion consistently to all of your model drawing studies. Constant proportion can be achieved by setting up horizontal folds as landmarks for different parts of the body. As for the previous exercise, have the model wear a leotard with a contrasting color belt to emphasize the movement of the waist. Using masking tape or chalk, mark off the Center Front line on her body. Working with charcoal pencil and light-colored crayon or pastel on newsprint:

1 Hold a sheet of the newsprint in landscape orientation and fold the paper horizontally, accordion-style. The number of folds should correspond to the number of heads that you have determined as the height of your stylized figure. For example, a traditional proportion for a women's fashion figure would call for nine folds. Number the spaces on one side of the paper. Using a light-colored crayon or pastel, draw a horizontal line across the page to indicate landmarks for the shoulders, waist, hips, knees, and ankles.

2 During the quick warmup poses, use a second pale-colored crayon or pastel to capture the gesture. Begin by drawing the head, Centre Front line, and the opposing angles of upper and lower torso. Plot the location of the knees and feet. Take care to locate each of the body parts near to the established landmarks. Then go back and finalize it, working with charcoal pencil to fill in the details.

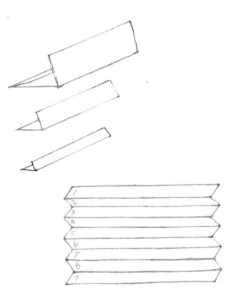

▲▶ *Fold the paper into nine equal divisions for a traditional fashion proportion (above). Drawing by Jillian Carrozza (opposite).*

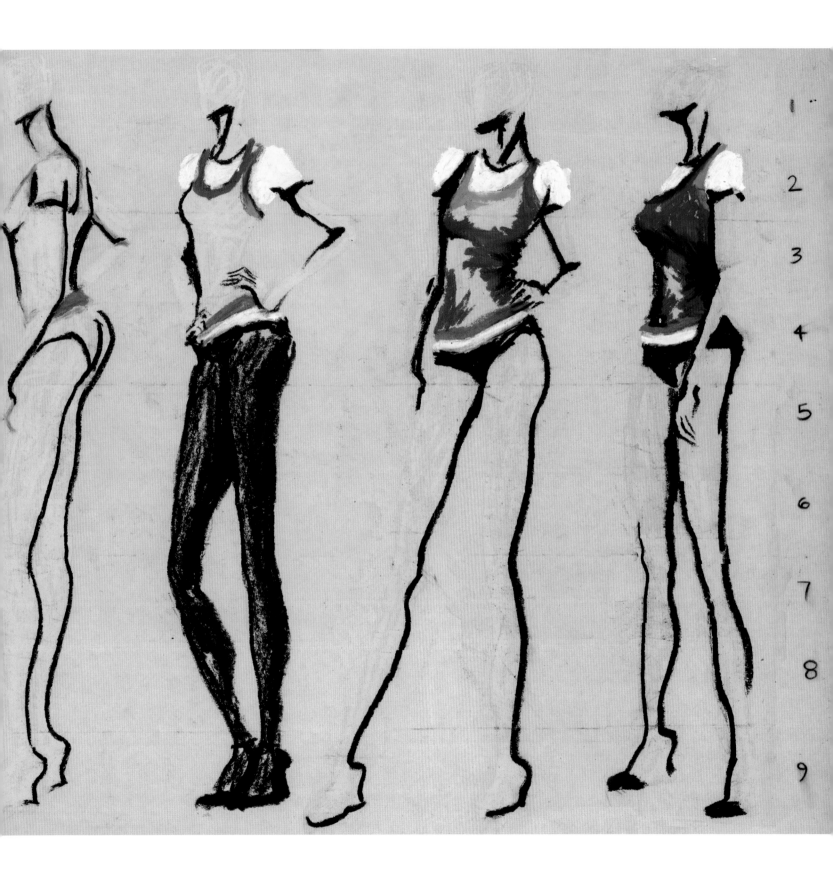

Balancing the Figure

In Chapter 1 you developed a figure in a high hip pose based on the rules of contrapposto. Working from the model will give you an opportunity to see firsthand how the figure is balanced.

As for the previous exercises, have the model wear a leotard with a contrasting color belt. Mark off the Center Front line on her body using tape or chalk. You can simulate the Balance Line by having the model suspend a plumb line—a string with a weight (bob) attached at the bottom—from the pit of her neck. Depending on the length of the string, she can tie it around her neck, or simply hold it with her hand. The suspended plumb line will help you determine which is the weight-bearing leg.

Referring to an anatomy chart, and even assuming the model's high hip pose yourself, will further your understanding of how the body moves.

1 Observe the movement of the model's body as she transfers her weight from one foot to the other. Notice how her hips move away from the plumb (the Balance Line) and work in opposition to the angle of the shoulders. Have her assume a front view high hip position with her free arm dangling at her side. Allow the plumb line to swing freely; when it stops, the bob will be hovering directly over the foot of the weight-bearing leg.

2 Using the method for maintaining constant proportion described in the previous exercise, draw the model in this high hip pose. Take a moment to analyze the pose before you begin drawing.
a. Which leg is bearing most of the weight? Remember that weight distribution is not always an all-or-nothing proposition—distribution may be 60–40, for example.
b. Locate her head, the Center Front line, and the high hip; this will help you find the S-curve—the essence of the overall gesture.
c. Determine the opposing angles of her hips and shoulders.
d. Make a mental note of the location of her feet in relation to her head.

3 Have the model shift her weight to the other leg and draw her in this position. The drawings created in steps 1 and 2 can be used as the basis for all variations of the high hip pose.

4 For the next pose, have the model turn slightly and shift her weight again, this time placing one of her hands on her hip. This is the same pose used for the exercise on pp. 56–57.
a. Sketch her head, torso, and legs and feet.
b. Next, draw the overall shape of her hand on her hip.
c. Using a bold-colored crayon or pastel, block in the negative space defining the inside of her arm. Using charcoal, draw the outside of her arm.
d. Draw the second arm and remaining details to complete your sketch. Continue working in this manner, experimenting with shifting weight and arm and leg positions.

▲ Have the model change into a T-shirt and a pair of five-pocket jeans so that she can pose with her hands in her pockets. Drawing by Whitney Newman.

Evaluate your completed drawing using the following checklist:

✓ Does the figure look like it is falling over?

✓ Are the shoulders and hips at opposing angles?

✓ Is the weight-bearing leg on the same side as the high hip?

✓ Is the foot of the weight-bearing leg directly under the head?

✓ Is the angle of the knees parallel to the angle of the hips?

✓ Are the apex and neckline parallel to the angle of the shoulders?

✓ Are the leg openings for her leotard at the same angle as her hips?

✓ Are the knees located at the vertical midpoint of the legs?

✓ Are the elbows at the vertical midpoint of the arms?

✓ Are the hands and feet drawn skillfully?

✓ Does the garment look attractive? Is it prioritized in the drawing?

✓ Is it accurately drawn?

✓ Did you use an economy of line?

✓ Did you edit visual information appropriately?

✓ Did you stylize the figure in a pleasing way?

Turning and Foreshortening the Figure

Working with a model will give you an opportunity to observe the foreshortening described in Chapter 1 (see pp. 54–55). The model should be dressed in a leotard and pantyhose, with her waist, Center Front, and Center Back delineated with chalk or tape. Toward the end of the session have her add a shrug and leg and arm warmers in contrasting colors.

1 Beginning with a front view high hip pose, have the model turn to a three-quarter view. Observe the movement of the Center Front line and how the parts of her body that turn away appear to shrink. Conversely, the parts of her body that are closest to you will appear larger.

2 Practice drawing several variations of the three-quarter turned pose. Be sure to accurately indicate the Center Front line in red on each drawing.

3 Next, have the model turn so that she is seen in profile. Observe the location of the Center Front line; it now becomes the defining edge for the side of the body turning from view. Practice drawing variations of the profile view, again indicating the Center Front line in red on each drawing.

4 Have the model rotate to a back view pose with her weight evenly distributed on both feet. Observe the movement of her hips and Center Back line as she shifts her weight from side to side. Draw her in a back view high hip pose indicating the Center Back line in red.

5 For your final drawing, have the model assume the same pose as for step 3. Sit on the floor as close to the platform as possible. Using the flat sight drawing technique (one eye closed to assist you), draw this extremely foreshortened view. Compare the proportion of this drawing to the one from step 3. Can you see the effect of foreshortening? The head will be smaller, the legs longer, the feet larger, and so on. You can also have the model sit down so that your eye level is raised up and looking down on her.

As you become aware of the effect of repositioning your line of sight, you can employ different and extreme points of view to control (and vary) the way in which you stylize your fashion figure. Try different points of view, working above, at, and below eye level to gauge the effect of different points of view on your drawing.

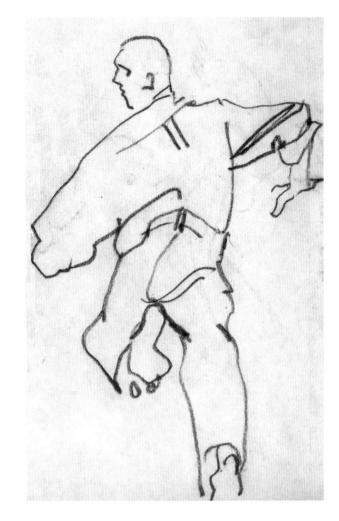

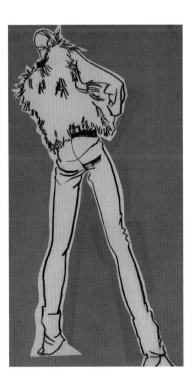

◀▲ *Exaggerated foreshortening can be used to add drama to a drawing.*

◀◀ *Because the lens of a camera can precisely focus at only one distance, there is a decrease in sharpness on either side of that focused distance. Jillian Carrozza takes a cue from photography and uses a selective focus in her drawing to create a hierarchy of information and sense of depth.*

Drawing Faces, Hands, and Feet

Drawing faces can often be especially challenging. It is possible that you are very accomplished at drawing a single face, but are unable to do variations beyond that one good face. The ability to draw faces—that is, capture a likeness and put it down on paper—is a function of the right hemisphere of the brain (more about that later in this chapter). For this exercise, drawing faces with your less dominant hand will require a leap of faith, but trust that it will help you to access the right brain for a task it does better.

Keep in mind that because artists typically draw the figure from the top down, concentration often becomes dissipated by the time they get to the feet. It is also possible to form bad habits. If, no matter what is put in front of you, the drawing looks the same, you will need to shake things up a bit. Drawing from the bottom up can lift you out of a rut as well as help you to accurately draw feet and shoes.

Determine what you want emphasized, then establish a selective focus in your drawing by prioritizing certain details. There is a normal tendency to avoid the parts of the figure that are problematic to draw. It is important to meet this challenge head-on by emphasizing what is most difficult to draw, using size and heavier line weights to accentuate these trouble spots.

For this session, make sure you hire a model with a versatile look. Have them bring simple garments with necklines and collars that frame the face, as well as a variety of hats, hair ornaments, sunglasses, shoes, patterned gloves, and hosiery.

1 For the warmup, draw only the model's face, capturing a wide variety of facial expressions/gestures (happy, sad, surprised, yawning, etc.).

2 Working with your left hand (right hand for left-handed people), draw three studies of the head wearing a variety of hats, sunglasses, and hairstyles.

3 As slowly as you possibly can, draw the entire figure (with either hand) working from the bottom up, emphasizing feet, hands, and face (leave the rest in silhouette). Be aware of the difference between big shoes and big feet! A shoe ultimately has to snugly fit the foot; it is the shape of the toe, platform, and heel which creates the appearance of a big shoe (such as combat boots).

4 Have the model wear patterned gloves and hosiery while in a seated pose. Working with color, block in the pattern only (no line) using it to define the hands and feet. Use a contour line to draw the remaining parts of the figure.

▲▼ *It is important to experiment with drawing a variety of hats, eyeglasses, and accessories. These observations will inform subsequent drawings created without the benefit of a model. Illustrations by Howard Tangye (top left), Megan Schwarz (top right), and Richard Rosenfeld (below).*

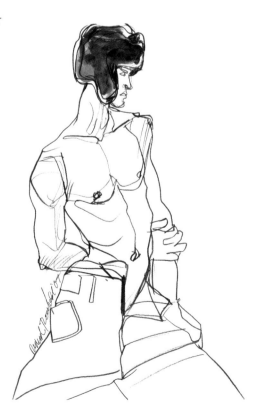

The Effect of Gravity, Compression, and Expansion on Garment Drape

Use this model drawing session to observe the basic principles of gravity, compression, and expansion, which govern garment drape. (For more information about basic garment drape see Chapter 6.)

1 Have the model wear a striped leotard and pantyhose for the warmup.

2 Layer a basic flared skirt over the leotard and have the model shift her weight to one leg. Observe how the skirt swings in the direction of the high hip and how the angle of the hemline corresponds to the angle of her hip. Draw her in this high hip position, accurately blocking in the stripes with color and reserving line work exclusively for the skirt.

3 Repeat step 2 with a coat or a loose shift, observing how the angle of the hemline now corresponds to the angle of the shoulder. Then draw a simple pair of pants, observing the effects of gravity, compression, and expansion.

4 Repeat any or all of steps 2 and 3 with an alternative point of view.

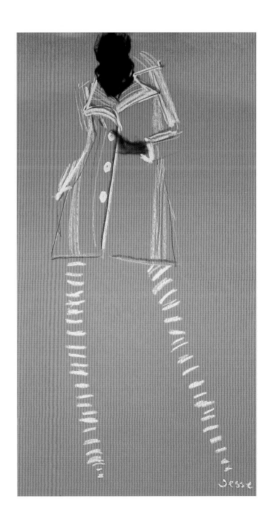

▲▶ Use stripes to map the form and movement of the body. Illustrations by Sara Harper (above) and Jesse Lee Burton (right).

Understanding How the Brain Processes Visual Information

It may surprise you to learn that the greatest benefit to be derived from life drawing is the ability to control the shift in consciousness that enables you to draw what you see. The exercises that follow are intended to encourage this cognitive shift. Studies of neurological function have shown that the inability to see the less obvious solution to a problem is tied to visual closure. When you draw from life, you are in fact cultivating an open mind. As the technology woven into our daily lives edges out manual tasks and non-verbal brain activities, it is that much more important to develop the visual (for most people) right hemisphere of the brain. Which is not to say that your left brain is the enemy; the right brain is often simply less accessible. The two sides of your brain view reality in very different ways and it is important to integrate both; to be able to freely access the appropriate cognitive mode for the task.

The right hemisphere is responsible for visual perception and unbiased observation—useful for drawing exactly what you see. The left hemisphere is host to words and symbols that can interfere with the ability to see what is right before your eyes (literally, mind chatter.) The left brain is, however, indispensable for creating something out of thin air; vital to conceiving and illustrating that which does not yet exist.

You have already experienced how drawing faces with your less dominant hand helped to capture a likeness. Essentially, the lack of dexterity with your hand slowed your eye down to a point where the left brain timed out. Very often, when an artist is "blocked," they simply cannot access their right brain. The left brain reliably makes very general assumptions about what is seen and then turns it into a symbol, thereby interfering with objective perception of the model. Professional artists cannot afford the luxury of a bad day and it is perhaps the greatest challenge to control mental shifts under these circumstances.

The following exercises will help you to access and balance right and left brain function.

Experimenting with Mass and Negative Space

In the previous exercises you drew the model by delineating her edges. Now, you will experiment with drawing the shapes of spaces. The perception of "negative" space is integral to the development of drawing skills. Because you cannot name a negative space, the left-brain mode defers to the right and both seeing and drawing are made much easier.

For this exercise have the model bring garments that create simple graphic silhouettes. A solid color drape in the background will help define the negative space.

1 Working with paint or pastel on a color ground (inexpensive craft or construction paper is fine) block in the entire negative shape that surrounds and defines the figure. Block in interior "parts" with color, taking care to use mass only, no line. For the next pose, block in the model's overall positive shape, but this time with color. Treat her as if she were a backlit silhouette.

2 For the next drawing, block in the negative shape with paint. Let the color of the paper work as the flesh tone and, using your less dominant hand, complete the interior parts with line.

3 Light the model so that cast shadows form defined shapes. Try to view the pose as a series of abstract shapes. Work back and forth using line or mass to describe the different parts of your drawing. Do not draw any one part with both line and mass.

▶ Both fine art and illustration offer solid examples of using negative shapes to maximum effect. Looking at Coles Phillips's "Fadeaway Girls" featured on p. 11, note how the dress is carved out of the negative space in the absence of a holding line. The background and parts of the dress are defined by the same color and so she appears to fade away in the areas where the two meet. In this painting by Alex Katz, there is almost a complete elimination of line. Katz relies on color and mass to portray his subjects, cropping them to further abstract the image.

◀ ▼ *Color blocking allows you to see the model more abstractly. Note how the ground color of the paper can be used to define one of the interior shapes. Illustrations by Jesse Lee Burton (left) and Carla Cid de Diego (below).*

Breaking Down Visual Impressions into Manageable Parts

Imposing a system on your drawing will have the effect of slowing down your eye and increasing your concentration (again, the left brain times out). For this exercise, you will break down visual impressions into manageable parts. Use media that give you an expressive line in a wide variety of colors. Have the model wear clothing with some sort of intricate pattern or construction details.

1 Take a moment to locate absolutely the smallest thing you can see. Using one of the colors, begin your drawing with that minute shape. Build the drawing one small piece at a time, changing colors as you locate each part in relation to the one that came before. Your finished drawing will have a mosaic-like quality.

2 Next, you will further abstract the figure by cropping and rotating the image. Draw a small rectangle to set the boundaries of your composition. Fit the drawing into this shape by zooming in to a point where your composition does not feature any of the model's outside edges.

3 Draw the model's Center Front line on the page. Working with a combination of wet and dry media, draw from the inside out, drawing everything on the left with the dry media and everything on the right with the wet media. Work backward and forward developing both sides in tandem.

▼◢ ▶ *Illustrations by Janet Shin (below), Juan Mota (below right), and Olga Baird (right) feature the background color as the flesh tone.*

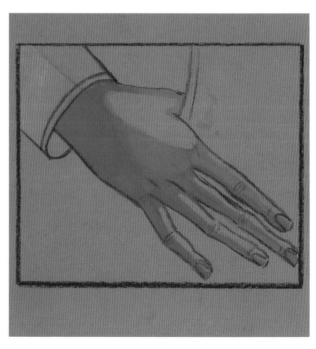

Balancing Observation with Imagination

It is equally important for the right brain not to dominate the left. In this exercise you will add invention to your observations from life. Experiment by adding irrational and symbolic imagery to your drawing. Try changing the model's orientation on the page (see p. 176)—feel free to defy gravity. Anything goes!

 Use nonsense color.

 Re-examine what "ugly" means to you. Challenge your sense of what is beautiful by creating a "fashion miss" (by a mile!). Exaggerate and relocate some detail in your drawing, utilizing a scale that defies relative proportion and good taste. Juxtapose otherwise unrelated images to suggest a narrative.

3 Use non-traditional paper such as accounting ledger, graph paper, wallpaper, gift wrapping paper, or sandpaper for your drawings.

▼ *In this imaginative drawing, seams on stockings sprout vines and flowers. Illustration by Kristin Shoemaker.*

▼ *Carolina Zuniga-Aisa uses striped giftwrap paper as the background for her life drawing.*

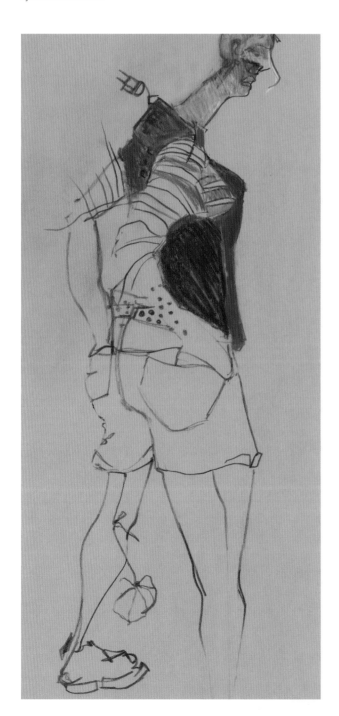

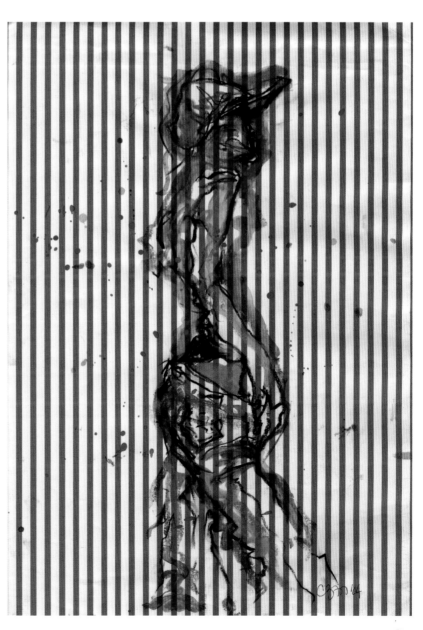

Working with Two Models

Working with two models will help you to see more abstractly. Try to find two models who like to collaborate. Opposite types—petite and plus sizes, male and female, mother and child—tend to play well off of one another. Have the two models assume a pose where they relate to one another and have physical contact. You will find that it is helpful to view their combined gesture as a composite of abstract shapes. Make sure to have a wider platform that can accommodate two people posing at the same time.

1 For the warmup have the models pose together; quickly capture their paired gesture.

2 Using color, block in the negative shape that surrounds the two models. The shape they make together is un-nameable and should be easier to draw.

3 Draw the two models posing together, but in this case one becomes "accessory" to the other and is featured only in silhouette.

4 Alternate models in solo poses for a continuous drawing workout.

5 Experiment with unisex clothing by having the two models:
a. Share the components of a suit (for example the man can wear the pants and the woman the jacket).
b. Dress in exactly the same garments (a shirt with French cuffs, tie, vest, suspenders, fedora, cummerbund, and **notched collar** jacket, for example).

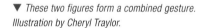

▼ *These two figures form a combined gesture. Illustration by Cheryl Traylor.*

▲ *The child's figure in the foreground is offset by the loosely sketched adult figure standing beyond her. Illustration by Cheryl Traylor.*

Drawing with Both Hands

Designers and illustrators derive significant benefit from drawing with both the right and left hands. The skills of each can be maximized in a variety of ways. For instance, the left hand can be used to search out the figure in a rough draft and the right for completion of the drawing. For this next exercise, it is helpful to have two different art supplies (perhaps hold a brush pen in one hand and a charcoal pencil in the other).

1 Working with a combination of wet and dry media, use both hands simultaneously to draw the model. Use your less dominant hand to draw the outlines with the wet media. Use your more dominant hand to block in shadows with the dry media.

2 Do a left-handed drawing (or right-handed for left-handed people), then render it with your right hand.

▶ *Drawing with your less dominant hand can help to prolong and sharpen concentration.*

Bringing It All Together

In the concluding exercises you will polish the details and incorporate your studies from life in an artful multi-page composition.

Creating Innovative Compositions

Changing the scale of your work on a regular basis will help you to remain flexible. For this exercise, work smaller than usual in a bound book with accordion-fold double-sided pages. You are less likely to give up and discard what you think is a bad drawing if you see it as part of a larger bound body of work. Complete this book over multiple sessions. Readymade accordion books, such as the Kolo brand, are usually found where photo presentation and scrapbooks are sold. You could also make your own book.

1 Make each drawing relate to the next in the context of the entire book.

2 Change the orientation of the page relative to the pose.

3 Integrate drawings from different sessions in a pleasing composition; while drawing a single figure, leave room on the page for figures to be completed in another session.

4 Revisit previous drawing premises. For example: while studying tailored clothing you might want to return to the premise in which the two models share a suit; exercises using the less dominant hand could serve you well on days when you feel blocked; when drawing a complex garment or pattern you could return to the exercise for breaking down visual impressions into manageable parts; you might want to revisit the exercises on color blocking and negative shape when studying gathers; and so on.

5 Make sure to fully document your process with all drawings (warmup gestures included) from several model-drawing sessions. The varying length of the poses will create an interesting rhythm in your book.

6 Render drawings fully and in color.

7 Working on the front and reverse side of pages, fill the book!

ASSIGNMENT 1

After the model drawing session is over, amend one of your drawings relying on memory and imagination to complete unfinished details and rendering (below). Add pattern, texture, and color with "rubbings" (see p. 346) and/or collage (opposite below). Introduce a new background by integrating your drawing with a photomontage.

▼ *The extended page width of the accordion format will allow you to begin and end your composition more organically. Illustrations by Elisabeth Dempsey.*

Amending Your Model Drawings

Drawings are not always completed by the end of the pose. Often you will have to rely on memory and invention to complete unfinished details and fully render your drawings. You can, for example:

1 Add pattern, texture, or color with "rubbings" (see p. 346) and collage.

2 Introduce a background by integrating your drawing with a photomontage. This can also be done digitally by scanning your drawing and exporting the image to Photoshop.

3 Make a point of drawing at a smaller scale. Observe how miniaturization restricts the amount of detail you can include in a drawing. Working with a photocopier or a computer, reproduce the small sketches at two or three times the original size. Working with the scaled-up image, invent the details previously omitted because of the restrictive size.

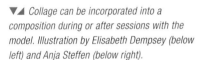 Collage can be incorporated into a composition during or after sessions with the model. Illustration by Elisabeth Dempsey (below left) and Anja Steffen (below right).

Sayumi Namba manipulates her life drawings in Photoshop, duplicating and reflecting the figures to surreal effect.

ASSIGNMENT 2

Manipulating drawings in Photoshop (above) after the live model session is over allows you to edit information that does not flatter the garment design (such as creases and folds). Scan one of your more successful model drawings and export it to Photoshop. If you think the proportion of the figure requires adjustment, select the part of the body in question and use the Transform command to enlarge or reduce its width and/or height. Once you are satisfied with the new figure proportion, experiment with different filters, adjustment layers, texture mapping, and the Paste Into command. For an extra challenge, group several drawings together, tweaking the scale of each to suggest depth in the picture plane.

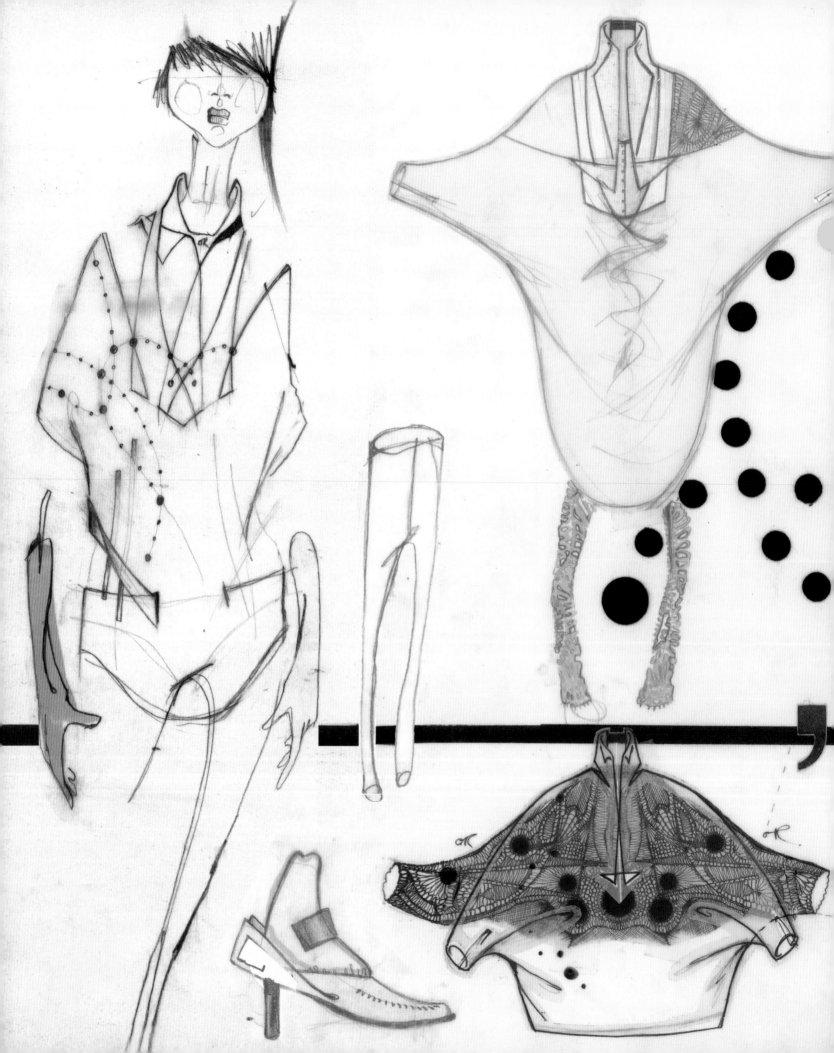

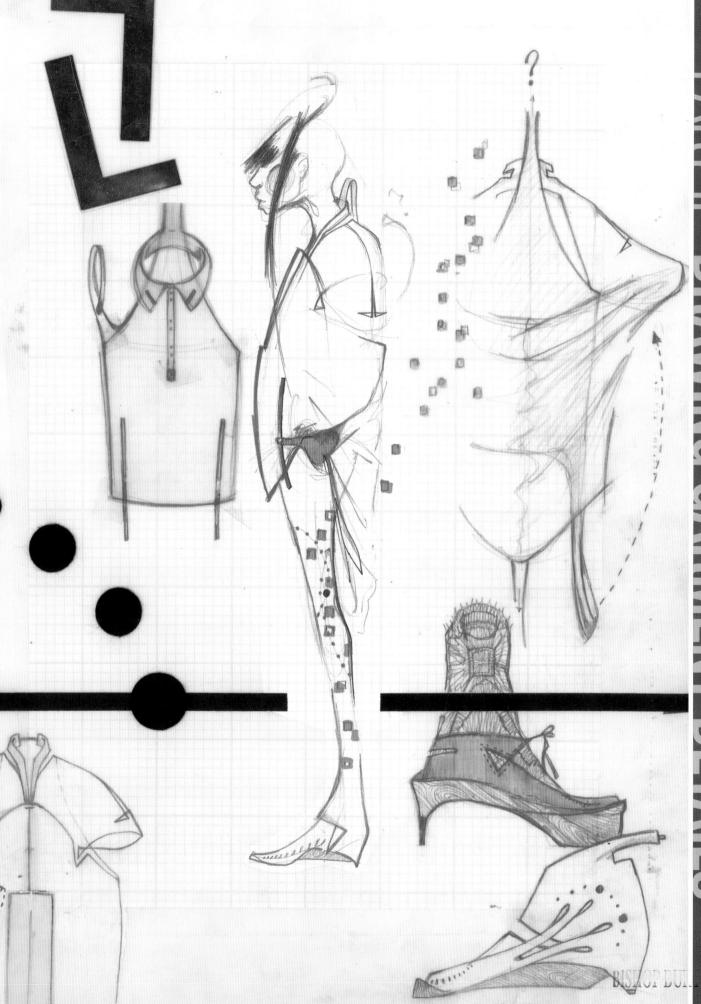

n this section you will use the fashion figures developed in Part I to realize your design concepts. To that end, the design process is introduced here and in the chapters that follow. Chapter 6 deals with drawing the most basic garment details and silhouettes. Because couture ateliers have traditionally been set up as two separate workshops—one for blouses and dresses and the other for more structured coats and suits—Chapter 7 covers draped garments and Chapter 8 tailored clothing.

The ability to draw a broad variety of garment details and silhouettes is integral to professional practices for fashion illustration and design. There are different circumstances under which you might be working and it is important to understand the specific requirements for each. For instance, you might be illustrating an existing garment for advertising or editorial purposes. You cannot assume that you will have the luxury of seeing the actual garment. An illustration is often commissioned instead of a photograph precisely because there is no access to the garment. The first sample may be in production in another country and therefore you have to work from a small fabric swatch and a rudimentary concept sketch. In order to do your job—visualize/idealize the garment—you must be able to identify and draw a broad variety of garment details from memory. It is also important to clarify just how much detail is actually required for the job. In some cases, drawings are intentionally kept vague to discourage knockoffs (copies).

Fashion designers face an even greater challenge—visualizing garments that do not yet exist beyond their imagination. Design development evolves over time with multiple phases of critical thinking and a different amount of detail will be required when moving from rough concept sketches to finished presentations and production sketches. Although designers strive to preserve freshness and immediacy in their work, successful "finishes" are often the end result of extensive trial and error.

Since fashion design students are likely to first attempt drawing garment details in a sketchbook, it would make sense to explore the formatting and contents of this book. As a new designer, it is important to set yourself up properly from the beginning and in advance of your investigation of garment details.

◀▼ *(Previous spread and below) For Jonathan Kyle Farmer, drawing is key to the exploration of ideas for fashion design.*

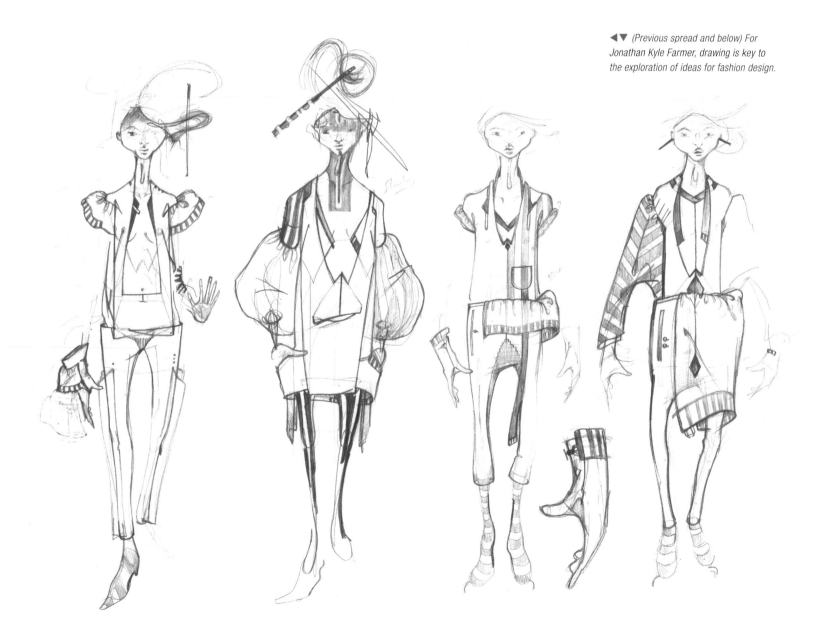

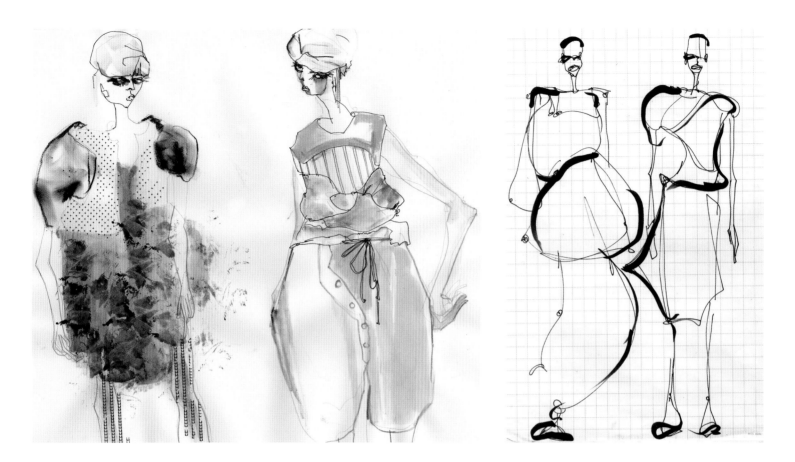

▲◤▼ ▶ *Design problem-solving for Sara Sakanaka begins on paper with a very general searching out of silhouettes.*

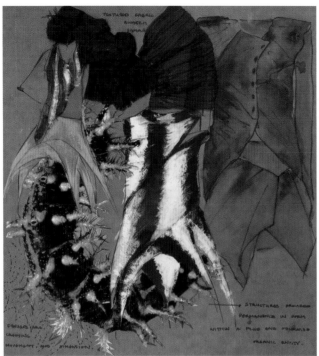

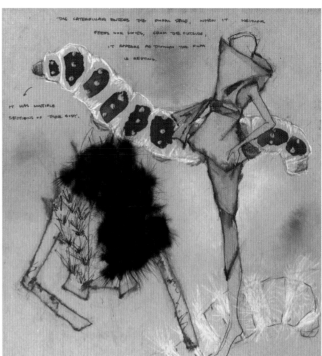

▲ In her presentation of a collection inspired by metamorphosis, Ji Eun Oh blurs the boundaries between portfolio and sketchbook.

▶ Jeffrey Williams' drawing style suits his quirky aesthetic.

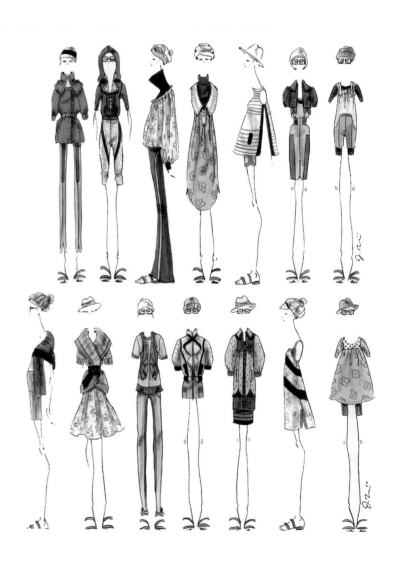

The Sketchbook

Like any other journal, the sketchbook is extremely personal in content and format. It serves as a window into your thoughts, process, and identity. It is in the sketchbook that concepts find their truest expression. A collection will reliably undergo a dramatic metamorphosis during the design development process, but it is also important to remain true to the proportion of the garments as first imagined in preliminary sketches. Changes made to designs should represent an improvement rather than an inability to visualize or construct the garment.

You will find your sketchbook to be an invaluable resource for communicating with a prospective employer or anyone else you might collaborate with. The sketchbook is also an important tool for self-assessment. If you are systematic in the organization and archiving of your design concepts, you can always return to an idea in days, weeks, or even years to come.

The boundaries between sketchbook and finished portfolio will vary with the individual. How your work is presented will largely be determined by the nature of your design and the segment of industry you intend to work in. For example, companies with a more conceptual design philosophy will be open to more esoteric presentations. You may also want to have a separate sketchbook tucked into a pocket at the back your portfolio. Some designers incorporate elements from their design development into the portfolio to add variety to visual presentations. In the end, it is up to you.

▶ *Desislava Zhivkova utilizes collage to explore new silhouettes in her sketchbook. Varying media choices can lead to new directions in design development.*

◢ *Fabric swatches and textile development are often incorporated in design sketchbooks. Here, Dylan Taverner includes the plotting of an intarsia knit pattern as part of the design development for a men's sportswear collection.*

Sketchbook Formats

The size of your sketchbook is a personal decision. You may find that one book is not enough. A small book can be used to record impressions on the fly, with a larger book reserved for in-depth research and design development. Do not limit your choices to manufactured bound or spiral books or even standard paper sizes. There may be a particular paper that you prefer to work with. Some artists find a blank white sheet to be intimidating and instead choose craft, color, or off-white paper. Give serious consideration to the various wet and dry media you might want to use in your sketchbook (gouache, collage, marker, pastel, etc.) and then select paper with an appropriate opacity, weight, and surface. (For more about media and paper choices see pp. 296–305.) You can have the paper trimmed and bound at a copy center—before or after you draw on it. Use a heavier weight cover stock or ad hoc material (such as plywood) for the front and back covers. An accordion-fold format allows the design development for many garments to be seen all at once (see p. 204). Another option is to use a three-hole punch and then bind the pages using Chicago screws (binding posts). Keep in mind that your sketchbook should be sturdy enough for the archiving of research, yarns, trims, fabric swatches, and treatments.

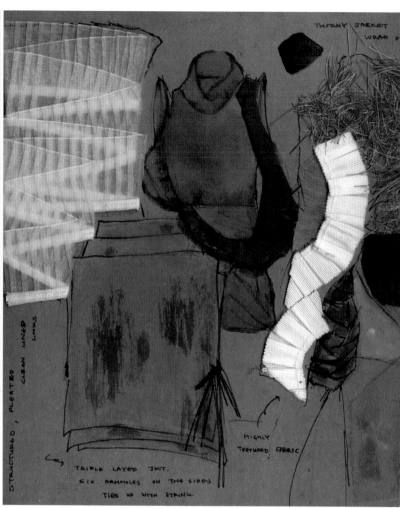

▲ Tactile considerations are an important part of design problem-solving for Ji Eun Oh, as documented in her sketchbook.

◣◤▼ *The mood page, consisting of visuals, yarns, and fabrics, is the jumping-off point for extensive design development of a knitwear collection by Dushane Noble.*

Sketchbook Content

Depending on the balance of art and commerce in your design practice, your process and documentation will vary. Designers who approach fashion as an art form independent of market trends will use their sketchbook to document the 2D and 3D (for example, photos of fabric pin drapes) exploration of ideas. More commercial designers are likely to adhere to prescribed phases of design development. The phases documented in the sketchbook can include: trend, inspiration, fabric and color research, developmental design sketches (on the figure and as flats), and a final edit. If you are designing in a commercial context, it is advisable to first determine the specific customer you have in mind for the collection. By collaging images in your sketchbook you can begin to conjure up an idea of who this person is. Try to imagine a typical day in his/her life, or even what his/her Facebook page might look like!

The design process can begin with **trend research** for inspiration, silhouette, color, textiles, and trim. **Forecasting services** such as Trend Union, Stylesight, and WGSN give seasonal presentations. Fiber companies (such as Invista, Cotton Incorporated, and Woolmark) also produce trend reports skewed to promote their products. A myriad of Web sites and blogs provide nearly realtime coverage of

couture and ready-to-wear runway shows. This information can jump-start the initial direction for your collection, but it must be filtered through a more personal design philosophy.

Having decided on your inspiration, you can then create a preliminary mood page in your sketchbook. Images may come from firsthand experiences captured with a digital camera. If you are working with a specific cultural or historic inspiration, be sure to use primary references such as books and visits to museums; do not rely exclusively on the Web. No matter how you go about acquiring your images, they must be assembled in an artful composition that speaks coherently to your inspiration.

Once your inspiration is set you can move on to fabric and color research, also to be documented in your sketchbook. If fabric swatches are not available in the colors you want to work with, you can include paint chips instead. The sample color cards available for house paint are readily available—and free! In professional practice, designers rely on the Pantone® standardized color system and use numbered swatches to accurately communicate color choices. (For more about color see pp. 306–9.) The availability of fabrics and trims at retail will vary depending on location; in some instances online vendors (and even eBay) will be your best and only resource. Make a note of the fiber content of fabrics, too, for

the purposes of garment care—you would not want to mix washable and dry-clean-only fabrics in a single garment.

The next phase of design development is the creation of quick design sketches. Here is where the ability to identify and draw garment details will be essential. As compared to "finishes," these sketches are smaller and quite impressionistic—a quick visual shorthand that allows you to freely traffic in ideas and convey concepts. Students are often shocked when they first learn of the number of sketches that designers generate prior to developing finished looks. For instance, six looks (with two or three garments per look) would be derived from approximately fifty sketches. But these fifty sketches are not of stand-alone ideas; instead they will represent approximately ten defined ideas with perhaps four subtle variations of each. These subtle differences help to establish a consistent design thread in a final collection. When grouped, the garments should not end up looking like a bunch of clothes, but rather a cohesive, well-coordinated collection. Indication of color, texture, and pattern is essential, although the thorough rendering of a finished sketch is not required.

This group of sketches is then culled for an edit: where six to ten of the most successful looks are redrawn at a slightly larger scale, with more comprehensive information about garment details, color, fabric, and trim. To facilitate the editing process, many designers use double-page spreads with accordion foldouts so that all of the sketches may be seen at a glance. Moving on to the final phase, larger "finishes" feature a more formal mood page, fully rendered figures, and flats.

▼ *Desislava Zhivkova uses an accordion-fold presentation for her edit of drawings originally made in a Moleskine journal.*

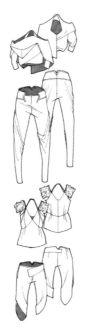

▲▼ *Artwork for finished presentations includes a mood page, figures, and flat sketches used to clarify garment details. Art and design by Jessica Ly.*

The Role of Observation

When it comes to visualizing garment details, relying on your imagination is a poor substitute for firsthand observation. Flat sketching garments from your own closet will help you to become familiar with a wide variety of silhouettes and construction details. An even better option is shopping the stores. Designers often conduct market research in the form of an illustrated shopping report. Visit several stores to see how the same collection is shopped and displayed differently in multiple retail venues (the designer's own store, a department store, a specialty boutique, and an online retailer, for example). Because sketching and photographing clothing in a store is inappropriate, this task will really test your visual memory, as well as your ability to draw a wide variety of garment details.

As you become acquainted with the various garment details and silhouettes, try to incorporate this information into your work with the fashion model. Be sure to devote some time during live drawing sessions to the firsthand observation of the basic garment details to see how the clothing is affected by the shape and movement of the body (and vice versa). Some general recommendations:

1 Sketch garments as flats to fully understand their construction prior to drawing a glamorized version of the same garment on the model. When the model is wearing the garment, observe the volume of the clothing and be aware of how different fabrics impact silhouette and drape. Allow for the dimension and behavior of the fabric in your drawing.

2 As mentioned in Chapter 1, sometimes turning a photo reference upside down facilitates the cognitive shift required for drawing. With that in mind, you may find that flat sketching the garment while it is hung upside down from a hanger with clips, allows you to see/sketch more accurately.

3 Experiment with layering multiple garments. When setting up the model, think of her as a mannequin in a prestigious store window where you would want to display as many garments as possible. Remember to prioritize/flatter the merchandise; it should always be the most important part of your drawing.

▲ Whenever possible, dress the model in your own creations. Use muslins (toiles) if finished garments are not available. Illustration by Felice DaCosta.

◄ A shopping report by Sylvia Kwan features illustrations and comprehensive notes and conclusions about trend, garment details and silhouettes, the fabric story, and how the garments were displayed.

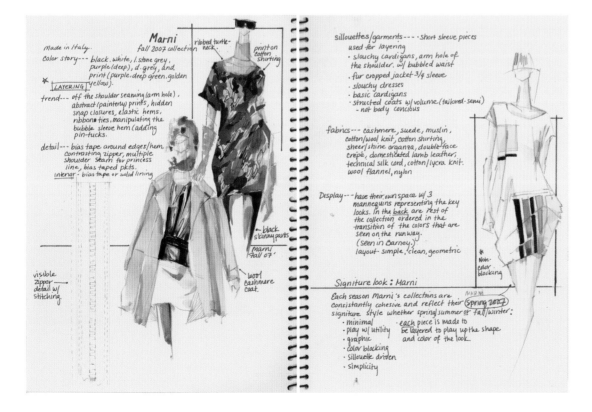

CHAPTER 6
BASIC GARMENT DETAILS

This chapter introduces basic garment details and the general principles that govern garment drape. You will see how body movement, gravity, location, and physical manipulation, as well as fabric weight and texture, can influence the appearance of garment details and silhouettes.

While it is possible that in the course of your design work you might come up with an entirely new garment detail or silhouette, for the most part there is no need to reinvent the wheel. Innovation lies in the proportion, fabrication, and combination of the various garment details. There are many tried and true methods for constructing silhouettes. Some garment details, such as **fit darts**, are used to achieve an overall shape that conforms to the body. Others, such as

gathers and **shirring** (**ruching**), are used to reshape and even camouflage the body. Garment details that are utilitarian in nature (such as the small change pocket on five-pocket jeans) require strategic placement. Some details are purely decorative (a scalloped hemline, for example) while others are both utilitarian and decorative (smile pockets with arrowheads on Western shirts).

Familiarity with the various garment details will give you an even greater appreciation for the body landmarks established for fit lines. For instance, the **princess line** (see p. 40) is useful for the placement of darts, belt loops, and pleats. The Center Front and Center Back lines will also be important; key to the placement of zippers, buttons, and snaps.

◀ ▶ *Hannah Hae In Lee's collection combines high fashion and functionality with the strategic placement of pockets, pulls, and draw-cords. Flat sketches provide comprehensive information for construction details and trim.*

As you begin the design process, you must consider specific garment details and silhouettes in tandem as one will often determine the other. For instance, if you wanted to design a skirt shaped like a bell, including gathers at the waistline seam would help to achieve that silhouette. Designing a dress shaped like an inverted trumpet might involve the insertion of triangular-shaped panels (**godets**) for additional fullness at the bottom hem (see p. 261). When sketching your designs, first consider the specific shape you have in mind and how it might be achieved with seaming, folds, and manipulation of the fabric grain.

▲ *The unique manipulation and combination of the most basic garment details by Osman Yousefzada; featuring, from left to right, round and square necklines, a **mandarin collar**, a layered **shawl** and **funnel collars**, a notched collar, and round and sweetheart necklines.*

▶ *Imagining a geometric shape is a good place to begin the design of a garment. Illustration by Ferdinand.*

Flat Sketching Basic Garment Details and Silhouettes

As a preliminary step toward drawing the clothed high hip figure, you will first identify and draw some basic garments as flats (technical drawings). Working with the static flats figure (see p. 41) will give you the opportunity to observe the most basic construction details and silhouettes without the complications that result from body movement and foreshortening.

Flat Sketching a Basic Shirt

For this exercise you will use a flats figure as a guide to maintain a relative proportion. Begin by folding a ½in. (1.5cm) flap from the topmost edge of a sheet of tracing paper. Position this flap over the top edge of your flats figure, securing it with masking tape on the back. If possible, work from a sample garment and begin your flat sketch:

NOTE The shirt front **extension** (where the two front sides of a shirt overlap) is gender-specific; closing proper right over left for women, and left over right for men.

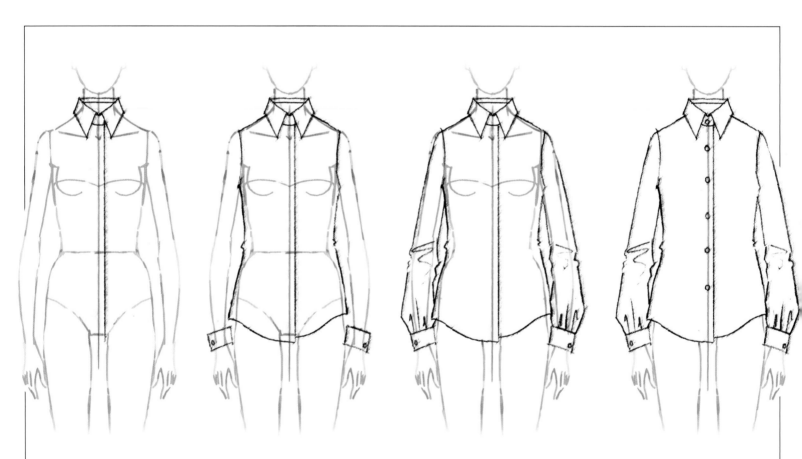

1 Draw the spread collar, indicating the seams where the collar attaches to the band and where the band attaches to the neckline. Then add a vertical line that is parallel and slightly to the side of Center Front.

2 Sketch the **set-in armholes** and then the overall silhouette. Add the shirttail hem and cuffs.

3 Sketch the sleeves, allowing for the fullness of the sleeve width where it is inserted into the cuff.

4 Position the buttons directly over the Center Front. Add buttonholes. Experiment with the different sleeves and construction details featured in the illustrated glossary at the end of this chapter.

There are many ways to finish a flats presentation:

• Inking the flats by hand using felt tip markers is a traditional method and a good technique to master for the times when you do not have access to a computer. Technical drawing tools such as circle and ellipse templates, French curves, and rulers can be combined with freehand drawing as appropriate for the different garment details (for example, drapery is best drawn freehand, structural details such as **plackets** with a ruler). Be sure to use a variety of stroke weights—reserving the heaviest for the outside edge, with progressively lighter stroke weights for seams and topstitching.

• When you are pressed for time, scan the pencil flat, clean it up in Photoshop, and export to Illustrator for a Live Trace. This preserves the spontaneity of the preliminary sketch, while converting the pencil sketch to a more finished "inked" drawing.

• Depending on your computer skills, you can also translate a scan of your pencil sketch in Illustrator using the various mechanical and freehand drawing tools—again as they relate to the different garment details. If you intend to render your flat, you must create closed paths that can be easily filled with pattern and color. Also, take care to create separate paths for the outside edges and construction details so that you can manipulate the hierarchy of stroke weights. This can be quite time consuming, but the end result will be "resolution independent"—meaning that the line will remain crisp no mater how much you reduce or enlarge the sketch. **Vector images** created in Illustrator also have the added benefit of having smaller file sizes that are easier to e-mail.

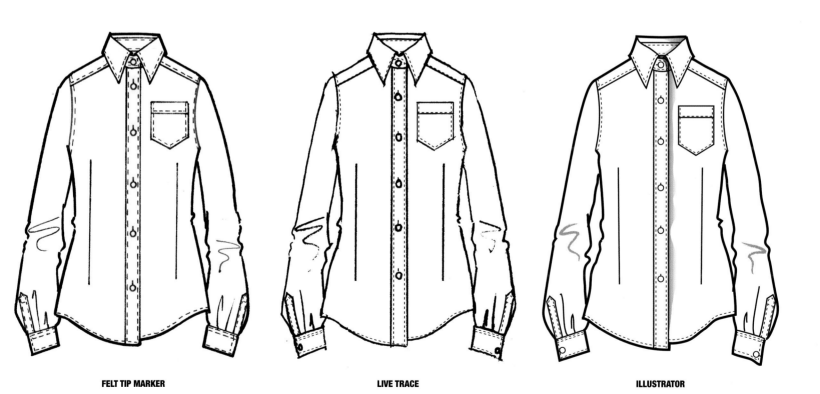

FELT TIP MARKER   **LIVE TRACE**   **ILLUSTRATOR**

Flat Sketching Low-rise Pleated Pants

The first design consideration for any bottom garment is the length of the seam that runs up the Center Front, as this will determine where the garment sits relative to the natural waist. On pants, or trousers, this seam is referred to as the **rise**. Pants with a long rise seam (with a **Hollywood waist** treatment perhaps) will sit higher in relation to the waist. Longer rise seams are also used for drop-crotch silhouettes such as **dhoti pants**. (For information about flat sketching dhoti pants see p. 255.) Pants with shorter rise seams sit lower on the body, beneath the natural waist.

For this exercise you will flat sketch basic low-rise pants with an extension waistband.

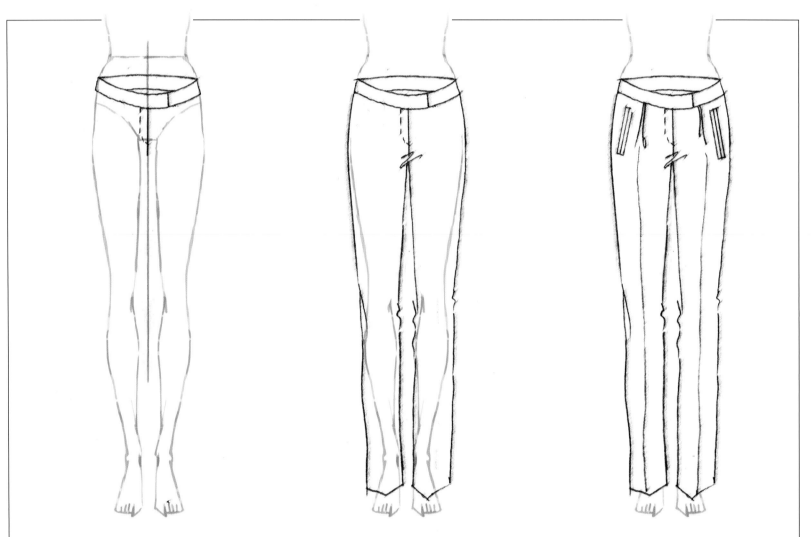

1 To begin, indicate the waistband for the pants with two parallel lines below the natural waist. Draw the rise seam directly on top of the Center Front line. Using a dashed line, indicate the zipper placket (fly) on one side of the Center Front line. The fly should end a considerable distance above the crotch (the intersection of the rise and inseam). Indicate the extension of the waistband (this line will be opposite the placket).

2 Sketch the overall silhouette of the pants. Indicate the bottom hem. The presence of a crease will affect the shape of the bottom hemline—round if left unpressed or pointed like the prow of a ship with a crease. You may also choose to have extra long pants that pool at the bottom, or a cuff, indicated with a line that is parallel to the hem.

3 Add inverted pleats and angled **besom pockets** (double-welt pockets). Develop different design variations by manipulating the scale and location of the different garment details (taper or shorten the legs, for example) and use the front view sketch as the basis for a back view. Finish the flat sketch using one of the methods described on p. 213.

ASSIGNMENT 1

Working with a flats figure, sketch different tops and bottoms using variations and combinations of garment details, experimenting with the basic armholes and necklines featured in the illustrated glossary at the end of this chapter. Proportion will be key. For example, you might use a high V-neck on a child's garment and a plunging V on a ladies' evening gown.

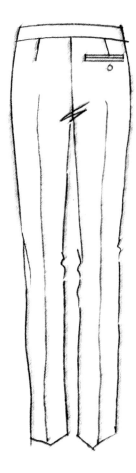

DESIGN VARIATION

BACK VIEW

▲ *Viktor and Rolf are famous for reconfiguring the classic shirt by skewing and reproportioning collar and cuffs. These details will look very different depending on their fabrication.*

Sketching Basic Garments on the Figure

Before you can begin drawing garment details on the figure, you must first give some thought to their placement. For instance, a waistline seam can be located above, below, or at the natural waist; a ruffled flounce can be used to trim a neckline, but also the bottom hem of a skirt, and so on. Garment details will have to be foreshortened in your drawing relative to eye level and/or rotation of the body. In order to fully understand the impact of location (point of view) on the appearance of various garment details, it is essential to first map the contours of your figure.

Cylindrical Analysis and Point of View

For this next exercise you will create a cylindrical analysis of the front view fashion figure with eye level established at the hip. Begin by folding a ½in. (1.5cm) flap from the topmost edge of a sheet of tracing paper. Position this flap over the top edge of your original figure drawing, securing it with masking tape on the back.

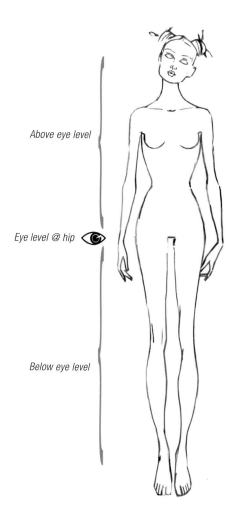

Above eye level

Eye level @ hip

Below eye level

▲ The location of eye level must be established for the lifelike depiction of garment details.

◀ Here, a floor-length striped dress by Gareth Pugh demonstrates the effect of body movement and point of view on fabric behavior.

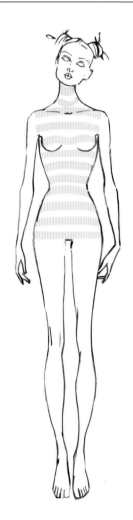

1 Working with a brightly colored broad tip marker, begin your cylindrical analysis on the tracing overlay. Start at the hip (eye level) with a straight line. As you work upward, above eye level, the lines will become convex (shaped like a frown). The stripes should carefully map the torso.

2 Continue the mapping for the legs (below eye level). These lines will be concave (shaped like a smile).

3 Next you will analyze the arms. The upper arm moves back in space and, as such, these lines will be concave. The forward movement of the lower arm is indicated with convex lines.

4 Use your completed cylindrical analysis to predict the appearance of various garment details. Draw a **jewel neckline,** set-in armhole, and various hemlines for sleeves and pants.

Variations

Repeat the exercise, analyzing the high hip, walking, and turned figures. Pay special attention to the manner in which upper and lower arm are positioned. The degree to which the arms advance or recede into space will dramatically affect the mapping of the contours. The same will also hold true for the cylindrical analysis of the upper and lower leg.

Note, too, how movement of the body changes the appearance of the garment details for the different views. For instance, in the high hip pose the angle of the neckline will correspond to the angle of the shoulders; the angle of the hemline will be parallel to the angle of the hips. The rotation of the body will also have a significant effect on the appearance of garment details. For example, a three-quarter turn will reveal the side and inseams and the garment details on the side turning from view will become foreshortened. Note the different appearance of the armhole seams in the front view compared to the turned figure. In the front view the two armhole seams look like open and closed parentheses. In the turned view, both armholes look like closed parentheses.

▼ A *float* (as compared to a flat) is a sketch of a garment as it would appear on the body, without actually including the figure in the drawing. Floats have more movement and can be used to add visual interest to a presentation. Here, floats of a basic T-shirt with a bateau neckline, set-in armhole, and straight sleeve illustrate how movement and rotation of the body can affect the appearance of even the most basic garment details.

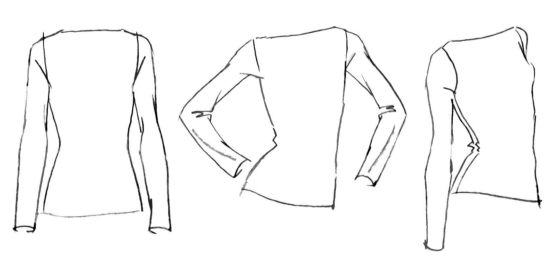

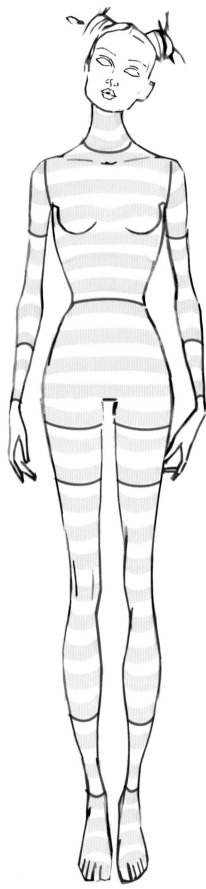

FRONT VIEW

HIGH HIP   **WALKING POSE**   **THREE-QUARTER VIEW**

The Combined Effect of Body Movement and Gravity

Garments will look very different depending on how the figure is posed. As previously mentioned in the chapters on figure drawing, the pose should always showcase garments to their best advantage. A tight-fitting garment will restrict body movement and therefore limit options for figure poses.

The action of the body will, in turn, influence garment drape. For instance, in the high hip pose the opposition of the upper and lower torso causes an area of compression to form at the waist on the weight-bearing side of the body. This compression will cause crush lines in a garment. As the torso expands on the opposite, non-weight-bearing side, there will be a smoothing of the garment drape. Because the hip and supporting leg are thrust in opposite directions, the tension between the two will also result in a crush line. Physical manipulation of the garment (such as the depression and crush lines formed by placing a hand on the hip or in a pocket) is also a consideration.

The arbitrary indication of crush lines in a fashion drawing can be visually confusing—make sure that the crush lines in yours are justified by compression or tension created by the movement of the body.

For your drawing of garment details to be convincing, the drape of the cloth must also appear to conform to the physical laws of nature. Gravity, which pulls all matter toward the center of the Earth, will alter the appearance of garment details and silhouettes. Length, volume, fabric weight, and texture will all determine the extent of gravity's impact.

The force of gravity combined with body movement will alter the appearance of garment details in many other ways too. The volume will reliably swing in the direction of the weight-bearing leg. The hemline (**sweep**) will be parallel to the angle of the hip. The closer the fit of the garment, the greater the influence exerted by the movement of the body. For example, the sweep of a fitted dress, such as a sheath, will be greatly affected by the action of the hips, whereas the sweep of a roomy trapeze dress will remain largely unaffected.

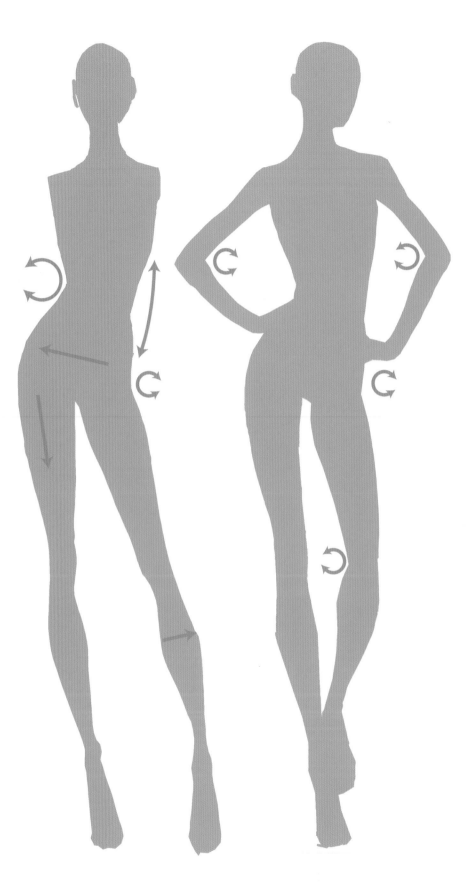

▲ Note how movement of the body forms areas of compression, expansion, and tension.

▲ The volume of a sleeve will fall below the arm, pulled by the force of gravity toward the floor. Moreover, the bending of the arm will form an area of compression, resulting in crush lines.

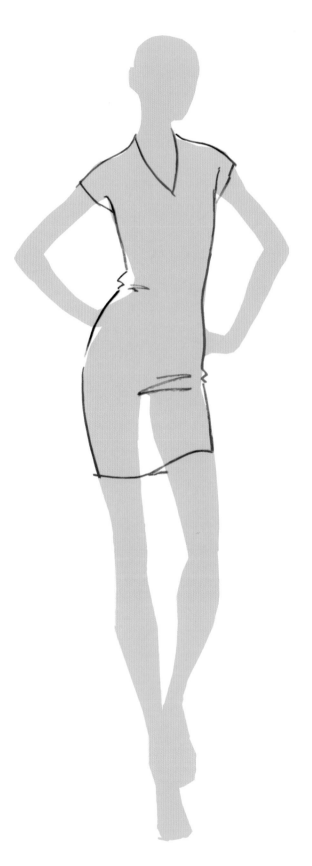

▲ Crush lines form in areas of compression.

Drawing a Shirtwaist Dress

Next, you will draw a shirtwaist dress, which will give you the opportunity to explore a variety of basic garment details found on both top and bottom garments. You will see how the appearance of garment details is altered by the movement of the body. For instance, the bottom hem will be parallel to the angle of the hips, the placket will follow the curve of the Center Front line, and so on. As you draw the dress, be sure to indicate the crush lines formed by areas of compression on the high hip side of the waist. Working with a tracing overlay and a front view walking figure:

1 Begin by indicating the jewel neckline and the set-in armholes. Draw the **self-belt** parallel to the angle of the waist. Add the hemline which is parallel to the angle of the waist. The volume swings in the direction of the high hip.

2 Sketch in the overall silhouette, excluding the sleeves. Add darts to the bodice and crush lines formed by areas of compression and tension.

3 Indicate the shirt placket on the Center Front.

4 Add the buttons and reinforced stitching in an "X" pattern at the bottom of the placket. Then fill in additional garment details: **yoke**, **patch pocket**, and **spread collar**. Take care that the pocket and collar points align with the angle of the shoulders.

5 Sketch the sleeves, indicating crush lines in areas of compression. Because of the force of gravity, the sleeves will cling to the tops of the arms and the volume will drape below. Add sleeve plackets and buttons to the outside edges of the cuff.

Performance apparel, clothing worn for a specific sport or athletic activity (below), is usually designed to fit very close to the body in order to enhance the wearer's performance when running, swimming, surfing, skiing, etc. The fabrics used for this type of apparel are usually high-tech stretch knits and garment designs require minimal seaming. Graphic color blocking (right) can be used to achieve the high visibility required for the safety and spectacle of competitive sports. Design a small collection of performance apparel utilizing three different jersey knit swatches. The color scheme can be either monochromatic (tints and shades of the same hue), complementary (opposites on the color wheel), or analogous (similar colors, sitting next to each other on the color wheel). (For more about color harmonies see p. 307.) Before you begin, research the requirements of the specific sport to better understand how your clothing design could enhance athletic performance.

▲ Designer Alexis Mabille uses color blocking as a key design strategy for this Spring/ Summer collection.

◄ For her senior thesis collection, Leslie Jones designed fashionable women's golf wear. Garments provide the necessary range of motion and conform with dress codes specific to the sport (both men and women must wear shirts with collars on the golf course).

Working with the illustrated glossary of necklines, armholes, sleeves, and bodice seams at the end of this chapter, draw a variety of dresses on figure poses (right). Experiment with relocating the waist seam above, at, and below the natural waist. Keep your designs very simple, focusing on the unique combination and layering of necklines and armholes. Try out different hemlines, such as knee-length, midcalf, and floor-length. Make sure that the garment details appear to be moving in relation to the body.

▶ The manipulation of a basic V-neckline is used as a connecting design element in this collection of dresses by Paul Negron.

Drawing Basic Pants

For this exercise you will draw basic pants on a front view high hip figure.

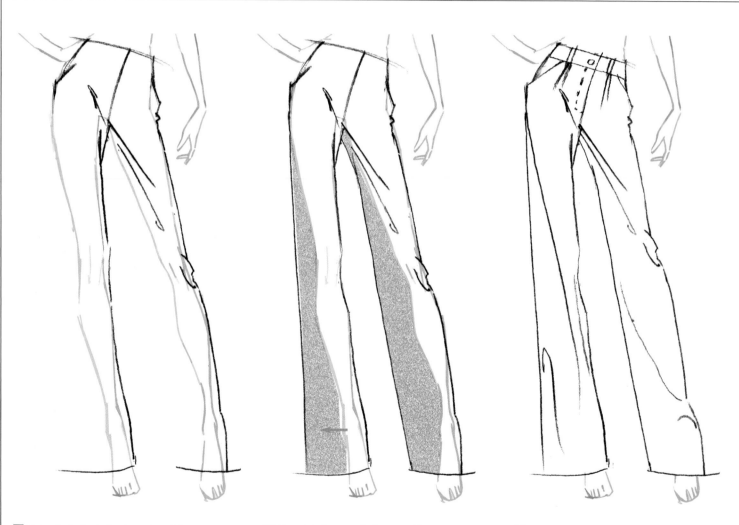

1 To begin, indicate the top edge of the waistband for the pants at the natural waist. The action of the hips will dictate the angle of the waistband. Draw the rise seam directly over the Center Front line. Sketch in the overall silhouette of the pants along both sides of the hips. Then draw the silhouette of the pant legs where the fabric comes into direct contact with the body. The pant hemlines will be parallel to the angle of the hips.

2 Complete the overall silhouette. The volume of the drape will swing in the direction of the weight-bearing leg. Be sure to indicate the crush lines that form in areas of tension and compression.

3 Using a dashed line, indicate the zipper placket on one side of the Center Front line. Draw the button to be centered over the zipper placket. Add belt loops and pleats.

Variations

Repeat this exercise, drawing a jumpsuit on a high hip figure. Then
draw the same jumpsuit on a three-quarter-view turned figure. When
drawing the garment on the turned figure, take care to include the
side and inseams and to foreshorten the garment details on the side
of the body turning from view.

FRONT AND THREE-QUARTER JUMPSUIT VIEW   **FIVE-POCKET JEANS**

▼ *Five-pocket jeans, an American basic that became popular during and after World War II, are both utilitarian and fashionable. Notice how extra long jeans can either be ruched at the bottom hem (left) or be rolled up in tall miner's cuffs (right). There seems to be an infinite number of variations—high- or low-rise, baggy or tight, bell bottom, bootcut, and so on.*

About Zippers

In the early 1930s, Elsa Schiaparelli was the first designer to use zipper closures for haute couture. Ever since, zippers have traditionally been inserted at the Center Front, Center Back, or side seams to facilitate entry into garments. They are key to the engineering of bottom garments such as pants and skirts which must be pulled up and over the hips and then fastened at a relatively narrower waist. Low-rise garments that hover at the hips do not have to accommodate this dramatic narrowing of the torso, so only a very short zipper is required for entry. Higher rise pants require at least a 7in. (18cm) zipper to accommodate the difference between the circumference of the waist and hips. Couture skirts and pants, designed to sit at or above the natural waist, sometimes feature two 3½in. (9cm) zippers inserted at the side seams. The pair of shorter zippers are easily concealed by a jacket. The combined length of the pair of shorter zippers equals 7in. (18cm).

At first, the illustration of the zipper placket (fly) and waistband extension can seem confusing. However, once you determine that the two elements are located on opposite sides of the Center Front, you should have no trouble at all.

> **ASSIGNMENT 4**
>
> Working with photo references for the garment details, draw a variety of pants on different figures (below). Compare how the hemlines drape, depending on the fullness of the pants and the height of the heels. Vary the length of the rise seams and experiment with details such as cuffs, pockets, and different locations for the zipper entry (side, or Center Back, for example).

▼ *Illustrate your designs on the figure or as floats, working with a variety of front and turned view figures.*

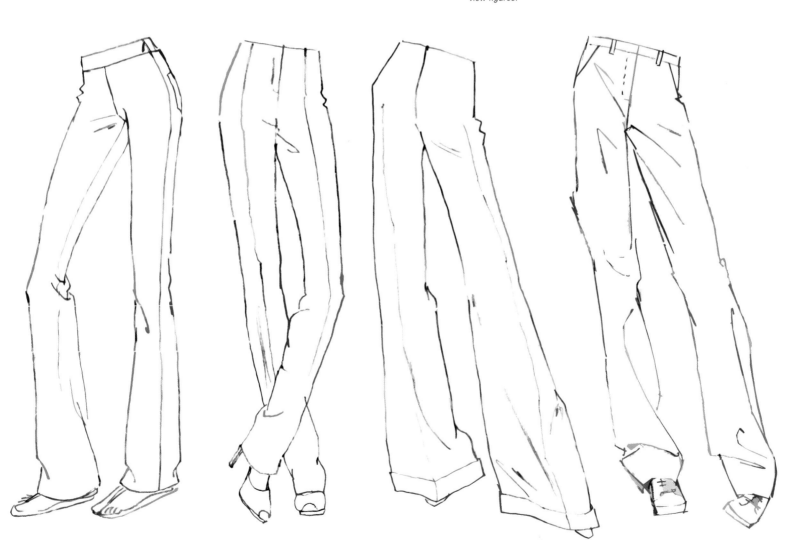

Illustrated Glossary of Garment Details

Jewel neckline
Cascading cap sleeve
Blouson

Scoop neckline
Petal sleeve
Button-through side entry

Crew neckline
Rib trim at apex
Straight sleeve

U-neckline
Cap sleeve

Square neckline
Kimono sleeve

Boat neckline
Drop shoulder

V-neckline
Batwing sleeve
Rib trim insert

Surplice neckline
Halter armhole
Empire waist

Cowl neckline
Epaulet
French dart

Gathered jewel neckline
Dolman sleeve

Keyhole neckline
Cap sleeve
Rib trim

Sweetheart neckline
Cap sleeve
Peplum

NECKLINES AND SLEEVES

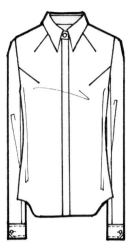

Mandarin collar
Raglan armhole
Bishop sleeve

Set-in armhole
Puff sleeve
Shoulder/waist darts

Shirt collar
Neckline/armhole darts
Fly front

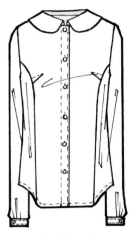

Peter Pan collar
Set-in armhole
Princess seam

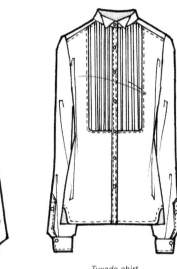
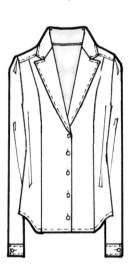
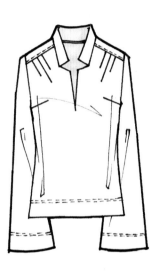

Convertible collar
Variation on bishop sleeve
Shirttail hem

Tuxedo shirt
Winged collar
Pleated bib

Notch collar
Princess seam
Shirttail hem

Open notch collar
Pagoda sleeve
Pleated yoke

Sailor collar
Epaulet
Flutter sleeve

Shawl collar
Set-in armhole
Bell sleeve

COLLARS AND SLEEVES

Dolman sleeve
Shirttail hem

Turtleneck
Cut-and-sew sweater
Rib sleeve

Shift
V-neckline
Waist dart

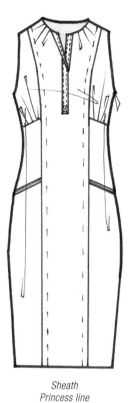

Sheath
Princess line
Empire waist

Trapeze
Cap sleeve
Empire waist

Bustier bodice
Elastic at waist and low hip

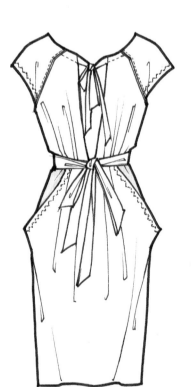

Belted shift
Saddle shoulder
Slash pocket

Jewel neck
Halter armhole
Empire peplum

DRESSES

Belted shirtwaist
Spread collar
Drop shoulder

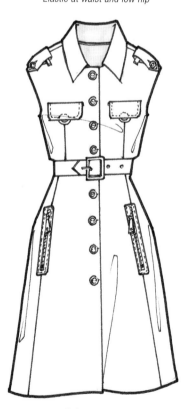

Safari shirtdress
Self belt
Onseam zipper pocket

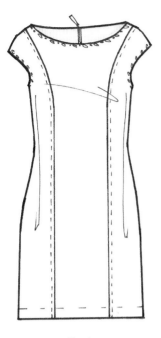

Chemise
Cap sleeve
Princess seam

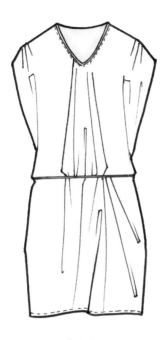

Sack dress
V-neckline

Cheongsam
Keyhole neckline
Raglan armhole

Sheath
U-neckline
Raglan armhole

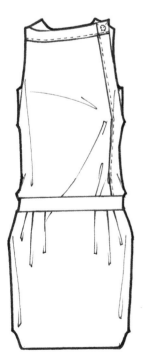

Asymmetric neckline
Drop waist
Shirttail hem

Sheath
Sailor collar
Peplum

Shift
Jewel neckline
3/4 sleeve

Shift
V-neckline
Capelet

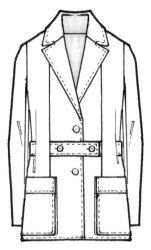

Norfolk jacket
Notched collar
Bellows pocket

Double-breasted blazer
Peaked lapel
Fishtail hem

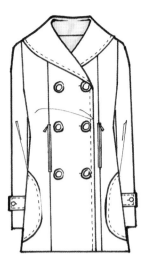

Peacoat
Shawl collar
Adjustable tab sleeve

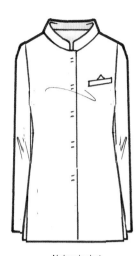

Nehru jacket
Mandarin collar
Angled welt pocket

Safari jacket
Epaulet
Flap patch pocket

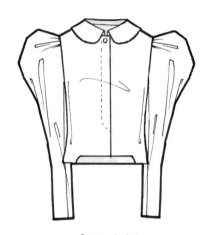

Bomber jacket
Flap patch pocket
Rib trim

Spencer jacket
Gigot sleeve
Fly front

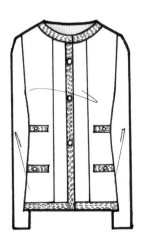

Varsity jacket
Angled besom pocket
Rib trim

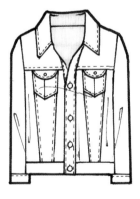

Jean jacket
Yoke
Flap patch pocket

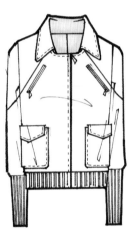

Chanel/Cardigan jacket
Grosgrain ribbon trim
Welt pocket

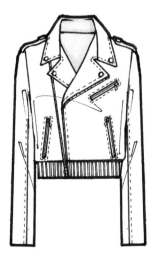

Motorcycle jacket
Epaulet
Asymmetric zipper closure

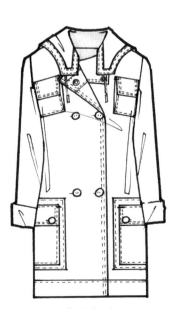

Hooded parka
Flap patch pocket

JACKETS AND COATS

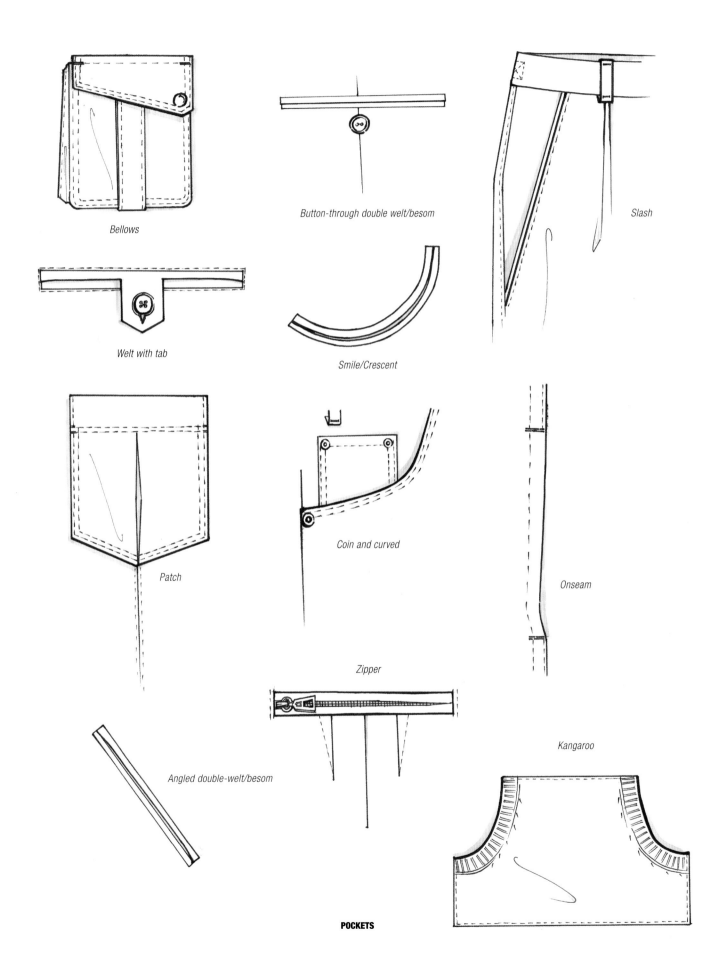

Bellows

Button-through double welt/besom

Slash

Welt with tab

Smile/Crescent

Patch

Coin and curved

Onseam

Zipper

Kangaroo

Angled double-welt/besom

POCKETS

A-line

Tiered

Sarong

Culotte

Layered handkerchief

Trumpet with godets

Straight

Fitted

Pegged

Flare

SKIRTS

Straight with peplum

Dirndl

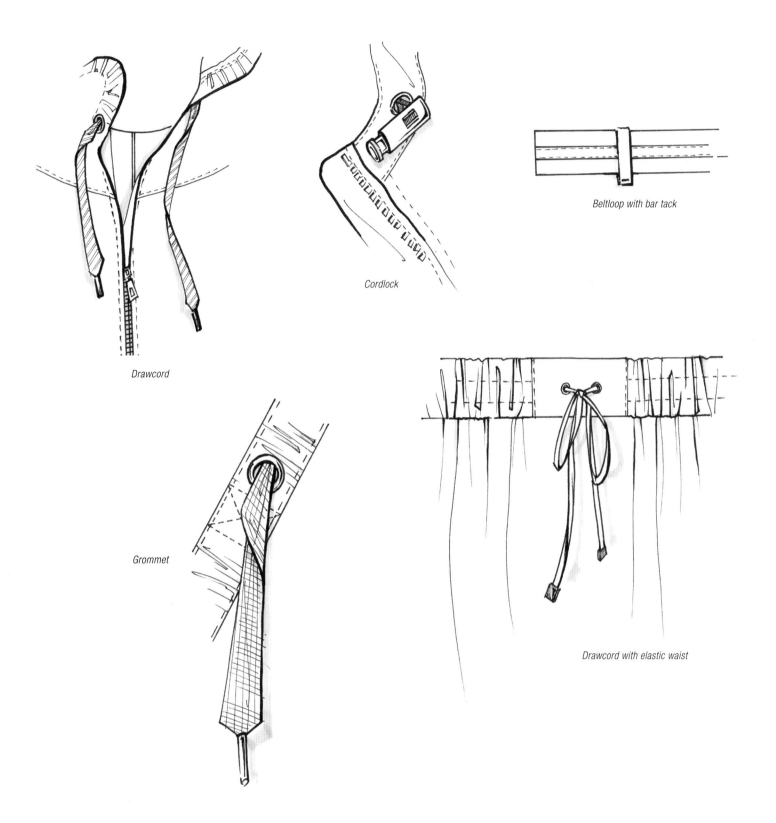

Drawcord

Cordlock

Beltloop with bar tack

Grommet

Drawcord with elastic waist

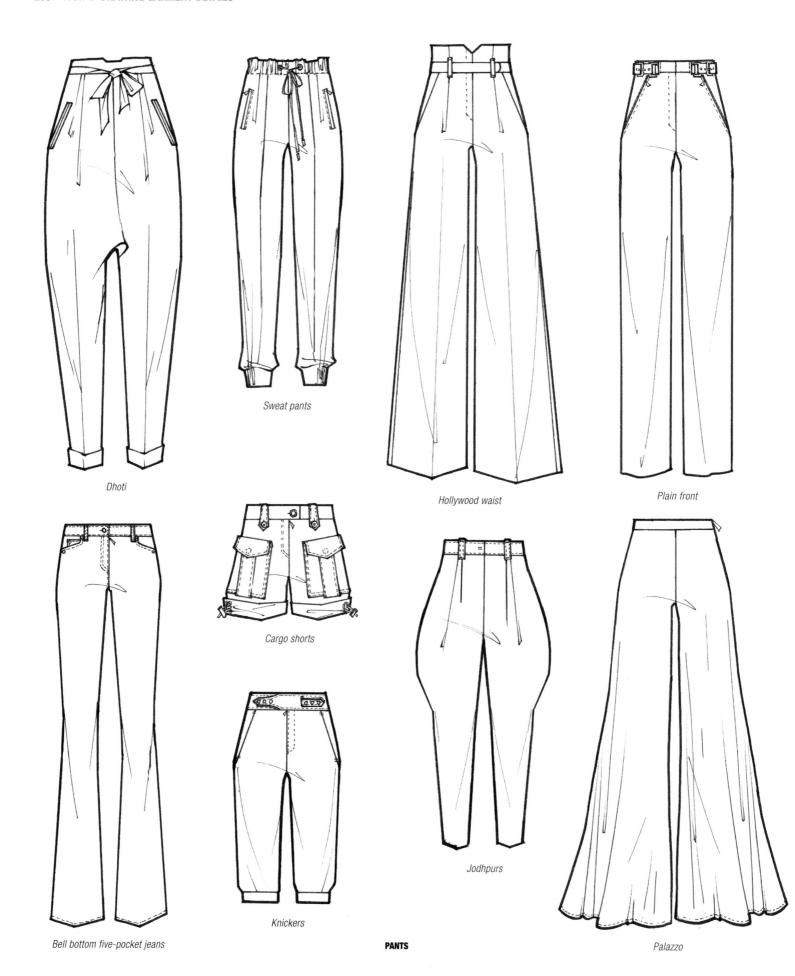

Dhoti

Sweat pants

Hollywood waist

Plain front

Cargo shorts

Knickers

Jodhpurs

Bell bottom five-pocket jeans

PANTS

Palazzo

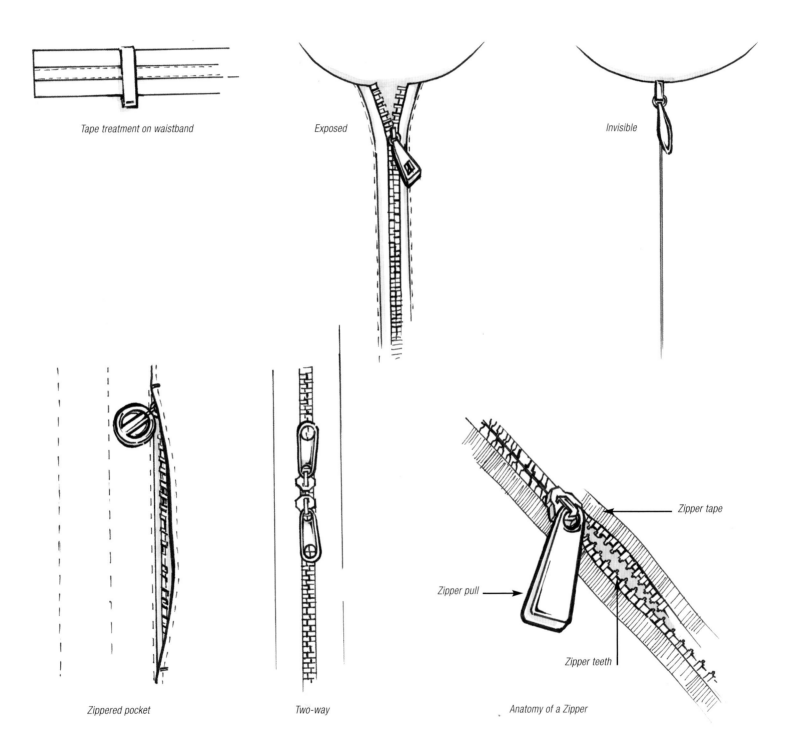

Tape treatment on waistband

Exposed

Invisible

Zippered pocket

Two-way

Anatomy of a Zipper

Zipper tape

Zipper pull

Zipper teeth

ZIPPERS

▲ In this illustration by Alfredo Cabrera, two figures on the left feature drapery formed by construction details. The drapery for the two figures on the right is the consequence of body movement and physical manipulation of the cloth.

▶ Timeless draped silhouettes by Norma Kamali as originally illustrated by Antonio Lopez in 1985.

CHAPTER 7
DRAPERY

▶ *Stella McCartney reproportions basic garment details to pleasing effect. Because the flounce on the blouse is positioned above eye level it is possible to see up and under the gathers.*

In this chapter you will learn about drapery—the manner in which suspended fabric hangs in soft, loose folds. As draped cloth drops and spreads, the force of gravity causes curved unstructured folds to form, each flowing from one to the other. The drapery lines will vary in shape and number depending on the weight and surface of the fabric. For instance, a dress made out of a "hard" fabric, such as a **brocade** or bulky wool, will only skim the body and have a limited number of rigid folds. The overall silhouette will be quite straight and angular. The same dress made out of a soft silk **georgette** will have a more fluid drape and fall closer to the body with a curvy silhouette. The texture, weight, and stiffness of a fabric can be illustrated via line quality. For example, a thick, soft wool can be conveyed with a fuzzy line, while a thin or transparent fabric would translate as a more delicate line. (For more about rendering see the chapters in Part III dedicated to specific fabric categories.)

The action of the body and physical manipulation of the cloth (for example, twisting, grabbing, and knotting) are also determining factors. Cross-grain (bias) and curvilinear pattern cutting are used to create trumpet-shaped silhouettes with individual tapered folds known as flares. Garment construction details, such as bell-shaped gathers created by increasing thread

THE NORMA KAMALI COLLECTION

tension, are used to engineer more permanent folds in a fixed position. The appearance of the folds will vary depending on where they are positioned on the body and according to the observer's point of view. For instance, you can see up and under draped folds at the neckline because they are positioned above eye level. Conversely, you would not be able to see underneath a flounce or ruffle applied to the sweep (bottom hemline) of a skirt or dress because of its location below eye level. Owing to the effect of gravity, flares and gathers will also have a different appearance depending on whether they are suspended from a horizontal or a vertical seam.

The history of draped garments dates all the way back to antiquity when Greco-Roman tunics, togas, and **chitons** were worn to celebrate and reveal the human form. Tailoring did not become popular until the early nineteenth century; prior to that time garment fit was achieved through curvilinear pattern cutting and gathers. Outerwear was also limited to draped garments, with cloaks and capes often doubling as blankets. Because draped silhouettes are perceived to be more feminine, sensual, and luxurious, they tend to re-emerge when there is a need for escape into ultra-feminine glamorous fashion.

▶ *Gathers are used to add volume; here, a pouf skirt illustrated by Richard Rosenfeld.*

◀ *Surreal draped fashion by Diana Lin.*

▼ A dramatic cascade is used to drape both the front and back of a jacket by Valentino.

▲ Sorcha O'Raghallaigh uses a featherweight line quality to convey dresses so light as to be practically airborne.

Basic Principles of Drapery

Garment drapery folds, similar to the swags and cascades you see on window treatments, radiate from a central hub known as the "point of suspension." The number and position of these points of suspension will determine the drape of cloth. The direction of the light source will dictate the position of shadows and highlights. Depending on the fabric and the degree to which it either reflects or absorbs light, each fold will have a highlight, middle value, and a shadow.

Direct observation is your best teacher, so take the time to do a series of draped fabric studies with different points of suspension. Working with a yard (about a meter) of fabric (plain muslin will do):

▼ *Because of the high shine of this metallic fabric, the soft folds of the cowl each have a highlight, middle value, and shadow. (For more about rendering shine see Chapter 9.)*

1 Loosely tack the drapery in one of the upper corners. Working with a medium to soft pencil draw the fabric draped in one-point suspension.

▼ *From left to right: one-, two-, and three-point suspension; bias two-point suspension.*

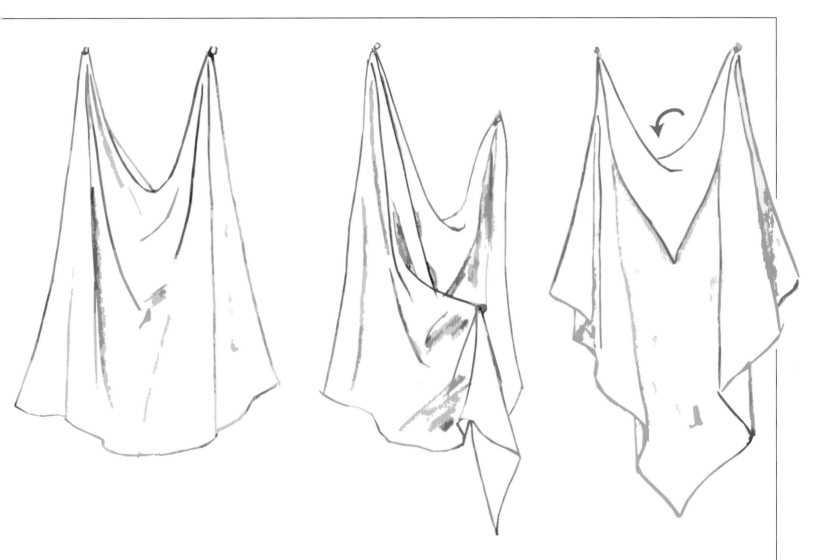

2 Add a second tack to the other upper corner of the fabric, leaving enough slack for a generous drape to form. Draw the fabric draped in two-point suspension.

3 Lower the upper right-hand tack, then add a third tack, using it to raise up the fabric somewhere at a midpoint. Draw the fabric draped in three-point suspension.

4 Unpin and rotate the fabric so that it will be suspended on the bias. When you pin the cloth at the two midpoints along the top edges, a pointy bottom edge will form. Draw the fabric in two-point suspension with bias drape.

Flat Sketching Basic Draped Garments

Next you will apply your observations of one-, two-, and three-point suspension from the previous exercise to flat sketching top and bottom garments with drapery. Before you begin each flat sketch, try to imagine that you are working with a specific fabric. For an added challenge, repeat the exercise working from a variety of fabric swatches.

Flat Sketching a Cowl Neck Blouse

For this exercise you will flat sketch a cowl neck blouse. Working with tracing paper and your flats figure as a guide:

  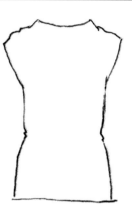 

1 Roughly sketch the overall silhouette of the blouse, indicating the soft folds expressed at the shoulder line. The back neckline will be visible in the front view flat sketch. Draw the neckline as if for a scoop, but with soft folds.

2 A **cowl neckline** is really just an application of two-point suspension. Using a soft expressive line, indicate the folds for the cowl. Experiment with the various line qualities by changing the angle of your pencil strokes.

3 Use the front view sketch as the basis for a back view.

4 Finish the flat sketch using one of the methods described on p. 213. Develop different design variations by making subtle adjustments to the proportion of the garment details.

Flat Sketching a Draped Skirt

For this exercise you will draw a slim miniskirt with a sheer draped overlay. (For additional information about rendering sheer fabrics see Chapter 12.) Working with your flats figure and a tracing overlay:

1 Roughly sketch the waistband and then the overall A-line silhouette. Include two fit darts on the princess line so the skirt will conform to the shape of the body.

2 Based on your observation of two-point suspension in the previous exercise, add the draped overlay. Indicate soft folds.

3 Make subtle changes to develop several alternative design variations.

Drawing Drapery on the Figure

Next you will explore how body shape and movement influence the appearance of draped garments. As you begin drawing drapery on the figure, try to imagine how fabrics with different weights, flexibilities, and textures would change the look of the garment.

Drawing a Draped Jumpsuit

For this next exercise you will draw a draped jumpsuit on the figure. Working with a tracing overlay:

1 Draw the neckline and silhouette of the top of the jumpsuit; then the waist seam and outside edge of the bottom of the garment.

2 Indicate the soft folds in the fabric. Fewer crush lines and folds form in the areas where the body makes direct contact with the garment. Gravity will cause the folds to fall downward and parallel to the Balance Line.

3 Finish the overall silhouette of the drop-crotch pants.

Gathers and Ruffles

Gathers are created by increasing the thread tension on stitching. They are often used to form a ruffle—a long narrow piece of cloth with gathers on one or both of the horizontal edges. Because increased thread tension compresses the width of the cloth at the stitchline, the silhouette of the single-edge ruffle will be tapered at the top and swell out in a bell shape to the wider bottom edge. The ruffle is then attached to another piece of fabric in order to add volume and a soft organic edge to the garment. Ruffles can be inserted into either a straight or a shaped seam. There are many variations of gathers and ruffles (see p. 249).

▼ *Jonathan Kyle Farmer uses gathers to soften tailored clothing.*

Variations of Gathers and Ruffles

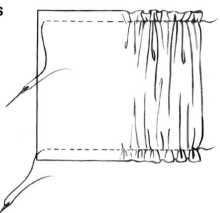

▶ *A double-edge ruffle has gathers at both top and bottom.*

◀◣ *By increasing the tension on the thread, soft, round, bell-shaped folds are formed. A basic single-edge ruffle has gathers on top, with the bottom edge draping freely.*

◀ *Multiple single-edge ruffles can be overlapped in tiers.*

▶ *Increased tension on multiple parallel rows of stitching will form "shirring." Shirring, which is also called "ruching," can follow free-form stitch lines for the formation of a more organic pattern.*

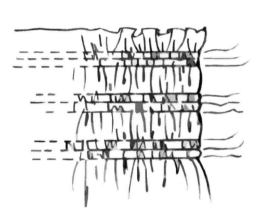

◀ *Shirring on vertical seams will have a different appearance owing to the effect of gravity on the drape.*

▶ *The addition of tunnels with elastic or drawcords also generates gathers.*

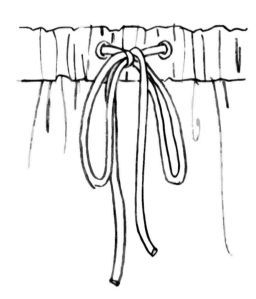

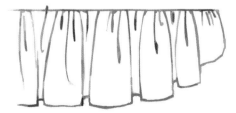

◀ *A single-edge ruffle with a shaped hem.*

As previously mentioned, gathers will have a different appearance depending on whether they are positioned above or below eye level. Before attempting to draw a garment with gathers on the figure, first study a single-edge ruffle from two different points of view:

Drawing a ruffle above eye level

Begin with a ruffle as it would appear, above eye level (at the neckline, for example).

1 Draw a horizontal line for the seam and below it a double guideline for the bottom edge.

2 Drop the drapery lines to form soft bell shapes.

3 Add the curved lines for the bottom hem, using the topmost guideline for the projecting folds and the bottom guideline for the recesses of the folds. Draw the inner folds.

4 Add individual gathers at the seam line.

1

Seam

Guidelines for ruffled hem

2

3

4

Drawing a ruffle below eye level

Then draw a ruffle as it would appear below eye level (at the hemline of a skirt or dress, for example).

1 Draw a horizontal line for the seam and below it, a double guideline for the bottom edge.

2 Drop the drapery lines to form soft bell shapes.

3 Add the curved lines for the bottom hem, this time using the topmost guideline for the recesses of the folds and the bottom for the projecting folds.

4 Add individual gathers at the seam line.

1

Seam

Guidelines for ruffled hem

2

3

4

Designing with Gathers

Gathers add volume, softness, and movement to garment silhouettes. The use of gathers in apparel for men and boys is usually reserved for details such as drawcords and elastic used at the waist and hemlines of pants, and jackets. Tiny ruffles can be applied to the placket of a formal shirt to be worn with a tuxedo. Voluminous ethnic looks with adjustable fit often feature gathers. The use of gathers is far more predominant in fashion for women, girls, and babies. Since gathers occur where there is stitching, they are usually inserted at the neckline, waistline, armhole, princess, or side seams.

Ruffles are often attached to the hemline of sleeves, skirts, and dresses. Drawcords and elastic facilitate an adjustable fit. For instance, a vertical drawcord passing through a tunnel on the outseam of a pair of pants allows the length to be adjusted for flats or heels. The increase in volume created by gathers can extend the wearer's range of motion.

Gathers can also be used strategically to increase volume in a way that makes another part of the body appear smaller by comparison. For instance, gathers inserted at the armhole seam of a jacket add fullness to the shoulder without sacrificing femininity. The increased shoulder presence has the added effect of making the waist appear relatively smaller. Gathered bustles featured in the back of skirts also diminish the appearance of the front-to-back dimension of the waist.

▲ Gathers inserted on side seams add volume and femininity.

◄ Gathers can be used to camouflage figure flaws. Here, a curvier girl wears a dress with ruching on the side seams. As with all body-hugging fashion, it is a good idea to first map the contours of the figure in order to more accurately predict the location and distribution of drapery.

▲ *Here, in a collection by Kelly Yeunh Li-Xia, anime is the inspiration for both the drawing style and the garment designs.*

▶ Because gathers and ruffles are perceived as quite feminine and romantic, they are often used for dresses and intimate apparel. Miyuki Ohashi uses a light touch for party dresses.

◀ Sungeun Kim uses gathers to create feminine details for play clothes for toddler girls.

MIYU

Flat Sketching Garments with Gathers

Now that you have an understanding of what gathers are and how their appearance is affected by placement, you can begin to apply this construction detail to garments. As you flat sketch examples of top and bottom garments, note how the gathers are used to create additional volume and soften the silhouette.

▲ *Use the folding method to achieve a more symmetrical sketch.*

Flat Sketching an Empire-waist Dress

For this exercise, you will flat sketch a dress with gathers inserted at the **empire waistline** (above the natural waist). Working with a flats figure and a tracing overlay:

1 Sketch one half of the garment, beginning with a scoop neckline, set-in armholes, and the empire waistline. Draw the overall silhouette of the dress—a soft bell shape. Indicate crush lines for gathers at the waist seam, then drop the drapery lines.

2 Fold the sketch in half on the Center Front line; then trace the other half of the garment. This method ensures that the drawing will be symmetrical. Draw the recesses and protrusions of the soft folds at the bottom hemline.

3 Center the placket over the Center Front line and add buttons and buttonholes. Experiment with other design variations. Build the back view based on the front view sketch. Finish the sketches using one of the methods outlined on p. 213.

Flat Sketching Draped Pants

Next you will draw a fashionable variation of traditional dhoti pants. Gathers inserted into the waist seam will allow for a looser fit through the hips and upper legs with a gradual tapering toward the bottom hem. An elongated rise seam is used to achieve a dropped crotch. All of these features make the pants quite comfortable and similar in appearance to pajamas. Working with your flats figure and a tracing overlay:

▲ Each soft fold is inserted into the next.

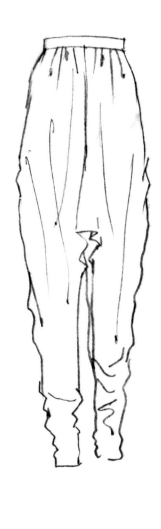

1 Draw two parallel lines for the waistband. Draw the silhouette of the pants to just below the hips. Indicate the shapes of the two draped panels so that their overlap is directly over the Center Front line.

2 Add crush lines for the gathers. Working upward from the outseam, draw the soft folds formed by the pannier drape.

3 Draw the soft outer edge of the pants, making sure to insert each soft fold inside the next. Finish the bottom hemline.

4 Create a back view based on the front; finish using one of the methods described on p. 213.

Drawing Gathers on the Figure

Next you will explore how the shape and movement of the body combines with gravity to influence the appearance of gathers and silhouettes. As you begin drawing gathers on the figure, try to imagine how fabrics with different weights, flexibilities, and textures would change the look of the garment.

Drawing a Tied/Wrap Skirt

For your first drawing of gathers on the figure, begin with a simple bow-tied wrap skirt. Select one of your drawings of a front view high hip figure for a woman or a girl. Working with a tracing overlay:

1 Block in the waistband and bell-shaped silhouette of the skirt. Imagine the Center Front line continuing in the same direction beyond the torso. The volume of the skirt will be equally distributed on either side of the line and swing in the direction of the high hip. Lightly sketch in a double guideline for the sweep (hemline). Note the angle of the hips and their effect on the waistband and hemline; make sure the side seams are of equal length.

2 Draw the bow and indicate the drapery lines, taking care to not make them too uniform. Draw the recesses and protrusions of the soft folds at the bottom hemline.

3 Add the small crush lines at the waist seam to indicate the individual gathers.

Drawing a Pouf Skirt

Next you will draw double-edge gathers for a pouf skirt.

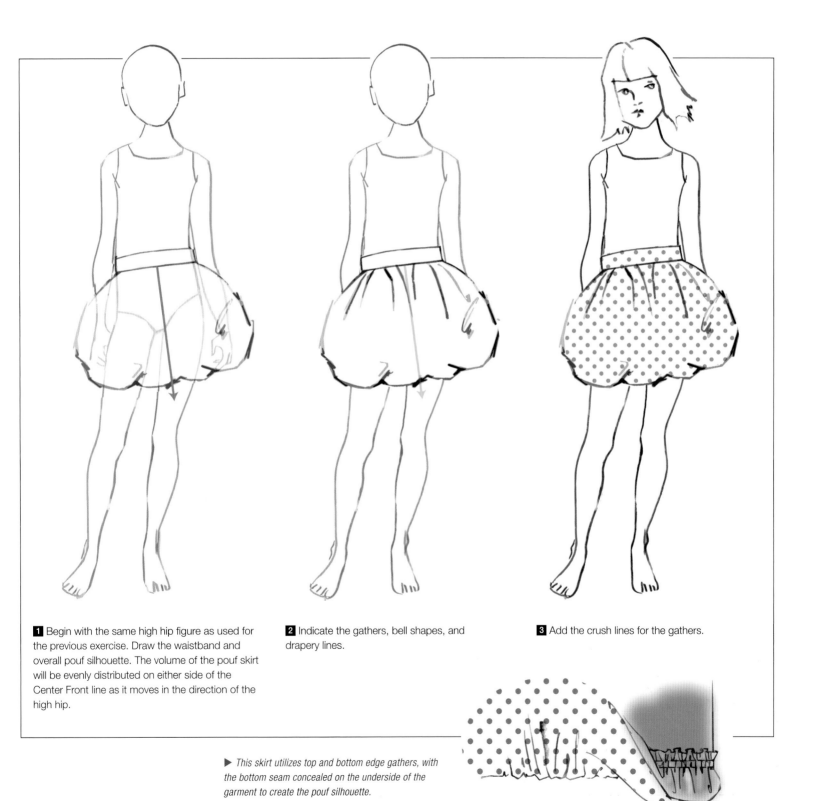

1 Begin with the same high hip figure as used for the previous exercise. Draw the waistband and overall pouf silhouette. The volume of the pouf skirt will be evenly distributed on either side of the Center Front line as it moves in the direction of the high hip.

2 Indicate the gathers, bell shapes, and drapery lines.

3 Add the crush lines for the gathers.

▶ This skirt utilizes top and bottom edge gathers, with the bottom seam concealed on the underside of the garment to create the pouf silhouette.

Drawing Ruffles

For this exercise, you will experiment with drawing gathered ruffles on the turned figure above and below eye level. The volume of the skirt and individual bell shapes will be slightly foreshortened on the side turning from view. (For more about foreshortening see p. 54.) Working with a high hip figure and a tracing overlay:

1 Begin by drawing a **surplice neckline** and a dropped-waist seam. Sketch the overall silhouette of the skirt, taking into consideration the action of the hips and how the position of the arms compresses the outer folds. Drop the drapery lines and indicate the recesses and projections of the gathers at the hemline.

2 Indicate the crush lines for the individual gathers at the waist seam. Draw the gathered ruffle at the neckline, beginning with a loopy curved line. Because the gathers are positioned above eye level, you can see up and under the ruffle.

3 Drop the drapery lines and indicate whatever folds you would see up and under the ruffle.

4 Finalize the drawing by adding crush lines for individual gathers.

1

2

3

4

Flares and Bias Cut

Whereas gathers must emanate from a seam, flares are created by manipulating the fabric grain and through curvilinear pattern cutting. The result is an overall silhouette and individual flares that are shaped like an inverted trumpet—quite slim at the top with an increase in volume at the bottom.

The term "fabric grain" refers to the lengthwise arrangement of threads in a woven fabric. Bias garments are cut with this grain running on the diagonal. The angle can vary, but only garments that are cut with the grain running at a 45-degree angle to the major seams are considered to be "true bias." Because cutting on this angle increases the elasticity of the fabric, bias-cut garments require fewer seams for fitting and closely hug the shape of the body.

Flares can also be created by adding a curvilinear piece of fabric, known as a flounce, to seams and hemlines. When the shorter incurved top edge is straightened and stitched to another piece of fabric, trumpet-shaped flares are formed and add fullness to the bottom edge. As compared to a straight-cut flounce, a circular flounce will produce a greater number flares and, consequently,

▲ Haider Ackermann challenges traditional notions of tailored clothing with bias and curvilinear pattern cutting. Silhouettes take on the form of an inverted trumpet.

◄ Bias-cut silhouettes are quite slim at the top with an increase in volume at the bottom. . Illustration by Laura Laine.

▲ Madeleine Vionnet, thought to be the inventor of the bias cut, began experimentation with cutting fabric on the diagonal grain in the twenties. The feminine bias cut would find acceptance with the general public in the thirties, when the popularity of swing dance prompted a fashion for floor-length white dresses. Here, a Vionnet bias-cut dress for the twenty-first century.

more volume. A circle of fabric is cut out at the center and then split, spread, and applied to another piece of fabric along the shorter inset edge. A flounce applied to a vertical seam will respond to gravitational pull with a soft **cascade drape** (named for its resemblance to a waterfall). Multiple flounces can be layered to form tiers. The flounce can also have a shaped bottom hem.

Like gathers, flares will have a different appearance depending on whether they are positioned above or below eye level. Before attempting to draw a garments with flares on the figure, first study a flounce from two different points of view (see p. 262).

◀ *Unlike voluminous gathers, which can be used for camouflage, bias-cut garments hug and reveal the body. Few, if any, foundation garments can be worn with bias-cut silhouettes. Illustration by Jinsol Kim.*

▼ *The seam allowance for curved and circular flounces is clipped to allow for application to a straight or shaped seam.*

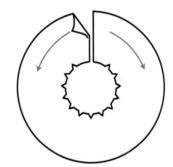

◀▲ *A godet (left) is a section of a circle that can be inserted into a seam or slash to increase the circumference of the bottom edge. Zac Posen inserts multiple godets to increase the sweep of a skirt (above).*

Drawing Flares

Before attempting to draw a garment with flares on the figure, first study the application of a flounce from different points of view.

Flares above eye level

Begin with a flounce that would be featured on a top garment, above eye level (at the neckline, for example).

1 Draw a horizontal line for the seam and below it, a double guideline for the bottom edge.

2 Drop the drapery lines to form soft trumpet-shaped flares. Flares are organic in nature and so their size, shape, and distribution should not be too uniform.

3 Add the curved lines for the bottom hem, using the topmost guideline for the projecting folds and the bottom guideline for the recesses. Draw the inner folds visible when positioned above eye level.

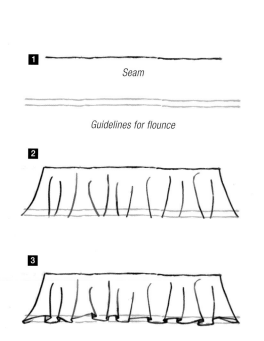

1
Seam

Guidelines for flounce

2

3

Flares below eye level

Then draw a flounce for a bottom garment positioned below eye level (at the hemline of a skirt or dress, for example).

1 Draw a horizontal line for the seam and, below it, a double guideline for the bottom edge.

2 Drop the drapery lines to form soft trumpet-shaped flares, taking care to vary their shape, width, and distribution.

3 Add the curved lines for the bottom edge, this time using the topmost guideline for the recesses of the folds and the bottom for the projecting folds.

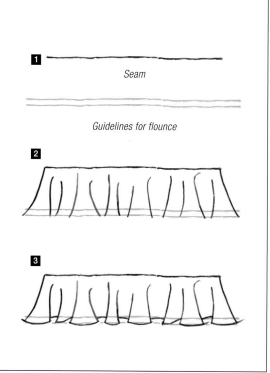

1
Seam

Guidelines for flounce

2

3

Vertical cascade drape

Next you will draw a cascading flounce applied to a vertical seam.

1 Begin by drawing a vertical line for the seam. This will be the single point of suspension for the individual cascading flares.

2 Draw the edge of the flounce with a squiggly line. The irregular loopy shapes should resemble puzzle pieces and straddle both sides of the seam.

3 Drop drapery lines for one-point suspension using the seam as the point of origin for each one of the flares.

1 **2** **3**

Designing With Flares and Bias Cut

The first design consideration for apparel cut on the bias is the increase in yardage required as compared to a garment cut on the straight. Solids are somewhat easier to deal with; woven and print patterns must be carefully matched. The bias cut can be used to create an asymmetrical hemline (such as a **handkerchief hemline**). If you do choose to include an asymmetric hem, be sure that your figure pose—specifically the action of the hips—does not contradict the asymmetry of the hem. Interesting effects can be achieved by mixing both straight and bias cuts in a single garment. For instance, a sleeve cut on the bias will form a trumpet shape, which can be a soft counterpoint to a bodice cut on the straight. Decisions about cutting and the direction of the fabric grain should not be made arbitrarily. It is advisable to cut the parts of garment that bear the most weight on the straight for greater stability of the weave.

▼ *Customer profile is always a significant issue, but especially so for bias-cut garments that reliably hug and reveal the figure—and all of its flaws.*

▼ *This dress features a layering of multiple flounces created with curvilinear pattern cutting. Illustration by Alfredo Cabrera.*

Flat Sketching Flares and Bias-cut Garments

Next you will flat sketch top and bottom garments that have been constructed using curvilinear and bias pattern cutting. When flat sketching the garments, indicate the grain of the fabric with a striped pattern to reinforce your understanding of bias and straight-grain pattern cutting.

Drawing a Waterfall Cardigan/Jacket

For this exercise you will draw a fit-and-flare waterfall jacket. Working with your flats figure and a tracing overlay:

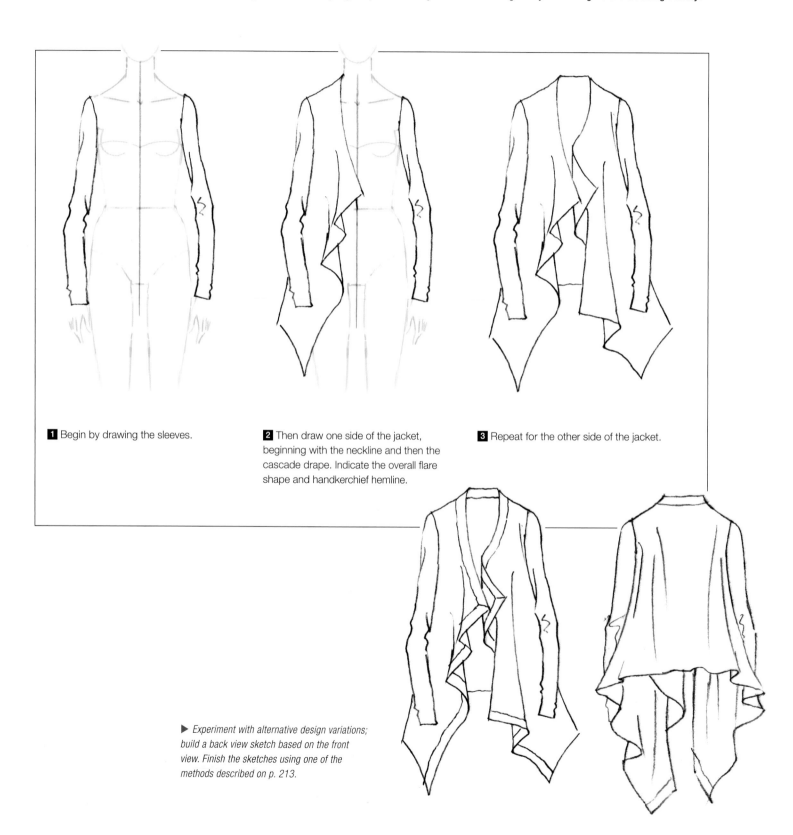

1 Begin by drawing the sleeves.

2 Then draw one side of the jacket, beginning with the neckline and then the cascade drape. Indicate the overall flare shape and handkerchief hemline.

3 Repeat for the other side of the jacket.

▶ *Experiment with alternative design variations; build a back view sketch based on the front view. Finish the sketches using one of the methods described on p. 213.*

Flat Sketching a Circle Skirt

Wide **swing skirts** with poodle **appliqué** are one of the most enduring symbols of the fifties.
These voluminous skirts are constructed by cutting out two semicircles and joining the
selvedges for a complete circle. Working with your flats figure and a tracing overlay:

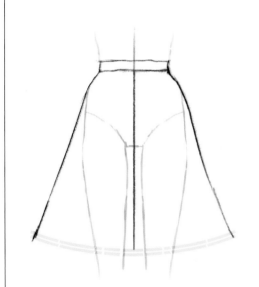

1 Begin drawing the skirt with two parallel lines for the waistband. Add the Center Front seam and overall flared silhouette. Create two guidelines at the bottom hem (sweep).

2 Draw the soft folds that form the flares. Take care to make them appear random in width and distribution.

3 Indicate the expression of the flares at the bottom hem.

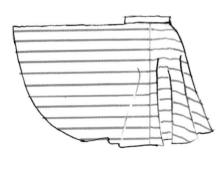
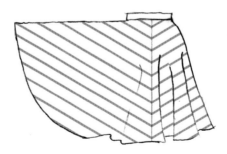

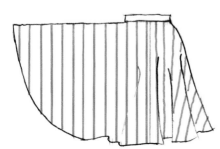
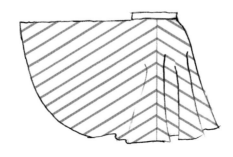

◀ *Stripes and plaids can be manipulated in a variety of ways for circle skirts. Left top and bottom, with a semicircle cut on the straight grain; right top and bottom, with the semicircle cut on the bias so that stripes form a miter. (For more about rendering pattern see pp. 342–55.)*

Drawing Flares and Bias-cut Garments on the Figure

The shape and movement of the body will exert enormous influence over clothing cut on the bias because of the increased elasticity of the fabric and the way it clings to the body. Therefore, the illustration of bias-cut clothing will really test your figure drawing skills.

Drawing a Floor-length Bias-cut Skirt

For this exercise you will draw a simple floor-length skirt cut on the bias. The drape will be quite liquid. Working with a high hip pose and a tracing overlay:

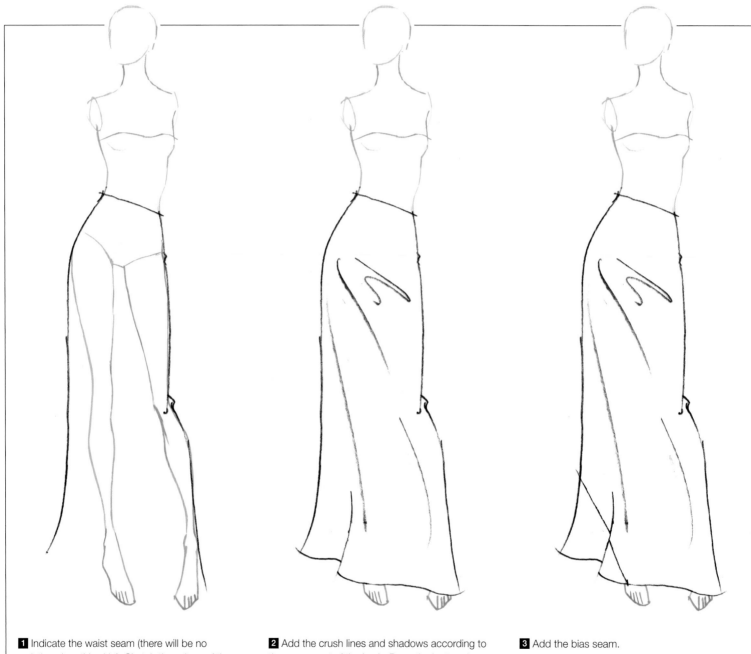

1 Indicate the waist seam (there will be no waistband on this skirt). Sketch the edges of the skirt in the areas where the fabric comes into direct contact with the body. Because it is cut on the bias, the skirt will flare slightly as you get closer to the bottom edge.

2 Add the crush lines and shadows according to the movement of the body. Draw the bottom hem so that the angle corresponds to the movement of the hips.

3 Add the bias seam.

Drawing an Eight-gore Skirt

A gore is a section of a skirt, shaped like a piece of pie, used to provide a tapering at the waist and fullness at the hem. A four-gore skirt has seams at the sides, Center Front, and Center Back; a six-gore skirt has seams at the princess lines (front and back), and sides.

For the next exercise you will draw an eight-gore skirt with seams at the Center Front, princess line (front and back), Center Back, and sides. Imagine that the skirt is made of a crisp medium-weight fabric. Working with a front view high hip pose and tracing overlay:

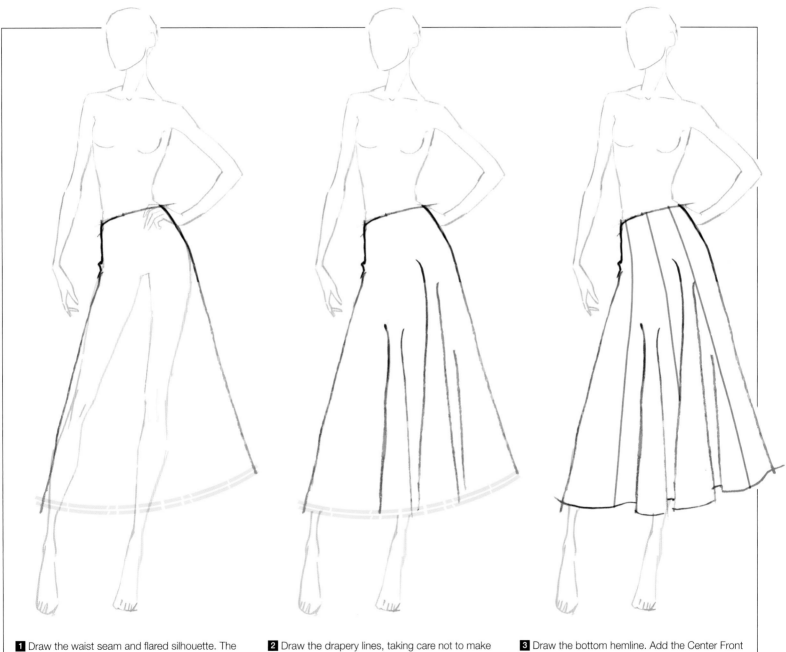

1 Draw the waist seam and flared silhouette. The volume of the skirt will swing in the direction of the high hip. Lightly sketch in a double guideline for the sweep (hemline).

2 Draw the drapery lines, taking care not to make them too uniform.

3 Draw the bottom hemline. Add the Center Front and princess seams to complete the four gores visible from the front view.

◀ ▶ *Diana Lin's dresses for Summer (left)
and Fall (opposite).*

ASSIGNMENT 1

Working with a specific customer profile and three to five fabric
swatches, design a small Spring/Summer collection of dresses or
intimate apparel with lots of drapery (above). The collection should
look coherent. Include a design element such as color, silhouette,
and/or construction details to serve as a connecting thread between
the garments. Once you have completed the Spring/Summer dresses,
design a second delivery that carries over these same design
sensibilities reinterpreted in fabric weights and colors suitable
for Fall (opposite left).

NOTE For more information on color
rendering, please see the
chapters dedicated to specific fabrics and
techniques in Part III.

ASSIGNMENT 3

Design a collection of dresses as an homage to a designer, working past or present, known for using innovative pattern cutting to achieve drape. For instance, you might want to draw inspiration from Charles James, who masterfully engineered drapery over hidden armatures in the fifties. The romantic flowing dresses that launched the careers of designers such as Steven Burrows and Ossie Clark in the late sixties would also be a good choice. You may want to consider practitioners of exquisite dressmaking working today such as Maria Cornejo, threeASFOUR, Alber Elbaz, Vivienne Westwood, or doo.ri. Have a specific customer and occasion in mind and use lots of flares and/or gathers for your dress designs (below).

▼ *The number, scale, and location of ruffles must be adjusted for a petite figure. Design and Illustration by Wyatt Hough.*

ASSIGNMENT 2

In the twenties, designer Jeanne Lanvin became famous for dressing her clients from infancy to adulthood. Her sophisticated mother/daughter dresses featured small waists and full gathered skirts. As per Jeanne Lanvin, for this assignment you will design a small collection of dresses for women and then adapt the garments for little girls. Children outgrow their clothing in the blink of an eye. Can you think of a way in which design features could extend garment life cycles?

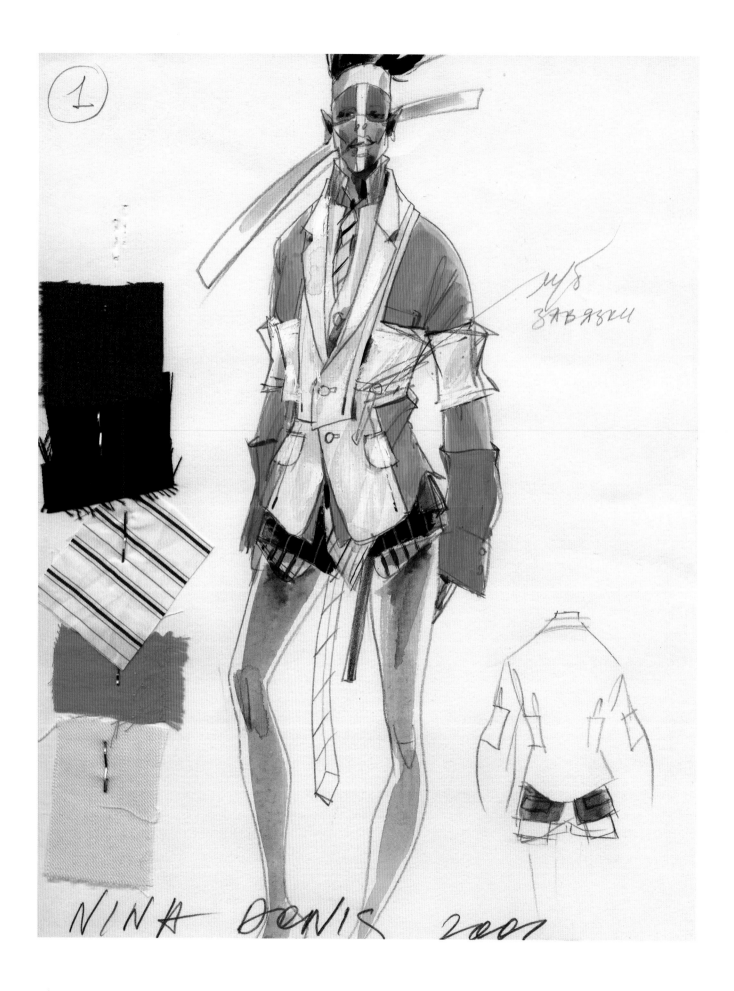

NINA DONIS 2001

CHAPTER 8
TAILORED CLOTHING

The term tailored clothing refers to menswear-style jackets and the shirts, vests (waistcoats), pants, and skirts that go with them. These garments can be paired as suits or coordinated as mix-and-match separates. While all garments begin as a flat piece of cloth, tailored clothing must be precisely engineered for the garments to smoothly conform to the shape of the body. Pattern cutting and structural elements, such as shoulder pads and a chestpiece, are used to mimic and flatter the figure according to the current ideal. "Bespoke" menswear (which originated in the epicenter of tailoring—Savile Row in London) goes so far as to not only fit, but actually design an entirely unique suit for each individual.

The design of tailored clothing is largely derived from military uniforms and clothing for equestrian sports. Tailored styles for women have followed those for men. Garments are therefore both masculine and utilitarian in nature. The popularity of "tailor mades"

at the turn of the twentieth century evolved as a consequence of women's emancipation and increased participation in sports, travel, and professional endeavors.

Historically, the innovation of new tailored looks has often been a carryover from wartime. For example, the habit for utilitarian dressing during and immediately following World War I laid the groundwork for Coco Chanel's introduction of tailored looks for women "borrowed from the boys." In the twenty-first century it is hard to imagine tailored clothing for women as being revolutionary. Yet, as recently as the late sixties, Yves Saint Laurent's "Safari" and "Le Smoking" pantsuits dramatically upended dress codes for women. From British Mods to dotcom geek chic, the streamlined appearance of tailored clothing has also been synonymous with modernity and "power dressing."

◀▶ Although tailored clothing is most often associated with career and formal dressing, trends in popular culture have also produced more subversive and even ultra-hip looks. Examples from the past of tailored clothing for the counterculture include zoot suits for jazz "hepcats," the "drape" preferred by British "Teddy Boys," and "Rat Pack" sharkskin suits. Here, fashion-forward tailoring by Moscow design team Nina Donis features an innovative layering and reproportioning of garments.

▶▶ Trench coats, originally military issue, became fashionable for civilian dress in the years immediately following World War I. Here, a high-fashion trench coat by Lanvin.

Drawing Tailored Jackets and Coats

There are a wide variety of jacket and coat styles. The blazer is perhaps the most popular and versatile, taking a cue from whatever garment happens to be paired with it. Single-breasted blazers have one row of buttons on the Center Front and, typically, some variation of a notched collar lapel. Double-breasted blazers, which have two vertical rows of buttons equidistant from Center Front, are considered to be more formal. Asymmetric and zipper closures offer additional design options. The shoulder line can be quite natural or extended, depending on the jacket design. Because the armhole seam allowance is usually turned in the direction of the sleeve, there will be some "shoulder presence" with or without the addition of padding.

Flat Sketching Blazers

In order to fully understand the construction of tailored jackets, you will first identify and draw single- and double-breasted blazers as flats. Work from sample garments to observe how overall silhouettes are achieved by manipulating the shoulder presence and fit lines. The scale, shape, and location of collar, lapels, and pockets are also integral to design development. Also note how the garments are finished (with single or multiple rows of topstitching in self or contrast colors, for example).

◀ *Satin trim peak lapels add a formal touch to a feminine tailored look by Vionnet.*

▶ *Tailored clothing is associated with power and modernity. Illustration by Paul Negron.*

Drawing a Single-breasted Blazer

Working with a men's flats figure and a tracing overlay, draw a
single-breasted blazer based on observations of a sample garment.

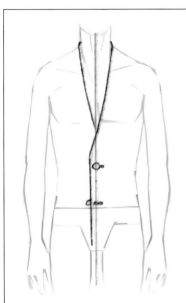   

1 Begin by drawing a curved line for one side of the neckline and lapel roll, continuing slightly beyond the Center Front. Indicate the edge of the front closure by dropping the line down parallel to the Center Front. Sketch the other side of the neckline to mirror the first, and overlap at the Center Front. Draw two buttons on the Center Front.

2 Next you will draw the lapels. The lapels are actually part of the front of the jacket and have two layers of the outer "shell" fabric plus another layer of **interfacing**—a total of three layers. In order to indicate the dimension of these layers, use soft shadows and rounded lines wherever the lapel rolls.

3 Draw the collar to meet the lapels at the **gorge** seam. The collar is a separate pattern piece also comprised of three layers of fabric. Be sure to convey this volume as soft folds. Establish the shoulder line, armholes, and bottom hem, indicating the overlap of the two sides of the jacket at the hemline with soft shadows.

4 Sketch in the overall silhouette. Draw the sleeves, keeping mind that even a straight arm will have a slight bend. A well-made jacket will typically have a two-piece sleeve construction; depending on the market price point, you may need to indicate this seam.

NOTE The horizontal distance between the center of the button and the opening edge of the jacket is called the "extension."

▶ Experiment with design variations and use the front view sketch as the basis for a back view. Finish the flat sketch using one of the methods described on p. 213.

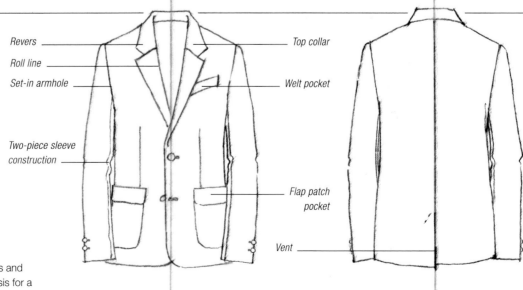

Revers

Roll line

Set-in armhole

Two-piece sleeve construction

Top collar

Welt pocket

Flap patch pocket

Vent

DESIGN VARIATION

BACK VIEW

Flat Sketching a Double-breasted Blazer

The method for drawing a double-breasted garment is not that different from the single-breasted. The two styles are distinguished by the size of the extension—increased in width for the double-breasted to accommodate two rows of buttons. Working with a flats figure, a sample garment, and a tracing overlay, draw a double-breasted blazer. Throughout the exercise be sure to allow ample volume for the layering of coordinating garments underneath the blazer.

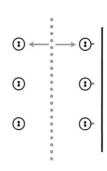

◀ *Buttons are equidistant from the Center Front and button through only on the side of the closing edge.*

▶ *The collar and lapel join to form a notch. Here, a classic application of topstitching.*

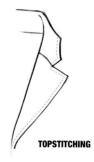

TOPSTITCHING

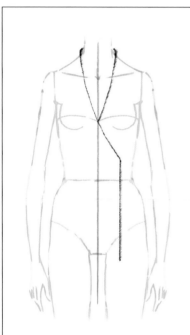

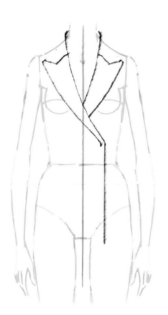

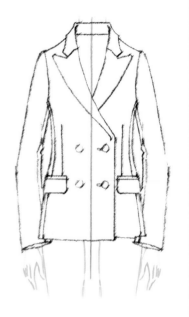

1 Begin by drawing a curved line for one side of the neckline and lapel roll, this time continuing the line farther beyond the Center Front line. Indicate the edge of the front closure by dropping the line down parallel to Center Front. Sketch the other side of the neckline to mirror the first and overlap at Center Front.

2 Next draw the peaked lapels.

3 Draw the collar to meet the lapels at the gorge seam. Establish the shoulder line and armholes. Sketch the overall silhouette and princess seams.

4 Draw the sleeves, indicating the seam for two-piece sleeve construction. Add two rows of buttons, making sure they are equidistant from Center Front. Indicate buttonholes. Develop alternative design variations by manipulating the shape and size of the collar, lapel, sleeves, and pockets from the illustrated glossary on pp. 230–39.

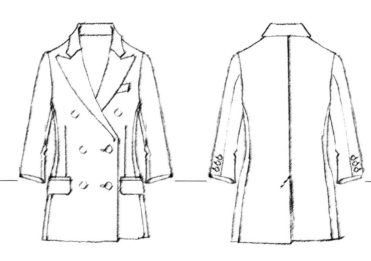

DESIGN VARIATION

BACK VIEW

◀ *Use the front view flat sketch as the basis for the back view and finish both using one of the methods described on p. 213.*

Drawing Tailored Jackets and Coats on the Figure

Before you begin sketching jackets and coats on the figure, give some thought to choosing an appropriate pose. Tailored clothing is more structured and so garments can limit the wearer's range of motion. For instance, you will need to position the arms near to the torso so as to accommodate closely set-in sleeves. As mentioned in Chapter 6, the movement of the figure affects the appearance of garments. Crush lines will form wherever opposition of the shoulders and hips creates an area of compression. The design details on the upper portion of the garment (collar and lapel points, handkerchief pockets, etc.) will fall parallel to the angle of the shoulders. The hemline and design details located below the waist will be aligned with the angle of the hips.

◄ A crisp tailored blazer designed by Gene Mayer.

► The collar and lapel points align with the angle of the shoulders; the pockets and hemline align with the angle of the hips.

▼ A casual approach to tailored sportswear for juniors by Jonathan Kyle Farmer.

Drawing a Single-breasted Blazer on the Walking Figure

Working with a walking pose and a tracing overlay, draw a single-breasted blazer.

NOTE Be sure to include buttonholes or your buttons may be interpreted as snaps (press studs).

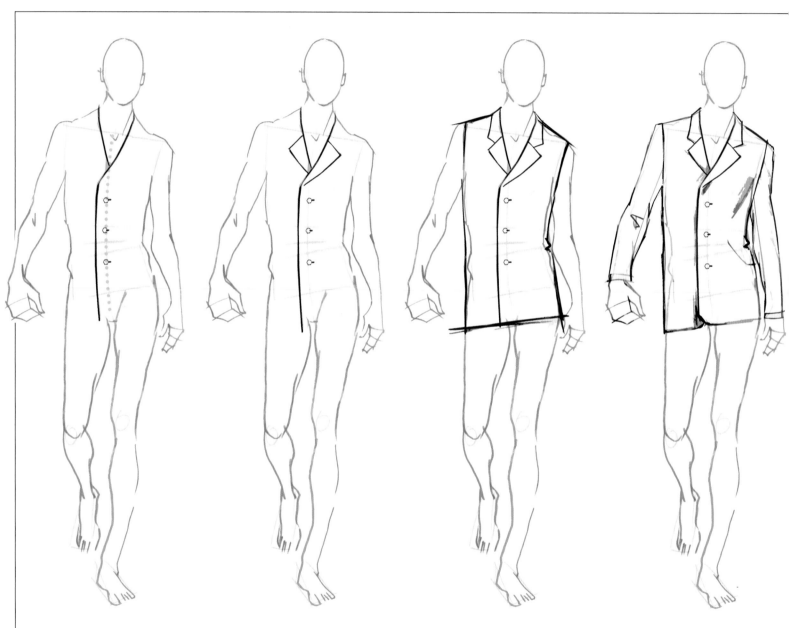

1 Begin by drawing a curved line for one side of the neckline and lapel roll, continuing slightly beyond the Center Front. Indicate the edge of the front closure by dropping the line down parallel to Center Front. Sketch the other side of the neckline to mirror the first, overlapping at Center Front. Draw three buttons.

2 Next you will draw the lapels. Take care to line up the lapel points with the angle of the shoulders.

3 Draw the collar to meet the lapels at the gorge seam. Take care to line up the collar points with the angle of the shoulders. Establish the shoulder line and armholes. Sketch the overall silhouette, indicating the crush lines at the waist on the high hip side of the figure.

4 Emphasize the overlap of the two sides of the jacket at the hemline with soft shadows. Draw the sleeves, keeping in mind that even a straight arm will have a slight bend. Indicate crush lines in the areas of compression (e.g. the crook of a bent elbow). Indicate the two-piece sleeve construction.

▶ *When you draw tailored clothing on the figure, you have an opportunity to show how the garments in your collection can best be coordinated. Draw the jacket open to show off the various layered pieces. Design and illustration by Nina Donis.*

5 Add flap pockets, taking care to align them with the opposing angles of the shoulders and hips.

Drawing a Double-breasted Trench Coat on the Figure

Working with a front view high hip pose and a tracing overlay, draw a belted double-breasted trench coat. Throughout the exercise be sure to allow ample volume for the layering of coordinating garments underneath the coat. The opposition between the shoulders and hips will affect the placement of the buttons, pockets, and other garment details; use the cylindrical analysis of the figure to help you map their location.

1 Draw a curved line for one side of the neckline and lapel roll, continuing the line beyond Center Front. Indicate the edge of the front closure with a line parallel to it. Sketch the other side of the neckline. Draw the lapels, lining up the points with the angle of the shoulders.

2 Draw the collar to meet the lapels at the gorge seam. The collar points should also line up with the angle of the shoulders.

3 Establish the shoulder line by drawing the epaulets and then the armholes. Sketch the overall silhouette and the belt.

4 Draw the sleeves, belt details, and angled **welt pockets**.

▼ *The opposition between the shoulders and hips will affect the placement of stripes and plaids, so it is important to map the garment before you render the fabric. (For more about rendering patterns see pp. 342–55.)*

5 Add buttons and buttonholes.

Drawing a Zippered Jacket on the Turned Figure

In selecting a turned figure for this exercise, can you predict how foreshortening will affect the appearance of the jacket? As noted in Chapter 1, an object will take on a different appearance depending on its location in space; a receding object will appear to grow smaller and, conversely, an advancing object will appear to grow larger. As the figure rotates in space, the side of the body that turns away from view will appear to shrink. Garment details will also become foreshortened as they turn away from view (necklines and pockets will appear to narrow, for example).

For this exercise, select a turned pose. Give added consideration to the foreshortening of design elements on the side of the body turning from view. Working with a tracing overlay:

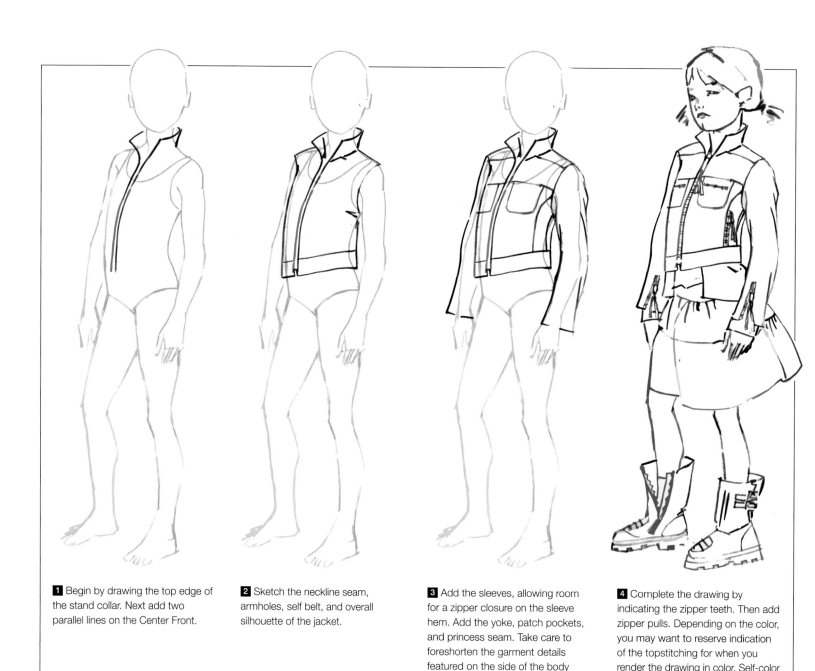

1 Begin by drawing the top edge of the stand collar. Next add two parallel lines on the Center Front.

2 Sketch the neckline seam, armholes, self belt, and overall silhouette of the jacket.

3 Add the sleeves, allowing room for a zipper closure on the sleeve hem. Add the yoke, patch pockets, and princess seam. Take care to foreshorten the garment details featured on the side of the body turning from view.

4 Complete the drawing by indicating the zipper teeth. Then add zipper pulls. Depending on the color, you may want to reserve indication of the topstitching for when you render the drawing in color. Self-color topstitching is traditionally rendered with a fine dashed black line.

Designing Tailored Clothing

Most tailored jackets and coats are a variation of the basic garments illustrated in the previous section. Innovation lies in manipulating the scale and location of garment details such as the top collar, lapels, gorge, button stance, pockets, and so on. These elements can be utilized to effect an idealized body shape. For example, at the end of the 1930s, the use of wider lapels and a lowered gorge seam had the effect of emphasizing a large torso (see p. 16).

The fabric, trim, and structural elements should be selected in the very beginning stages of your design development as this will obviously have a significant impact on the overall look of the garments. If you are designing a suit, the fabric chosen must work for both top (jacket and vest) and bottom (pants or skirts) garments. These fabrics are referred to as **suitings**.

▶ *Nina Donis transform classic shapes by manipulating the scale of garments and details.*

▼ *The relative proportion between the coordinating garments is key. High-fashion tailored sportswear by Jonathan Kyle Farmer.*

◢ *When designing tailored clothing, careful consideration must be given to the layering of coordinating garments.*

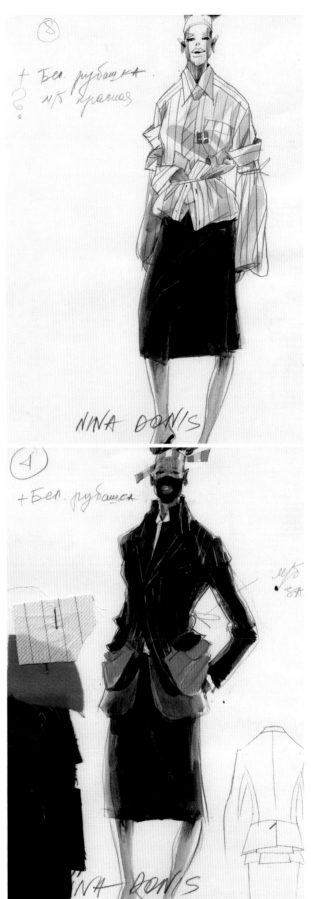

▲◥ Here, two single-breasted suits reflect entirely different design sensiblities. The one designed by Prada (left) has a closer fit and uses

more structural fabrication, while the other, designed by Lanvin (right), has a more relaxed fit and softer fabrication.

▲ Designers must give consideration to the basics and soft pieces that go underneath structured tailoring.

If the collection is to include garments that can be coordinated in different ways, you will be working with two different groups of fabrics: top- and bottom-weights. **Top weights** are for coats, jackets, and vests; **bottom weights** are for pants and skirts. While woven fabrics are typically used for tailored clothing, a strategic mixing of knits and wovens can facilitate a more precise fit—especially for mass-market fashion. (For more on rendering wools see Chapter 10.) If the jacket is to be fitted closely to the body, construction details such as fit darts will be required to achieve the shaping of the garment. For women's jackets, the princess seam is an option, as is the addition of feminizing flares and gathers (such as bias-cut cascading lapels or a gathered peplum at the bottom hem). The addition of topstitching in self or contrast color can significantly change the look of a jacket, making it seem more or less casual.

Since the jacket will be layered over (and possibly under) other garments, the proportion will be key to the look of the entire

▶ ▶▶ *Here, two double-breasted jackets have an entirely different fit and proportion: Zac Posen (right) shapes his jacket close to the body for a sexy look; Junya Watanabe (far right) creates a boxier silhouette in his recalling of the British Raj.*

◀ *The jacket sets the proportion for the entire look and, as such, should be your first design consideration.*

collection. Therefore, it makes sense to design the jacket first. In order to convey the nesting and volume of multiple layers, indicate the topmost layers as having a relatively looser fit. Thinner fabrics are typically used for base layers, with progressively heavier fabrics for outer layers. The line quality you choose for your drawing can convey this. Practitioners of exquisite twenty-first-century tailoring include Kris Van Assche, Karl Lagerfeld, Paul Smith, Jil Sander, Roland Mouret, Yohji Yamamoto, Thom Browne, and Helmut Lang.

Anna Kiper

◀ ▼ ▲ *Feminine tailored looks for day into evening designed by Anna Kiper for Maggie Norris.*

ASSIGNMENT 1

For this exercise you will design a small collection of tailored clothing inspired by a vintage blazer. If possible, work with an actual garment. Use a maximum of five fabric swatches combining top- and bottom-weights. Working in your sketchbook, accurately flat sketch the jacket as it is and then begin to make subtle and gradual changes. Sketch 15 variations, adapting fabrication and construction details for a modern customer profile. Select the most successful jacket design and build a collection of seven coordinating garments (including the jacket). Illustrate your final presentation on three figures. For an added challenge, design the pieces to be coordinated in such a way as to be worn from day into evening (opposite).

ASSIGNMENT 2

In the 1830s, French novelist Amandine Aurore Lucile Dupin, Baroness Dudevant (better known by her nom de plume "George Sand") was one of the first women to wear men's clothing in public. For this assignment, design a collection of tailored clothing that George Sand would wear if she were alive today. You may want to draw additional inspiration from well-dressed men ("dandies") of the period (below). For an added challenge, design the garments to be unisex; worn by either men or women. What does androgeny look like in the twenty-first century?

▼ *Design development for Mia Grimaldi's collection is inspired by dandyism.*

Pleats

Unlike the free-form drapery discussed in Chapter 7, pleating involves folds that are carefully and permanently engineered. The number and distribution of the pleats is precisely measured, with folds sharply creased or left unpressed. Stitching is used to permanently secure the folds.

▼ *The immediacy of Nina Donis's quick sketching technique nonetheless conveys specific garment details and volume created by fine pleating.*

Flat pleating techniques:

● Knife (or side) pleats are folds turned in a single direction that have been leveled to lay flat.
● Inverted pleats are formed by pairs of inward facing under-folds.
● Box pleats are formed by pairs of outward-facing under-folds.

Projecting pleating techniques:

● Accordion pleats are alternately folded in and out so that the pleats project like a bellows. Sunray pleats are a variation cut on the bias to produce a fanned effect.
● Fortuny or broomstick pleating is actually more of a wrinkled surface treatment than a pleat. The folds vary in size and direction and are discontinuous from top to bottom.

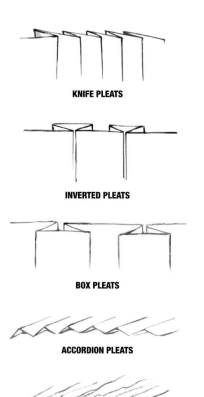

KNIFE PLEATS

INVERTED PLEATS

BOX PLEATS

ACCORDION PLEATS

FORTUNY (BROOMSTICK) PLEATS

Flat Sketching a Skirt with Knife Pleats

For your first drawing begin with a knife-pleat skirt with one-way flat folds. Working with a flats figure, tracing overlay, and a sample garment:

1 Block in the waistband and overall silhouette of the skirt with two guidelines at the bottom hem. Using the Center Front line as a guide, divide the skirt in half.

2 Subdivide half of the skirt in two. Repeat on the other side for a total of four subdivisions. Continue subdividing until the pleats are of the desired number and width.

3 Using a zigzag line, indicate the single direction and leveling of the folds at the bottom hem. Finish using one of the methods described on p. 213.

▶ *Rei Kawakubo deconstructs a kilt for Comme des Garçons.*

Flat Sketching a Skirt with Inverted Pleats

Next try drawing a skirt with inverted pleats—two-way flat folds. Working with a flats figure, tracing overlay, and a sample garment:

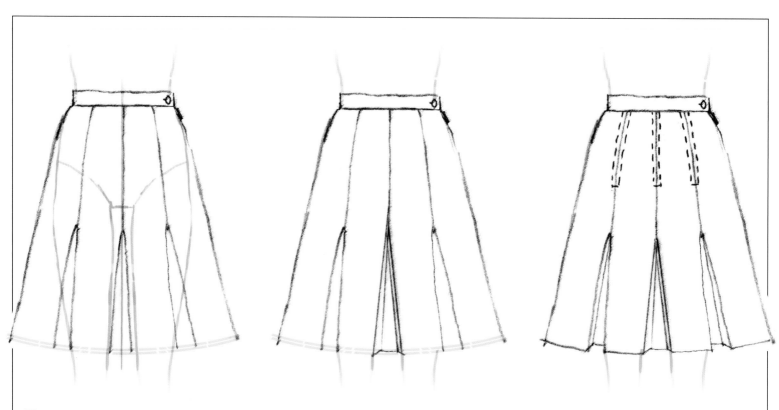

1 Block in the waistband and overall silhouette of the skirt. Lightly sketch in a double guideline for the sweep. Divide the skirt in two using a narrow upside-down Y shape positioned on the Center Front. Draw two additional inverted Ys on the princess lines.

2 Draw a tall narrow triangle recessed within the center pleat. Indicate the inner folds with a stepped line for the hem.

3 Draw a second inverted pleat on one side of the skirt (there will only be a partial view of this pleat). Sketch the hemline, indicating the inner folds. Draw the mirror image of the pleat on the opposite side of the skirt. Add topstitching so that the pleats release below the hipline.

Drawing Accordion Pleats on the Figure

The next exercise involves drawing an accordion-pleat skirt with projecting folds on a high hip figure. Working with a tracing overlay, and a sample garment:

1 Begin with a basic silhouette as for a flared skirt (see p. 267). Sketch several soft flares. Add vertical guides from the waistband to the hem at the Center Front and princess lines.

2 Add fine accordion pleats to each of the flares. Locate the Center Front of each flare and work outward to indicate each parallel projecting pleat.

3 Refine the sweep with a zigzag line to express the projection of the accordion pleats at the bottom hem.

Drawing Fortuny Pleats on the Figure

Fortuny pleating is often used for body-conscious silhouettes constructed from lightweight fabrics such as silk chiffon. For this next exercise you will draw a slim ankle-length skirt with Fortuny pleats and a curly "lettuce" edge. Working from a tracing overlay and high hip figure:

1 Begin by sketching the waistline and overall silhouette of the skirt. Indicate the contour of the body underneath the skirt by adding soft shadows for the legs. Use the same soft shadows for the crush lines formed by the movement of the hips.

2 Following the action of the body, add the irregular pleating.

3 Sketch the lettuce edge for the bottom hem.

Designing with Pleats

Vertical, horizontal, and zigzag pleating can be used to shape both top and bottom garments and even accessories (such as men's cummerbunds). The pleats can be secured with stitching at the top, bottom, or both, and the pressing of the folds is also left to the designer's discretion. Pants often feature inverted or box pleats incorporated into waist treatments. The most common use of pleats is for skirts. Knife pleats are often used on the back of kilts, knee-length tartan skirts that originated as traditional dress in the Scottish Highlands. Pleating for kilts can be engineered to coincide with individual stripes or full repeats woven into the fabric. High-tech whole-garment pleating is another option. Garments are cut and sewn together at two and a half to three times larger than the finished size. The whole garment is then fed into a heat press for permanent pleating.

▲ As with all garment details, proportion and fabrication of the various pleats will determine overall design. Pleated mini-dress by Valentino.

◀ As with all garment details, proportion and fabrication of the various pleats will determine overall design. Illustration and design by Paul Negron.

▶ A little girl's dress with a box-pleated flounce, designed and illustrated by Sungeun Kim.

ASSIGNMENT 3

For this assignment, try a more casual approach to tailoring by applying the garment details featured in this chapter to a denim collection (right). Because denim is so durable it is integrated into many fashion market categories and constantly updated with different fits, washes, and treatments (e.g. distressed, acid washed, or bleached). The amount of water consumed in the production of the various washes is an environmental concern, although new technologies, such as Jeanologia waterless wash, provide sustainable alternatives. Depending on your area of specialization, design a small denim collection for women, children, or men, working with four to six fabrics. Be sure to include finer garment details such as one or more rows of topstitching in self or contrast color (right).

▲ Jennifer Chun's denim collection features many functional garment details such as tabs, epaulets, and D-rings that afford adjustable fit.

▼ Tailored garment details can be used for informal apparel. Here, Eri Wakiyama's whimsical drawing style suits her presentation of casual separates; denim does not have to be blue.

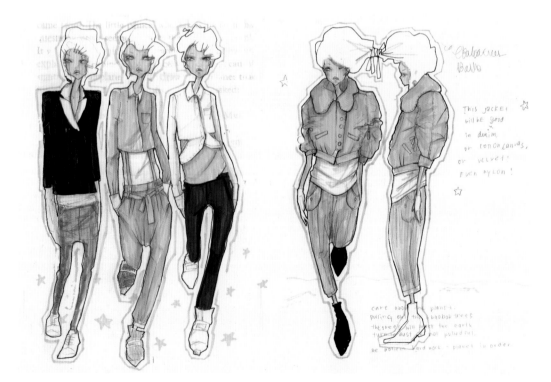

ASSIGNMENT 4

In Japan, one of the first measures taken to combat global warming was to turn down the air-conditioning in offices during the summer months. Dress codes were revised to accommodate higher indoor temperatures; workers were no longer required to wear suits and ties over the summer. For this assignment, design a collection of tailored clothing to be worn for business attire in warmer environments. Clothing that can be worn multiple ways and for multiple seasons is perceived to have added value. Can you think of any other way to make your designs more sustainable? For an added challenge, design your collection as an homage to a couturier known for innovative tailoring (below). Be sure to include pleats!

▼ *A collection of tailored clothing designed by Hyo Kyung Lee as an homage to Chanel.*

Communicating a fashion design concept on paper can be as much of a challenge as coming up with the idea in the first place. In addition to the visual component, there are also tactile considerations. The same **muslin**, or **toile**, interpreted in one fabric can look entirely different in another. While the nature of the line quality in your drawing will vary in order to communicate the weight, cut, and drape of the fabric, rendering will ultimately convey information about texture, color, and pattern.

Getting Started

Throughout this section you will find examples and demonstrations of a broad variety of rendering techniques. Media choices can include paint, colored pencil, marker, rubbing, collage, pressure-sensitive graphics, and combinations thereof. There is no one right way to use them. The selection of art supplies is predicated on what is actually being rendered. For instance, corduroy might be best rendered using a rubbing technique with colored pencil.

These unlimited options can raise just as many questions! Do you prefer digital techniques or hand rendering? Should you limit yourself to commercial art supplies? How tight or loose will your rendering be? Is overall coverage required or will a partial rendering do? Answers to these questions will depend on personal drawing style and the job description. The illustration of fashion can serve various purposes such as design development, production, or presentation, and each will have its own requirements.

◀ (Previous spread and left) Myrtle Quillamor emphasizes fabric behavior with a contoured mapping of textures and patterns in the presentation of her garment designs.

▲ If you are rendering a floral print that has the appearance of a watercolor, you might use transparent paint or marker to simulate the hand of the textile. Illustration by Anna Kiper.

While comprehensive rendering for finished presentations has a certain virtuosity (and can be gorgeous!), design concept sketches tend to have a more immediate indication of color, texture, and pattern—just enough to establish the balance of each in the collection. Partial renderings of pattern and texture are also used when full coverage would otherwise obscure garment details. For the most part, extensive rendering should be reserved for finished presentations. As you progress from roughs to edits to finished presentations, drawing and rendering should become increasingly more refined and provide more information about garments and fabrication. There is no point in repeatedly drawing and rendering designs with the same specificity. Each iteration should add to the one that came before.

Because of the quick turnaround required for **fast fashion**, designers often hand render a photocopy of the black-and-white line art, thereby preserving original flats and figures for future use. Pencil sketches can also be easily reproduced using a scanner and a printer; just be sure that the paper feed can accommodate larger sheets, such as 11 x 14in. or A3 (11.69 x 16.54in./297 x 420mm) and that the ink will not cause line work to smudge when marker or paint is applied. It is also important to note that design briefs have different criteria regarding "original art," and your work must conform to requirements. When using a mix of hand and digital techniques there may only be virtual art. Before you begin, determine whether hard copy is required for the project or if digital formats will do.

▼ *A partial rendering is appropriate for design development in a sketchbook. Design and illustration by Nina Donis.*

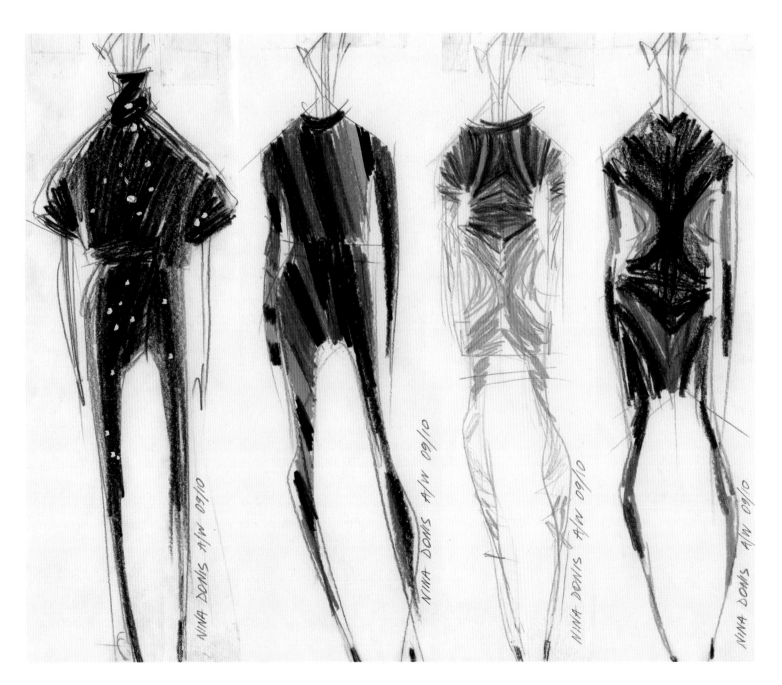

Albert Elia

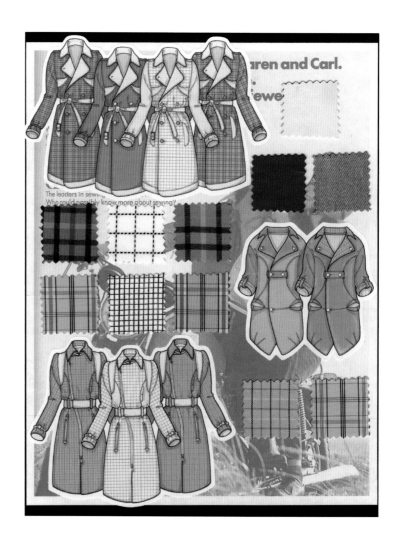

◀ Albert Elia's editorial illustration, first published in 1976, recalls the costume plates of Leon Bakst and the Art Deco preference for decorative flat rendering. At the time of publication, Elia's combining of handwork with graphic reproduction (photocopies) was both visionary and indebted to sixties' Pop Art.

▲ Because of the technical nature of outerwear, formal presentations are often done on flats. The same flats will also be used as line art without fabric rendering to provide construction details on **spec sheets**. Design and illustration by Makoto Takada.

▶ Here, an editorial illustration features very little information about garment details. Tanya Ling is more concerned with creating an impression and providing context for fashion.

Materials

Before you begin selecting papers, pencils, and paints, your first concern is the anticipated life cycle of the project. Will archival materials (such as acid-free paper and tape, stable pigments) be required in order to preserve the artwork over a longer period of time? "Economical" choices should be made with the knowledge that over time papers will begin to yellow and disintegrate. Inks and paints may also fade or change color. On the other hand, less expensive non-archival materials may work perfectly well for short-term projects.

Another consideration before you go shopping for art supplies is the size and scope of your project. The quality of your presentation will depend on the accuracy and consistency of color which can only be achieved with an adequate supply of papers, markers, and paints on hand. Always take the time to test new art supplies before buying anything in large quantity. Buy individual markers and tubes of paint (not sets) and paper by the sheet. Once you know what really works for the project, buy a bit more than you actually need so you will have backup. Running out of paper or paint or having a marker go dry when working to a tight deadline is a disaster you can easily avoid.

The most important aspect of working with color is choosing the right light source for your workstation. When mixing and matching colors, be sure to use a "color correct" combination of cool (fluorescent) and warm (incandescent) light. Luxo (Anglepoise) lights are a good investment and will facilitate accurate color matching.

So, in what order should you choose paint, pencil, or paper? It is best to first have a general idea about the paints or pencils you intend to use, since this will influence your paper choices. But do reserve color selection for after the paper is purchased, since the exact same color can look entirely different when applied to different types of paper.

▶ *Watersoluble colored pencils and crayons. Changing media choices is key to the exploration and evolution of personal drawing styles.*

◀ *Charcoal sticks in a variety of thicknesses. They are also available in pencil form.*

▼ *A selection of pens, including markers, ballpoints, and fineliners.*

▼ *A selection of pastels.*

Paper

Before you buy paper, you should think ahead to the size of the portfolio you intend to use to present your finished work. This can be especially vexing for those who study abroad, as European and American paper sizes have different aspect ratios. International students often return home with work that does not fit into portfolios available in their country. And since a portfolio is a work in progress, consideration should be given to where work will be done, ongoing, so as to accommodate available paper sizes. For instance, if you are a student from the U.S. studying in the E.U., you could purchase A3 size paper—11.69 x 16.54in. (297 x 420mm)—and then trim the paper down to 11 x 14in. (279 x 356mm), a standard size for paper and portfolio inserts in the U.S. If you intend to feature your work in a digital presentation, make sure that your artwork is of a size that can be scanned in a single pass on a flatbed scanner.

▼ *Hae Won (Anna) Lee uses a combination of wet and dry media to render her artful fabric mix.*

▶◢ *Here, Alfredo Cabrera applies a variety of marker colors for flesh tones, with multiple values (shades and tints) for each. Shadows are positioned consistently with regard for an overhead light source. A color photocopy is incorporated as collage for the "itsy" floral on the girl third from the left.*

Once you have determined the size for your work, choices about paper surface come next. The finish and weight of the paper must be compatible with the paints, pencils, or markers chosen to work with. For instance, a rough surface that allows color and glue to adhere to the paper might interfere with fine line work. Therefore, media and paper choices will to some extent depend on which fabrics are being rendered. Wet media, such as paints, inks, and dyes, require heavier-weight paper. Paper with a cold press (rough) finish, such as Bristol board, works best for transparent watercolor, whereas a hot press (smooth) finish works for opaque gouache. Both sides of the Bristol have a workable surface. Other terms used to describe the finish of the paper include **plate** (smooth) and **vellum** (a slight tooth). All-purpose paper is another alternative that can be used with both wet and dry media. Heavier-weight papers that are more durable can withstand repeated erasures and the layering of paints, colored pencil, and pressure-sensitive graphics. Because of the opacity of heavier papers, you must either draw directly on the page or use a preliminary underdrawing viewed with a light box. Using an underdrawing will keep your finished art free of preliminary pencil marks and the end result much cleaner. Saral transfer paper is another option that can be used to transfer roughs onto opaque paper.

Because of their tendency to bleed, water- or alcohol-based markers require stock created specifically for that purpose. Bleedproof marker paper is available in a variety of weights. Semitransparent layout paper, such as Bienfang Graphics 360 Marker Paper, offers many advantages. Marker can be applied to both the front and back of the page for interesting effects. Because the front and back will take color differently, you must take care that the same side used is consistent throughout multipage presentations. This lighter-weight paper will also allow you to capture textured surfaces using rubbing techniques (see p. 346). But this type of layout paper is also quite fragile and projects requiring extensive rendering can look shop-worn before they are even completed. Paris Bleedproof Paper is a more durable alternative for working with markers. Although similar in weight and finish to plate (smooth) Bristol, this paper is specially designed to take marker.

Tinted paper can be used to dramatize white garments. Canson Mi-teintes comes in multicolor packs of dual-surface sheets—rough on one side for pastel, smooth on the other for detail work with pencil or ink. Painted and printed papers, such as Coloraid and Pantone® brands, can be used in much the same way with opaque pencils, gel pens, pastels, and paints.

Translucent vellum, a high-quality, heavyweight tracing paper, is another alternative with workable surfaces on both the front and back of the page (see p. 398). This semitransparent paper is especially effective for rendering patterns with small light-colored motifs superimposed on a dark ground. Working with marker you can put the darker ground color on the back. Then after turning the page over, light-colored pencil can be added to illustrate motifs. Try scribbling charcoal or pastel on a piece of scrap paper (this will serve as sort of a palette). Then smudge the scribble with a paper stump and apply to your drawing for shadows. You can also work with a single-edge razor blade to scratch away areas of color to simulate fabric structure (such as twill weaves).

Clear acetate, one more transparent option, can be used alone or layered over other papers and media. You can draw directly on "treated" acetate with brush or pen and ink.

Finally there are textured papers (embossed snakeskin, mesh, corrugated board, and so on) on which rubbing techniques and collage can be used.

Dry Media

Commercial art supplies typically used for "dry" fashion rendering include Stabilo or Prismacolor pencils, NuPastels, pastel pencils, PanPastels, and Caran d'Ache Neocolor I (wax) and II (water-soluble) crayons. There are also Chartpak and Letraset brand pressure-sensitive graphics (solid and patterned adhesive-backed film, transfer lettering, and tape). Whenever possible, stick to a single brand so that the various materials will be color matched. Cray-Pas oil crayons can be used both dry or wet when combined with mineral spirits (white sprit). Paper-wrapped China markers (grease, or Chinagraph, pencils) come in a variety of colors and will write on practically any surface. Charcoal pencils also come paper-wrapped—take care not to drop them as the charcoal inside is easily shattered. Keep in mind that art supplies that smudge easily may require the application of aerosol fixative. Fixatives come in different finishes and the workable varieties allow for the continued reworking of a piece. When using any aerosol, be sure your workspace is well ventilated and free of open flame.

Wet Media

Although markers are the industry standard, paint allows for the greatest control of color; you can mix an infinite number of colors and more accurately match paint to a fabric. Choices largely revolve around a personal preference for opaque versus transparent color. Transparent watercolors are available in tube or cake form. Brands such as Winsor & Newton, Pelikan, and Grumbacher have a variety of color series ranging in costs. Some of the higher-end series can be quite expensive, so take care when choosing colors. Dr. Ph. Martin's or Luma transparent dyes are concentrated liquid watercolors that come in dropper bottles. These colors are particularly brilliant and a little bit goes a very long way when mixed with water. Opaque watercolor, known as gouache, also comes in individual tubes with differently priced color series. The tubes of transparent and opaque watercolors look quite similar to one another (as well as to oil and acrylic paints), so make sure you choose the appropriate product. Recommended colors for your initial purchase include the primaries (red, yellow, and blue), black, and Van Dyke brown. As your budget allows, other useful colors include the secondary hues (violet, orange, and green). Also buy opaque bleedproof white. It is not necessary to buy the highest priced paints, but do avoid amateur craft sets.

As for brushes, quality and price are variable with synthetic hair, such as white "erminet," at the bottom tier and natural hair, such as sable, at the top. Get yourself a

▼ *Myrtle Quillamor uses soft pencil laid over wash for a tactile fabric rendering.*

good mix of sizes and shapes (round and flat) according to what your budget will allow. An initial purchase can include two moderately priced round brushes; #1 or #2 for smaller areas and #6, #7, or #8 for greater coverage. Brushes should be treated as an investment, so do take care of them. Never leave brushes soaking in water for any period of time. Also, when transporting brushes, protect them in a brush holder (sushi mats tied with a ribbon work really well for this).

Markers, which are more commonly used in the fashion industry, come in alcohol-, oil-, and water-based varieties. You do not have as much control over color mixing with markers as you do with paint. "Storebought" color may only come close to matching your fabric swatch. However, some marker colors are keyed to the Pantone Matching System® and are faster and more convenient to apply than paint. Brands of professional-quality alcohol-based markers include Prismacolor, Letraset, Sharpie, and Chartpak AD. Most are double- or triple-tipped with chisel, brush, and extra-fine points. Copic brand markers (a favorite with manga artists) have the advantage of being refillable. Copic ink can also be used straight from the bottle, applied with a cotton swab (cotton bud), or cotton ball for greater coverage. Colorless blenders can be used for gradient effects and to smooth out the graininess of colored pencil. Many of the marker brands can be used in conjunction with cans of compressed air for special airbrush effects.

Oil-based opaque pigment markers, developed for craftmaking uses such as scrapbooking and the decoration of three-dimensional objects, work with a valve action (meaning that you have to shake them up). Brands such as Marvy DecoColor, Sakura Permapaque, and Sharpie are waterproof and can be applied to just about any surface. Because of their opacity these oil-based pens can also be used to layer light colors over dark.

Alcohol- and oil-based markers give off strong fumes and so it is very important to work in a well-ventilated space. You may instead prefer less toxic water-soluble brands, such as Tombow and Le Plume dual-tip brush pens, which can be dipped in water for interesting watercolor effects. "Gel" pens, which are also water-based, come in white, "milky" pastels, and metallics. Since the gel pens are also semi-opaque, they can be used to layer light colors over dark.

You will find that the key to successful rendering with markers is to work with several values (shades and tints) of the same hue (color), so buy as many as you can afford. For your initial purchase, avoid buying sets until you determine which varieties and brands best suit your needs. Pick out only the specific colors required for the project. Also buy a

range of colors that will work for flesh tones and hair colors; do not limit your choices to colors specifically named for skin tones. Also buy at least three values (percentages) for cool and warm grays. Blenders are invaluable but be forewarned that mixing brands can yield unpredictable results. Always test markers on the paper you intend to use as colors will look very different on various types of paper. If possible, look at your color choices in color-correct light before you buy them.

And finally, some brief advice about adhesives. Double-sided tape, which comes with or without a wax liner in a variety of widths, is perhaps the most reliable and least toxic choice. Dry mount adhesive sheets are great for the

▼ *Andrew Yang's experimental media mix includes a combination of charcoal, pen and ink, collage, and stencil/ airbrush effects.*

presentation of fabric swatches and collage. If you apply the adhesive sheet first and then cut the fabric, the swatch will not fray*. Temporary glue sticks allow for repositioning and so are handy for preliminary layouts. However, a more permanent adhesive is required for finished presentations. Rubber cement (Copydex) comes in two varieties—single and two coat (the latter requires application of the adhesive to both surfaces). You can clean up the excess with a rubber cement pickup. Both the liquid and fumes are flammable and toxic, so take care when storing and working with rubber cement. Aerosol adhesives such as 3M Spray Mount should be used in a well-ventilated area. Spray adhesives can irritate the eyes and skin; moreover, inhalation of the fumes can be harmful. Residue from overspray can damage surfaces, so take the time to protect the work area in advance with newspaper.

▼ *Hannah Hae In Lee skillfully applies transparent watercolor for her finished presentations.*

▲ *Temporary glue sticks are fine for searching out layout, but a more permanent adhesive is required for final presentations. Here, a spontaneous collage is created by Meiling Chen during a timed fashion model drawing.*

*NOTE Pinking shears or scissors should be reserved exclusively for cutting fabric. Paper-cutting implements recommended include X-Acto (craft) knives and single-edge razor blades.

▲ *Sungeun Kim uses a combination of manual drawing and digital rendering to present her winter sportswear collection for tweens. Pencil sketches were scanned and exported to Illustrator for a live trace; fabrics were scanned, scaled, and used as a pattern fill.*

NOTE   FIBER VERSUS FABRIC: A fiber is the raw, hairlike material that is spun into thread and yarn. Natural fibers, such as wool, cotton, silk, and linen, are derived from animal and vegetable sources. Synthetic fibers, such as nylon, polyester, and spandex (Lycra®), are derived from chemical sources. Fabric is formed by manipulating the fiber threads via knitting, weaving, knotting, felting, and so on. When describing a textile, the name of the fiber usually precedes the name of the fabric (wool challis, cotton twill, etc.).

About Computer Rendering

Although it is important to first master hand rendering in order to fully understand the basic concepts of color, pattern, and drape, you may choose to export a hand drawing to Photoshop or Illustrator for completion. Computer rendering is seldom as simple as it seems. Achieving more sophisticated effects can be quite time consuming and will require intermediate or advanced skills. You must also be prepared for the times when you do not have access to a computer and so must render by hand. Preferences for the use of technology versus evidence of the hand also cycle in and out of fashion.

That said, when rendering complex patterns and textures, you might want to work on the computer. Check out online tutorials and the Help menu for Paste Into, Offset Filter, and Displacement Maps in Photoshop. You can also investigate pattern swatches and editing patterns as mesh objects in Illustrator. Make sure that your deadline allows for the steep learning curve involved in perfecting new computer skills. Working digitally will allow you to create a virtual mix of art supplies that would otherwise be incompatible in reality. For instance, applying a watercolor wash over a charcoal pencil sketch would probably result in a muddy mess. Instead, working with a light box, slip your charcoal drawing under a separate sheet of watercolor paper and apply the wash. Then scan both the sketch and the color wash and incorporate the two as separate layers in a Photoshop file with the topmost layer mode set to Multiply.

With or without inclusion of digital techniques, the possibilities for rendering are limitless!

Developing a Swatch Library

Before attempting a rendering, be sure to have sizable swatches of the fabrics you will be working with. Fabrics come in different weights and are categorized according to use; top weights for jackets and coats are heavier, bottom weights for pants and skirts are lighter, while suitings work for both top and bottom garments. A swatch library comprised of different weights, fiber contents, surface structures, and patterns is a vital resource for designers and illustrators.

Your access to good suppliers for fabric will vary according to location. Many fabric stores have specific swatching hours and policies, so call ahead. Online resources are especially good for hard-to-find vintage and eco-friendly fabrics. Technical fabrics used for performance apparel (e.g., for snowboarding and skiing) can be particularly hard to find, as these textiles are often proprietary— developed by or licensed to apparel manufacturers for exclusive use. Online resource lists provided by fiber companies such as Invista and Ingeo are a good place to start your research. The Earth Pledge Future Fashion textile library (see p. 210) is an invaluable online resource for sustainable fashion.

As you begin to collect swatches, it is a good idea to establish some kind of a system for organization. You can mount swatches with staples or double-sided tape onto index cards and store the cards in a metal container designed for that purpose. The multi-pocketed plastic inserts used by photographers to sort slides are also user-friendly for fabric swatches and can be archived in a common three-ring binder. Record information such as fiber content (e.g. wool, rayon), fabric description (e.g. **gabardine**, **organza**), source, and price on adhesive labels affixed directly to the back of each swatch. It is also helpful to collect tear sheets of high-fashion images that demonstrate innovative use of a particular fabric. You should never avoid designing with a specific fabric because you think it will be too difficult to render!

Working with Color

Working with color is an integral part of fashion design. Because the name given to a color affects the viewer's perception of it, the descriptive language used to communicate and achieve accurate color must be quite precise. Much of the terminology used for fashion is derived from scientific theory, and so that is a good place to begin exploring color as a function of fashion.

Scientific Color Theory

There are many different systems for organizing color. RYB deals with pigment, such as paint; CMYK is named for the cyan, magenta, yellow, and (key) black inks used to achieve colors in printing; RGB deals with color as light. Subtractive color systems, such as RYB and CMYK, deal with color achieved by mixing pigments and dyes. Additive color systems, such as RGB, deal with color as light (as the colors appear on computer monitors).

Although color theory dates back to the fifth century BC, the most significant system for organizing color is credited to Sir Isaac Newton. In 1672, Newton discovered that when white light passes through transparent mediums of different densities (e.g., from air to a glass prism) the light is broken down into different wavelengths. As a result, a spectrum of color is produced. Perception of the different colors is determined by the size of the various wavelengths (red has the longest wavelength and violet has the shortest). The acronym ROYGBIV (red, orange, yellow, green, blue, indigo, and violet) is used to help remember the name of the spectral colors in descending order of wavelength. Newton then took the bar of colors created by the diffraction of white light and translated it into a segmented circle. This **color wheel** was subsequently expanded to include 12 hues, categorized as groups of **primary**, **secondary**, and **tertiary colors**. Properties such as **hue**, **value**, and **intensity** are used to describe color. Specific combinations, such as **monochromatic**, **complementary**, **split complementary**, **triadic**, and **analogous color schemes**, are thought to be harmonious.

Categories of Color

Primary colors (consisting of red, yellow, and blue) are pure and do not have to be mixed; these are the source of all the other colors.
Secondary colors (consisting of orange, green, and violet) are the product of mixing two primary colors.
Tertiary colors (consisting of red-orange, yellow-orange, yellow-green, blue-green, blue-violet, and red-violet) are the product of mixing a primary and a secondary color. When naming these colors, the primary color always comes first.

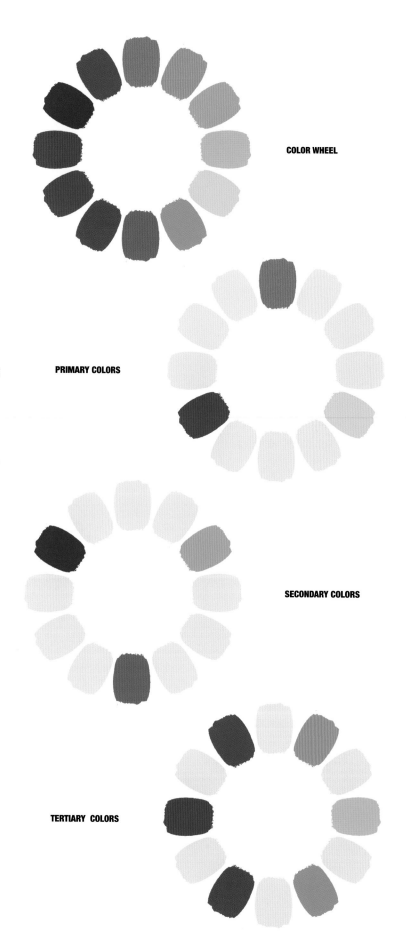

COLOR WHEEL

PRIMARY COLORS

SECONDARY COLORS

TERTIARY COLORS

Properties of Color

Hue is the name of a color. There are three different categories of color: primary, secondary, and tertiary.

Value is the lightness or darkness of a color. Lighter colors (hue + white = tint) are higher in value; darker colors (hue + black = shade) are lower in value.

Intensity is the saturation of a color. When mixing paint, the intensity of a hue can be diminished by adding the complement of the color. "Neutrals" have a low level of intensity.

Color Schemes

Monochromatic: a combination of colors comprised of tints and shades of a single hue.

Analogous: a combination of colors that are adjacent to one another on the color wheel.

Complementary: a combination of colors that are opposite one another on the color wheel (including tints and shades of the two colors).

Split Complementary: a combination of the color, and the two colors adjacent to the complement.

Triadic: a combination of colors that are equidistant from one another on the color wheel (e.g., every fourth color).

The perception of a color will depend on its relationship to the other colors in a composition. For instance, the intensity of a color will appear to be amplified when the hue is placed next to its complement. This is why team sports use complementary color schemes for uniforms viewed from afar in stadiums and arenas (the Los Angeles Lakers' team colors are violet and yellow, The New York Knicks' team colors are blue and orange, and so on).

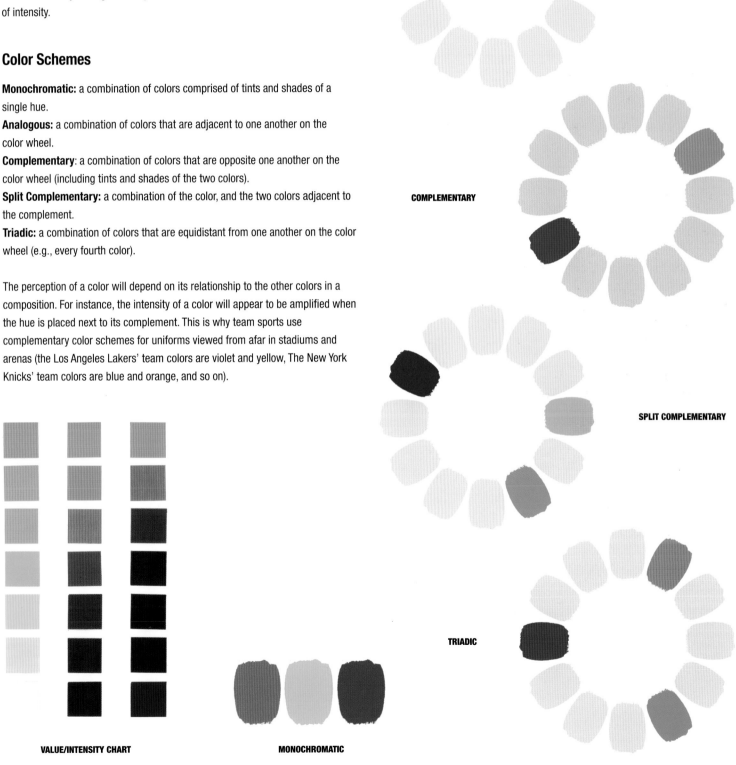

ANALOGOUS

COMPLEMENTARY

SPLIT COMPLEMENTARY

TRIADIC

VALUE/INTENSITY CHART

MONOCHROMATIC

The Symbolic and Psychological Meaning of Color

The symbolic and psychological meaning of color varies according to custom in different parts of the world. For instance, in the western hemisphere white symbolizes purity and is therefore worn by brides at wedding ceremonies. In China, white is thought to be the color of mourning and is worn for funerals. Red, which is associated with risqué behavior (and even scandal) in the West, is preferred for bridal costumes in India.

Colors are described according to temperature, perceived as either cool (colors such as blue, violet, and green) or warm (colors such as red, yellow, and orange). Color also affects the appearance of an object. Warm colors will cause an object to appear closer (and as a consequence, larger) to the viewer. Cool colors will cause an object to recede. Cool colors are thought to be calming in nature whereas warm colors are thought to agitate and excite. For example, red tablecloths are used in restaurants to encourage faster customer turnover.

▶ *A color palette for a design collection can be derived from an exquisite image, such as this photograph of the* Rosa rubiginosa *variety by Edvard Koinberg.*

▼◢ *The Raw Color research project explores extracting color from natural resources. Lab dips (below right) are used to achieve subtle variations in color.*

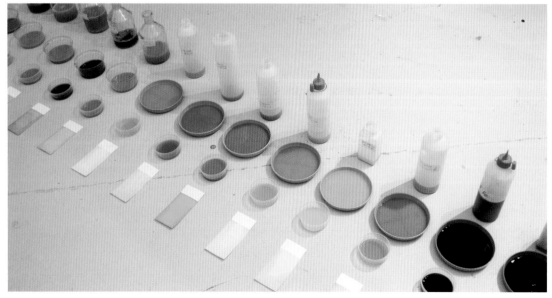

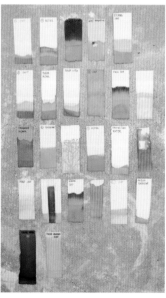

Color as a Function of Fashion

When making decisions about color for fashion, a designer must consider customer profile, geography, season, market, and price point. While there are no hard and fast rules, lighter colors tend to be more popular in warmer climates and seasons. For instance, in New York the first delivery for a Fall collection arrives in stores prior to the arrival of cold weather. Therefore, Fall I collections usually feature fabrics that are relatively light in weight (such as tropical worsted wool) in darker fall colors to accommodate transitional weather. Color for infants and children is gender-specific (pink for girls and blue for boys) and children tend to wear brighter colors than adults. Consideration must also be given to the event or activity where the clothing will be worn. For instance, a classic male customer who would otherwise wear subtle colors for business might wear brightly colored clothing on the golf course. Designers also work with different colors for top and bottom garments (some colors are not flattering to the face; advancing colors are less suitable for bottom garments and so on). A solid garment will typically be offered in more than one color. These **colorways** should merchandise well with other coordinating pieces and not fight each other for sales.

Fashion color forecasting is a very specialized field. Services such as Trend Union assess social and cultural undercurrents to determine seasonal colors well in advance of other aspects of garment manufacture. Pantone also produces color forecasts 18 months in advance of the selling season for women's, men's, and childrenswear.

These color cards contain swatches of dyed cotton from the PANTONE® Fashion + Home Color System, which provides a standardized method of matching colors in the industry. Since choosing yarn color precedes the manufacture of cloth, which in turn precedes the design of garments, color forecasters are truly working at the forefront of fashion. Once a designer chooses a color palette for the season, they are often required to oversee/approve **lab dips** where a swatch of fabric is dyed to match a specific color. Full spectrum color correct lighting (a combination of warm and cool lights) and a comprehensive color vocabulary are essential to this process.

CHAPTER 9
RENDERING SHINE

When you think about shine, the first thing that probably comes to mind is special occasion dressing and eveningwear—looks with lots of "bling" for red carpet moments. But lustrous fabrics are in fact used for a much wider variety of apparel categories (**silk dupioni** for tailored suiting, vinyl for outerwear, metallic yarn for knitwear, and so on).

In order to skillfully render any fabric, the visual properties of the cloth (texture, weight, and flexibility) must first be evaluated for their effect on garment drape and silhouette. For instance, more flexible fabrics such as silk **charmeuse**, **panne velvet**, and **lamé** jersey form softer silhouettes, while stiffer fabrics, such as taffeta and vinyl, form more structural silhouettes. There are also shiny fabrics with embossed patterns such as croqué satin (a puffed novelty similar to **seersucker**) and python leather. A brocade, which is a **jacquard** woven from matte and shiny threads, is another example of combining pattern and shine. Embellishments such as sequins, **paillettes**, and beads also add luster to garments.

Because shiny fabrics clearly demonstrate the fundamental principles of shadow and light, they are a good starting point for learning how to render. Moving from light-absorbing to increasingly reflective surfaces, the exercises that follow demonstrate rendering techniques for a variety of lustrous fabrics. You will discover the pattern of shadows and highlights formed by each and the colors and values required to convey the different surfaces.

But before you begin, it is important to first investigate the physical nature of shine.

◀ *Jun Hyung Park incorporates fabrics and embellishments with high shine to lend a futuristic twist to his collection.*

▶ *Swarovski supports young designers through wide sponsorship of special projects utilizing crystals for embellishment. Here, an entry by Hannah Hae In Lee for a competition at Parson's School of Fashion, New York.*

The Physical Nature of Shine

Luster is produced when a fabric or embellishment reflects light. The degree to which the surface either absorbs or reflects light will determine the amount of shine. Fabrics with a "soft" shine, such as velvet, absorb light and have highlights, midtones, and shadows that are close in value. Fabrics with a "hard" shine, such as patent leather, reflect light and therefore have highlights, midtones, and shadows with values set much farther apart. You can wrap a fabric swatch around your finger to get a sense of whether light is absorbed or reflected.

For a better understanding of how shadows and highlights are produced, it is helpful to think about the effect of a directional light source on the basic geometric forms (see opposite). On a cylinder, for instance, the highlight runs from top to bottom in a single thin line. On a sphere, the highlight forms a small circle nearest to the source of light. On a cone, the highlight runs from top to bottom in a single thin diagonal line. The darkest shadows are located at a slight recess from the outer edge of all the forms. When rendering, leave a small margin of white space near the edge of a form to suggest dimension.

▶ *Depending on the purpose of the sketch, the rendering of shine can be comprehensive or an abbreviated indication of fabric. Here, Eri Wakiyama makes an impressionistic rendering of panne velvet.*

▼ *Desislava Zhivkova's garment designs are embellished with oversized paillettes. Her presentation incorporates digital manipulation of a hand-rendered collage.*

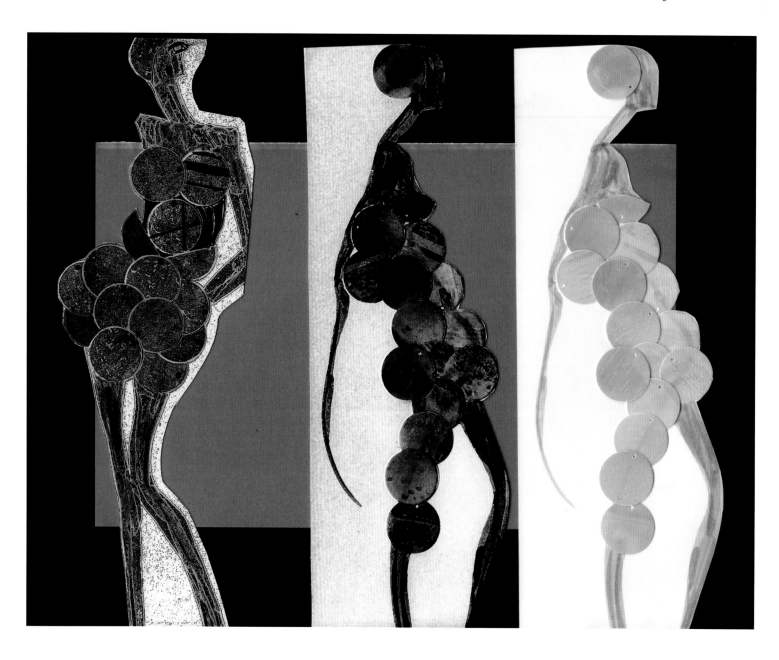

this velvet is very nice. →

Sometimes see through, sometimes i can't see through you.

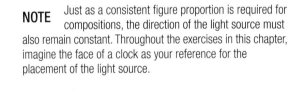

NOTE Just as a consistent figure proportion is required for compositions, the direction of the light source must also remain constant. Throughout the exercises in this chapter, imagine the face of a clock as your reference for the placement of the light source.

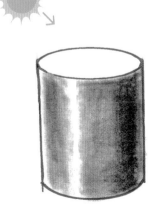

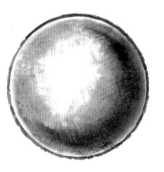

▲ Vinyl raincoats can be categorized as a "hard" shine.

SHADOWS AND HIGHLIGHTS FOR THE BASIC GEOMETRIC FORMS

Drapery and Shine

When you are rendering an illustration and do not have a firsthand experience of the garment, you must conjure up memories of real life observations so that you can describe the garment's structural form with shadows and light. The close observation of a variety of draped fabrics will therefore be useful for future reference. Buy half a yard (about half a meter) each of inexpensive fabrics with varying light-reflecting qualities, flexibilities, and textures (such as velvet, charmeuse, taffeta, and **pleather**). As your budget allows, purchase the fabrics in both light and dark colorways, as each will present a special challenge for rendering.

Rendering Draped Satin

Required Materials:

- Bleedproof marker paper
- HB or #2 pencil
- Markers in 20%, 30%, and 50% gray*

---

*NOTE   Approximate values, as different marker brands will vary. Grays come in cool, warm, and neutral ranges; when choosing your markers, stick with a consistent color cast.

For this next exercise you will do a black-and-white study of a light-colored satin fabric draped in two-point suspension. Satin has a "soft" shine that can be rendered using three values. The dark value is found at the edges and recesses of soft folds. The highlight value is found at the peaks of the folds closest to the light. Pin the fabric to the wall or a dress form with a single light source positioned at 10 o'clock. Observe the abstract shapes formed by the pattern of shadows and highlights.

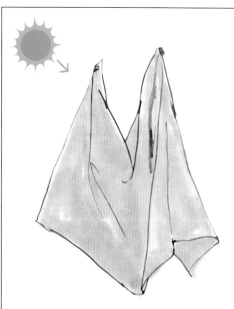

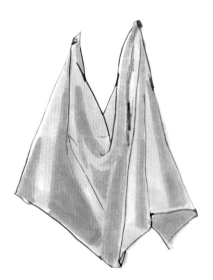

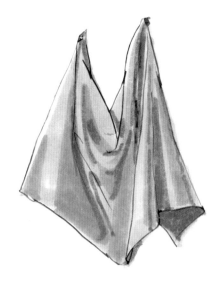

1 Sketch the draped satin in pencil, then apply the highest value (lightest) gray marker to your sketch, leaving a small margin of white at the outer edges of the folds.

2 Allow adequate drying time for the first layer of marker and then block in the middle value.

3 Allow adequate drying time for the second layer of marker and then complete the study by blocking in the shadows using the lowest value (darkest) gray marker.

Rendering Draped Taffeta

Required Materials:

- Bleedproof marker paper
- HB or #2 pencil
- Markers in 50% and 70% gray
- Marker blender
- 90% cool gray colored pencil

Next, you will repeat the previous exercise using a slightly less flexible fabric. Pin a dark-colored taffeta draped in two-point suspension to the wall or a dress form. Make sure the light source is coming from a single direction and forms dramatic highlights and shadows (at 10 o'clock). Notice the angularity of the folds, shadows, and highlights as compared to the curvy lines of the softer satin.

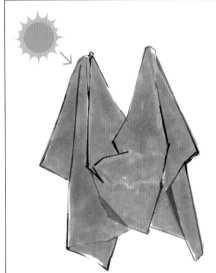   

1 Do a pencil sketch of the draped taffeta. Apply the highest value (lightest) gray marker to your sketch, leaving a small margin of white at the outer edges of the folds.

2 Allow adequate drying time for the first layer of marker and then block in the middle value.

3 Allow adequate drying time for the second layer of marker and then block in the shadows with a 90% cool gray colored pencil.

4 Working with the marker blender, blend the colored pencil for a more continuous tone.

COLOR INTERPRETATION OF DRAPED SATIN   **COLOR INTERPRETATION OF DRAPED TAFFETA**

Rendering Garments with Shine

Your observations of the drapery will help you to predict patterns of highlights and shadows when rendering garments. Not only is the draped figure a more complex form, but you must also search out how the shape of the body finds expression on the surface of the garment. Protruding forms, such as the bust and hips, are closest to the light and are therefore areas where you would expect highlights to form. Highlights are also more likely to occur wherever the garment comes into close contact with the body. In a walking pose, for instance, highlights would form in the forward thrust of the limbs. Shadows fall in the recesses of the folds and in the areas farthest from the light source. By analyzing the figure in this way, you can begin to predict a pattern of highlights and shadows.

As discussed in Chapter 6, the heavier the cloth, the greater the effect of gravity on garment details and silhouette. For instance satin, a flexible fabric with a soft shine, comes in a variety of weights from light crepe to the heaviest duchesse satin. Also keep in mind that a dress made from any type of cloth will look quite different if cut on the bias as compared to the straight grain. The appearance of various garment details, such as gathers and flares, will depend on the weight, flexibility, and light-reflecting properties of the fabric.

ASSIGNMENT 2

Look at fashion photos to determine the shapes of highlights and shadows for both "hard" and "soft" shine (right). Keep in mind that the direction of the lighting varies from one photo to the next. Make a diagram of the shapes of the shadows and highlights (the end result should resemble a paint-by-numbers canvas).

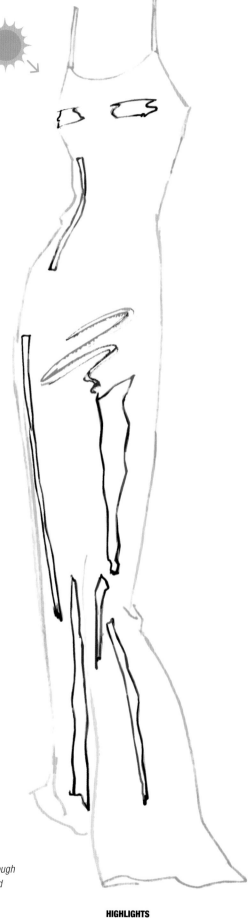

▶ *The planes of the body are expressed through the garment—here, highlights, midtones, and shadows as they would fall on a floor-length satin dress on a turned high hip figure.*   **HIGHLIGHTS**

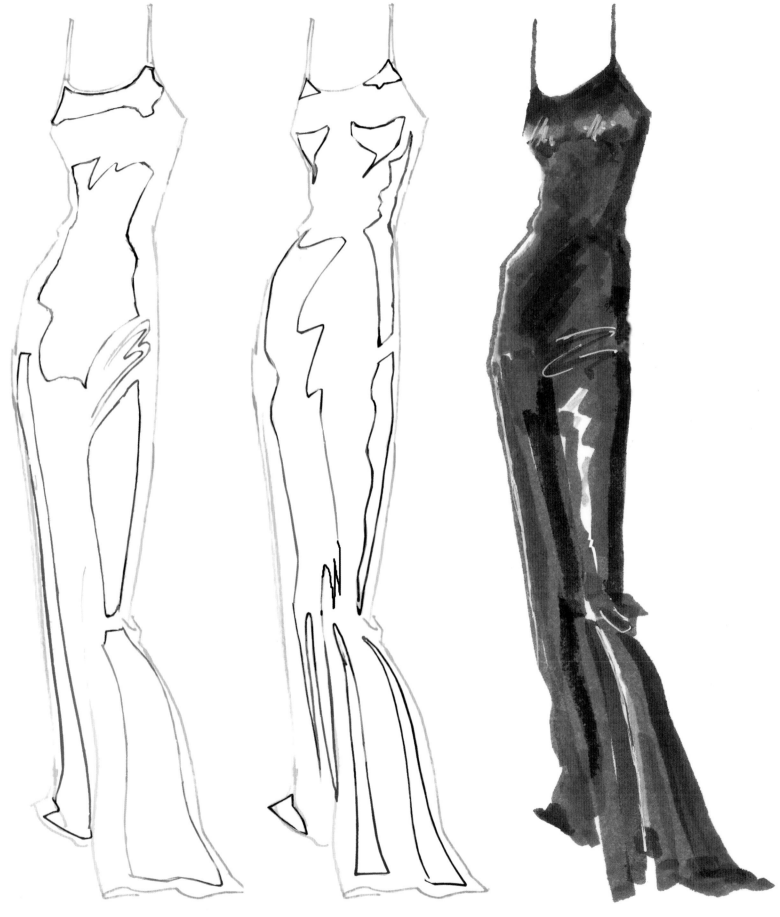

MIDTONES   **SHADOWS**   **FINISH**

Rendering Black and White Fabrics

Required Materials:

- Bleedproof marker paper
- HB or #2 pencil
- Black broad or brush tip marker
- White and 90% cool gray colored pencils
- White gel pen

Rendering all-black and all-white garments presents special challenges. Illustrations of white garments can look unfinished without the description of light and shadows. However, if the shadows are handled too heavily the garment will not look white. The values for black clothing must also be handled carefully. Without gutsy darks, the garments can look gray instead of black. But a heavy-handed application of black can obscure garment detail. For this next exercise, you will render the exact same garment in a "soft" black velvet and then again in a "harder" white taffeta with a **moiré** pattern.

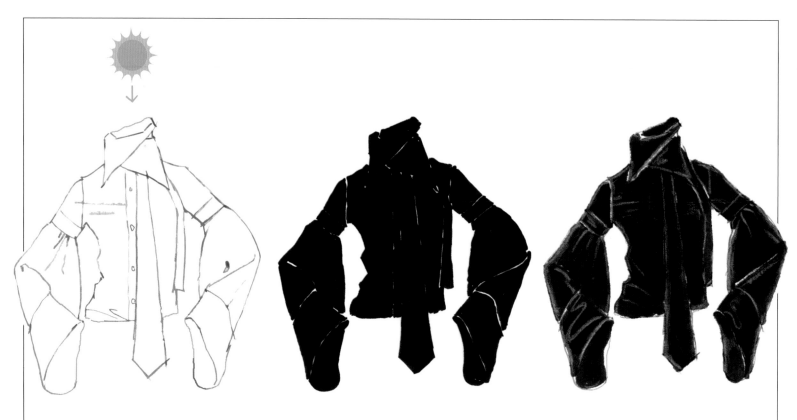

1 Sketch a float of a button-down shirt. The line quality of the silhouette and drapery should convey the softness of the pile fabric. Place the light source directly overhead at 12 o'clock.

2 Working with a black marker, fill in the individual shapes within the overall silhouette one at a time. Leave a wide margin of white at each edge to avoid bleeding.

3 Because of the depth of the pile, velvet absorbs light at the center and has a very soft shine. The number of shadows and highlights are limited and fairly close in value. Use a white colored pencil to indicate soft highlights at the edges of the indivdual shapes and the overall silhouette.

Next you will render the same garment in white taffeta moiré.

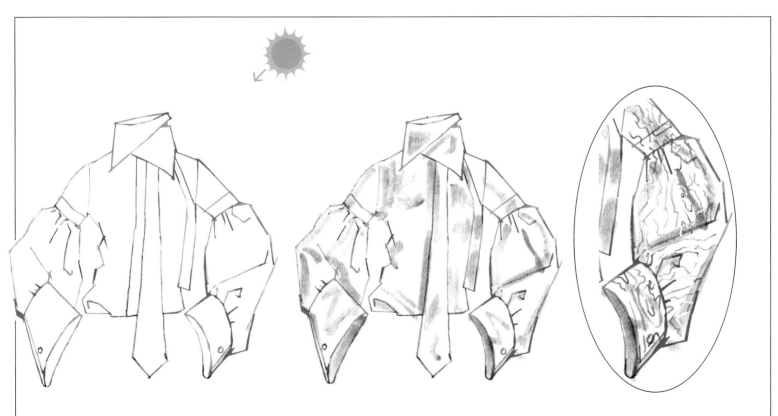

1 Because the properties of taffeta are so different from velvet, it will be necessary to redraw the shirt using a more angular line quality for the silhouette, folds, and crush lines. Place the light source at 2 o'clock.

2 Indicate the shadows using a light gray marker.

3 Add a moiré pattern (similar to wood grain) using a partial rendering. Indicate the texture with a white gel pen in the areas of shadow and, conversely, with gray pencil in the areas of highlight.

Rendering Velvet

Required Materials:

- Bleedproof marker paper
- HB or #2 pencil
- Markers in two values of brown and pale blue
- Indigo colored pencil

For this next exercise you will work with a high/low mix of fabrics by combining a dressy velvet blazer with utilitarian distressed denim jeans. This time you will render the highlights of the velvet with a marker in a higher value of the base color. Sketch a single-breasted blazer with shawl collar, shirt, and jeans on a men's figure in a walking pose. Position the light source at 1 o'clock and then render as follows:

1 Apply the base color of the jacket leaving a substantial white margin within the edges of the garment details and silhouette, and with consideration for the direction of the light. Allow for adequate drying time.

2 Using a higher value (lighter) marker, indicate the soft highlights in the margins. Allow the lighter marker to function as a blender; the intermingling of the two colors will create diffused highlights.

3 Apply a light blue marker to the shirt and jeans.

4 Using an indigo colored pencil, indicate the shadows and color variations on the jeans (the worn/distressed areas of the denim will be lighter in color). Place a textured surface underneath the marker paper so that the pencil strokes will capture the relief.

Rendering Lustrous Jersey

Required Materials:

- Bleedproof marker paper
- HB or #2 pencil
- Markers in red and 30% gray
- Semi-opaque white marker
- White gel pen

Jersey, a knitted fabric constructed of looped stitches, is often made from shiny silk or rayon yarns. Knits have lots of stretch and so jersey garments can be made to conform to the body with minimal fit darts and seaming. Draw and render as follows:

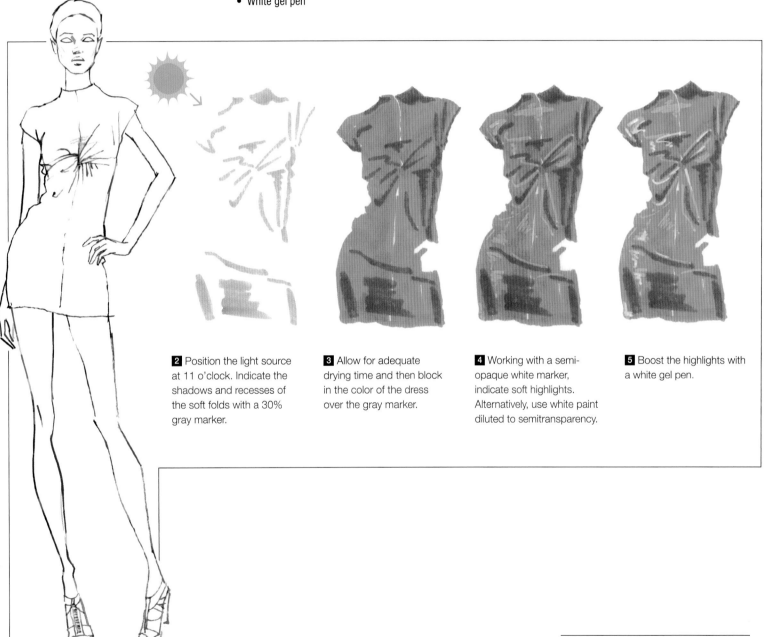

1 Sketch a simple jersey dress on a high hip figure.

2 Position the light source at 11 o'clock. Indicate the shadows and recesses of the soft folds with a 30% gray marker.

3 Allow for adequate drying time and then block in the color of the dress over the gray marker.

4 Working with a semi-opaque white marker, indicate soft highlights. Alternatively, use white paint diluted to semitransparency.

5 Boost the highlights with a white gel pen.

NOTE You may want to work with a photocopy of your sketch on marker paper so that you can experiment with different rendering techniques.

Rendering Gold Lamé

Required Materials:

- Bleedproof marker paper
- HB or #2 pencil
- Golden yellow marker and blender
- Sepia colored pencil

Lamé is a woven or knit fabric made of metallic yarns. Although there are plenty of metallic markers and pencils readily available, these pigments are difficult if not impossible to reproduce graphically (inkjet printers and photocopiers do not have metallic ink). Instead, render highly reflective surfaces with a dramatic shift in values for well-articulated shadows and highlights. Practice rendering lamé with your pencil drawing of the wrap skirt from Chapter 7 (see p. 256). Establish a light source at 11 o'clock.

1 Apply the yellow marker as the middle value of the skirt. The high luster of the fabric will create well-articulated highlights, to be left white.

2 Use the sepia colored pencil to indicate shadows in the recesses of the folds. Treat the individual flares as if they were cylinders.

3 Soften the colored pencil with the blender marker for a smoother, more continuous tone. You can achieve this same high luster for any metallic fabric by using values that are set far apart—either yellow cast for gold, gray cast for silver, orange cast for copper, and so on.

Rendering Iridescence

Shiny fabrics woven with different color warp and weft threads will have color shimmer in the areas of highlight. For this next exercise, you will render a dress with nipped-in waist and full skirt in iridescent taffeta. Pencil sketch a dress on bleedproof marker paper. Working with an **iridescent** fabric swatch, match two markers (a tint and a shade of the same color) for the middle and shadow values. White highlights will be achieved by omission. A third marker in another color will be used to convey a hint of iridescent shimmer. Position the light source at 11 o'clock.

1 Apply the middle value marker to the dress, working one shape at a time and leaving an appropriate margin of white to suggest highlights.

2 Allow for drying time and then apply the darker marker to the recesses and shadows.

3 Indicate the second yarn color as a shimmer by applying marker to the areas of highlight.

Rendering Patent Leather

Required Materials:

- Bleedproof marker paper
- HB pencil
- Markers in black and 50% gray

Patent leather is a hard shine with the most light-reflecting qualities. Highlights and shadows are well defined and angular. The values used to render hard shine are set very far apart. Shadows are black (the lowest possible value) and highlights are white (the highest possible value). The middle value is the color of the fabric. For this exercise, you will render patent leather boots. Sketch the boots in HB pencil on bleedproof marker paper. Place the light source at 9 o'clock and then:

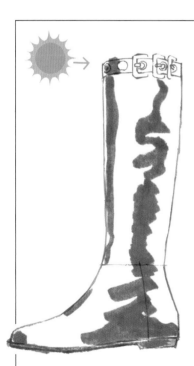 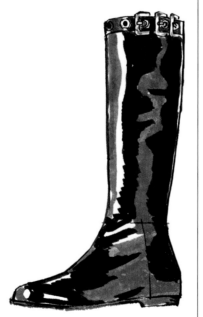

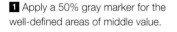 Apply a 50% gray marker for the well-defined areas of middle value.

2 Apply black marker to the areas of shadow, taking care to preserve well-defined areas of white for the highlights.

▲ *Pleather pants are another example of hard shine. The effect is achieved with well-articulated areas of highlights and shadows defined by dramatically different values for each.*

Combining Shine with Pattern and Texture

Among the many variations of light-reflecting fabrics are those which also incorporate texture and pattern. For example, there is silk dupioni, which has a **slub**, and brocade, a jacquard pattern woven with matte and shiny threads. As previously mentioned, a partial rendering is usually best for indicating texture. It is a simple matter of using a darker value to indicate texture in the highlight areas and, conversely, using a lighter value to indicate texture in the shadow areas. To finish off the rendering, the values are reversed for randomly scattered lights and darks.

Rendering Silk Dupioni

Required Materials:

- 2- or 3-ply Bristol with vellum finish, or watercolor paper
- HB or #2 pencil
- Gouache
- Brushes

Next, you will render a silk dupioni suit using opaque watercolor—gouache—working from light to dark, layering the three values. In order to avoid a thick buildup of paint the base layer of color should have a thinner consistency than subsequent layers. The light source will be positioned directly overhead at 12 o'clock.

1 Mix up paint to match the three values of a silk dupioni fabric swatch. Quickly and evenly apply the highest (lightest) value to the entire suit.

2 Allow for adequate drying time and then paint in the middle value.

3 Add shadows after allowing adequate drying time for the middle value.

4 Indicate slubs with a partial rendering using the middle value in the areas of highlight and the highlight value in the areas of shadow.

Rendering Sequins

Required Materials:

- Bleedproof marker paper
- HB or #2 pencil
- Markers in 30% and 60% gray
- Semi-opaque white pen
- White gel pen

For this exercise you will render a gray matte jersey dress embellished with silver sequins. Again, it is best to simplify with a partial rendering of the sequins. Sketch a jersey dress with a boat neck and long sleeves on a women's figure in a walking pose. Position a light source at 2 o'clock and render as follows:

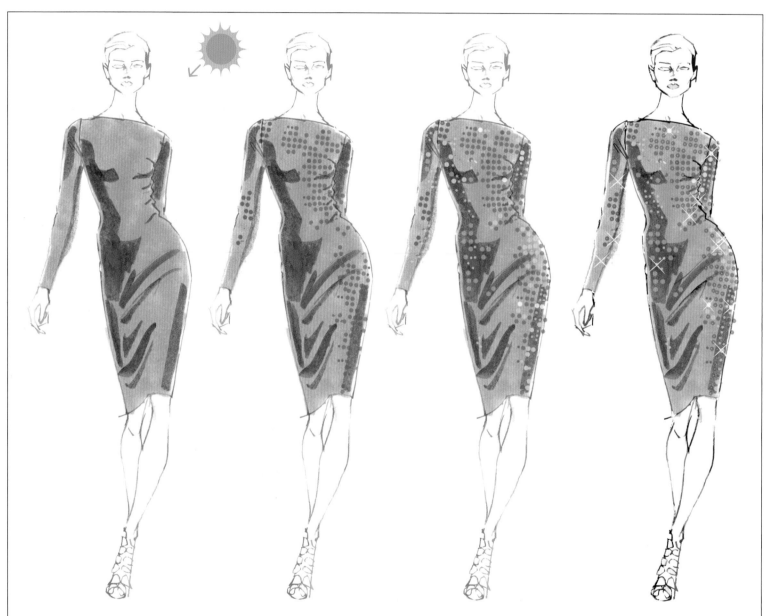

1 Apply marker for shadows and middle value. Because the jersey has a matte surface there will be no highlights. Allow adequate drying time between applications of marker.

2 Use the 60% gray marker to indicate the sequins as small dots sparsely distributed in the areas of middle value. Some of the dots should go slightly outside the holding line to create dimension. Distribute a few stray dots in the areas of shadow.

3 Use the white semi-opaque pen to indicate additional sequins in the shadow areas. Because of the transparency of the pen, the dots will appear to be light gray. Place a few stray dots in the areas of middle value.

4 Using the white gel pen, place a small white dot in the center of the sequins and then add an "X" pen stroke for random sparkle.

◀ *You can reduce the size of the dots to gradually diminish the distribution of the sequins.*

Rendering Studs

Next you will render square studs, an embellishment standard for motorcycle jackets and other heavy-metal goth accessories. Begin by drawing five small squares and render as follows:

Required Materials:

- Bleedproof marker paper
- HB or #2 pencil
- Markers in 20%, 30%, and 40% gray
- Fine tip black marker

1 Block in the background color around the rectangular shapes of the studs.

2 Working with the fine tip black marker draw a frame and an "X" in the middle of each stud.

3 Fill in a middle value gray as indicated.

4 Fill in shadow value with a fine tip black marker.

5 Complete by drawing a frame within the frame using the fine tip black marker.

ASSIGNMENT 3

Working with a combination of fabrics with soft and hard shine, design a small collection of short cocktail or party dresses (right) inspired by a designer who worked either in the ultra-feminine fifties (such as Charles James, Jacques Fath, or Cristóbal Balenciaga) or androgynous sixties (André Courrèges, Paco Rabanne, or Mary Quant).

▶ *This collection of dresses by Paul Negron features a pattern of colorful shiny embellishments specifically engineered to each of the garments. (For more about engineered placement of patterns see p. 364.)*

▶ *Embossed papers can be used to create collage, but you must be careful that the scale of pattern is not too big. Illustration by Pierre-Louis Mascia.*

ASSIGNMENT 4

Design a sportswear, outerwear, or accessories collection using a mix of lustrous patterned and/or embellished fabrics. Utilize an appropriate mix of media choices to produce the best possible finished presentation (right).

Rendering Embossed Leather and Vinyl

Both real and faux leathers are often embossed to simulate the hide of a rare or endangered animal. The same approach used to render other lustrous textures can be applied to a marker rendering of an embossed python pattern. For this excercise, the light source will be positioned directly overhead at 12 o'clock. Working with a sketch of a fashionable shoe on bleedproof marker paper:

1 Apply three values of gray marker for highlight, midtone, and shadow.

2 Working with a 90% cool gray colored pencil indicate the pattern in the areas of highlight.

3 Working with a white colored pencil, indicate the pattern in the areas of shadow.

4 To complete the drawing, use a white gel pen to dot in random highlights in the centers of the scales to suggest relief.

SPECIALIZATION: Accessories

The design of shoes, handbags, belts, gloves, and eyewear is a specialized practice with different markets in each of the product categories. There are sport-specific shoes and accessories, children's accessories, bridal accessories, and so on. Accessories enhance and reinforce design statements and can be the greatest source of revenue for luxury brands. The aspirational shopper, for whom the price of designer clothing is normally out of reach, will often invest in a luxury brand accessory. Worn daily, such investment pieces are thought to elevate the wearer's overall appearance. Because handbags in particular do not have to conform to the shape of the body, both consumers and designers are more likely to view them purely as art objects.

The manufacture of accessories requires specialized materials such as leathers, reptile skins, plastics, and high-tech textiles. The same drawing and rendering skills required for garment design will have application for accessories. As you move through the various stages of the design process, drawings will become increasingly focused—moving from vague conceptual roughs to refined sketches. Exploded views are used to provide information about custom hardware, trim, and construction details. There are also specialized CAD applications used to create presentations and specification sheets.

When illustrating a group of accessories, be sure to use a relative proportion and some semblance of perspective for the various pieces. Position an accessory with a degree of rotation that best displays important design features. For instance, although shoes are typically drawn in outermost profile, distinctive features (such as Christian Louboutin's signature red soles) will require multiple angles and exploded views.

▼ *The design of accessories is inextricably linked to that of the garments they are paired with. Jonathan Kyle Farmer utilizes an unconventional combination of materials (eyelets, lace, and wood) for his innovative footwear designs.*

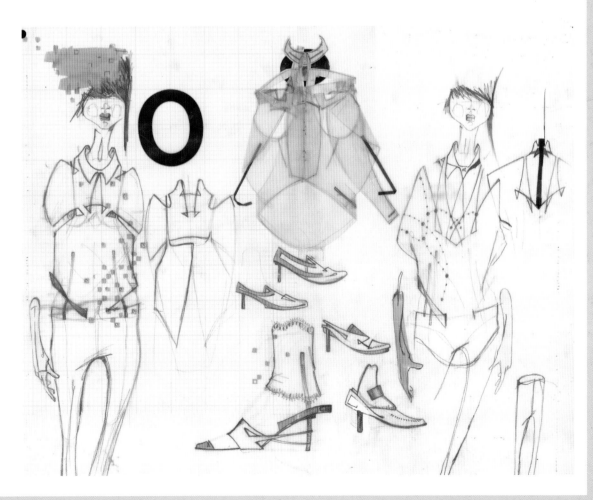

▼ *Accessories designer Frank Nathan draws inspiration from the sea.*

▼ Here, everyday objects, such as paper clips, are the inspiration for an accessory collection by Frank Nathan.

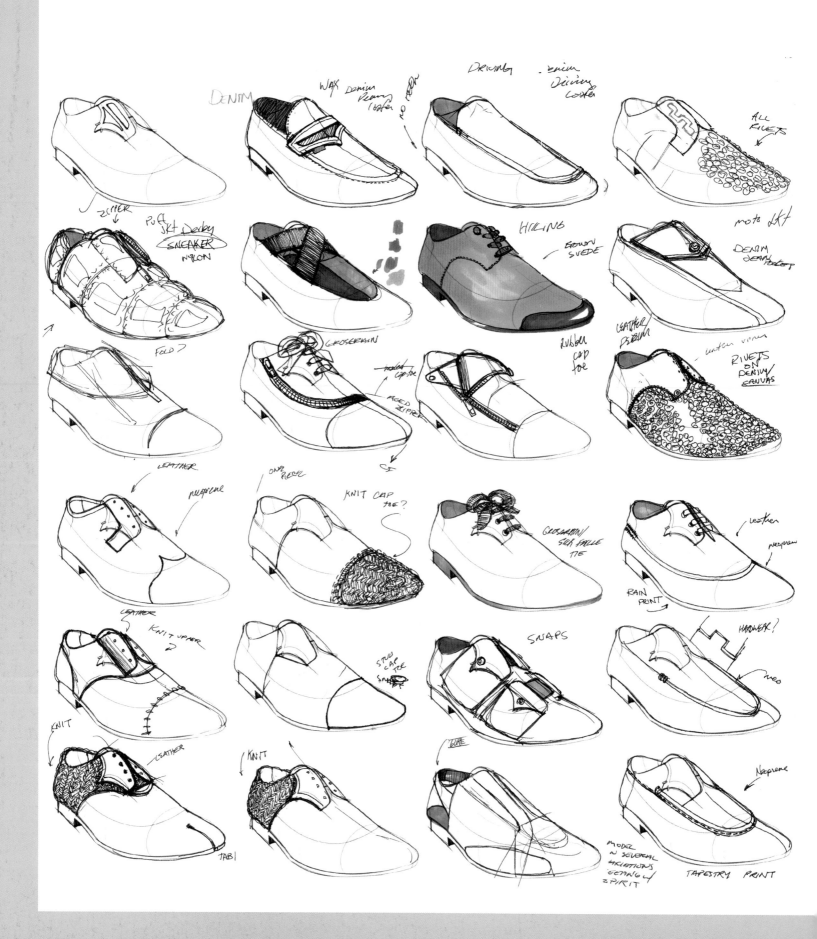

◀▲▶ *The degree of detail in accessory sketches will vary depending on the stage of design development. Here, preliminary rough sketches are by Benyam Assefa.*

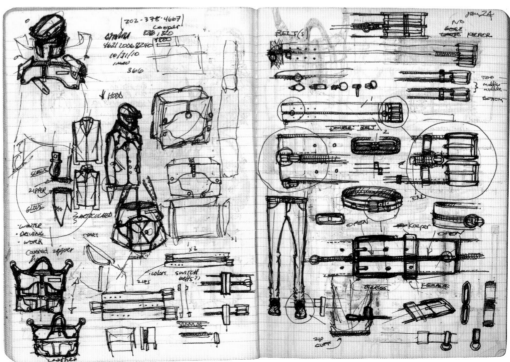

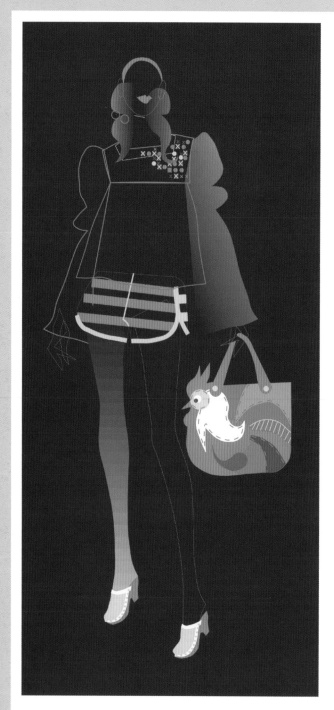

ASSIGNMENT 5

Referring to one of your previous fashion design collections, use the same inspiration to design a small group of coordinating accessories (left). The hats, handbags, belts, and so on should be consistent with the established design philosophy, season, and customer profile. What construction details might be carried over from the garment design? Will these accessories be used for everyday wear, a special occasion, or travel? How durable do the accessories need to be? Think about incorporating decorative custom hardware to convey a branding strategy across the different product categories.

▲ *Ferdinand uses a selective focus to establish a visual hierarchy in his illustrations; here, accessories are prioritized.*

▶◥ *Benyam Assefa uses specialized CAD applications for the presentation of his footwear designs.*

Illustrated Glossary of Fabrics with Shine

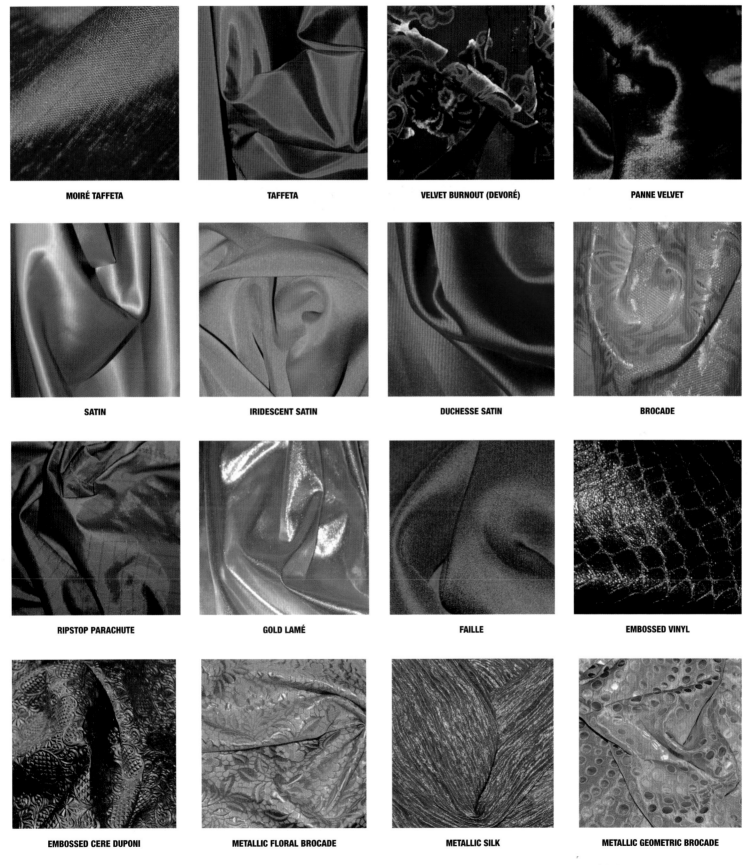

MOIRÉ TAFFETA

TAFFETA

VELVET BURNOUT (DEVORÉ)

PANNE VELVET

SATIN

IRIDESCENT SATIN

DUCHESSE SATIN

BROCADE

RIPSTOP PARACHUTE

GOLD LAMÉ

FAILLE

EMBOSSED VINYL

EMBOSSED CERE DUPONI

METALLIC FLORAL BROCADE

METALLIC SILK

METALLIC GEOMETRIC BROCADE

CHAPTER 10
RENDERING WOVEN WOOLS

This chapter focuses on the rendering of woven fabrics—cloth formed by the interlacing of vertical (**warp**) and horizontal (**weft**) yarns. There are many different ways to interlace the yarns, each resulting in a different weave pattern (including plain, rib, twill, satin, and dobby). Pile weave patterns have loops of yarn on the surface; the loops can be cut or left as is. The resulting raised threads are referred to as the **nap** of the fabric. Woven fabrics come in a variety of weights that are categorized by intended use: top weights for jackets and coats; bottom weights for pants and skirts; and suitings, which work for both top and bottom garments.

Rendering Woven Wool Solids

Rendering wool solids, which may seem easy in theory, in fact requires a high level of skill for the smooth application of color to a very large area. Consideration must also be given to fabric weight, weave, and surface (lightweight, smooth gabardine vs. heavier, hairy mohair, for instance). The line quality in your drawing must be chosen carefully to accurately define the outside edges of the garment. You can get a sense of what this would be like by folding your swatch and examining the folded edge.

◄ *Jannelle Russ uses expressive brushstrokes and the elimination of outline to convey wooly texture.*

◄ *Tiffany Ju's incorporation of machine stitching into her illustration emphasizes and reinforces her deconstructed design concept.*

Rendering Woven Wool Solids on Flats

Required Materials:

- Bleedproof marker paper
- HB or #2 pencil
- Markers to match colors of fabrics, plus markers in 20%, 40%, and 60% gray, and a colorless blender
- Colored pencils and fine tip markers in highlight and shadow values for base color
- Solid color fabric swatches for wool crepe, camel hair, **bouclé**, and mohair

Flat sketch four versions of the same jacket with a relative line quality that expresses the four different fabric swatches. Then render as follows:

Wool crepe

Begin by establishing a direction for the light source and plot soft shadows using a gray marker. Because wool tends to be a light-absorbing surface, there will be no hard defined highlights.

Quickly fill in the overall color of the garment with a marker color matched to your swatch. Choose a marker with a fairly broad nib or brush tip for faster coverage. Keep in mind that transparent marker colors can look very different when layered with another color. When working with new "juicy" markers, limit your rendering to just inside the edge of the outline to allow for bleeding.

Camel hair

Follow the same steps as for wool crepe and then, working with a brown colored pencil, indicate the fabric texture avoiding the edges to suggest dimension; finish off the rendering by smoothing out the colored pencil using the colorless blender.

Bouclé

Follow the same steps as for wool crepe and then, using a fine tip marker in a lower value, indicate the loopy wool fibers; using a colored pencil in a higher value indicate the highlights for the loop structure.

Mohair

Follow the same steps as for wool crepe, then using a brush marker in a lower value of the base color, indicate the hairy fibers with downward strokes; use colored pencil for additional values, maintaining a single direction for all strokes.

▲ *To render wool solids on the flat, start with a sketch that uses a line quality specific to the fabric weight and texture. Here, the same jacket silhouette is interpreted (from left to right) in wool crepe, camel hair, bouclé, and mohair.*

Cool gray 40% marker

Raspberry marker

WOOL CREPE

Green gray marker

Brown pencil and slump

Clay marker

CAMEL HAIR

Cool gray 40% marker

Parrot green marker

Blue green marker

Blue green pencil

BOUCLÉ

Indian red pencil

Dark brown pencil

Dark brown brush marker

MOHAIR

Rendering Woven Wool Solids on the Figure

Required Materials:

- Bleedproof marker paper
- HB or #2 pencil
- Markers in 20%, 40%, and 60% gray
- 90% cool gray colored pencil
- White gel pen

To render wool solids on the figure, start with a pencil sketch that uses a variety of line qualities to convey the different surfaces in your drawing. For instance, the line quality used for defining the face and legs should be different from the line used to describe the garment silhouette. Sketch a tweed sports coat and flannel trousers and render as follows:

1 Establish a direction for the light source (here it is at 2 o'clock) and plot soft shadows using the 20% gray marker.

2 Working on a second sheet of translucent marker paper laid over the drawing, fill in with a darker value of the jacket color. The color will bleed through the paper to the drawing underneath, creating a textured effect. Dispose of the overlay.

3 Fill in the overall color of the garment by quickly and evenly applying marker. The jacket will be in a lower (darker) value gray.

4 Indicate the texture of the tweed with the 90% gray colored pencil and white gel pen.

ASSIGNMENT 1

Working with at least three different solid wool fabrics (such as bouclé, felt, and gabardine) design a small collection (approximately three looks) of coordinated tailored separates. The collection may be conceived as an "homage" to a particular design house (right) (Balenciaga, Dior, Chanel, etc.). Think about a specific occupation and how it might dictate apparel choices for your target customer. When rendering your finishes, consider fabric weight, cut (bias or straight), and texture and their combined effect on the overall silhouette.

▲ Jinsol Kim uses fabrics and garment details associated with the House of Chanel in her mini-collection of tailored clothing.

◀ Paint, pencil, and scanned imagery are combined to special effect in a collection designed and illustrated by Kelly DeNooyer.

ASSIGNMENT 2

You might want to try your hand at rendering a design concept using collage (left). Dry mount adhesive sheets work very well for this. Remember that the design process does not necessarily end with garment construction; consider post-construction design elements such as whole-garment felting, overdying, pleating, etc., all of which present additional challenges for rendering.

Rendering Woven Wool Patterns

In order to render wool patterns properly, it is important to understand the difference between **yarn-dyed** and printed patterns. Unlike a print, where patterns are superimposed after the cloth is manufactured, yarn-dyed patterns are produced by interweaving different color warp and weft threads. When rendering patterns, wovens will be distinguished from prints by an indication of this structure. Because yarn-dyed patterns must conform to the weave of the textile, they tend to be more geometric in nature. Which is not to say that there are no printed stripes and checks. You can determine whether a patterned fabric is a print or a yarn-dyed woven by simply looking at the back of the swatch; prints will have the pattern only on one side, yarn dyes will have color on both front and back.

Fashion designers and illustrators seldom have the luxury of working with a generously sized swatch. Commitments for fabric purchases are usually made at a later stage of design development when merchandising considerations have been resolved and there is a better sense of the collection as a whole. At the beginning of the design process, fabric choices are speculative and, in all likelihood, you will be working with a very small swatch with only a partial **repeat** of the pattern (for more on repeats see p. 367). You must rely on your imagination (and stored observations) to construct the whole repeat and predict the drape of the pattern. To do so, it is helpful to have an understanding of the basic woven patterns (see p. 344).

Rendering patterns can seem complex at first, but if you take the time to analyze stripe color, order, and width, you will find it is not as difficult as you might think. The single most important thing to remember when rendering any pattern is that while your swatch is life size, your figures and flats are drawn at a much smaller scale. Scale is what differentiates apparel fabric from home furnishing textiles, which feature much larger stripes, plaids (tartans), and motifs suitable for upholstered furniture and window treatments. So when rendering a garment in a pattern meant for apparel, it is important to first hold the fabric swatch up to a person or dress form to see how many times a bar of color would repeat across and up and down the body.

This relationship should be carried over to your drawing. Some artists photocopy the fabric at a reduced scale (25 percent is a good rule of thumb) and use it for reference in order to maintain an accurate and consistent proportion for the pattern. Again, tracing is not advised! You can also create a rough guide directly on your drawing using a hard pencil (4H) line that will disappear behind subsequent color rendering. If you have a light box, graph paper slipped under your drawing can also be helpful for keeping motifs and the spaces between them consistent in size. Maintain a light, loose touch. The amount of visual information you include is also key to your success. All patterns are "reduced" or simplified for fashion rendering. Walk five big steps away from the pattern—whatever you cannot see at this distance should be eliminated from your rendering.

When working with plaid take care to respect the aspect ratio of shape formed by the intersection of the stripes. Do they form a square or a rectangle? Determine whether the rectangle is taller than it is wide or vice versa.

Just as for wool solids, a combination of media may be required for rendering a specific pattern or trim. Aspects such as transparency, order of layering, and drying time for wet media must also be considered. When building up layers of color, artists traditionally work from light to dark. The color of your fabric may, however, call for a different approach—for instance, if you were rendering a fabric with a white pinstripe on a dark-gray ground (see p. 346). Transparent media such as marker or watercolor would be used first to lay in the ground color. Opaque media, such as gouache, colored pencil, oil-based marker, or gel pen would then be applied on top for the lighter-colored stripe. Take care to accurately plan the placement of the stripes, working outward from the center of each on the collar, lapels, pockets, and body of the jacket.

◀ *A pattern is reduced to its simplest elements in Nina Donis' painterly rendering of a woven check.*

▼◥ *In this series of quick sketches by July Choi, an abbreviated rendering of the fabrics (see above right) is used to visualize the design development of coordinated separates.*

Fall I   Fall II

Dress   Blouse +   Dress   Cape   Dress   Coat   Tee   JK   Legging   JK Sweater
         Sk   Jumpsuit Pants   Pants   SK   Dress   Leggings

Rendering Simple Wool Patterns

Required Materials:

- Bleedproof marker paper
- 30% gray marker with dual tip
- Fine tip black marker

To begin rendering yarn-dyed woven patterns, you will start with the simplest two-color (meaning motif plus ground color) patterns: a basic check, houndstooth, herringbone, and Glen plaid. Take the time to analyze each pattern before rendering. Place a sheet of marker paper over the grid provided (below left) and follow the steps indicated for rendering a small test square of each of the patterns.

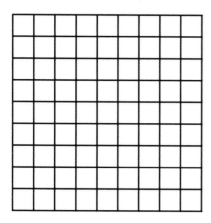

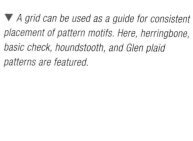

▼ A grid can be used as a guide for consistent placement of pattern motifs. Here, herringbone, basic check, houndstooth, and Glen plaid patterns are featured.

▲ When patterns are rendered on the figure, the size of the motif is reduced dramatically to correspond with the scale of the drawing. Design and illustration by Diana Lin.

◄ Before attempting to render patterns, take the time to form a plan for how the pattern will lay out on the different parts of the garment (such as collar, lapels, and pockets).

▲ Working on lightweight marker paper, apply dark gray marker to cover the entire garment. Then, with corrugated board placed underneath the drawing, apply white pencil with a light, rapid motion to capture the relief. Rotate the corrugated board incrementally so that the angle of the stripes is relative to the action of the body. This is especially important for high hip positions, where there is opposition between the upper and lower torso.

▼ High-relief surfaces such as corrugated board and embossed papers can be used for rubbing techniques.

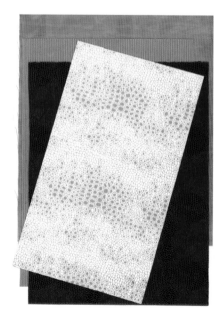

Illustrating Draped Wool Patterns

Required Materials:

- Bleedproof marker paper
- HB or #2 pencil
- 20% gray marker
- Fine tip markers in red and blue
- One yard (about a meter) each of muslin and plaid fabric

As previously mentioned, in all likelihood you will probably find yourself illustrating a plaid garment without the benefit of seeing a large swatch with a full repeat. Before you begin speculating about the effect of drapery on your plaid, it is important to investigate what you already know, based on preconceived notions and past observations.

1 Pin the muslin to the wall using two-point suspension (see p. 314). Position a light source to create well-defined shadows.

2 Do a still-life pencil sketch of the draped fabric, thoroughly exploring the shadows created in the recesses of the folds.

3 Then imagine that there is a single weft (horizontal) thread in a contrast color running across the cloth. Draw the path of this thread as it appears in your mind's eye, going across and over, in and out of the different peaks and valleys of the width of the draped fabric.

4 Then imagine a single warp (vertical) thread in a contrast color and follow its path up and down the fabric.

Now it is time for a reality check.

1 Pin the plaid fabric to the wall using the exact same two-point suspension.

2 Do a pencil sketch of the drapery. Then add a color rendering based on careful observation of the draped plaid.

Go back and look at your sketch of the solid fabric from the previous exercise. How accurate was your prediction? Observation and acquired knowledge of pattern drape will help you to create a believable fiction. And since this observation allows you to more accurately predict the effect of drape on pattern, the next challenge is a contoured rendering of plaid on a garment.

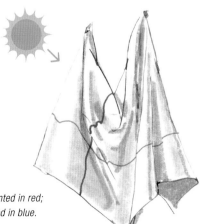

▶ A single weft thread is represented in red; a single warp thread is represented in blue.

▲ Daisy de Villeneuve's illustration of a Vivienne Westwood plaid suit features a loosely contoured mapping of the pattern.

Rendering Multicolor Tartan Plaids

A tartan plaid is really just a multicolor check. Color combinations are often said to be derived from specific Scottish clans and regiments. Perhaps owing to the fact that the wearing of plaid was once outlawed in Scotland, designers such as Vivienne Westwood and Alexander McQueen have incorporated plaid into more subversive punk looks. Experimental designers such as Rei Kawakubo and Junya Watanabe use plaids and checks to map the human form.

Rendering Iconic Plaid on Flats

Required Materials:

- Bleedproof marker paper
- HB or #2 pencil
- Markers in champagne, 10%, and 20% gray
- Fine tip markers in red and 40% gray

The iconic Burberry plaid is a good simple pattern for a first attempt at rendering plaid. Working with a flat sketch of a trench coat, establish the direction of the hypothetical light source and lay in shadows for the folds using the 10% or 20% gray marker. Then, follow these steps for rendering the plaid:

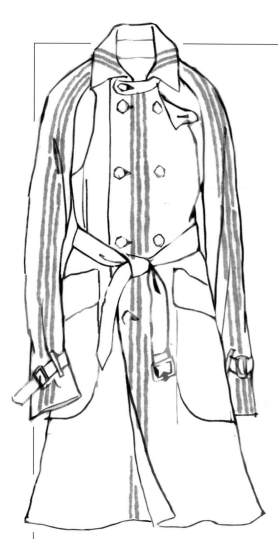  

1 Block in the vertical gray triple stripe using the 40% gray marker. Begin by plotting the first stripe on the Center Front of the garment. Similarly, plot a prominent vertical stripe on the center line of the sleeves. Distribute the remaining vertical gray stripes with respect for the repeat and in relation to the scale of your flat sketch.

2 Beginning at the hemline of coat, plot the horizontal gray stripes to be roughly perpendicular to the vertical stripes already established in your drawing. Then add stripes to the sleeves, aligning them with the stripes on the body of the coat. Fill in the negative spaces with a champagne-colored marker.

3 Next, using a fine tip marker, render the vertical and horizontal thin red stripes.

4 Use a second pass with your gray marker wherever the gray vertical and horizontal stripes intersect.

▲ *Burberry plaid rendered on the figure.*

Rendering a Dark Plaid on the Figure

Required Materials:

- Bleedproof marker paper
- HB or #2 pencil
- Green broad tip marker
- Markers in green, indigo, 20%, and 50% gray
- Fine tip black marker
- 90% cool gray colored pencil

Darker plaids such as Black Watch tartans require a layering of opaque color over transparent darks. For the next exercise, research or create a dark plaid at www.houseoftartan.co.uk. You can also work from fabric swatches in the illustrated glossary of fabric at the end of this chapter. The fabrication for the pants is corduroy, which is often paired with wool in Fall/Winter collections. Sketch a young man's figure, with evenly distributed body weight, wearing a jacket with a notched collar and lapels. Establish the direction of the light source and block in the shadows on the garments using a light gray marker. Then render as follows:

1 Block in the background color for your plaid using the broad tip green marker.

2 Allow adequate drying time and draw a prominent indigo vertical stripe on the Center Front of the garment. Then do the same for the center line of the sleeves. Distribute the remaining vertical stripes, working from the center out and with consideration for the repeat and any foreshortening created by rotation of the figure.

3 Position a prominent horizontal stripe at the hemline of the coat. Distribute the remaining horizontal stripes on the body, working from the bottom up and with consideration for the repeat and scale of your drawing. Then add stripes to the sleeves, aligning them with the stripes on the body of the coat.

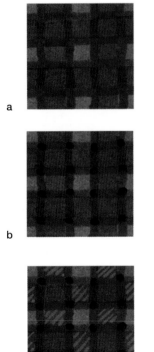

a

b

c

a

b

c

4 **a.** Add secondary vertical and horizontal stripes.
b. Take another pass with the marker wherever the secondary vertical and horizontal stripes intersect.
c. Working with an opaque medium (such as oil-based marker or gouache) in the same color as the ground, indicate the weave structure for the plaid.

5 Then render the corduroy pants:
a. Block in the base color of the pants with a 50% gray marker.
b. Indicate the corduroy whales with a 90% cool gray colored pencil, using continuous vertical strokes.
c. Take a second pass with the colored pencil in segments of the whales to indicate the pile surface of the corduroy.

BLACK WATCH TARTAN

Rendering a Light Plaid on the Figure

Required Materials:

- Bleedproof marker paper
- Tracing paper
- HB or #2 and 4H pencil
- Markers in deco pink, cocoa, olive drab, and 20% gray
- Pink colored pencil

For this exercise, you will observe how the movement of the body causes plaid to fall in different directions. You will have to adjust the angles of the horizontal and vertical stripes incrementally while preserving their perpendicular relationship. The effect of compression and expansion must also be considered, as well as foreshortening created by rotation of the body. Sketch a single-breasted blazer layered over pants on a turned high hip figure. Establish a direction for the light source and block in the shadows using the light gray marker.

Then create a loose guide for the plaid directly on your drawing by working with a hard pencil (4H). Alternatively, plan your plaid on tracing paper to be used as an underdrawing viewed with a light box. Begin with

the placement of a prominent horizontal stripe just above and parallel to the hemline for the pants. Next plot a horizontal stripe at the knee. Then plot a horizontal stripe at the high hip. Distribute the remaining horizontal stripes with consideration for the repeat as well as the scale of your drawing. Continue your plan by plotting a prominent vertical stripe on the Center Front and then down the center line of the two pant legs. Take care to preserve the perpendicular relationship between the horizontal and vertical stripes. Then distribute the remaining vertical stripes with consideration for the repeat and any foreshortening created by rotation of the figure. Now render the plaid pants as follows:

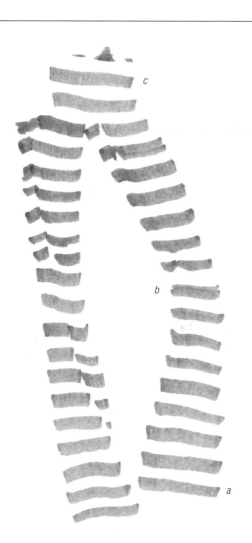

1 Render the prominent horizontal stripes with the olive marker, following the same order as for your plan (see a, b, and c).

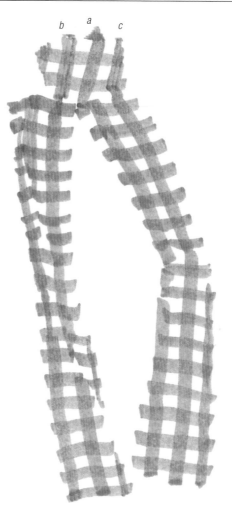

2 Allow for adequate drying time and then render the prominent vertical stripes with the same marker (see a, b, and c).

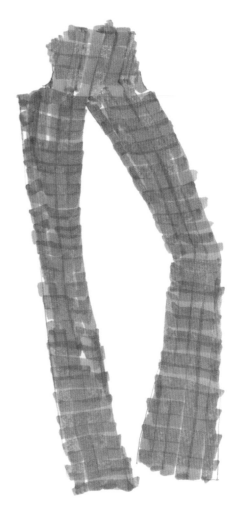

3 Fill in the ground color around the stripes with the cocoa marker.

▶ Note how the plaid has been scaled down for the illustration as compared to the swatch.

Pink marker

Cocoa marker

Bush marker

Pink colored pencil

4 After the marker dries, add the remaining stripes using the pink colored pencil.

▲ Render the jacket with deco pink marker. To add a light finishing touch, indicate weave structures and embellishments as a partial rendering with colored pencil.

Illustrating Brushed Patterns

Required Materials:

- Semitransparent bleedproof marker paper
- Graph paper
- HB or #2 pencil
- Brush marker in burnt umber
- Markers in clay, pink, deep orange, and 30% warm gray
- Opaque markers in cream yellow and blush pink
- Pink colored pencil

Sometimes, the only way to achieve an exact color match is with a strategic layering of art supplies. Knowledge of color theory is integral to finding the perfect mix. For instance, imagine you have a pink marker that is just a little too intense to match your fabric swatch. Working with semitransparent bleedproof marker paper, you could apply a tint of the complementary color (in this case, pale green) on the back of the paper to lower the intensity of the pink.

For this next exercise you will systematically build up layers of color in order to render a brushed-wool pattern from the fabric swatch provided. Pencil sketch a girl's figure wearing a double-breasted overcoat with princess seams, epaulets, and angled welt pockets. Then render as follows:

 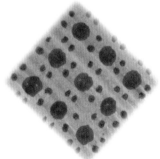 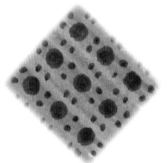 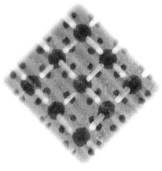

1 Place a sheet of graph paper, rotated at a 45-degree angle, underneath your drawing to be used as a guide to the placement of the dots. Render the pattern in burnt umber brush marker.

2 Apply clay marker to the back of the paper, filling in the ground color.

3 Turn the paper to the good side and apply pink marker in stripes as per the pattern.

4 Render the cream yellow pattern with opaque marker.

NOTE   If ready-made graph paper is not of the appropriate scale, you can always create a graph working with the Grid tool in Illustrator.

HERRINGBONE AND BRUSHED WOOL PATTERNS

Clay marker

Pink marker

Deep orange marker

Cream yellow opaque marker

Blush pink opaque marker

Burnt umber brush marker

Cream colored pencil

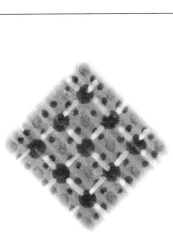

5 Dot in circles with deep orange marker.

6 Use opaque pink marker to dot in the pattern.

7 Apply a final layer of pink pencil to the entire garment to create a slight blur, suggesting a brushed surface. Render the herringbone pattern on the pants by layering burnt umber hatch marks over a 30% warm gray ground.

NOTE Color selections were made with consideration for the cumulative effect of the final overlay of pink pencil.

SPECIALIZATION: Outerwear

Outerwear for women, men, and children is a thriving segment of the fashion industry. Categories include fashion, casual, and performance outerwear. Fall/Winter is obviously the busiest season, although there is also a focus on rainwear for Spring. In the past, when more formal dress codes were in place, coats were designed in tandem with tailored suits. After World War II, when leisure time increased and lifestyles became more active, so too did apparel. Army surplus, which was originally the only alternative for snow sports, was quickly replaced with "technical" outerwear and gear designed for this and other sports. Ever since, there has been an enormous cross-pollination between fashion and performance outerwear. Formal overcoats designed to be paired with suits still have their place, but sportier coats that double for or borrow from active sports are more popular.

Design Considerations for Outerwear

First and foremost, outerwear is designed to keep the wearer warm and dry. Coats can be long, mid-length, or short. Since outerwear is worn daily, overcoats must coordinate with various garments that will be layered underneath (think about impact on color and silhouette). Outerwear must slip on and off easily, so closures should work efficiently; zippers and buttons must be placed where they can be easily reached (not below the knee or on the back of the garment, for example). There are many other design decisions to be made, such as choices for shell and lining fabrics, interlining, insulation, and fabric treatment (such as lamination to repel water).

Fashion outerwear design is often inspired by military apparel (the field jacket or trench coat), industrial apparel (coats worn by emergency medical service workers and firemen), and the culture at large (the Perfecto motorcycle jacket worn by Marlon Brando in the movie *The Wild Bunch*). Street style is also enormously influential.

In recent years, one of the most significant developments in performance outerwear has been the replacement of bulky, voluminous "hard shell" jackets with layering systems. As an alternative to overly warm, "Michelin Man" puffy looks, new breathable "soft shell" jackets are designed for multiple climate conditions and can be worn with a packable, lightweight waterproof shell for heavy rain. Silhouettes that are closer to the body resist abrasion and use stretch wovens to facilitate this closer fit and range of motion. "Smart" clothing incorporates technology right into the cloth (with heated polar fleece, fiber optics, GPS, and antimicrobial silver filament, for example). Features such as solar panels can be used to collect energy and power small electronic devices. Multiple fabrications in a single garment enhance functionality (such as water repellent fabric for the back yoke, stretch wovens for side panels, and wind resistant fabrics in front).

Despite strong cross-pollination between the performance and fashion markets, there are significant differences between the two. For casual outerwear, designers work from a fashion perspective and design decisions can be more arbitrary. The design of performance (also known as technical) outerwear, however, requires form to more closely follow function (will the jacket be worn for snowboarding, skiing, team sports, etc?). What works for fashion may not be suitable for performance wear. For example, deconstructivism and ad hoc seaming can be quite appealing design elements for fashion, but would not work for performance since every seam creates an opportunity for wind, cold, and rain to penetrate the outer surface. Draping features and projecting embellishments compromise aerodynamics and create hazard for active sports, and so minimizing seaming and stitching using new technologies such as lamination, microstitching, and welding with radio waves is important.

▼▲ *Silhouettes that are closer to the body can be layered under more voluminous coats with unisex appeal. Design and illustrations by Alfredo Cabrera.*

◀▶ *Garments with drapery and relief can be hazardous when worn for snow sports. Here, designer Angela Lee uses distinctive prints, which can be seen from afar, to more safely embellish clothing and gear. (For more about prints see Chapter 11.)*

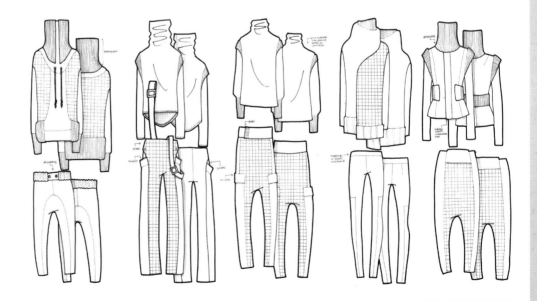

Special Challenges for Illustrating Outerwear

Both fashion and performance outerwear will be layered over other garments and it is the illustrator's job to convey volume. Take care to accurately illustrate seams that are strategically placed. As previously mentioned, there are often multiple fabrications used in a single garment and care should be given to distinguishing each in your rendering. Sketches for outerwear can be quite technical because of the many design and functional features. Figure drawings must be supported with very detailed flat sketches, specifiying shell fabric, interlining, insulation, and trim (such as cordlocks, zipper teeth, and tape).

For perfomance outerwear, athletic poses can be used to convey lifestyle and garment functionality. But be sure that your poses are not overly ambitious and that they do not obscure garment details. Background can be used to suggest lifestyle and narrative. In some cases, high-tech garments can be literally beyond belief. For instance, although a bulky coat may not be the optimum choice when compared to a high-tech, body-hugging silhouette, it may be perceived by consumers as providing the best protection from winter's cold. It is the illustrator's job to communicate to buyers the functionality of new features which in many cases may not even be visible.

ASSIGNMENT 3

Design a small collection of coordinated sportswear (this page and opposite). Finishes should be supported by front- and back-view flats that feature magnified views of important garment details. For your fabric story, you can use swatches or work from the illustrated glossary of wool fabrics on pp. 360-61. You can incorporate technical fabrics and features if your collection is to be aimed at the more active market. Depending on your computer skills, textures and patterns can be developed in Photoshop, Illustrator, or a proprietary CAD system such as U4ia.

▶▼ *Shannon Adam's performance apparel presentation includes in-depth information about fabric, trim, and garment details.*

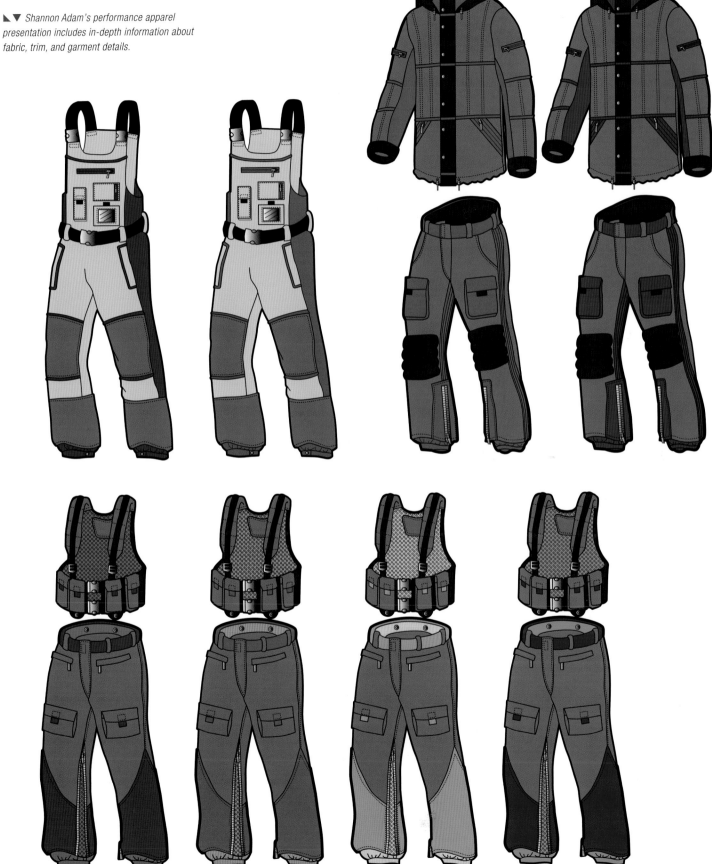

Illustrated Glossary of Wool Fabrics

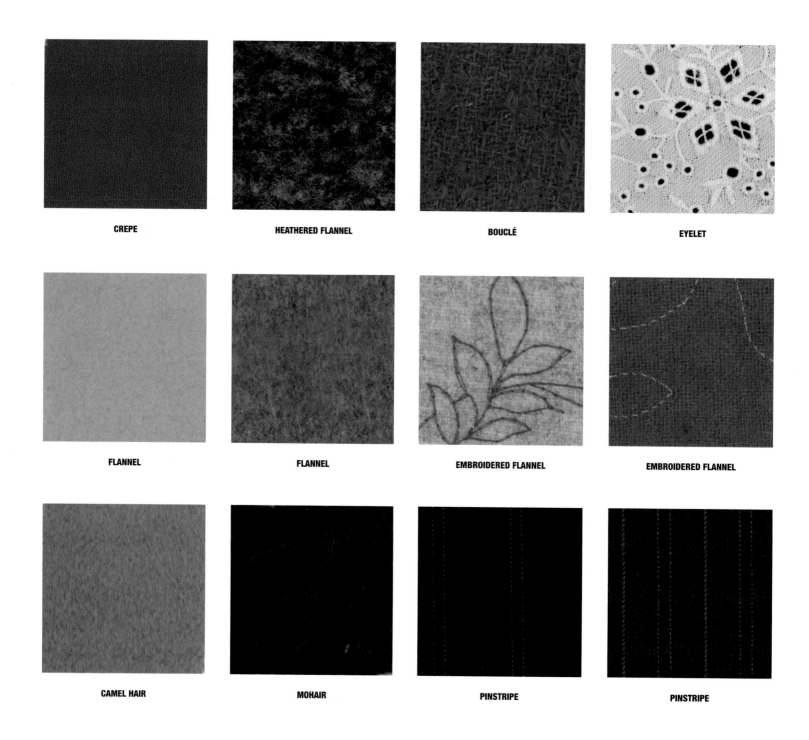

CREPE	**HEATHERED FLANNEL**	**BOUCLÉ**	**EYELET**
FLANNEL	**FLANNEL**	**EMBROIDERED FLANNEL**	**EMBROIDERED FLANNEL**
CAMEL HAIR	**MOHAIR**	**PINSTRIPE**	**PINSTRIPE**

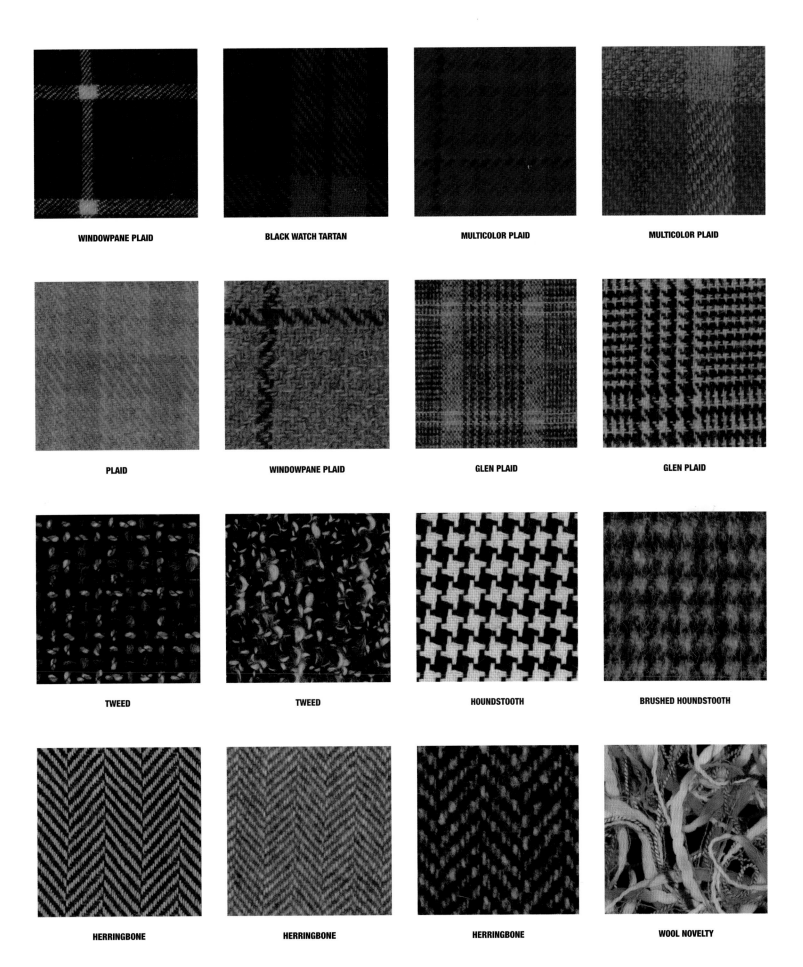

WINDOWPANE PLAID

BLACK WATCH TARTAN

MULTICOLOR PLAID

MULTICOLOR PLAID

PLAID

WINDOWPANE PLAID

GLEN PLAID

GLEN PLAID

TWEED

TWEED

HOUNDSTOOTH

BRUSHED HOUNDSTOOTH

HERRINGBONE

HERRINGBONE

HERRINGBONE

WOOL NOVELTY

Carmen Chen Wu.

CHAPTER 11
RENDERING PRINTS

While patterned cloth may be produced through a variety of techniques, (weaving, appliqué, embroidery, intarsia knitting, etc.) this chapter is concerned with the rendering of prints. You can distinguish between print and yarn-dyed patterns by checking the back of the fabric. If the pattern is featured on only one side, it is probably printed—although prints with highly saturated colors can bleed through to the back of the fabric. Hawaiian shirts, for instance, often feature inside-out "reverse prints" to simulate the sunbleached colors worn by surfers.

Well-known manufacturers of quality printed fabrics include Liberty of London, Etro, Marimekko, and IVANAhelsinki.

Motifs

A print consists of a motif, such as a flower or geometric shape, and a ground, the solid area behind the pattern. The scale of the motif and the way in which it repeats are key design elements. The density of the distribution of the motifs will also vary by design.

Some of the many different types of motifs include geometrics (stripes, dots, and stars perhaps), animal prints (leopard, zebra, tiger, and snakeskin), and florals. Print motifs can also be abstract, such as the boomerang shapes popular in the fifties. Designers often incorporate ethnic motifs, such as mudcloth, batik, and paisley, into their own signature dressing. There are pastoral scenes rendered in fine line work known as **toile de Jouy**. It is also possible to create a print from a licensed image (Hello Kitty or any of the other Sanrio characters). Novelty prints which feature unusual motifs are often referred to as **conversationals**. Digital and photo prints are created with graphic reproduction technologies. For examples of the different types of motifs, see the illustrated glossary of print fabrics at the end of this chapter.

▶ *Daisy de Villeneuve's decorative drawing style works well for fashion illustration and surface designs.*

◀ *Carmen Chen Wu uses a partial rendering for floral prints so as not to obscure garment details.*

Placement

There are three basic categories for print fabrics based on the placement of the various motifs. **Allover prints** feature motifs that are distributed throughout the yardage. Engineered prints require specific placement of the motifs on a garment. Pattern pieces are often cut and then printed prior to construction of the garment. A screen-printed T-shirt with a large image centered on the chest is a good example of an engineered print. Border prints are a very specific type of engineered print which feature placement of the motifs at the edge of the fabric. When constructing the garment, the motifs are usually placed at the bottom hem of shirts, pants, and skirts. Skirts and pants with border prints at the hemline can only be shortened by manipulating the waist seam, or by cutting and reattaching the bottom edge.

▶ *Engineered prints are a key design element for this pre-Fall collection by Vionnet.*

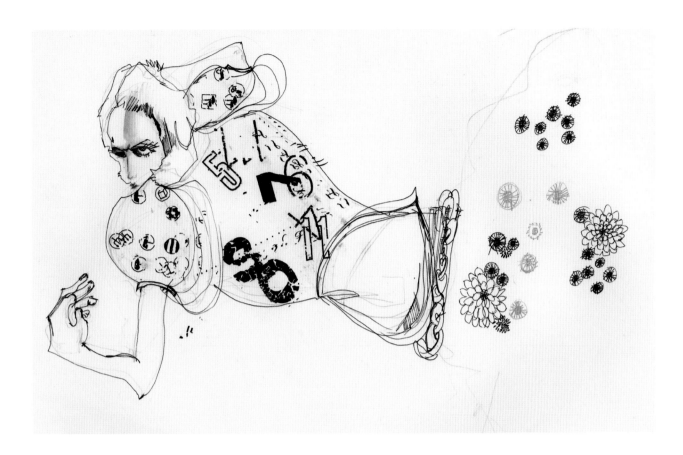

▲ *Sara Sakanaka designs her allover prints in tandem with garment silhouettes.*

▶ *Exclusive status prints, a mainstay of luxury manufacturers, feature motifs that reflect activities associated with the upper classes (horseriding and sailing perhaps).*

▶ ▶▶ *(Middle) Licensed images, such as this one by David Horvarth for YoyaMart, are commonly used for childrenswear. These illustrations combine hand drawing with digital imagery. (Far right) Many designers work with royalty free clipart.*

◄ *Bold engineered stripes are key design elements in this developmental sketch by Nina Donis.*

Repeats

A print typically starts out as a painting or a digital image. This artwork must then be duplicated over and over again on the fabric. In order to achieve a seamless repetition, textile designers must engineer one or a group of motifs in a repeat. Some repeats are random while others are directional. Home furnishing fabrics typically feature single-direction repeats whereas apparel fabrics usually have non-directional repeats for more efficient use of yardage. Different types of repeats include:

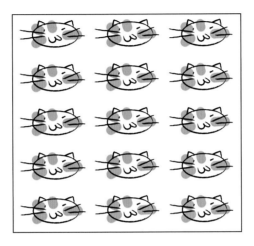

ONE WAY

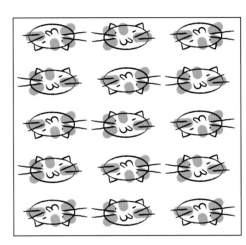

TWO WAY

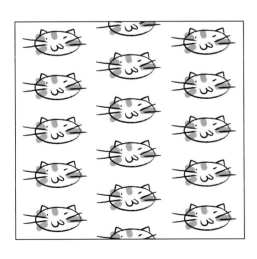

HALF-DROP VERTICAL SHIFT

HALF-DROP HORIZONTAL SHIFT

TOSSED

Rendering Print

In order to effectively render a print, you must first try to capture the "hand" of the artwork. If the print is painterly, you will want to use paint. Digital prints will require some sort of graphic reproduction (a hard copy of a scan of the print can be reduced to scale and incorporated into the illustration as collage). The hand of the textile design must also be filtered through your own drawing style. A loose interpretation is preferable—stylize the print just as you would the figure. Keep in mind that an exquisitely detailed rendering of a print may obscure construction details that distinguish garment design. Establish a hierarchy in your drawing, prioritizing silhouette, garment details, or fabric as appropriate for the specific design. The job description will ultimately dictate the amount of detail required.

Experiment with a broad variety of media to discover your own unique way of representing prints. More than one art supply may be required for garments with multiple textures and patterns. You should have a strategy for combining wet and dry as well as opaque and transparent media for maximum effect. Choose media that convey the surface texture and opacity of the cloth. Make sure that the media combination is truly compatible (for example, take care that laying in a wash will not make the marker line work bleed).

A good print rendering starts with a sizable swatch, one that gives you some idea of how the pattern will repeat. To determine the size of the motif in relation to the body, pin the swatch to a dress form, garment, or even your own body. How many times would you see the motif repeat across the shoulders? How many times would it repeat from the top to bottom of the torso? This relationship should be replicated in your illustration of the garment.

Because the scale of your illustrations will be so much smaller than the actual size of the swatch, it will be necessary not only to shrink the size of the pattern, but also to simplify it. This is known as "reducing a print." Walk at least five feet (1.5 meters) away from the swatch to predict how it will look when scaled and reduced. Anything you cannot see from that distance should be eliminated from your rendering. You can also scan or photocopy your print

▶ *Illustrator Camilla Dixon takes a more graphic approach to rendering, as appropriate for the hand of this particular print.*

at 25 percent of the original size to approximate how it will look on your illustration. The scaled-down reproduction can be used loosely as a guide. If you choose to do a partial rendering on a developmental sketch, or you do not want the print to obscure garment details, 70 percent coverage is a good rule. Follow the curves of the body but be careful that you do not create the appearance of an engineered print or high shine.

Planning, which is essential even for loose rendering, can be done with a hard pencil applied directly to your drawing or to a rough sketch used as an underdrawing (this will require a light box). The latter tends to give a better result—keeping your drawing and colors cleaner.

The plan for the placement of the print should reflect the garment's construction. First determine the grain of the fabric (and thus the direction of the print) to be used for different parts of the garment. Then center a predominant motif on the body of the garment as well as on the edges of the collar, hem, or pocket top. The biggest and most common mistake made when rendering prints is to work from one side of the garment to the other—you end up with an odd placement of motifs, an indication of poor garment construction. Instead, you must begin at Center Front and work outward. As you draw the motifs, make sure to maintain a consistent scale and distribution relative to the repeat, body movement, and garment drape.

▼ ▶ *In the design development for her resort collection, Julia Blum features signature prints inspired by traditional Mexican embroideries. Her rendering reduces the prints to their most basic elements.*

Rendering a Two-color Stripe

Required Materials:

- Bleedproof marker paper
- HB or #2 pencil
- Markers to match fabric swatch and T-shirt, 20% gray
- Stripe fabric swatch

For this next exercise, you will render a two-color horizontal stripe. Sketch a turned figure wearing a T-shirt and dhoti pants. Establish a direction for the light source and, using a 20% grey, render the shadows and folds of the draped fabric. Working with your chosen fabric swatch, determine the scale of the stripe relative to the proportion of your sketch. You can photocopy the swatch at a reduced scale and use it as a visual reference—but do not trace!

1 Position the predominant stripe at the midpoint of the garment (here, just above the dropped crotch). If possible, render this stripe with a single stroke of the marker.

2 Working upward and downward, fill in the stripes following the contours of the fabric drape and adjusting the angle of each stripe to correspond to the movement of the body and fabric drape.

Rendering a T-shirt Graphic

You will complete the illustration by adding an engineered print to the T-shirt. When the hand of a print is difficult to capture, collaging a photocopy or computer printout gives the best result:

1 Scan or photocopy artwork for the print. Scale this image as appropriate for your drawing and print out on marker paper.

2 Tracing off the exact shape from your figure drawing, draw the silhouette of the body of the T-shirt around the image.

3 Render the ground color and cut out the T-shirt shape as if it were for a paper doll.

4 Working with a permanent adhesive, such as rubber cement, paste the "paper doll" shirt onto the illustration.

NOTE If you do not want the cut paper doll effect, as an alternative method, you can reproduce the print on self-adhesive film. Brands such as Chartpak, Letraset, and Tekra manufacture film made especially for laser and inkjet printers. Take care to render shadows and ground color before positioning the film, as the slick surface prohibits the additional application of markers and paints. Then, using a craft knife, cut and peel off a piece of the film slightly larger than the area you intend to cover. Position and press the film into place. Carefully cut away the excess with the knife, applying only enough pressure to remove the excess film. Then burnish the film in place.

Rendering a Multicolor Stripe

Required Materials:

- 2-ply vellum-finish Bristol
- HB or #2 pencil
- Gouache and brushes
- Multicolor stripe fabric swatch

Next you will render broad stripes with variable colors and widths. As you can see from the diagram (below), one of the design features of the dress will be the multidirectional use of the stripe.

Sketch a figure in a walking pose wearing a floor-length, empire-waist dress with handkerchief hem. You may want to do a preliminary rough sketch on tracing paper and then, using a light box, redraw the figure on the Bristol. Working with gouache, mix up paint to match the four colors of the stripe. Before you begin your rendering, determine the scale and placement of the stripes relative to the proportion of your sketch. Begin with the vertical placement of the most prominent stripe near to the Center Front and then work outward. Then indicate the most prominent horizontal stripe at the midpoint of the garment and work upward and downward. When plotting the print take care to use a light hand as these lines will eventually be erased so as not to be confused for seams. The manner in which you draw the stripes should reflect the fabric drape and body movement. Make sure that the order and width of the different bars of color remains consistent with the repeat.

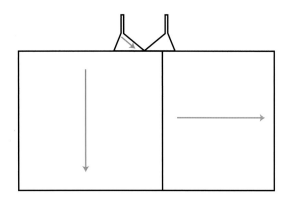

▲ Determine the grain of the fabric for each pattern piece and then plot the print.

NOTE When painting stripes or plaids, it is extremely helpful to work with a flat brush or felt tip marker point that approximates the width of the stripe in a single stroke.

1 Working with pencil, locate the important seams on the dress.

2 Paint the central vertical stripe.

3 Working outward from the center, paint the remaining vertical stripes; the paint for each adjacent stripe should be dry before you begin the next bar of color.

4 Next paint the most prominent horizontal stripe.

5 Paint the remaining horizontal stripes, working upward and downward. Complete by adding shadows for soft folds; intensify the line art as necessary.

ACTUAL SIZE AND ORIGINAL COLORWAY

Rendering a Floral

Required Materials:

- Bleedproof marker paper
- HB or #2 pencil
- Markers to match colors substituted for fabric swatch and 20% gray
- Colored pencils in henna and cool gray 90%
- Floral fabric swatch

Designing with printed fabrics often involves manipulation of the print. A **pitch sheet**, which features a full repeat of the pattern and a precise description of colors (using chips), will often include the systematic substitution of colors for alternative or second colorways. For this next exercise you will recolor a floral and then render the print. Sketch a little girl's figure in a high hip position wearing a two-piece playsuit. Then render as follows:

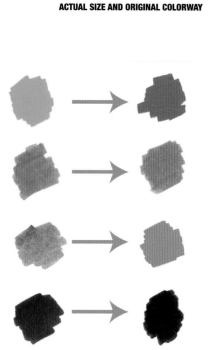

▲ Systematically substitute each of the colors for the print.

1 Block in the shadows created by the soft folds of the fabric and movement of the body. Roughly pencil in the print, beginning with placement of the most prominent motif on the Center Front.

2 Complete placement of the print, working outward.

3 Render the print with color-matched markers, working from light to dark and leaving a thin white margin at the outer edges of the garment to suggest dimension. Reinforce the outline.

Rendering Paisley

Required Materials:

- 2-ply vellum-finish Bristol
- HB or #2 pencil
- Gouache and brushes

Next you will render a paisley pattern with a dark ground. Working from the image of the fabric swatch provided, determine the scale of the print relative to the size of your drawing. Roughly sketch a girl's figure wearing a double-breasted, empire-waist jacket layered over a ruffled blouse and jeans. Working in pencil, create a plan for placement of the print. Mix up gouache to match the motifs and ground color. The ground color will be easier to work with if it is somewhat transparent, so dilute the paint as much as you can without changing its value (it should still appear dark brown). Add a bit of white to the lighter colors to boost their opacity. Begin rendering the paisley as follows:

ACTUAL SIZE

1 Paint the ground color. Ideally, your pencil plan for the paisley should show through. Alternatively, work with an underdrawing and a light box.

2 Allow for adequate drying time and add the different colors for the motifs, working in layers from light to dark. Remember to reduce the print by eliminating the smaller details. Add the final layer of color (see right).

3 Add the final layer of color. Create a "twin print" for the shirt by extracting some element from the paisley, (this can be as simple as a polka dot).

NOTE Graph paper can be used as a guide for the even placement of prints—for example, polka dots can be uniformly spaced by placing the dots at the intersection of the grid lines. The Grid tool in Illustrator can be used to create graphs of different sizes.

Rendering Camouflage

ACTUAL SIZE

Required Materials:

- 2-ply vellum-finish Bristol
- HB or #2 pencil
- Gouache and brushes

Next you will render camouflage—a print intended to disguise the wearer in a specific location (for example, desert camouflage will feature bleached-out motifs and ground colors). Working with the image of the fabric swatch provided, mix gouache to match the motifs and ground color in the print. Sketch a young man's figure wearing a cardigan layered over a button-down shirt and Bermuda shorts. Then render as follows:

1 Fill in the ground color. Indicate shadows and crush lines with light gray paint. Allow sufficient drying time before moving on to the next step.

2 Begin rendering the motifs, starting with the lightest color.

3 Working from light to dark, paint the different color motifs, allowing for sufficient drying time between layered applications of color. Reinforce line art as necessary.

▼ *Camouflage prints were originally created with the military and hunting sports in mind. These patterns have now come across from functional apparel into urban streetwear and even high fashion. Here, camouflage by Bernhard Willhelm on the catwalk.*

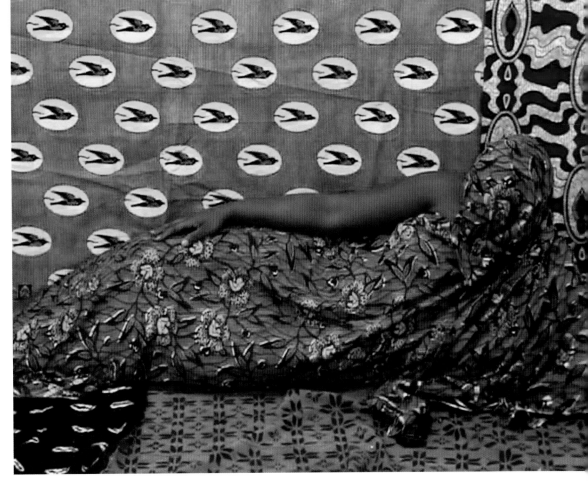

▲ *In Grace Ndiritu's* The Nightingale, *allover ethnic print fabrics are draped on a reclining figure so as to recall Matisse's odalisques. Tribal influences carry over into fine art and then into fashion.*

ASSIGNMENT 1

Create a camouflage print (left) specific to a unique location. Think about how pattern, texture, and silhouette might allow the wearer to blend in with the environment. Then design and illustrate a layered system of garments using the camouflage print.

Rendering an Animal Print

Required Materials:

- 2-ply vellum-finish Bristol
- HB or #2 pencil
- Luma or Dr. Ph. Martin's dyes in slate gray and bright orange
- Brushes

As previously mentioned, engineered prints require specific placement on the garment. Here you will render a tiger stripe on a romper with a band of color engineered at the bottom hem. Sketch a simple dress or short jumpsuit on a high hip figure. Add shadows and crush lines with a light gray wash. Then render the engineered print as follows:

1 Working within the silhouette of the bloomer, use a round brush to saturate the paper with water. Then quickly lay in a bright orange wash at the bottom hemline, creating a gradient effect.

2 Allow for adequate drying time before moving on to the next step. Using a fine tip brush and slate gray watercolor, add the tiger stripes.

3 Add flesh tone and haircolor; as necessary, reinforce the outline.

◄ *A collection by July Choi utilizes twin prints and alternative colorways.*

▼ *Select a scarf as the inspiration for an allover print for apparel.*

ASSIGNMENT 2

Working with a swatch for an allover print, design a small collection of coordinated separates (approximately five looks). Extract a motif from this swatch to create a second "twin" print. Your collection should include at least two prints and three solid fabrics (above).

ASSIGNMENT 3

Scarves often feature decorative patterns engineered to a prescribed shape and size. As compared to continuous apparel patterns used as yardage, there is no requirement for the motifs to repeat. Working with a print scarf, adapt the pattern for an allover print for a dress (right). Follow all of the steps previously established for rendering print on the figure.

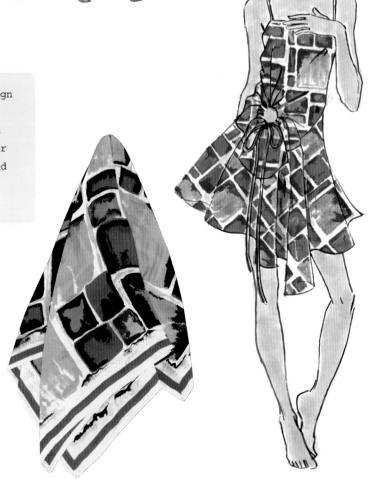

SPECIALIZATION: Childrenswear

Childrenswear is an important and fast-growing segment of the retail apparel market. Many fashion schools offer a separate course track for this specialization. There is an enormous range of styles and prices for childrenswear. Just like adults, girls and boys of all ages need clothing for different occasions: active sport, more formal apparel for school, special occasion party clothes, and sleepwear. Childrenswear follows trends in adult fashion, although with some modifications (for example, sexy/provocative looks would be inappropriate for young girls). Rules regarding gender-specific garment details and colors are pretty much a thing of the past—just about anything goes. Clothing designs must appeal to both parent and child and accommodate growing bodies experiencing progressive developmental changes (garments for toddlers that have not been potty trained must have snap crotches, for instance). Garment care is paramount, with wash-and-wear preferred. Safety issues, such as requirements for flame-retardant fabrics for sleepwear, are also important concerns. Because childrenswear is outgrown so quickly, parents appreciate designs that extend garment life cycles. With an eye to the future, forward-thinking childrenswear designers combine fashion-conscious styling with eco-design and socially conscious manufacturing practices.

Whimsical prints, a key component of childrenswear, must be designed according to trend, customer profile, and season. For instance, a print used for infantwear would be deemed too babyish for big kids. Imagery for tweens' prints tends to be more rebellious, inspired by grafitti, manga, and pop music. There is a huge business in character licensing for childrenswear—garments with engineered and allover prints automatically benefit from the popularity of a character from a TV series, movie, or book.

ASSIGNMENT 4

Design a small childrenswear collection utilizing licensed images or clip art (below). Be sure to use characters or motifs that are suitable for the selected age range.

◀ *Gothic and sweet Lolitas prefer a wild mix of prints. Originating in Japan, the trend has had enormous staying power and become a worldwide influence for girls', tweens', and junior fashion.*

▶ *Jonathan Kyle Farmer's clothing and accessory collection for tweens features age-appropriate allover and engineered prints.*

Special Challenges for Illustrating Childrenswear

Strong graphic design skills are an important asset for childrenswear; put to use in the creation of prints, embroideries, appliqué, flats, and hang tags. CAD systems are often required to create tech packs with instructions for the size and placement of prints.

Presentations for childrenswear can include garments for more than one age category and so your stylization of the different children's figures must reflect a relative proportion. (For more about children's age categories and figure proportions, see Chapter 3.)

If sustainability is prioritized in the collection, you must use materials in your presentation that convey this message. It is not simply a matter of finding non-toxic, natural, or recycled materials; your presentation must actually look eco-friendly.

◀▼ *A concept sketch and realization of Sungeun Kim's print-driven thesis collection.*

Illustrated Glossary of Print Fabrics

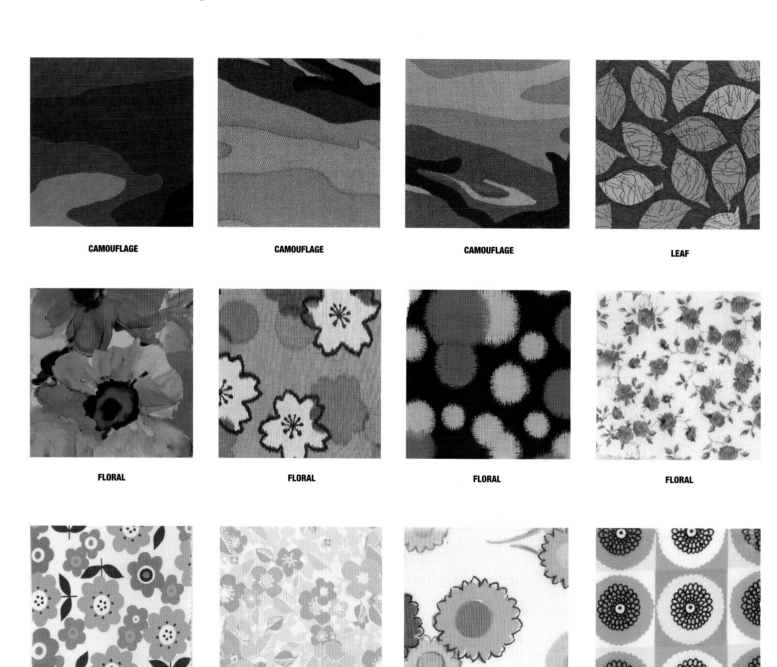

CAMOUFLAGE   CAMOUFLAGE   CAMOUFLAGE   LEAF

FLORAL   FLORAL   FLORAL   FLORAL

FLORAL   CORDUROY   GEOMETRIC TWIN PRINT   GEOMETRIC

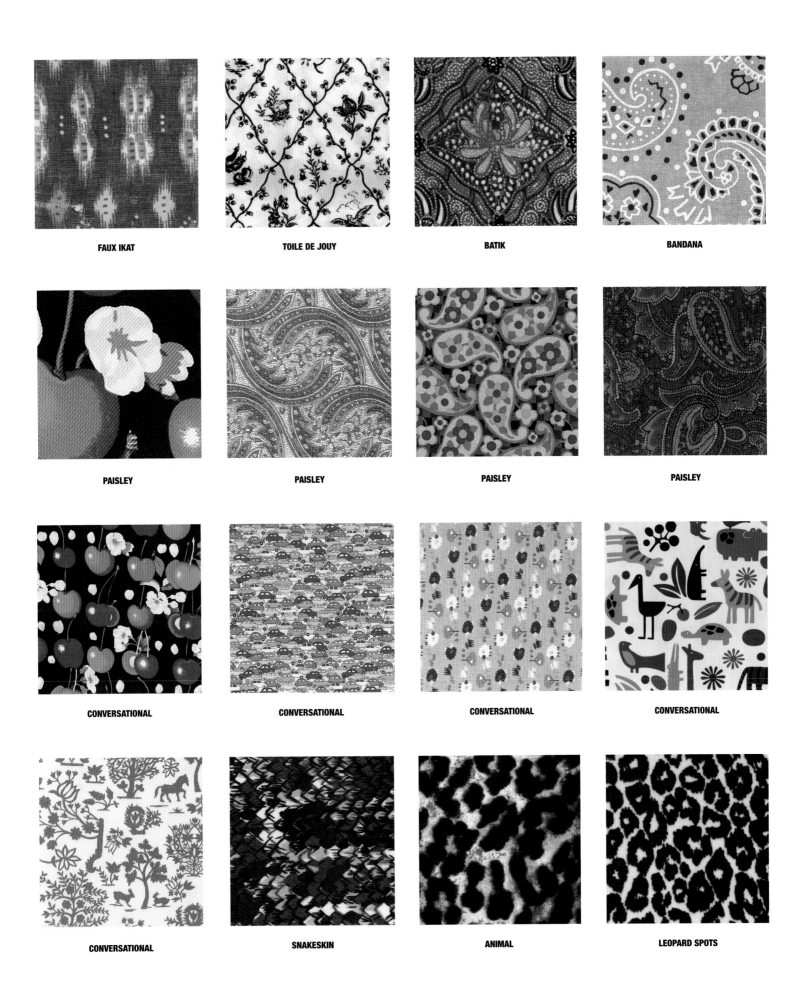

FAUX IKAT

TOILE DE JOUY

BATIK

BANDANA

PAISLEY

PAISLEY

PAISLEY

PAISLEY

CONVERSATIONAL

CONVERSATIONAL

CONVERSATIONAL

CONVERSATIONAL

CONVERSATIONAL

SNAKESKIN

ANIMAL

LEOPARD SPOTS

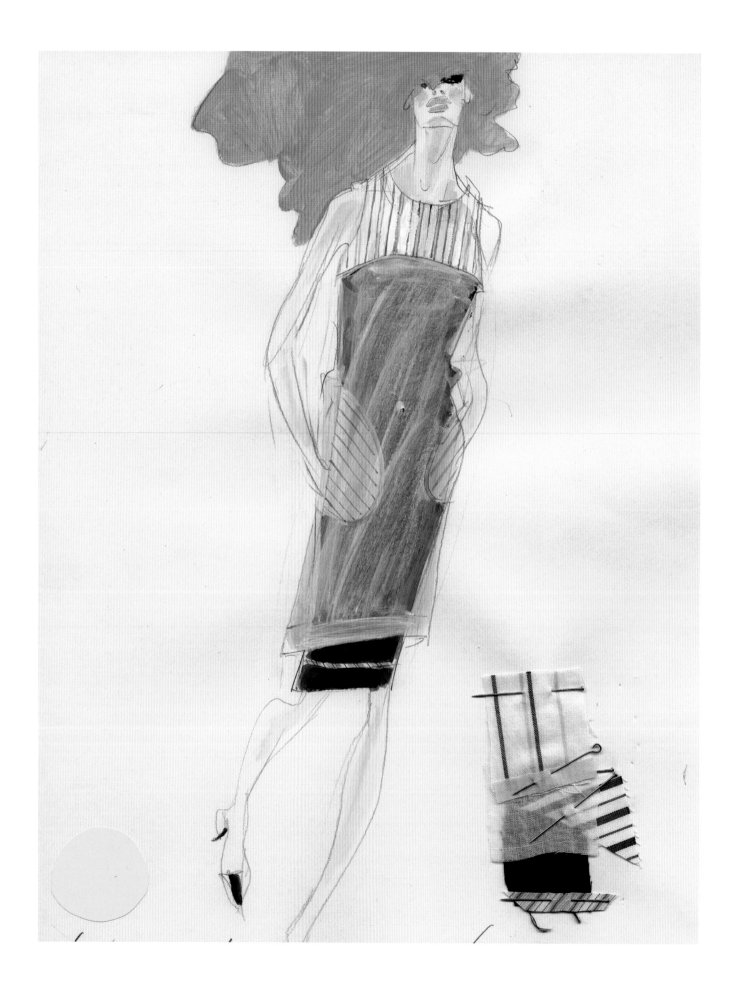

CHAPTER 12
RENDERING SHEERS

Sheer fabrics come in a broad variety of weights and textures. For example, chiffon, gauze, voile, and ultrafine jersey are light as a feather; net and mesh are more structured; openwork knits, eyelet, laser cutwork, **devoré burnout**, and lace have peekaboo characteristics. These different properties will produce altogether different silhouettes, conveyed by the quality and, in some cases, elimination of, the line in your drawing. Just as for the other fabric categories, the appearance of sheers is determined by weight, texture, and light-reflecting properties, but also by what the fabric is layered over. For instance, a red chiffon blouse will look quite different if layered over a nude camisole as compared to layering the same garment over a black bodysuit. White lace can look quite different when layered over white or black fabric.

Because translucent fabrics reveal so much of the body, they are often associated with intimate apparel—a specialization explored at the end of this chapter. But ever since 1966, when Yves Saint Laurent caused an uproar with his see-through blouses (sans undergarments), sheer fabrics have been used for all garment categories. Design strategies for working with sheer fabric must include artful layering. Seam allowances will be partially, if not fully, visible, and so the number of seams is often kept to a minimum; sheer garments also require special consideration for seam finishing and hems are often left raw.

▶ *When rendering sheer fabrics in Photoshop or Illustrator, transparency can be achieved by manipulating Opacity Sliders and Layer Blending Modes (Multiply vs. Normal). Illustration by Ferdinand.*

◀ *The appearance of sheers is significantly affected by whatever fabrics they are layered over. Here, an artful layering of sheers over stripes for sporty separates by Nina Donis.*

▶ *Harder sheers, such as vinyl, are often used for outerwear to create interesting layered effects. Observation of hard and soft fabric behavior on the model will inform all of your subsequent drawings. Model drawing by Ivy Chen.*

▲ *Andrew Yang's artful composition utilizes a variety of rubbing and stencil techniques to illustrate sheers.*

▶ *Only a loose indication of surface and pattern is required for developmental sketches. Illustration by Eri Wakiyama.*

▼ *When working with embossed papers for rubbing techniques, keep in mind that the two sides of the paper have different textures and so will give different results.*

Basic Principles for Rendering Sheers

Just as you were able to envision the look of lustrous, wool, and print fabrics, the appearance of sheer fabrics is also predictable—determined by the order and number of layers of cloth. Based on your understanding of how body movement affects garment drape, you should be able to anticipate where soft folds will form and the fabric will overlap; these layered areas will be either higher or lower in value depending on the base color of the garment. For instance, when rendering a black or dark-colored chiffon blouse, you would use a lower value of the base color for areas with multiple layers of fabric, such as the cuffs, collars, and yoke. Conversely, for white fabrics, areas with layered fabric would be of a higher value.

Net and mesh have more structure and texture, as compared to chiffon. When rendering the texture it is important to maintain a consistent line weight, spacing, and angle for the pen strokes. One way of doing this is with rubbing techniques using a tulle swatch or another textured surface.

Rendering Chiffon

Required Materials:

- Bleedproof marker paper
- HB or #2 pencil
- Markers in flesh tone, hair color, 20%, 30%, 40%, 50%, and 70% gray*
- 90% cool gray colored pencil

▼ *The overlapping of different colored sheer fabrics has the same effect as layering transparent watercolors.*

For this next exercise you will render a simple black chiffon cowl-neck blouse with cap sleeves. Sketch the blouse on a cropped high hip figure in pencil on the bleedproof marker paper. Then render the drawing as follows:

*NOTE Approximate values, as different brands will vary. Grays come in cool, warm, and neutral ranges; when choosing your markers, stick with a consistent color cast.

1 Block in the flesh tone and apply the highest value (lightest) gray marker to the blouse. Use the 70% gray to block in the color of the leggings.

2 Allow adequate drying time for the first layer of marker and then erase the holding line for the blouse. Block in the silhouette of the body visible under the blouse using the second value gray marker.

3 Allow adequate drying time and then block in areas where the fabric overlaps with the third value gray marker. Use the fourth value for areas where more than two layers of fabric overlap.

ASSIGNMENT 1

Design a small group of dresses utilizing fabrics in different colors and opacities. The layering of the transparent fabrics in multiple colors will be very much like mixing paint. You can use your knowledge of color theory (see pp.306-7) to predict the appearance of areas with overlapping colors. For instance, the layering of sheers in complementary colors will result in lowered intensity in the areas where the two fabrics overlap (left).

Rendering Tulle and Eyelet

Required Materials:

- Bleedproof marker paper
- HB or #2 pencil
- Markers in flesh tone, hair color, and 40% gray
- White colored pencil
- A surface for rubbing with appropriate texture and scale
- Red fine point marker

Next you will render a long-sleeved T-shirt with a white eyelet flounce layered over a white tutu. For this illustration block in a neutral color for the background to best offset the white garments. Working with a girls' figure, lightly pencil sketch the garments and render as follows:

1 Block in the background using a 40% gray marker.

2 Allow for sufficient drying time and then block in the flesh tone on the face and legs. Erase the holding lines in the areas of the body that will be covered by the skirt.

3 Working with a textured surface placed underneath your drawing, render the tulle using a rubbing technique with the white color pencil. Be sure to use heavier pressure for the areas with overlapping layers of fabric so that they are defined by a higher (lighter) value.

4 Add cutwork to the eyelet flounce using pencil and light gray marker. Complete the drawing by rendering the stripes, dots, and hair color.

Rendering Athletic Mesh

Required Materials:

- Bleedproof marker paper
- HB or #2 pencil
- Markers in flesh tone, hair color, olive drab, and indigo blue
- White and flesh colored pencils
- A textured surface for rubbing
- 90% cool gray colored pencil
- White gel pen

Athletic mesh is one of the more durable sheers used for women's, men's, and children's apparel. If you can find an appropriate surface with the correct scale for your drawing, a rubbing technique works quite well for this. Pencil sketch a junior boy wearing a short-sleeved athletic mesh Henley shirt layered over a white tank top and dark-wash denim five-pocket jeans. Then render as follows:

1 Block in the T-shirt with the olive drab marker, then fill in the face and arms below the sleeve hemline with the flesh tone marker. Allow the marker to dry completely.

2 Working with a textured surface placed underneath your drawing, do a rubbing with the flesh tone color pencil in the areas where the body would show through the sleeves of the T-shirt. Do a second rubbing, this time in white colored pencil, in the areas where the T-shirt overlaps the white tank top. Block in the color of the jeans using the indigo blue marker.

3 Allow for sufficient drying time and, using a 90% cool gray pencil, indicate the weave of the denim with a series of diagonal strokes. Add haircolor, contrast stitching in white gel pen, and shoe details to finish the drawing.

Rendering Point D'Esprit

Required Materials:

- Bleedproof marker paper
- HB or #2 pencil
- Markers in flesh tone, fuchsia, 20%, 30%, and 40% gray
- 90% cool gray colored pencil
- A textured surface for rubbing
- Fine tip black marker

Next you will tackle a more complex layering of garments. Working with a high hip figure, loosely sketch underwear and hosiery inspired by vintage lingerie. Then render as follows:

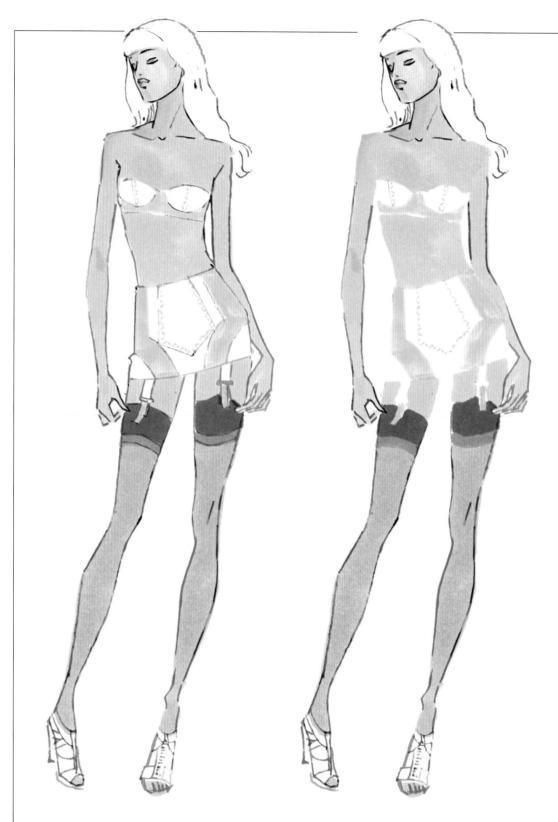

1 Working with markers, fill in the flesh tone and color-blocked areas of the underwear. Render the hosiery using the gray markers.

2 Erase the pencil line work that separates the different values on the stockings as well as the areas on the body that will be covered by the dress.

3 Lightly sketch a cap-sleeve minidress. Use a rubbing technique with the 90% gray colored pencil to indicate the mesh, applying greater pressure where the fabric overlaps.

4 Working with the fine tip black marker, add the **point d'esprit** dot pattern to the net ground. Add finishing touches. (To render studs see p. 327.)

Rendering Fishnet

Required Materials:

- Bleedproof marker paper
- HB or #2 pencil
- Markers in flesh tone, red, 20% and 70% gray
- 90% cool gray and white colored pencil
- White gel pen
- Red, gray, and black fine tip markers
- A surface for rubbing with appropriate snakeskin texture and scale
- Adhesive pattern film (e.g. Screentone by Letraset)
- Craft knife or single-edge razor blade
- Red gouache and fine brush

The next rendering will require a wide variety of media, including pressure-sensitive graphics, for the various textures and patterns of this Gothic Lolita outfit. Working with a junior girl figure, pencil sketch a zipper-front halter vest layered over a tank top, bralette, and pouf skirt. Be sure to include the requisite combat boots! Then render as follows:

1 Render the skin with flesh tone marker, including areas of the body that will be revealed beneath the fishnet tank top. Block in the hosiery with red marker. Use white pencil and 20% gray marker for highlights and shadows on the legs.

2 Working with the 70% gray marker, fill in the trim for the tank top and the combat boots. Add red marker to the bralette. Do a rubbing with the 90% cool gray colored pencil for the snakeskin vest.

3 Add cast shadows on the torso. Render the red plaid using the white gel pen and red, gray, and black fine tip markers.

4 Work with the pattern film to render the fishnet tank top and stockings. Use a razor blade to cut and peel off a piece of film slightly larger than the area you intend to cover. Position and press the film into place. Carefully cut away the excess and burnish the film in place. Add topstitching to the vest with red gouache. Finish with rendering of hair and makeup.

Rendering Lace

Lace is an openwork fabric thought to have evolved from embroidery. Many varieties, such as Chantilly, Valenciennes, and Battenberg, are named for their geographic origin. Lace is a decorative pattern with a mesh or net ground. Motifs can also be positioned in a way that allows for the base cloth to be dissolved, leaving an open structure connected by bars. The lace pattern can be distributed as an allover repeat or engineered with specific placement on the garment. Laces such as Venice and guipure (Cluny)—both bar varieties—have raised surfaces. Mesh lace may also be re-embroidered for added color and relief.

In the past, intricate lace and embroidery were associated with quaint domesticity. As compared to other textile techniques, embroidery allows for placement of threads in any position or direction on a base cloth, and can therefore be used for the most experimental manipulations of cloth. In recent times, lace-making has been radically reinvented by experimental artists and designers who marry traditional methods with new technologies and materials.

Many of the general considerations for designing with sheer fabrics will apply to lace. Lace is used for whole garments as well as for edgings and insertions. Individual motifs (known as "medallions") can be clipped from lace yardage and used as an appliqué. Lace garments will often feature a scalloped edge left, or reattached, at the hems of sleeves, skirts, and so on.

There are many different techniques for rendering lace. Just as with the rendering of prints, lace patterns must be scaled and reduced. The indication of the motifs should be handled delicately. Lace with raised surfaces will require multiple pen widths. Before you begin rendering, take the time to analyze the lace pattern and form a plan for the application of line and color.

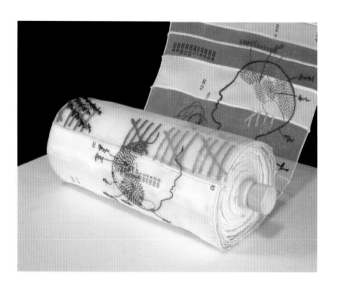

▲ *Jiseon Lee Isbara combines inkjet printing with hand and machine embroidery on silk and linen fabrics.*

▼ *Laura Splan's lace doilies are based on microscopic images of dangerous, often lethal, viruses such as SARS.*

▼ *Karen Nicol resurfaces existing textiles to create innovative patterns and textures.*

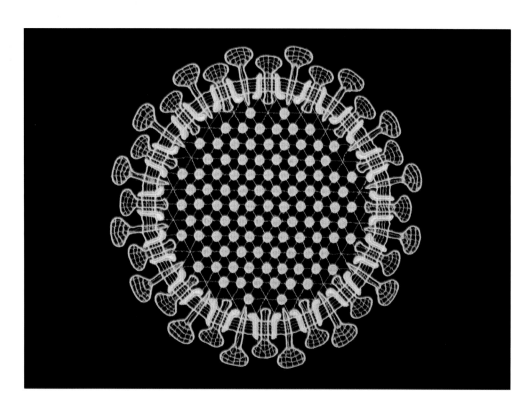

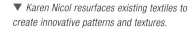

Rendering Black Lace

Required Materials:

- Bleedproof marker paper
- HB or #2 pencil
- Markers in flesh tone, 20%, and 50% gray
- Fine point black markers in three different stroke widths
- 90% cool gray colored pencil
- A black lace swatch

Like all sheer fabrics, the appearance of lace is affected by what it is layered over. For the next exercise you will render black lace layered over white satin. Working with a high hip women's figure, pencil sketch a simple slip with demi-cup bra top. Then render as follows:

1 Block in the skin with the flesh tone marker. The white slip should be a bit shorter than the lace overlay—render the legs accordingly.

2 Using the 20% gray marker, fill in the areas where the lace will be layered over the white slip and legs. Fill in remaining areas with 50% gray marker.

3 Add the lace pattern, using various black pen widths relative to the different motifs (for example, the scalloped hemline will require a heavier stroke weight).

Rendering Color on Color

Required Materials:

- Bleedproof marker paper
- HB or #2 pencil
- Markers in flesh tone, turquoise, and 20% gray
- Fine point red marker and matching red colored pencil
- A surface for rubbing with appropriate fine mesh texture and scale
- A red lace fabric swatch

Rendering colored lace layered over a second color slip can present a challenge. The fine line work required for the motif is difficult to achieve with opaque media such as brush and paint. While fine tip markers are perfect for fine line work, their transparency makes it difficult to layer one color on top of another. For this next exercise you will use a fairly simple method for rendering color on color. Pencil sketch a strapless empire-waist dress on a high hip figure. Then render the lace as follows:

1 Indicate the shadows in the soft folds on the dress with the 20% gray marker.

2 Use the fine tip red marker to render the pattern of lace motifs. Indicate loose threads at hemline.

▲ Sheer fabrics are often used for veils. Here, an unconventional bride by Vivienne Westwood.

3 Working with the textured surface placed underneath the drawing, do a rubbing, applying light pressure with the red pencil to create the fine mesh ground.

4 Working on the back of the marker paper, loosely add turquoise marker in and around the motifs, fading out the density of the color as you move toward the outside edges of the dress. Add turquoise with highlights and shadows for the satin belt. Finish by adding the flesh tone.

ASSIGNMENT 2

Because handmade lace is an expensive luxury, both fabric and trim are often handed down from one generation to the next. For this next assignment use online historical databases or source vintage lace from thrift and antique stores. Design a small collection of party dresses. You might want to design the wardrobe for a wedding party: dresses for the bride (above), maid of honor, bridesmaids, flower girl, etc. Research different wedding rituals from around the world. Also consider how inherited lace might be used to add sentimental value to a design.

SPECIALIZATION:
Intimate Apparel

Sheer fabrics are key to the design of intimate apparel—a segment of the fashion industry that includes underwear, foundation garments, and sleepwear. Underwear, a sometimes visible and stylish part of daily clothing that must be both comfortable and flattering, includes garments such as bras, panties, slips, camisoles, teddies, bodysuits, and hosiery. Foundation garments include corsets, girdles, suspenders (also known as garter belts), and shapewear. Sleepwear includes nightgowns in various lengths, pajamas, and bathrobes.

Historically, attitudes about undergarments have been in a constant state of flux. For instance, Christian Dior's edict that "without foundations there can be no fashion" held sway throughout the fifties into the sixties. But by the late sixties, the women's liberation movement called for the elimination of any and all restrictive undergarments. Then in the eighties, postfeminists called for the return of extremely sexy unmentionables to be worn in public. To this day, intimate apparel, such as camisoles and corsets, continues to do double duty, crossing over and being worn as outerwear. The French refer to this as *dessus-dessous*, which basically means "underwear as outerwear."

Design Considerations for Intimate Apparel

While lace and chiffon are perhaps the first fabrics that come to mind for intimate apparel, state-of-the-art mesh weaves, spandex (Lycra®), and smart microfibers are also used to provide comfort, moisture management, and support. High-tech construction plays a major role in modern design, with innovations such as laser cutting and seamless knit technologies. Foundation garments and underwear require seam finishes, stitching, and trim (such as aglets, busks, and suspender grips) specific to intimate apparel. Foremost design considerations for sleepwear include flame resistance and garment care.

Just as for other areas of the fashion industry, intimate apparel is designed for different price points and with specific branding strategies. Companies such as Agent Provocateur, Kiki de Montparnasse, Victoria's Secret, and Frederick's of Hollywood manufacture romantic and seductive intimate apparel. Berlei takes a more practical approach, focusing on fit, function, and comfort for women of all ages, shapes, and sizes. La Perla is all about luxury and elegance, with styling that includes lots of handmade lace and embroidery. Wolford is also a luxury brand, but with a more modern and streamlined aesthetic that relies on the latest technology to achieve the best possible fit and feel. VPL (an acronym for "visible panty line") by Victoria Bartlett offers a subversive alternative to "barely there" underwear with iconoclastic design references to medical gauze, bandages, and hospital uniforms.

◀ There are intimate apparel garments for everyday wear and more provocative versions designed for special occasions (see pp. 400–2). Here, illustration by Barbara Pearlman.

▼ ▼ Reciprocal influence and inspiration between innerwear and outerwear is apparent in all market categories. Design development for a versatile innerwear/outerwear children's collection by Chanmaly Sivongxai. "Pajama Party" illustrated by Antonio Lopez (above left).

▲ Men's lingerie was once designed with only necessity and practicality in mind. Today, style and fashion are incorporated with functional details.

Special Challenges for Illustrating Intimate Apparel

Because so much of the body is revealed by "barely there" garments, the greatest challenge for illustrating intimate apparel is perfecting your figure drawing skills. Cropped figures work well for underwear and allow you to zoom in on details such as trim and stitching, which must be accurately illustrated. Coquettish or provocative poses can be used relative to customer profile. Background can be used to suggest the fantasy and romance associated with this market category.

◀ Intimate apparel has very specific stitching details and trim, which must be accurately illustrated. Intimate apparel design and illustration by Anna Kiper.

▶▼ Leslie Jones's intimate apparel collection features the engineered appliqué of laser-cut dots—a high-tech alternative to lace and traditional embellishment.

ASSIGNMENT 3

Foundations determine the shape of outerwear by sculpting the body into an idealized form. But the design of silhouettes for outerwear also dictates the requirements for innerwear. There is clearly reciprocal influence and inspiration between the two. Design a small collection of intimate apparel that can double as, or be incorporated into, outerwear (this page). Since the structure of modern corsetry garments is not all that different from Victorian times, you may want to utilize a historical inspiration, but you must design for a modern lifestyle. Incorporate design details and trims such as sliders, elastics, and zigzag stitching, borrowed from the architectural quality of vintage underwear.

◣ ◤▼ *Julia Blum's elegant and risqué thesis collection blurs the boundaries between market categories and earned her the distinction of Parson's Designer of the Year. Preliminary design development (left) and realization on the runway (above and below).*

Illustrated Glossary of Sheer Fabrics

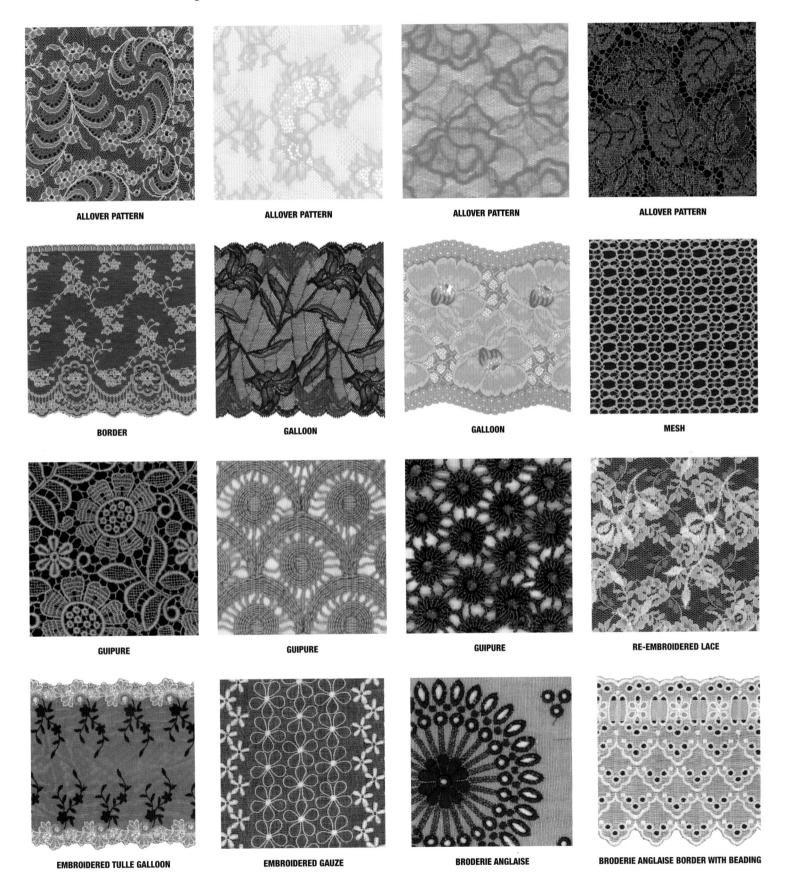

ALLOVER PATTERN

ALLOVER PATTERN

ALLOVER PATTERN

ALLOVER PATTERN

BORDER

GALLOON

GALLOON

MESH

GUIPURE

GUIPURE

GUIPURE

RE-EMBROIDERED LACE

EMBROIDERED TULLE GALLOON

EMBROIDERED GAUZE

BRODERIE ANGLAISE

BRODERIE ANGLAISE BORDER WITH BEADING

Glossary

Allover print

A printed fabric with a pattern of motifs repeated from selvage to selvage, and therefore across the whole surface of a garment. See also ENGINEERED PRINT.

Analagous color scheme

Uses combinations of colors that are next to each other on the COLOR WHEEL.

Anime

Refers to Japanese animation. In Japanese the word denotes any style of animation. See also MANGA, OTAKU.

Apex

The highest point of the bust. On a pattern this can also refer to the point at which any dart terminates.

Appliqué

A decorative effect created by sewing or fusing small patches of fabric onto a garment.

Art Deco

A decorative arts movement which originated in Paris and became popular in the 1920s and 1930s. It was based on strong colors, new materials, and geometric shapes and organic motifs.

Avatar

A computer user's online alter ego or representation of themselves: their chosen name, image, or 3D model.

Balance Line

Or "plumb" line; a vertical line dropped down through the center of a figure. Used as a point of reference to determine the center of gravity and balance of the figure.

Besom pocket

A pocket cut into a garment, finished with piping along each edge of the length of the opening. Also known as a "double welt" pocket.

Bias cut

Fabric which is cut at 45 degrees to the warp threads to create draped garments which have greater stretch and hug the body.

Bottom weights

Fabrics which are used to make skirts and pants. See also TOP WEIGHTS.

Bouclé

A textured fabric made from bouclé yarn. The yarn is made of several plies—usually three—one of these being looser than the others, so that it creates loops which are then visible in the finished fabric.

Bridge collection

An "affordable" clothing collection released by a designer in order to "bridge" the price gap between designer and mass-market fashion. Also called "diffusion line."

Brocade

A heavy woven fabric featuring raised designs. Often made from lustrous yarns. See also JACQUARD.

Cascade drape

A bias-cut ruffle that is attached vertically to a garment so that it hangs down like a waterfall.

Center Back

The vertical center down the back of a garment.

Center Front

The vertical center down the front of a garment. A reference point for the position of buttons, zippers, etc.

Charmeuse

A lightweight fabric with a satin finish.

Chemise

A short, loose-fitting dress, cut straight at the sides. Based on the undergarment of the same name. See also SACK DRESS, TRAPEZE DRESS.

Chiton

A tunic worn in ancient Greece by both men and women, consisting of a single rectangle of fabric, draped around the body and secured with fastenings at one or both shoulders and a belt.

Color wheel

A visual tool with the 12 spectrum colors arranged in a circle.

Colorways

The chosen range of available colors for a garment or a collection. Also applies to the range of colors available for a printed textile.

Complementary color scheme

Uses combinations of colors that are opposite one another on the COLOR WHEEL.

Contrapposto

A pose in which a model rests most of their weight on one leg. As the weight shifts, the angles of the head, shoulders, and hips adjust to compensate, working in opposition.

Conversational

A printed fabric featuring unusual themes and motifs.

Cool hunting

Gathering information on emerging street trends and styles. See also TREND RESEARCH.

Cowl neckline

A "draped" neckline, of varying depths, created by using two-point suspension. A cowl bodice is usually BIAS CUT.

Croquis

An alternative term for "figure."

Customer profile

A description of the (intended) buyer of an item in terms of demographics and taste.

Devoré burnout

A chemical process used to destroy one of two different fibers in a fabric to create relief patterns. Most commonly used on velvet, removing the pile in places to leave just the backing. From the French *divorer*, meaning "to devour."

Dhoti pants

Loose pants with a dropped crotch which taper toward the ankle; named after the traditional loose loincloth worn by Indian men.

Diffusion line See BRIDGE COLLECTION.

Directoire

Paul Poiret's (1879–1944) clothing line, inspired by the fashions of the Directoire period in France (1795–99), featuring dresses with high waists and loosely flowing skirts. See also EMPIRE WAISTLINE.

Dolman sleeve

A sleeve cut as an extension of the bodice without an armhole, as opposed to a set-in sleeve.

Empire waistline

A waistline seam located above the natural waist on the body. See also DIRECTOIRE.

Engineered print

A print which has motifs intended for a specific area of a garment. Also called a "placed print." A border print is a type of engineered print. See also ALLOVER PRINT.

Extension

The horizontal distance between the center of a button and the opening edge of the garment.

Fast fashion

An approach to fashion employed by mass-market (high-street) stores whereby trends featured on the catwalks are quickly and cheaply imitated/designed, manufactured, and then placed in stores in large quantities.

Fit dart

A stitched-down, tapering fold used to allow fabric to follow the contours of the body more closely.

Fit model

A person who is used by a designer or clothing manufacturer to test the fit and look of sample garments. The model's proportions will adhere to the target customer's measurements.

Flat

Or flat sketch. Also known as "technical drawing." A black-and-white sketch used to communicate designs for presentation and production. The garment is shown off the body, including any construction details and technical information.

Float

A sketch of a garment as it would appear on the body, but with the body not shown in the sketch. See also FLAT.

Forecasting services

Research that aims to predict future trends, often a season or more ahead. See also COOL HUNTING.

Foreshortening

Creating the illusion of depth in a drawing. An object, or part of an object, that is receding from the viewer's perspective will look smaller, while an advancing object will look larger. As a figure turns away, that side of the body farthest from view will seem to shrink and vice versa.

Funnel collar

A jacket collar, creating a funnel up the neck if fastened, and two large triangular flaps at the front when unfastened.

Gabardine

A stiff, durable, twill-weave fabric with a tightly woven diagonal pattern. Made of cotton, wool, silk, viscose, and synthetic fibers.

Georgette

A sheer, plain-weave lightweight crepe fabric made of silk, wool, viscose, or synthetic fibers.

Godet

A triangular-shaped piece of fabric, inserted into a garment to create added fullness.

Gorge

The seam which joins a collar to a lapel.

Handkerchief hemline

A garment with soft folds of fabric ending in points, like the corners of a handkerchief, at the hemline.

Haute couture

French for "high dressmaking." Custom-made (as opposed to ready-to-wear) clothing of original design. Only those meeting the strict requirements of the Chambre Syndicale of the Fédération Française de la Couture in Paris are permitted to use the term.

High hip figure see CONTRAPPOSTO.

Hollywood waist

A waist treatment for bottom garments without a separate waistband. High-waisted styles feature belt loops secured at the natural waist.

Hue (of a color)

The intrinsic property of a color that defines its name and place in the spectrum; e.g. its redness, blueness, or purpleness, as opposed to the VALUE or INTENSITY of that color.

Interfacing

A fabric sewn in between the layers of a garment to provide extra strength or shaping. Interfacing is either sewn in place or ironed on (fusible).

Intensity (of a color)

The brightness or dullness of a color; ranging from pure color, to gray. Achieved with paint by adding the complement. See also HUE, VALUE.

Iridescent

Fabrics with different-colored warp and weft threads. They display changing colors when seen in different lights or from different angles.

Jacquard

A fabric with an intricate woven pattern, such as BROCADE. Named after the mechanical loom invented by Joseph-Marie Jacquard (1752–1834), which uses a series of hole-punched cards to control the weaving of complex patterns.

Jewel neckline

A simple round neckline.

Lab dip

Used to test-dye a swatch of fabric in order to match an exact color specified by a designer before production begins.

Lamé

A shiny fabric, made from metallic yarns.

Layette

A collection of clothing and bedding for newborns.

Licensing

Granting another manufacturer the rights to use a trademark or image on a specific product category in exchange for royalties.

Mandarin collar

A standing collar on a shirt or jacket based on traditional Asian designs; open at the front and rising 1–2in. (2.5–5cm) vertically. Also called a NEHRU COLLAR.

Manga

Japanese comic strip and print cartoons, with a distinctive visual style, shared by ANIME. See also OTAKU.

Masstige

"Prestige for the masses." Products which can be considered premium but which are available at more affordable prices.

Moiré

(Fabric with) a wavelike pattern.

Monochromatic color scheme

Uses colors comprised of tints and shades of a single HUE.

Muslin

A test version of a garment, often made of muslin (hence the name) and used to test pattern and fit. Also called a "toile."

Nap

Fabric with a nap has a raised pile which lies flat in one direction and so affects the way it reflects light. A garment made from napped fabric must have all its pattern pieces laid out facing the same direction on the fabric to avoid variations in color. Fabrics with a nap include velvet and corduroy.

Nehru collar

The small, standing collar featured on a Nehru jacket, as famously worn by Jawaharlal Nehru (1889–1964), first Prime Minister of independent India. Also called a MANDARIN COLLAR.

"New Look"

A silhouette introduced by Christian Dior (1905–1957) at his first couture show in 1947. The look featured a fitted jacket with a nipped-in waist and a full, calf-length skirt billowing out below.

Notched collar/lapel

Typical in blazers and coats, with a triangular notch cut or formed where the lapel joins the collar.

Organza

A sheer, crisp plain-weave fabric often used in bridalwear and eveningwear.

Orientalism

The influence of Eastern cultures, or the "Orient," on the arts. Orientalism in fashion was introduced in the first decade of the twentieth century, with designers such as Paul Poiret designing exotic clothes with cylindrical silhouettes and intricate prints and embellishments.

Otaku

A derogatory term used in Japan reclaimed from its negative connotation by a fan base having an obsessive interest in ANIME and MANGA.

Paillette

A small round metal or foil object larger than a sequin and used as embellishment, generally in clusters; spangles.

Panne velvet

A soft, stretchy, high-luster velvet with its pile flattened to one side. Also called "crushed velvet."

Patch pocket

A flat pocket created by sewing a pre-cut piece of material onto a garment.

Peacock Revolution

The movement in men's fashion, beginning in Britain in the early 1960s, toward a less conservative, more colorful and flamboyant look.

Peplum

A short extension of a bodice attached to the waist of a jacket, blouse, or dress. Can include gathers, pleats, or flares.

Picture plane

The flat surface on which an image is captured; in an imaginary plane perpendicular to the viewer's line of sight.

Pitch sheet

A reference sheet, showing a full REPEAT of the pattern and including samples of the colors to be used for the print.

Placket

A piece of fabric used to bind an opening, e.g. at the neckline or cuffs, usually with buttons.

Plate

An ultra smooth-finished paper, made by pressing the paper between metal plates.

Pleather

"Plastic leather"; an affordable synthetic leather substitute.

Point d'esprit

A mesh fabric covered with small dots, usually regularly spaced. Most commonly available in black or white.

Primary color

Red, yellow, or blue. These colors cannot be created by mixing other colors; they are themselves mixed to create all other colors.

Princess line

A fitted bodice or dress, created by using princess seams—curved vertical seams—rather than darts to create fullness and fit over the bust and a long, slim outline; the seam lines used to create this silhouette.

Raglan armhole

An armhole which extends all the way up to the neckline. The seam for this kind of sleeve starts at the neckline and extends diagonally down to the underarm.

Raster image

A computer image formed using a grid of small dots (pixels); used for photographs and image editing. The resolution of the image is determined by the number of dots per inch. See also VECTOR IMAGE.

Repeat

A motif or pattern which is duplicated along the length of a piece of fabric.

Rise

The center front length from the crotch to the waist on a pair of pants, or trousers. See also HOLLYWOOD WAIST.

Ruching see SHIRRING.

Sack dress

A style created by Cristobal Balenciaga (1895–1972). A simple, loose-fitting dress which hangs straight from the shoulder to the hem.

Secondary color

Orange, green, or violet. Colors which are created by mixing together two PRIMARY COLORs.

Seersucker

A cotton fabric that is woven using a process of alternating tight and slack weaves so that the fabric has a puckered, wrinkled appearance in certain places. Usually striped or checked.

Self belt

A belt made from the same fabric as the garment it is worn with.

Set-in armhole

An armhole that is attached to the body of a garment at or near the natural edge of the shoulder and eased to fit the armhole.

Shawl collar

A wide, turned-over collar on a sweater, jacket, or robe that incorporates the lapels and so extends in one unbroken line down the chest, forming a "V."

Shirring

A kind of machine gathering usually stitched in rows across the fabric and using an elastic bobbin thread to provide stretch. Also called "ruching."

Silk dupioni

A stiff silk fabric made from two intertwined yarns woven together, to create a shimmering effect. The threads used are uneven, which results in a "slubbed" decorative texture. Also called "shantung" and "raw silk." See also SLUB.

Slub

A soft lump or irregular thickening in yarn which is either considered an imperfection or is retained for decorative effect.

Smile pocket

An upward curving, set-in pocket, seen on Western-style shirts; often piped or embroidered with arrows at the corners.

Spec sheet

"Specification sheet." A document given to a pattern cutter to ensure correct execution of a first sample garment; including technical diagrams, measurements, grading formulas, and fabric yields.

Spread collar

A variation on a standard men's shirt collar, with a wide spread between the points.

Split complementary color scheme

Color scheme that uses the combination of a hue and the two colors adjacent to its complement.

Suitings

Fabrics used to make suits, therefore appropriate for both top and bottom garments. See also BOTTOM WEIGHTS, TOP WEIGHTS.

Surplice neckline

A neckline created from the two front sides of a bodice overlapping diagonally, forming a deep "V."

Sweep

The circumference of a hem.

Sweetheart neckline

A low-cut, plunging neckline, featuring two curves over the bust line, suggesting a heart shape.

Swing skirt

A retro-style circle skirt popular in the 1950s, fitted at the waist and hips with a wide flare at the hem.

Swipe file

A collection of images used as a ready reference for drawing figures and garment details. See also TEAR SHEET.

Tear sheet

A page cut or torn from a magazine or other publication, to be used as reference and included in a SWIPE FILE. Also called a "swipe."

Technical drawing see FLAT.

Tech pack

A document given to a manufacturer by a designer, stipulating all the relevant measurements and instructions for making a particular garment. Can also include distribution of colors and sizes for first samples; specifications for hang tags, labels, and packaging.

Tertiary color

Red-orange, yellow-orange, yellow-green, blue-green, blue-violet, or red-violet. Colors created by mixing together a PRIMARY COLOR and a SECONDARY COLOR.

Toile see MUSLIN.

Toile de Jouy

A fabric that was first manufactured in Jouy-en-Josas, France. A pastoral, Oriental, or floral themed pattern is printed in a single color on a white or off-white background.

Top weights

Fabrics that are appropriate for top garments—coats, jackets, and vests (waistcoats). See also BOTTOM WEIGHTS.

Trapeze dress

A style created by Yves Saint Laurent (1936–2008) for Dior. A loose-fitting dress that is narrow at the bust and flares out toward the bottom hem.

Trend research

The forecasting of themes, styles, and colors; published or commissioned to support designers and retailers. See also COOL HUNTING, FORECASTING SERVICES.

Triadic color scheme

Uses a combination of colors that are equidistant from one another on the COLOR WHEEL.

Value (of a color)

The lightness or darkness of a color; ranging from light, to dark, to black. See also HUE, INTENSITY.

Vector image

A computer image formed using anchor points and connecting paths to form shapes rather than pixels; resolution-independent and smaller in file size. See also RASTER IMAGE.

Vellum

A heavy, high-quality translucent paper resembling parchment.

Vintage chic

An approach to fashion that involves sourcing secondhand or antique items, which are often worn mixed with modern garments.

Warp

The lengthwise yarns of a woven fabric. The warp yarns are stretched on the loom first, then the WEFT yarns are woven through them.

Weft

The widthwise yarns of a woven fabric. Weft yarns are woven through the WARP threads at right angles to them, from selvage to selvage.

Welt pocket

A set-in pocket with one lip (or finished edge), 3/8–1in. (1–2.5cm) in width, at the opening. Commonly used for handkerchief pockets on blazers.

Yarn-dyed

Fabrics which are made of yarns that have been colored before they are woven or knitted into fabric.

Yoke

A shaped piece of fabric at the top of a skirt or on the shoulder of a shirt or jacket onto which other fabric is attached.

Further Reading

General

Books

Cally Blackman. *100 Years of Fashion Illustration*. London: Laurence King, 2007

Laird Borrelli. *Fashion Illustration by Fashion Designers*. San Francisco, CA: Chronicle Books, 2008

Sass Brown. *Eco Fashion*. London: Laurence King 2010

Hywel Davies. *Fashion Designers' Sketchbooks*. London: Laurence King 2010

Editors of Phaidon Press. *Sample: 100 Fashion Designers—010 Curators—Cuttings from Contemporary Fashion*. London: Phaidon, 2006

Clive Hallett and Amanda Johnston. *Fabric for Fashion: The Swatch Book*. London: Laurence King 2010

Sue Jenkyn Jones. *Fashion Design (2nd edition)*. London: Laurence King 2005

Bradley Quinn. *Textile Designers at the Cutting Edge*. London: Laurence King 2009

Magazines

A Magazine, Bloom, Dansk, Dazed & Confused, Elle, Flair, Flare, i-D magazine, L'Officiel, Numéro, Oyster, Pop, Purple Fashion, Rendezvous, Selvedge, 10 Women, V, Velvet, View on Colour, Viewpoint, Visionaire, Vogue, VS

Websites

www.morefashiondrawing.com

agencies and associations

www.agent002.com
www.art-dept.com
www.cwc-i.com
www.dutchuncle.co.uk
www.fashionillustration.or.kr
www.fashionmission.nl
fashion.parsons.edu/
www.trafficnyc.com

blogs and individual designers

www.ashadedviewonfashion.com
www.costumes.org
designerman-whatisawtoday.blogspot.com
www.ecofashiontalk.com
www.julieverhoeven.com
www.mamienbaby.com
www.showstudio.com
www.sparked.biz
www.stylewillsaveus.com/blog.php
www.thesartorialist.blogspot.com
zerofabricwastefashion.blogspot.com

news and trendwatching

www.catwalking.com
www.coolhunting.com
www.dazeddigital.com
www.drapersonline.com
www.firstview.com
www.firstviewkorea.com
www.hintmag.com
www.jcreport.com
www.peclersparis.com

www.refinery29.com
www.style.com
www.stylesight.com
www.trendunion.com
www.WGSN.com
www.wwd.com

historical dress

www.fashion-era.com
fashionmuseum.fitnyc.edu/code/emuseum.asp
www.kci.or.jp/archives/index_e.html
www.marquise.de
www.museumofcostume.co.uk

resources

www.human-anatomy-for-artist.com
www.pbs.org/newshour/infocus/fashion/whatisfashion.html

retail

www.colette.fr
www.doverstreetmarket.com
www.kirnazabete.com
www.newpeopleworld.com
www.openingceremony.us
www.projectno8.com
www.10corsocomo.com

Chapter 1 Drawing Women

Books

Michele Wesen Bryant. *WWD Illustrated*. New York, NY: Fairchild Publications, 2004

Juan Eugene Ramos. *Antonio: 60, 70, 80 – Three Decades of Fashion Illustration*. London: Thames and Hudson, 1995

Jenó Barcsay. *Anatomy for the Artist*. London: Little, Brown, 2008

Robert Beverly Hale and Terence Coyle. *Albinus on Anatomy*. New York, NY: Dover Publications; Reprint edition 1989

Chapter 2 Drawing Men

Books

Cally Blackman. *100 Years of Menswear*. London: Laurence King, 2009

Farid Chenoune. *A History of Men's Fashion*. Paris: Flammarion, 1996

Hywel Davies. *Modern Menswear*. London: Laurence King, 2008

D. Hastings-Nield. *Basic Human Anatomy*: introductory CD-ROM from *The Anatomy Project* series. New York, NY: Parthenon Group, 1998

David K. Rubins. *The Human Figure*. New York, NY: Viking Press, 1976

Fritz Schider and Bernard Wolf. *An Atlas of Anatomy for Artists*. New York, NY: Dover Publications, 1957

Magazines

AnOtherMan, Arena Hommes, Esquire, Fantastic Man, GQ, Vogue Hommes, L'Officiel Hommes, Numéro Homme

Websites

www.aitorthroup.com
www.brooksbrothers.com
www.fantasticman.com
www.hickeystyle.com
www.gq.com
www.nylonguysmag.com

Chapter 3 Drawing Children and Young Adults

Books

Henry Darger, ed. Michael Bonesteel. *Henry Darger: Art and Selected Writings*. New York, NY: Rizzoli International Publications, 2001

Garan, Gina. *Blythe Style*. San Francisco, CA: Chronicle Books, 2004

Eadweard Muybridge. *The Human Figure In Motion*. New York: Dover 1955

Magazines

FADER, FRUiTS, Girl's Life, Seventeen, Teen Vogue, Vogue Bambini, Yellow Rat Bastard

Websites

trade shows:

Fimi Feria, Valencia: www.fimi.es
Pitti Bimbo, Florence: www.pittimmagine.com/en/fiere/bimbo
Bubble, New York: www.bubblenewyork.com

infants and toddlers:

www.babesta.com
www.bonnieyoung.com
www.gap.com *(babyGap)*
www.zutano.com

children:

www.americangirl.com
www.brycewear.com
www.florahenri.com
www.jcrew.com *(crewcuts range)*
www.oililyshop.com
www.us.allsaints.com/children

tweens and juniors:

www.55dsl.com
www.abercrombiekids.com
www.bape.com
store.delias.com
www.drjays.com

general reference:

www.dccomics.com
www.enchanteddoll.com
www.gaiaonline.com
gorillaz.com
www.herakut.de
www.honeyjam.co.uk
www.kidrobot.com
www.kouklitas.com
www.lost.art.br/osgemeos.htm
www.manhattantoy.com
www.nick.com
www.secondlife.com
www.whyville.net
www.yoyashop.com

Chapter 4 Zooming In

Books

Fly. *Peops: Portraits and Stories of People*. Brooklyn, New York: Soft Skull Press, 2003

Hans Silvester. *Natural Fashion: Tribal Decoration From Africa*. London: Thames and Hudson, 2008

Websites

www.allaboutshoes.ca/eng
www.albertusswanepoel.com
www.stephenjonesmillinery.com

Chapter 5 Working from Life

Books

Gerald M. Ackerman, Charles Bargue, Jean-Léon Gérôme. *Drawing Course*, Courbevoie, Paris: ACR, 2003,

Betty Edwards. *The New Drawing on the Right Side of the Brain*. New York, NY: Jeremy P. Tarcher/Putnam, 1999

Kimon Nicolaides. *The Natural Way to Draw*. New York, NY: Mariner Books, 1990

Websites

www.springstudiosoho.com
www.lifedrawingsociety.co.uk

Chapter 6 Basic Garment Details

Books

Bill Dunn. *Uniforms*. London: Laurence King, 2009

Mary Brooks Picken. *A Dictionary of Costume and Fashion: Historic and Modern*. Mineola, NY: Dover Publications, 1999

Michele Wesen Bryant and Diane DeMers. *The Spec Manual, 2nd Edition*, New York, NY: Fairchild Publications, 2004

Websites

www.polyvore.com

Chapter 7 Drapery

Books

Marie-André Jouve. *Balenciaga*. New York, NY: Assouline, 2004

Richard Martin. *American Ingenuity: Sportswear 1930s–1970s*. New York, NY: Metropolitan Museum of Art, 1998

Richard Martin. *Charles James*. New York, NY: Assouline, 2006

Richard Martin and Harold Koda. *Haute Couture*. New York, NY: Metropolitan Museum of Art, distr. Abrams, 1995

Tomoko Nakamichi. *Pattern Magic*. London: Laurence King, 2010

Charlotte Seeling. *Fashion: The Century of The Designer 1900–1999*. Cologne: Konemann, 2000

Judith Watt. *Ossie Clark: 1965–74*. London: V & A Publications, 2006

Norah Waugh. *The Cut of Women's Clothes*, London: Routledge, 2007

Kohle Yohannan and Nancy Nolf. *Claire McCardell: Redefining Modernism*, New York, NY: Harry N. Abrams 1998

Chapter 8 Tailored Clothing

Books

Cally Blackman. *100 Years of Menswear*. London: Laurence King, 2009

Amy Spindler. "Critic's Notebook. The Power Suit and Other Fictions." *NY Times* March 25, 1997

Colette Wolff. *The Art of Manipulating Fabric*. Radnor, PA: Chiltern Book Co., 1996

Websites

www3.fitnyc.edu/museum/tailorsart/contemporarytailoring.htm
www.cesarani.com
www.chesterbarrie.co.uk
www.craigrobinsonnyc.com
www.dege-skinner.co.uk
www.gievesandhawkes.com
www.henrypoole.com
www.historyinthemaking.com
www.krisvanassche.com
www.nortonandsons.co.uk
www.tombrowntailors.co.uk

Chapter 9 Rendering Shine

Books

Francesca Sterlacci. *Leather Fashion Design*. London: Laurence King 2010

Websites

www.lineapelle-fair.it
www.lostartnyc.com

Chapter 10 Rendering Woven Wools

Books

Jeffrey Banks and Doria de La Chapelle. *Tartan Romancing the Plaid*. New York: Rizzoli International Publications, Inc., 2007

Matilda McQuaid. *Extreme Textiles: Designing for High Performance*. New York, NY: Princeton Architectural Press, 2005

SGMA. *Sport Apparel Dictionary of Performance Fibers, Fabrics and Finishes*. North Palm Beach, FL: Sporting Goods Manufacturers Association, 1997

Websites

www.house-of-tartan.scotland.net
www.invista.com
www.ispo.com

www.pittimmagine.com/en/fiere/filati/
www.schoeller-tech.com/en.html
www.snowsports.org
www.strathmorewoollen.co.uk
www.21stcenturykilts.com
www.wool.com

Chapter 11 Rendering Prints

Books

Melanie Bowles and Ceri Isaac. *Digital Textile Design*. London: Laurence King 2009

Stephen Calloway. *Liberty of London: Masters of Style & Decoration*. London: Little, Brown, 1992

Shirley Kennedy. *Pucci: A Renaissance in Fashion*. New York, NY: Abbeville Press, 1991

Jonathan M. Woodham. *Twentieth-century Ornament*. New York, NY: Rizzoli, 1990

Websites

www.design-library.com
www.eleykishimoto.com
www.ivanahelsinki.com
www.liberty.co.uk
www.research.amnh.org/anthropology/database/collections

Chapter 12 Rendering Sheers

Books

Katie Dominy. *Contemporary Lingerie Design*. London: Laurence King, 2010

Robert Doyle. *Waisted Efforts: An Illustrated Guide to Corset Making*. Halifax, Nova Scotia: Sartorial Press Publications, 1997

Malu Halasa and Rana Salam. *The Secret Life of Syrian Lingerie: Intimacy and Design*. San Francisco, CA: Chronicle Books, 2008

David Revere McFadden. *Radical Lace & Subversive Knitting*. New York, NY: Museum of Arts & Design, 2007

Harriet Worsley. *The White Dress: Fashion Inspiration for Brides*. London: Laurence King 2009

Websites

www.agentprovocateur.com
www.foundationsrevealed.com
www.kikidm.com
www.lace.lacefairy.com
www.laperla.com
www.lingerie-uncovered.com
www.mode-city.com
www.princessetamtam.com
www.solstissbucol.com
www.the-lingerie-post.com
www.triumph.com
www.underfashionclub.org
www.venacavadesign.co.uk

Resources

Museums, galleries, and libraries

Museums

Australia
Powerhouse Museum
500 Harris Street
Ultimo
NSW 1238
Tel. +61 (0)2 9217 0111
archive@phm.gov.au
www.powerhousemuseum.com

Belgium
MoMu
Antwerp Fashion Mode Museum
Nationalestraat 28
B-2000 Antwerpen
Tel. +32 (0)3 470 27 70
info@momu.be
www.momu.be

Canada
The Bata Shoe Museum
327 Bloor Street West
Toronto ON
M5S 1W7
Tel. +1 (0)416 979 7799
www.batashoemuseum.ca

France
Fondation Pierre Bergé Yves Saint Laurent
5 avenue Marceau
75116 Paris
Tel. +33 (0)1 44 31 64 00
www.fondation-pb-ysl.net

Institut Français de la Mode (IFM)
36 quai d'Austerlitz
75013 Paris
Tel. +33 (0)1 70 38 89 89
ifm@ifm-paris.com
www.ifm-paris.com

Musée des Arts de la Mode et du Textile
Palais du Louvre
107 rue de Rivoli
75001 Paris
Tel. +33 (0)1 44 55 57 50
www.ucad.fr

Musée de la Mode et du Costume
Palais Galliéra
10 avenue Pierre 1er de Serbie
75116 Paris
Tel +33 (0)1 56 52 86 00

Musée de la Toile de Jouy
54 rue Charles de Gaulle
78350 Jouy-en-Josas
Tel. +33 (0)1 39 56 48 64

Le Musée des Tissus et des Arts Décoratifs
34 rue de la Charité
F-69002 Lyon
Tel. +33 (0)4 78 38 42 00
info@musee-des-tissus.com
www.musee-des-tissus.com

Germany
Deutsches Historisches Museum
Unter den Linden 2
10117 Berlin
Tel: +49 (0)30 20304 0
www.dhm.de

Lipperheidesche Kostümbibliothek
Kunstbibliothek
Staatliche Museen zu Berlin
Matthäikirchplatz 6
10785 Berlin
Tel. +49 (0)30 266 42 4242
service@smb.museum
www.smb.museum

Italy
Fondazione Antonio Ratti
Villa Sucota
Via per Cernobbio 19
22100 Como
Tel. +39 (0)31 233111
info@fondazioneratti.org
www.fondazioneratti.org

Fondazione Cerratelli *(Theatrical Costume Collection)*
Via G. di Vittorio 2
San Giuliano Terme, 56017
Tel. +39 (0)50 817900
fondazione@fondazionecerratelli.it
www.fondazionecerratelli.it/home.html

Galeria del Costume
Palazzo Pitti
Piazza de' Pitti 1
50125 Florence
Tel. +39 (0)55 238 8611

Museo Fortuny
Palazzo Fortuny
San Marco 3958
Venice 30124
Tel. +39 (0)41 520 09 95
www.museicivicveneziani.it

Museum Salvatore Ferragamo
Palazzo Spini Feroni
Via Tornabuoni 2
50123 Florence
Tel. +39 (0)55 3360 456
museoferragamo@ferragamo.com
www.museoferragamo.it

Triennale Design Museum
Viale Alemagna 6
20121 Milan
Tel. +39 (0)2 724 341
www.triennaledesignmuseum.it

Japan
Kobe Fashion Museum
9, 2-chome
Koyocho-naka
Higashinada
Kobe 658-0032
Tel. +81 (0)78 858 0050
www.fashionmuseum.or.jp/english/index.html

Kyoto Costume Institute
103, Shichi-jo Goshonouchi Minamimachi
Shimogyo-ku, Kyoto
600-8864 Japan
Tel. +81 (75)-321-8011
www.kci.or.jp
info@kci.or.jp

Spain

Museu d'Art Contemporani de Barcelona (MACBA)
Placa des Angels, 1
08001 Barcelona
Tel. +34 (0)93 412 08 10 (ext 366)
bibliote@macba.es
www.macba.es

The Netherlands

Centraal Museum Utrecht
Nicolaaskerkhof 10, Utrecht
Tel. +31 (0)30 2362362
www.centraalmuseum.nl
infocentrum@centraalmuseum.nl

Gemeentemuseum Den Haag
Stadhouderslaan 41
Postbus 72
2501 Den haag
Tel. +31 (0)70 3381111
www.gemeentemuseum.nl
info@gemeentemuseum.nl

U.K.

Museum of Costume
Assembly Rooms
Bennett Street
Bath BA1 2QH
Tel. +44 (0)1225 477173
fashion_bookings@bathnes.gov.uk
www.museumofcostume.co.uk

Somerset House Trust
Strand
London WC2R 1LA
Tel. +44 (0) 20 7845 4600
www.somersethouse.org.uk
info@somersethouse.org.uk

Victoria and Albert Museum (V&A)
Cromwell Road
South Kensington
London SW7 2RL
Tel. +44 (0)20 7942 2000
vanda@vam.ac.uk
www.vam.ac.uk

U.S.

Cora Ginsburg LLC
19 East 74th Street
New York, NY 10021
Tel: +1 212 744 1352
info@coraginsburg.com
www.coraginsburg.com

Costume Gallery
Los Angeles County Museum of Art
5905 Wilshire Boulevard
Los Angeles
CA 90036
Tel. +1 323 857 6000
publicinfo@lacma.org
www.lacma.org

Costume Institute
Metropolitan Museum of Art
1000 5th Avenue at 82nd Street
New York
NY 10028-0198
Tel. +1 212 535 7710
www.metmuseum.org

Drexel Historical Costume Collection
Antoinette Westphal College of Media Arts & Design
603, Nesbitt Hall
33rd and Market Streets
Philadelphia, PA 19104
Tel. +1 215-571-3504
www.drexel.edu

Museum at the Fashion Institute of Technology
7th Avenue at 27th Street
New York
NY 10001-5992
Tel. +1 212 217 7999
museuminfo@fitnyc.edu
www.fitnyc.edu

Museum of the City of New York
Costume and Textile Collection
1220 5th Avenue at 103rd Street
New York, NY 10029
Tel. +1 212 534 1672 (ext 3399)
research@mcny.org
www.mcny.org/

Smithsonian Cooper-Hewitt, National Design Museum
2 East 91st Street
New York, NY 10128-0669
Tel. +1 212 849 8400 (General)/849 8452 (The Textile Collection)
tex@si.edu
www.cooperhewitt.org

Fabric libraries

U.K.

The Design Library
11 Sandringham Court
Dufours Place
London, W1F 7SL
Tel. +44 (0)20 7287 7336
kdenham@design-library.com

U.S.

American Textile History Museum
491 Dutton Street
Lowell, MA 01854-4221
Tel. +1 978 441 0400
www.athm.org

The Design Library
400 Market Industrial Park, Suite 1
Wappingers Falls, NY 12590
Tel. +1 845 297 1035
info@design-library.com
www.design-library.com

Earth Pledge Foundation
Future Fashion Textile Library
122 East 38th Street
New York, NY 10016-2602
www.earthpledge.org/ff
info@earthpledge.org

Galleries and archives specializing in fashion illustration

Galerie Bartsch & Chariau GmbH
Galeriestrasse 6
D-80539 Munich
Germany
Tel. +49 (0)89 295557
galerie@bartsch-chariau.de
www.bartsch-chariau.de

Fashion Illustration Gallery
The Mayor Gallery
22A Cork Street
London W1S 3NA
Tel. +44 (0)20 8543 6731
info@fashionillustrationgallery.com
www.fashionillustrationgallery.com

Gallery Hanahou
611 Broadway Suite 730
New York, NY 10012
Tel. +1 646 486 6586
info@galleryhanahou.com
www.galleryhanahou.com

Anna-Maria and Stephen Kellen Archives
Parsons The New School for Design
66 Fifth Avenue, lobby level
New York, NY 10011
Tel. 212-229-5942
library.newschool.edu/speccoll/kellen/
kac@newschool.edu

The Frances Neady Collection/ Special Collections
The Gladys Marcus Library at FIT
7th Avenue at 27th Street, E-Building
New York, NY 10001-5992
museuminfo@fitnyc.edu
www3.fitnyc.edu/museum/artful_line/ neady.htm

Museums for children

U.K.

V&A Museum of Childhood
Cambridge Heath Road
London E2 9PA
UK
Tel: +44 (0)20 8983 5200
moc@vam.ac.uk
www.vam.ac.uk/moc

U.S.

American Visionary Art Museum
800 Key Highway
Baltimore, MD 21230
Tel. +1 410 244 1900
info@avam.org
www.avam.org

Museum of the City of New York
(NY Toy Stories)
1220 5th Avenue at 103rd Street
New York, NY 10029
Tel. +1 212 534 1672
info@mcny.org
www.mcny.org/exhibitions/current/new-york-toy-stories.html

Mercer Museum
84 South Pine Street
Doylestown, PA 18901-4999
Tel. 215 345 0210
info@mercermuseum.org
www.mercermuseum.org

Lacemaking

Le Musée des Beaux-Arts et de la dentelle, Calais
(history of lacemaking in Calais)
25 rue Richelieu
62100 Calais, France
Tel. +33 (0)3 21 46 43 14
www.musee.calais.fr

Competitions

All Japan Fashion Teachers Contest
295 Madison Ave.
New York, NY 10017-6304
+1 (212) 685-4971

Arts of Fashion Foundation competition
www.arts-of-fashion.org

Concept Korea fashion collective
www.conceptkorea.org/main

Council of Fashion Designers of America (CFDA)
www.cfda.com/scholarship-program
www.cfda.com/liz-claiborne-scholarship-lookbooks
www.cfda.com/geoffrey-beene-design-scholar-award

ITS Fashion Competition/Diesel Award
www.itsweb.org/jsp/en/fashion/index.jsp

Mittelmoda/The Fashion Award
Mittelmoda International Lab
Via Cotonificio, 96
33030 Torreano di Martignacco (Udine)
Italy
Tel. 00353 862478170
www.mittelmoda.com
sopelza@tiscali.it

Riccione Moda Italia
www.riccionemodaitalia.it

Triumph Inspiration Award *(intimate apparel design competition)*
www.triumphinspirationaward.com

Villa Noailles festival
www.villanoailles-hyeres.com

Stores and suppliers

(art supplies unless otherwise indicated)

Australia

Brandcorp
www.brandcorp.com

NSW Leather
www.nswleather.com.au

Textile & Lace Imports
48 Princess Ave, Rosebery, NSW 2018
Tel. +61 (02)9662 4566

Belgium

Schleiper
www.schleiper.be

Denmark

Creas A/S
www.creas.com

Finland

Tempera
www.tempera.com

France

Bazar de l'Hôtel de Ville (BHV) *(art supplies, trim, hardware, yarn)*
www.bhv.fr

Bouchara *(fabrics)*
www.bouchara.com

Créa
www.crea.tm.fr

Dominique Kieffer *(fabrics)*
www.dkieffer.com

La Droguerie à Paris *(trimmings, knitting patterns, and supplies)*
www.ladroguerie.com

Le Géant des Beaux Arts
www.geant-beaux-arts.fr

Marché Carreau du temple *(fabric and clothing market)*
rue Perrée
75003 Paris

Marché St Pierre *(fabrics)*
www.marchesaintpierre.com

Mokuba *(ribbons)*
www.mokuba.fr

Moline Tissus *(fabrics for interiors)*
1 Place Saint-Pierre
75018 Paris
Tel. +33 (0)1 46 06 14 66

Pierre Frey *(fabrics and furnishings)*
www.pierrefrey.com

Tissus Reine *(end-of-line fabrics)*
www.tissus-reine.com

Le Rouvray *(patchwork and craft supplies)*
www.lerouvray.com

Tombées du Camion *(bric a brac)*
www.tombeesducamion.com

Librairie 7L *(bookstore owned by Karl Lagerfeld)*
7 rue de Lille
75007 Paris
Tel. +33 (0)1 42 92 03 58

The Netherlands
Harolds Grafik B.V.
www.harolds.nl

De Vlieger Amsterdam B.V.
www.vliegerpapier.nl

Peter Van Ginkel
www.petervanginkel.nl

Van der Linde
www.vanderlinde.com

Van Beek
www.vanbeekonline.com

Ireland
Bradbury Art Store
www.bradbury-graphics.co.uk

Italy
Arte 3
www.arte3.it

Vertecchi
www.vertecchi.com

Japan
Ito-ya Ltd.
www.ito-ya.co.jp

Korea
Atom Trading Co.
Namdaemun4-ga 20-1
Jung-gu, Seoul, 100-094

Dongdaemun Complex Market *(fabrics and trims)*
Jongno6-ga 289-3
Jongno-gu
Seoul
South Korea 110-701

Homi Art Co.
www.homi.co.kr

New Zealand
The French Art Shop
www.thefrenchartshop.co.nz

NSW Leather
www.nswleather.com.au

Spain
Tot en Art
www.totenart.com

Switzerland
Boesner GmbH
www.boesner.ch

Interproducts AG
Seefeldstrasse 224
8034 Zurich
Tel. +41 (0)44 422 70 23

art ware mail
www.artwaremail.ch

U.K.
Alma Leather
www.almahome.co.uk

Barnet & Lawson *(ribbons, lace, feathers, elastics)*
www.bltrimmings.com

Borovick Fabrics Ltd.
www.borovickfabricsltd.co.uk

Cass Arts
www.cassart.co.uk

Celestial Buttons
54 Cross Street
London N1 2BA
Tel. +44 (0)20 7226 4766

The Cloth House
www.clothhouse.com

The Cloth Shop *(fabrics)*
www.theclothshop.net

Creative Beadcraft (formerly Ells & Farrier) *(beads, sequins, and crystals)*
www.creativebeadcraft.co.uk

Eastman Staples Ltd. *(pattern-cutting equipment)*
www.eastman.co.uk

F. Ciment Pleating
www.cimentpleating.co.uk

George Weil and Sons Ltd. *(fabrics, dyes, printing equipment, books)*
www.georgeweil.co.uk

The Handweavers Studio *(yarns, fibers, dyes, books)*
www.handweavers.co.uk

London Graphic Centre
www.londongraphics.co.uk

MacCulloch & Wallis Ltd. *(fabrics, haberdashery, trimmings)*
www.macculloch-wallis.co.uk

Morplan Fashion *(stationers and cutting-room equipment)*
www.morplan.com

Pongees
www.pongees.co.uk

R.D. Franks Ltd. *(fashion books and magazines, tools, dress stands)*
www.rdfranks.co.uk

Rai Trimmings *(tailoring supplies)*
9–12 St Annes Court
London W1F 0BA
Tel. +44 (0)20 7437 2696

Rose Fittings (James & Alden)
Hannover House
385 Edgware Road
London NW2 6BA
Tel. +44 (0)20 8830 8008

Soho Silks
www.sohosilks.co.uk/home1.php

Whaleys (Bradford) Ltd. *(plain, natural, and greige cloth)*
www.whaleys-bradford.ltd.uk

William Gee *(linings, haberdashery, trims)*
www.williamgee.co.uk

U.S.
Active Trimming *(shoulder pads and trims)*
247 West 38th Street
New York, NY 10018-4447
Tel. +1 212 921 7114

Adel Rootstein USA Inc. *(display mannequins)*
www.rootstein.com

Alpha Trims Inc.
www.alphatrims.com

B&J Fabrics
www.bandjfabrics.com

Blick Art Materials
www.dickblick.com

Brewer-Cantelmo *(custom portfolios)*
www.brewer-cantelmo.com

Britex Fabrics
www.britexfabrics.com

La Button Boutique Ltd.
250 West 39th Street
New York, NY 10018-4414
Spandex House
www.spandexhouse.com/

Button Works
www.buttonworks.com

Buttonwood Corporation
www.woodbuttons.com

Fashion Design Books
www.fashiondesignbooks.com

Fermin's Fashion Inc. *(leather)*
265 West 37th Street
Suite 408
New York, NY 10018
Tel. +1 212 575 2088

General Bead Online
www.genbead.com

Global Leather
www.globalleathers.com

Kinokuniya Bookstore
www.kinokuniya.com

Lace Star, Inc.
www.lacestar.com

La Lame Inc. *(stretch and party fabrics, elasticated trims)*
www.lalame.com

Libra Leather, Inc.
www.libraleather.com

M&J Trimming
www.mjtrim.com

Mendels and Far Out Fabrics
www.mendels.com

Metalliferous *(metal trim, tools and supplies)*
www.metalliferous.com

Mood Fabrics
www.moodfabrics.com

NY Elegant Fabrics
www.nyelegantfabrics.com

Paron Fabrics
www.paronfabrics.com

Pearl Paint
www.pearlpaint.com

The Pellon Company *(interfacings and appliqués)*
www.pellonideas.com

Quick Fuse & Cut Inc
260 W 36th Street # 1
New York, NY 10018-7560
Tel. +1 212 967 0311

Reprodepot Fabrics
www.reprodepotfabrics.com

Sam Flax *(art supplies)*
www.samflaxny.com

Satin Moon *(fabrics)*
www.satin-moon.com

Service Notions
256 West 38th Street
New York, NY 10018-5807
Tel +1 212 921 1680

Snap Source
www.snapsource.com

Stanley Pleating & Stitching Company
www.stanleypleatingandstitching.com

The Strand Bookstore
www.strandbooks.com

Superior Model Form Co.
www.superiormodel.com

Swarovski Crystal Company
www.swarovski.com

Tender Buttons
www.tenderbuttons-nyc.com

Utrecht Art Supplies
www.utrechtart.com

Zipper Stop *(zippers and threads)*
www.zipperstop.com

Index

Page numbers in **bold** refer to picture captions

Picture Credits

The author and publisher would like to thank the following institutions and individuals for providing photographic images for use in this book. In all cases, every effort had been made to credit the copyright holders, but should there be any omissions or errors the publisher would be pleased to insert the appropriate acknowledgment in any subsequent edition of this book.

l = left, r = right, c = center, t = top, b = bottom, br = bottom right:

Front cover: Tina Berning, represented by 2agenten.com (Germany and Europe), CWC-i.com (North America), Synergyart.co.uk (UK) and CWC-tokyo.com (Asia)

1: © Laurie Marman
2–3: © Sylvia Kwan
4: © Richard Rosenfeld
5 t: © Eri Wakiyama
5 b: Drawing by Steven Broadway
6 bl: © Alfredo Cabrera
6 br: © Anna Kiper
7: © Laura Laine
8–9: © Alfredo Cabrera
10: Photo by Fernanda Calfat/Getty Images
11 br: © L & M Services B.V. The Hague 20100508
13: Colgate-Palmolive
15 tr: © ADAGP, Paris and DACS, London 2010
17, 20 l, 21 r: AKG Images/Gerd Hartung
20–21: © Alvin J. Pimsler
22: Original work by Jo Landis. Contracted by Don Wise Advertising, NYC for Junior Fashion Co., "Charlie Girls"
23: Courtesy Estate of Antonio Lopez and Juan Ramos and Galerie Bartsch & Chariau
24: © Barbara Pearlman
25 r: © George Stavrinos
26: © Albert Elia
27 l: © Sharon Watts
27 tr: Courtesy Estate of Antonio Lopez and Juan Ramos and Galerie Bartsch & Chariau
29: Illustrated and styled by Amy Davis
30: © Richard Haines
31 l: Mark Grady (Grady Echegaray www.strangepixels.net)
31 r: Pierre Verdy/AFP/Getty Images
32: © Eri Wakiyama
33: Firstview
34: © Niloufar Mozafari
35: Blumarine
36 l: Lunar Superstar from the series "Witch". Witch: The Book of Bananas, Forks, Spoons + Heartbreak © 2010 Andrea Marshall
36 r: © Laura Laine
41 bl, br: © Hae Won (Anna) Lee
42: © Jessica Strimbu
56 r: Firstview
58: stylesight.com
59: Firstview
63: Girl with Fan from the series "Psychedelica" © 2006 Andrea Marshall
64 r: Image by Kelly de Nooyer using pieces of clip art
65 r: © Eri Wakiyama
67 tr: © Elisabeth Dempsey
72 r: Pierre Verdy/AFP/Getty Images
73: Illustration by Muntsa Vicente originally published by Woman magazine (Spain)
74: www.ninadonis.com
75 l: Dylan Paul Moran Taverner
75 r: Firstview
76 l: © Howard Tangye
76 r: © Richard Haines
77: © Paula Sanz Caballero, Coredo 1 – hand stitched illustration, 2004
78 r: © Fernanda Guedes, São Paulo, Brazil. www.fernandaguedes.com.br, www.galeriamagenta.com.br
79: © Seksarit Thanaprasittikul
84 t: Photo: Peter Clark. Design by Peter Clark
84 b: © Diana Lin
86, 90, 91: © Richard Rosenfeld
92: Firstview
95: Dylan Paul Moran Taverner
96: © Howard Tangye
97: © Diana Lin
98: Scratch My Record, 2005. Mixed media on paper. www.illustrationweb.com/sarahbeetson © Sarah Beetson
99: © Sarah Beetson
100: © Sungeun Kim
101 l: Yuki Hatori c/o. CWC International, Inc. www.cwc-i.com, agent@cwc-i.com tel: +1. 646.486.6586. 611 Broadway, Suite 730, New York NY 10012, U.S.A.
101 r: © Sarah Beetson
108: © Kathryn Elyse Rodgers
109 l: Tina Berning, represented by 2agenten.com (Germany and Europe), CWC-i.com (North America), Synergyart.co.uk (UK) and CWC-tokyo.com (Asia)
109 tr: Courtesy Estate of Antonio Lopez and Juan Ramos and Galerie Bartsch & Chariau
109 b: Designer/artist: Joey Casey. The figures are croquis for a collection
118 c, bl: Courtesy Estate of Antonio Lopez and Juan Ramos and Galerie Bartsch & Chariau
119: Drawings by Steven Broadway
122 bl: © Lubo Vladov
124 bl: © Fernanda Guedes, São Paulo, Brazil. www.fernandaguedes.com.br, www.galeriamagenta.com.br
124 tr: © Eri Wakiyama
125 tr: © Lubo Vladov
125 c: © Richard Haines
125 r: Mark Grady (Grady Echegaray www.strangepixels.net)
128 l, c: © Marina Bychkova. Image editing by Chad Isley
128 r: Cinderella designed and made by Shona Reppe puppets. Photo: Esther Sundberg
129: © Herakut
134: © Tanya Ling 2009. Chanel RTW F/W 2009. Image Courtesy FASHIONILLUSTRATIONGALLERY.COM
135: Catwalking.com
136: © Julie Johnson www.juliejohnsonart.com juliejohnsonart@gmail.com, julie@juliejohnsonart.com
137 t: © Fabiola Arias
138 t: © Herakut
138 b: © Angelique Houtkamp
142 br: © Frank Nathan
143 t: © Eri Wakiyama
143 br: Richard A. Brooks/AFP/Getty Images
144 l: © Laurie Marman
144 r: © Elisabeth Dempsey
145 tr, br: © Richard Haines
146: David Bray represented by Private View www.pvuk.com, create@pvuk.com
147 tl: © Laurie Marman
147 r: Tina Berning, represented by 2agenten.com (Germany and Europe), CWC-i.com (North America), Synergyart.co.uk (UK) and CWC-tokyo.com (Asia)
151 tr: © Howard Tangye
152 l: Ferdinand (http://ferdinand.nowhasa.com)
152 r: © Wyatt Hough
155 t: Photo: Peter Clark. Design by Peter Clark
157 l: Dana de Kuyper www.damneddollies.com
157 r: © Herakut
160 l: © Marina Bychkova. Image editing by Chad Isley
160 r: © Herakut
161 l: Courtesy Estate of Antonio Lopez and Juan Ramos and Galerie Bartsch & Chariau
161 r: Ferdinand (http://ferdinand.nowhasa.com)
165 b: © Richard Haines
166 t: © Glen Tunstull Original in the private collection of Renaldo Barnette
173 t: stylesight.com
176: © Janae DeLaurentis
177 r: © Vasilija Zivanic, Vasilija Zivanic Design
178: © Noriko Kikuchi
179 bl: © Erika Kobayashi
180: © Sofia Enlund
181 r: © Sara Harper
183: © Jillian Carrozza
184: © Whitney Newman
185 bl: © Jillian Carrozza
186 tl: © Howard Tangye
186 tr: © Megan Schwarz
186 b: © Richard Rosenfeld
187 l: © Sara Harper
187 r: © Jesse Lee Burton
189 l: © Alex Katz, DACS, London/VAGA, New York 2010
189 tr: © Jesse Lee Burton
189 br: http://www.carlaciddediego.blogspot.com/
190 t: © Olga Baird
190 bl: © Janet Shin
190 br: © Juan Mota
191 l: © Kristin Shoemaker-Schmidt
191 r: © Carolina Zuniga-Aisa Model: Rael Cohen
192: © Cheryl Traylor
194 b: © Elisabeth Dempsey
195 tr: © Sayumi Namba
195 bl: © Elisabeth Dempsey
195 br: © Anja Steffen. Www.anjasteffen.com, info@anjasteffen.com
196–7: © Jonathan Kyle Farmer
198: © Jonathan Kyle Farmer
199: © Sara Sakanaka
200 tl, tr: © Ji Eun Oh, sole creator of the portfolio
200 b: © Jeffrey Williams
201 t: © Desislava Zhivkova
201 b: Dylan Paul Moran Taverner
202 b: Page in croquis book © Dushane Noble
203: Page in croquis book © Dushane Noble
204–5: © Desislava Zhivkova
206: © Jessica Ly
207 t: Felice DaCosta is sole owner and copyright holder of JA-C
207 b: © Sylvia Kwan
208: Hannah Hae In Lee
209: Hannah Hae In Lee
210–11: Osman S/S 2009. Photographer: Sam Mitchel
211 r: Ferdinand (http://ferdinand.nowhasa.com)
216 l: Catwalking.com
224 t: Catwalking.com
224 b: © 2010 Leslie Jones
225: © Paul Negron
230–9: © Sylvia Kwan
240: © Alfredo Cabrera
241 t: Catwalking.com
241 b: Courtesy Estate of Antonio Lopez and Juan Ramos and Galerie Bartsch & Chariau
242 l: © Diana Lin
242 r: © Richard Rosenfeld
243 l: Catwalking.com
243 r: © Sorcha O'Raghallaigh. Illustration completed as part of Nokia Young Designer of the Year award, 2006 (Dublin), in which Sorcha received the runner up prize
244 l: stylesight.com
248: © Jonathan Kyle Farmer
251 r: Photo by Rob Loud/Getty Images
252 b: © Sungeun Kim
252–3: Kelly Yeunh Li-Xia, Parsons New School for Design
253 r: © Miyuki Ohashi
260 l: © Laura Laine
260 c: Catwalking.com
260 r: stylesight.com
261 r: Catwalking.com
261 l: © Jinsol Kim
263 l: Catwalking.com
263 r: © Alfredo Cabrera
268: © Diana Lin
269 l: © Diana Lin
269 r: © Wyatt Hough
270, 271 l: www.ninadonis.com
271 r: Firstview
272 l: © Vionnet, tailored suit
272 r: © Paul Negron
275 l: © Gene Meyer
275 b: © Jonathan Kyle Farmer
277 r: www.ninadonis.com
281 l: © Jonathan Kyle Farmer
281 tr, br: www.ninadonis.com
282 l, c, r: Catwalking.com
283 c, tr: Catwalking.com
284: © Anna Kiper
285: © Mia Grimaldi
286 r: www.ninadonis.com
287 b: stylesight.com
291 l: © Paul Negron
291 tr: stylesight.com
291 br: © Sungeun Kim
292 t: © Jennifer Chun
292 b: © Eri Wakiyama
293: © Hyo Kyoung Lee
294–5: © Myrtle Quillamor
296 r: © Anna Kiper
296 l: © Myrtle Quillamor
297: www.ninadonis.com
298 l: © Albert Elia
298 br: © Tanya Ling 2000. Tanya Ling for Paper Magazine, December 2000. Image courtesy FASHIONILLUSTRATIONGALLERY.COM
298 tr: © Makoto Takada
299 bl, tr, c, br: Fredrika Lökholm and Martin Slivka, © Laurence King Publishing
300: © Hae Won (Anna) Lee
301: © Alfredo Cabrera
302: © Myrtle Quillamor
303: © Andrew Yang
304 l: Hannah Hae In Lee
304 r: © Meiling Chen www.meilingchen.com
305: © Sungeun Kim
308 t: © Edvard Koinberg
308 bl, br: Photo: Raw Colour, www.rawcolour.nl
309 l, c, r: PANTONE Colors displayed here may not match PANTONE-identified standards. Consult current PANTONE Color Publications for accurate color. PANTONE®, myPANTONE™ and other Pantone trademarks are the property of, and are used with the written permission of, Pantone LLC. Portions © Pantone LLC, 2010
310: © Jun Hyung Park, Class of 2009, Parsons New School for Design
311: Hannah Hae In Lee
312: © Desislava Zhivkova
313 t: © Eri Wakiyama
327 b: © Paul Negron
328 t: © Pierre-Louis Mascia
329: © Jonathan Kyle Farmer
330–1: © Frank Nathan
332–3: © 2010 Benyam Assefa
334 l: Ferdinand (http://ferdinand.nowhasa.com)
334 r, br: © 2010 Benyam Assefa
336: © Tiffany Ju
337: © Janelle S. Russ
341 l: © Kelly DeNooyer
341 r: © Jinsol Kim
342: www.ninadonis.com
343: Min Ae "July" Choi
345 t: © Diana Lin
347 r: Fashion Drawing of a girl dressed in Vivienne Westwood. Published in *Selvedge* magazine, January 2008
356 t: © Alfredo Cabrera
356 b: © Angela Lee
357 t: © Alfredo Cabrera
357 b: © Angela Lee
358: © Shannon Adam
359: © Shannon Adam
362: © Carmen Chen Wu
363: Fashion drawing of a girl dressed in Jean Muir. Published in *Selvedge* magazine, January 2008
364: Vionnet pre Fall 2010 collection, belted dress l, belted top with trousers r, © Vionnet
365 t: © Sara Sakanaka
365 bl: IRMA, www.irmasworld.com. Jasmin Khezri
365 bc: Little Yoya by David Horvath. Property of Yoyamart and David Horvath
366: www.ninadonis.com
368: © Camilla Dixon. Courtesy Taiko and Associates, Tokyo
369: © Julia Faye Blum
377 l: Catwalking.com
377 r: Photo: Grace Ndiritu, taken from the video titled "Still Life: Lying Down Textiles" by Grace Ndiritu
379 t: Min Ae "July" Choi
380 l: stylesight.com
380 r: © Jonathan Kyle Farmer
381: © Sungeun Kim
384: www.ninadonis.com
385 l: Ferdinand (http://ferdinand.nowhasa.com)
385 r: Drawn by Ivy Yen-Chu Chen, at Parsons New School for Design. Teacher Mr. Richard Rosenfeld, 2009
386 t: © Andrew Yang
386 b: © Eri Wakiyama
394 t: Photo: Courtney Frisse
394 bl: Laura Splan, Doilies (SARS), 2004. Free-standing computerized machine embroidered lace mounted on velvet. 8" x 8" doily dimensions/16.75" x 16.75" framed dimensions
394 br: Embroidered wall skirts by Karen Nicol. www.karennicol.com
397 r: Catwalking.com
398: © Barbara Pearlman
399 tl: Courtesy Estate of Antonio Lopez and Juan Ramos and Galerie Bartsch & Chariau
399 b: © Chanmaly Sivongxai
400: © Anna Kiper
402: © Julia Faye Blum
401: Chris Fennel – artist used for inspiration. © Leslie Jones 2010

The following images are © Michele Wesen Bryant: 6 t, 25 l, 28 bl, tr, br, 37, 38, 39, 40, 41 t, 43, 44, 45, 46, 47, 48, 49, 50, 51, 52, 53, 54, 55, 56 bl, 57, 60, 61, 62, 64 bl, 65 bl, 66, 67 bl, 68, 69, 70, 71, 72 bl, 78 l, 80, 81, 82, 83, 85, 87, 88, 89, 93, 94, 102, 103, 104, 105, 106, 107, 110, 111, 112, 113, 114, 115, 116, 117, 118 l, 120, 121, 122 c, r, 123, 126, 127, 130, 131, 132, 133, 137 bl, br, 139, 140, 141, 142, 145 l, 147 b, 148, 149, 150, 151 l, 153, 154, 155 b, 156, 158, 159, 162, 163, 164, 165 t, 166 b, 167, 168, 169, 170, 171 172, 173 b, 174, 175, 177 bl, 179 t, r, 181 tl, b, 182, 185 tr, br, 193, 212, 213, 214, 215, 216 r, 217, 218, 219, 220, 221, 222, 223, 226, 227, 228, 229, 244–5, 246, 247, 249
Drawings by Michele Wesen Bryant based on research by Colette Wolffe in *The Art of Manipulating Fabric*, 250, 251 l, 254, 255, 256, 257, 258, 259, 261 c, 262, 264, 265, 266, 267, 273, 274, 275 r, 276–7, 278–9, 280, 283 l, 286 l, 287 t, 288, 289, 290, 313 b, 314, 315, 316, 317, 318, 319, 320, 321, 322, 323, 324, 325, 326, 327 t, 328 b, 338, 339, 340, 344, 345 b, 346, 347 b, 348, 349, 350, 351, 352, 353, 354, 355, 365 bc, 365 br, 370, 371, 372, 373, 374, 375, 376, 378, 379 b, 387, 388, 389, 390, 391, 392, 393, 395, 396–7.

Author's Acknowledgements

I am grateful to many many people for their unwavering support during the five plus years—longer than anyone could have imagined— it took to birth this book.

Thanks to the team at Laurence King for their collective vision of what a fashion drawing textbook might be: Helen Rochester, Angus Hyland, Anne Townley, Zoe Antoniou, Paul Tilby, Emma Brown, Liz Jones, Angela Koo, and Sue Farr.

I was extremely fortunate to have had constructive input from thoughtful reviewers. This is a better book thanks to Andy Chan, Massachusetts College of Art; Laura Chapius, Wade College; Val Fisher, Arts University College, Bournemouth; Jane Gottelier, University College Falmouth; Hanna Hall, Kent State University; Johannes Reponen, University of the Creative Arts; Melanie Schmidt, Pratt Institute.

Thank you to all of the artists who have contributed their work so generously. It would not have been possible to demonstrate the personal and diverse nature of fashion drawing—the thesis of this book—without their participation.

Special thanks to Lee Ripley for getting behind the project early on.

Personal thanks to my parents Elayne and Phillip Wesen for the DNA, love, and encouragment to pursue a creative path from the very beginning; to Yayoi Tsuchitani and Piet Halberstadt for the exquisite meals and especially for listening. Grazie to Lisa Feuerherm for her collegiality.

Neverending thanks to my husband Stan Bryant for sacrificing almost all of his downtime for five years. I could not have completed this book without his loving support, good humor and infinite patience.